MW01241509

God in the Courtroom

American Psychology-Law Society Series

Series Editor
Ronald Roesch

Editorial Board
Gail S. Goodman
Thomas Grisso
Craig Haney
Kirk Heilbrun
John Monahan
Marlene Moretti
Edward P. Mulvey
J. Don Read
N. Dickon Reppucci
Gary L. Wells
Lawrence S. Wrightsman
Patricia A. Zapf

Books in the Series

Trial Consulting
Amy J. Posey and Lawrence S. Wrightsman

Death by Design
Craig Haney

Psychological Injuries
William J. Koch, Kevin S. Douglas, Tonia L. Nicholls, and Melanie L. O'Neill

Emergency Department Treatment of the Psychiatric Patient
Susan Stefan

The Psychology of the Supreme Court
Lawrence S. Wrightsman

Proving the Unprovable
Christopher Slobogin

Adolescents, Media, and the Law
Roger J.R. Levesque

Oral Arguments before the Supreme Court
Lawrence S. Wrightsman

God in the Courtroom
Brian H. Bornstein and Monica K. Miller

God in the Courtroom

Religion's Role at Trial

Brian H. Bornstein and Monica K. Miller

UNIVERSITY PRESS
2009

OXFORD
UNIVERSITY PRESS

Oxford University Press, Inc., publishes works that further
Oxford University's objective of excellence
in research, scholarship, and education.

Oxford New York
Auckland   Cape Town   Dar es   Hong Kong   Karachi
Kuala Lumpur   Madrid   Melbourne   Mexico City   Nairobi
New Delhi   Shanghai   Taipei   Toronto

With offices in
Argentina   Austria   Brazil   Chile   Czech Republic   France   Greece
Guatemala   Hungary   Italy   Japan   Poland   Portugal   Singapore
South Korea   Switzerland   Thailand   Turkey   Ukraine   Vietnam

Copyright © 2009 by Oxford University Press.

Published by Oxford University Press, Inc.
198 Madison Avenue, New York, New York 10016
www.oup.com

Oxford is a registered trademark of Oxford University Press.
All rights reserved. No part of this publication may be reproduced,
stored in a retrieval system, or transmitted, in any form or by any means,
electronic, mechanical, photocopying, recording, or otherwise,
without the prior permission of Oxford University Press.

Library in Congress Cataloging-in-Publication Data
CIP data on file
ISBN 978-0-19-532867-7

We dedicate this book to four individuals whose influence on our lives greatly exceeds their awareness of that fact:

To my uncles Alex Berman and Eddie Bornstein, for their example in religion, law, and things in between.

—Brian

To Grandpa and Grandma, whose hard work, sacrifices, and enduring love make me realize how lucky I am.

—Monica

Series Foreword

This book series is sponsored by the American Psychology-Law Society (APLS). APLS is an interdisciplinary organization devoted to scholarship, practice, and public service in psychology and law. Its goals include advancing the contributions of psychology to the understanding of law and legal institutions through basic and applied research; promoting the education of psychologists in matters of law and the education of legal personnel in matters of psychology; and informing the psychological and legal communities and the general public of current research, educational, and service activities in the field of psychology and law. APLS membership includes psychologists from the academic, research and clinical practice communities as well as members of the legal community. Research and practice is represented in both the civil and criminal legal arenas. APLS has chosen Oxford University Press as a strategic partner because of its commitment to scholarship, quality, and the international dissemination of ideas. These strengths will help APLS reach its goal of educating the psychology and legal professions and the general public about important developments in psychology and law. The focus of the book series reflects the diversity of the field of psychology and law, as we will publish books on a broad range of topics.

The role of religion in the legal process is a topic that has received little attention in the psychology and law literature. This latest book in the APLS series may serve to stimulate more interest in this important topic among the intended audience of researchers, practicing attorneys, and policy makers. As Brian Bornstein and Monica Miller show, religion influences the law in numerous but often subtle ways. They review legal developments and behavioral science research to show how religion affects the actions of jurors, judges, attorneys, and litigants. In criminal trials, this influence begins even before the start of a trial, as both defense and prosecution lawyers may use peremptory challenges to exclude potential jurors based on their presumptions about the relationship between religion and the decisions these potential jurors are likely to make. For example, they note that prosecutors may wish to exclude those high in evangelism and devotionalism, whereas defense attorneys will try to exclude those high in fundamentalism and literal interpretism. Bornstein and Miller review the research on this relationship and note that the findings are neither robust nor clear, and at times challenge the credibility of these hunches.

Bornstein and Miller provide answers to key questions about the impact of religion on the legal process. Does religion matter at trial? What role should religion play at trial? Should attorneys be able to use religion in voir dire? Should attorneys be allowed to make religious appeals during oral argument? Should factfinders be allowed to rely on religious texts and beliefs in making their decisions? What influence does religious affiliation have on decisions made by judges? What role does religion play when Catholic churches and priests are defendants in child sexual abuse litigation? Some of the answers may surprise readers. For example, the authors note that although legal scholars may not agree on whether biblical appeals should be admissible, research shows that they are either ineffective or may backfire.

This book also examines issues outside the courtroom, such as religion's role in legal training through the development of religious law schools, which explicitly incorporate religion and morality into law students' ethical training. Noting that the "Religious Lawyering Movement" is relatively new, they suggest research that could provide information on how this might impact the practice of law.

As with many areas of psychological research, clear conclusions about the role of religion in law are often difficult to reach. Bornstein and Miller are careful to identify the limitations of the research and, in the final chapter, lay out a blueprint for future research. Their thoughtful and comprehensive review of the strengths and limitations of our existing knowledge and the legal and policy issues that can be addressed by psychological research should stimulate the interest of researchers. As they note in their concluding chapter, Bornstein and Miller hope that this book will serve to inspire researchers to take on the challenge of focusing attention on religion and law. I believe this book will do just that.

Ronald Roesch
Series Editor

Acknowledgments

This book was a long time in the making. It began around 2001, when one of us (Monica) had the idea to do her dissertation on how attorneys' appeals to religion in oral arguments influence jurors' decision making. The other one of us (Brian) supervised that dissertation, the results of which we describe in Chapter 8. As the dissertation evolved and took on a life of its own after Monica's graduation, the research incorporated additional elements, such as defendants' use of religious conversion as a mitigating factor in sentencing (covered in Chapter 9). Gradually, this led us to realize that religion can influence courtroom outcomes in myriad ways and that we had a much larger topic on our hands than a single dissertation or line of research could accommodate. This book is our attempt to cover most of the ways in which religion affects the behavior of various courtroom actors.

We contributed equally to the project, and the book is a fully collaborative effort. Each of us took the lead on individual chapters, which the other then revised and added his or her own style to—with the intent of creating an integrated work with a single voice. We will know we succeeded if readers cannot tell which chapter was originally whose. The book solidified a friendship and collaboration that began many years ago as teacher–student. That deepening friendship was one of the best things about working on the project together.

For the period during which the book was being written, Monica received financial support from the University of Nevada, Reno College of Liberal Arts and Scholarly and Creative Activities Grants Program. Brian was supported by a faculty development leave from the University of Nebraska-Lincoln. The leave freed Brian from teaching and other day-to-day professorial responsibilities, enabling him to concentrate on this project. The leave also afforded the opportunity for travel to meet with colleagues at the University of Regina, the University of Nevada, Reno, the University of Texas-El Paso, and the University of Leicester. Colleagues at all of these institutions provided valuable feedback as the book began to take shape, and Brian thanks Jeff Pfeifer, Monica Miller, Chris Meissner, and Emma Palmer for arranging these visits. Portions of Chapter 6 were presented in October 2008 at a festschrift conference at Kansas University in honor of Larry Wrightsman. We received helpful comments from the audience and, as always, inspiration and encouragement from Larry himself, the *eminence grise* of psychology and law, whose professional and personal example we strive to emulate.

Any book is the product of many people's efforts, not just the authors'. These folks fall into several more-or-less discrete, though overlapping, categories: readers/commenters, research assistants, production personnel, and moral supporters. Several individuals gave generously of their time and expertise in reading drafts of chapters: Ani Aharonian, Mark Cambron, Christie Emler, Sam Lindsey, Kevin Miller, Marc Pearce, Samantha Schwartz, Alan Tomkins, and Sandi Zellmer. Thanks to their insights, the book contains fewer inaccuracies and less obfuscatory prose than it would have otherwise; they are not responsible for any inaccuracies and obfuscation that remain, but they share in the credit for any clarity we managed to achieve. The research assistance of several students saved us much time and helped locate relevant cases and articles. We gratefully acknowledge the research contributions of Joe Hamm, Jon Maskaly, Timmy Robicheaux, and Megan Schroeder. We are especially grateful to Ron Roesch, editor of the American Psychology-Law Society book series. Ron's patience, encouragement, and editorial acumen have been invaluable. And of course, the finished product could not have been made without the efforts of the kindly folks at Oxford University Press.

Finally, we cannot express strongly enough our appreciation for the numerous colleagues, friends, and family who supported us throughout this process. Whether simply asking "How's the book coming along? Is it done yet?," humoring us as we described the latest cool case or research findings, or enduring our absences with patient understanding, they contributed more to the final product than they can ever know. We will not attempt to mention them all by name, but hopefully they know who they are. There are, however, a special few who do deserve mention by name. Throughout the "year of Torah study," Marilyn Bornstein and Sandy Emler fostered a religious dialogue that provided an informative backdrop to many of the themes covered in the book. Joel Harrington has graciously and patiently answered questions about religious history for more than twenty years.

We are especially grateful to our spouses, Christie Emler and Kevin Miller, for their unwavering encouragement and support; and to Lillian and Melissa Bornstein, for affording so many good reasons not to work on the book but understanding when Daddy got more than his fair share of computer time. It would mean very little if we did not have you to celebrate our professional successes with, like the completion of this book.

Contents

God in the Courtroom

1

Introduction

> They came here to try revealed religion. I am here to defend it.
> —William Jennings Bryan, testifying in the Scopes
> monkey trial (Larson, 1997, p. 187)

"God in the courtroom." What does the phrase mean? Several images might come to mind: William Jennings Bryan defending religion against the tyranny of evolution in the famous Scopes monkey trial; a robed deity on the bench, passing divine judgment; the Ten Commandments on the courtroom wall; a witness, hand upon the Bible, taking an oath to tell "the truth, the whole truth, and nothing but the truth, so help me God"; or God as prosecutor accusing fallible mankind of various misdeeds. One might even imagine God as defendant, which he would have been had one Nebraska legislator had his way. In September 2007, Nebraska State Senator Ernie Chambers sued God, seeking a permanent injunction ordering God to cease making terroristic threats and causing widespread death and destruction. The suit accused God of injuring the plaintiff's constituents and causing "fearsome floods, egregious earthquakes, horrendous hurricanes, terrifying tornadoes, pestilential plagues, ferocious famines, devastating droughts, genocidal wars, birth defects and the like" ("State Sen. Ernie Chambers sues God," 2007). God's response—filed by an attorney from, fittingly enough, Corpus Christi, Texas—argued that the defendant was immune from prosecution and that the court lacked jurisdiction (Bratton, 2007; "'God' responds," 2007). The case was ultimately dismissed (Young, 2009).[1]

Such depictions are entertaining, and they illustrate some of the many ways in which religion and the courts are intertwined, perhaps inextricably so; but they are not scientific, and they are therefore not the focus of this book.

Rather, the present volume will review legal developments and behavioral science research concerning the effects of religion on legal practice, courtroom decision-making processes, and trial outcomes. Religion and law intersect in numerous, often subtle ways. For example, religious beliefs might influence the decisions of legal decision makers, such as judges and jurors. Attorneys might rely on religion, both in the way they approach their professional practice generally and in specific trial tactics (e.g., using a scriptural rationale in arguing for a particular trial outcome). This book will cover these and related topics in exploring how religion affects the actions of all of the major participants at trial: jurors, judges, attorneys, and litigants. In the remainder of this chapter, we give a thumbnail sketch of the place of religion in American life, explain why we should care about religion's role at trial, comment briefly on empirical issues, and provide an overview of the remainder of the book.

Religion in America: Briefly Sketching the Terrain

Recent surveys attest to the resurgence of religion in American life. Americans are among the most religious people on earth: Roughly 90–95% report a belief in God, approximately 90% affiliate with a congregation or religious group, and more are attending religious services than in previous decades (Baylor Institute for Studies of Religion, 2006; Pew Forum on Religion and Public Life, 2008; Spilka, Hood, Hunsberger, & Gorsuch, 2003). Meanwhile, more and more books, television shows, and movies center on religious themes, and media coverage of religion and religious-themed websites have increased dramatically (Riley, 2005). Former President George W. Bush is a born-again Christian who, while in office, was very open about his faith and implemented a number of faith-based initiatives.[2] Candidates' faith is a common issue in political campaigns, and sincere religious belief seems to have become a litmus test for holding high public office.

At the same time, highly publicized controversies threaten to divide religious institutions, such as the Catholic Church's sexual abuse scandal involving priests, the Episcopal Church's ordination of a gay bishop, and debates over homosexuality in many denominations. The growing importance of religion in American life has not gone unnoticed by the opposition. There has been a vocal backlash from nonbelievers, with several recent books published on the supposed evils of religion and folly of religious belief (e.g., Dawkins, 2006; Dennett, 2006). Concomitantly, some surveys have detected a wide, and possibly growing, "swath of secularism" (Kosmin, Mayer, & Keysar, 2001, p. 6).[3] These developments have created an unprecedented public debate over the virtues and vices of religion.

The American religious landscape is changing in other ways as well. For one thing, the growth in religious affiliation and appetite for religious materials and media have been fueled more by youth than by adults (Riley, 2005), suggesting that current trends are likely to continue into the foreseeable future. In addition, the nation's religious composition is changing. In the last two decades, membership in the mainline Protestant denominations has diminished, while membership in nondenominational and evangelical churches has increased substantially (Baylor Institute for Studies in Religion, 2006; Kellstedt, 1989; Kosmin, Mayer, & Keysar, 2001). For example, the Baylor study found that one-third of Americans affiliated with an evangelical Protestant faith. Evangelicals share certain core doctrinal beliefs (see Chapter 4), yet despite these shared beliefs, "evangelicalism is a multifaceted movement" (Kellstedt, 1989, p. 4), with groups ranging across the political spectrum. Evangelicalism should not be confused with fundamentalism, although the two overlap. The two groups share a number of features, such as the belief that eternal salvation is attainable only through acceptance of Jesus in one's life, but fundamentalists are more literal in biblical interpretation, are more likely to have had a "born-again" experience, and are more conservative politically (Kellstedt, 1989).[4]

Although only a relatively small minority (typically in the neighborhood of 5%) of Americans affiliate with a specific non-Christian religion (Baylor Institute for Studies in Religion, 2006; Kosmin et al., 2001; Pew Forum on Religion and Public Life, 2008), changing demographic patterns such as immigration and high birth rates have produced significant growth among some minority religions over the last several decades (e.g., Islam). By some accountings, there are now more Muslim Americans than Episcopalians and as many Muslims in the United States as there are Jews (Eck, 2001). There are an estimated 4 million American Buddhists and over 1 million Hindus, both from a number of different countries and distinct religious traditions (Eck, 2001). Thus, early twenty-first century America is religiously more diverse than ever before and arguably "the most religiously diverse nation on earth" (Eck, 2001, p. 4).

In addressing the role of religion, we treat it not as a single construct, but instead address the various elements that go into one's religion: affiliation (i.e., the particular faith one identifies with; see Chapter 3), degree of observance (often referred to as "devotionalism"; see Chapter 4), and specific religious beliefs (e.g., interpreting the Bible literally; see Chapter 4). The need for this multi-construct approach to religious expression reflects the fact that specific beliefs or levels of devotionalism might be more predictive of individuals' behavior than mere affiliation. For example, Orthodox Jews, fundamentalist Protestants, and conservative Catholics might have more in common with one another than each group does with its more liberal denominational brethren.

In addition, the classification of religious denominations varies depending on a number of doctrinal, social, and historical factors and is consequently somewhat arbitrary (Smith, 1990). One approach is to distinguish between "mainstream" and "marginalized" religions, yet it is not always so easy to identify the mainstream (Feldman, 2006). For example, American Jews are fairly mainstream in terms of cultural acceptance, but at less than 2% of the population, they are not mainstream numerically. This classification problem is particularly acute with respect to non-Catholic Christian denominations, among whom a single label (e.g., Lutheran, Baptist, Presbyterian) can encompass widely divergent worship practices and beliefs, ranging from liberal to conservative. Some denominations are more consistently evangelical than others (e.g., Baptists), but many denominations can have evangelical and nonevangelical branches. Some researchers attempt to solve the problem by distinguishing between "mainline" (or "high") and "evangelical" (or "low") branches of different Protestant denominations (e.g., Baylor Institute for Studies of Religion, 2006; Pew Forum on Religion and Public Life, 2008), but even that is a relatively crude taxonomy that different researchers implement differently. Moreover, no agreement exists on whether certain denominations (e.g., Mormonism, Unitarianism, Jehovah's Witnesses) are Protestant, "other" Christian faiths (i.e., neither Catholic nor Protestant but still Christian), or separate (non-Christian) faiths altogether. Good arguments also exist for treating historically Black Protestant churches separately (Kellstedt, 1989; Pew Forum on Religion and Public Life, 2008), although not all studies do so. Religious identification is also somewhat fluid, with 16% of U.S. adults reporting having switched their religion preference (Kosmin et al., 2001). Finally, there is a significant disparity between how many persons describe themselves religiously and how others view them (e.g., just a third of those in denominations commonly deemed evangelical actually refer to themselves as "evangelical"; Baylor Institute for Studies of Religion, 2006). This ambiguity in classification necessarily complicates any efforts at cross-religion comparison.

Religion is a politically salient factor in many parts of the world in addition to the U.S. (Bruce, 2003; Smidt, 1989): Europe (e.g., Ireland, Poland, the countries formerly known as Yugoslavia), Africa (e.g., Nigeria, South Africa), the Indian subcontinent (e.g., India, Pakistan), essentially the entire Middle East, and much of Latin America. In these countries, religion undoubtedly colors legal processes as well. But because of the legal issues raised by the topic, and because empirical answers to the sorts of questions we ask require some degree of religious diversity (for cross-religion comparisons), our emphasis is on American law. The central issues arise less often in countries that are less religiously diverse or that have an official state religion; nonetheless, we do include some material from other countries, especially those with related legal systems, such as the United Kingdom and Canada.[5]

Although the United States is, in many respects, a religiously diverse nation, surveys indicate that more than three-quarters of Americans identify themselves as Christian (Baylor Institute for Studies of Religion, 2006; Kosmin et al., 2001; Spilka et al., 2003).[6] These same surveys show that Americans affiliate with a plethora of Christian denominations. For example, the American Religious Identification Survey found that the question *"What is your religion, if any?"* elicited more than a hundred different responses, which could be classified into 65 categories (Kosmin et al., 2001). With the exception of Jews, little research in the social science of religion has addressed non-Christian religious groups (Spilka et al., 2003), and the research on religion's role at trial is no exception. We are therefore unable to present much systematic data on the treatment of these other religions in court. However, we do present legal cases involving members of minority religions and speculate about their treatment compared to members of more mainstream American religions. For example, we discuss trials involving Muslim defendants (see Chapter 9) and those in which Muslim prospective jurors have been excluded from jury service (see Chapter 2).

Why Religion's Role at Trial Matters

As the preceding discussion illustrates, religion is a prominent issue in the lives of the overwhelming majority of Americans. In one sense, then, religion will matter at trial simply because it matters everywhere else. Yet, in another sense, religion matters at trial because it raises a number of unique and intriguing issues in this particular context. Religion and law are intimately connected, if for no other reason than that religious values serve as the foundation for most, if not all, legal systems (Berman, 2000; Hamburger, 1993; Marty, 2005; Segrest, 1994). The statutory codification of religiously grounded morality means that religion indirectly finds expression in the law (e.g., "thou shalt not kill"). Jurors rely on their intuitions about what is morally just all the time, as in dispensing "commonsense justice" (Finkel, 1995, 2001) or in nullifying laws that they deem unjust (e.g., Horowitz, Kerr, & Niedermeier, 2002; Horowitz, Kerr, Park, & Gockel, 2006). Yet, a subtle distinction exists between using religiously tinged morality to decide the outcome of legal cases, which is generally legally permissible, and explicitly using religion to accomplish the same thing, which is generally not permissible. For example, it is unproblematic for a legal factfinder (i.e., a judge or jury) to condemn a murderer to death on moral grounds related to his culpability and the reprehensibility of his actions, and not merely because his actions broke the law. However, it *is* problematic if they explicitly justify that same sentence by citing the Bible (see Chapters 5 and 6). One could argue that this is a spurious distinction, that religion is influencing the factfinder's decision whether or not the religious influence is explicit, and that it is therefore better to acknowledge and potentially regulate it.[7] Nonetheless, the principle of church–state separation has generally been interpreted as barring the explicit use of religion in legal decision making.

Indeed, the best-known, and most widely written about, religion-and-law topics are those involving church–state separation and religious liberty, as embodied in the First Amendment's religion clauses. The Amendment states that "Congress shall make no law respecting an establishment of religion, or prohibiting the free exercise thereof." The former is commonly referred to as the Establishment Clause, and the latter as the Free Exercise Clause. A wealth of material has been written about these issues (for general sources, see Alley, 1988; Flowers, 2007; Hitchcock, 2004; Witte, 2005).[8] A focused legal analysis of religious liberties jurisprudence would be well beyond the scope of the present work; however, we do consider the First Amendment's religion clauses in several respects. Specifically, we discuss whether the outcome of religious liberties cases is influenced by the religion of the judges hearing such cases (Chapter 6), the attorneys litigating the cases (Chapter 7), or the claimants themselves (Chapter 9).

More broadly, we consider the many ways that religion can influence trial outcomes. Why do trials matter? Trials have always resolved only a small fraction of legal disputes (Galanter, 1990, 2004; Gross & Syverud, 1996). The number of trials has even declined in recent years, in both absolute terms and as a proportion of case dispositions (Galanter, 2004). For instance, Ostrom, Strickland, and Hannaford-Agor (2004) found that the percentage of civil cases in state courts of general jurisdiction that were disposed of at trial decreased from 36.1% in 1976 to 15.8% in 2002. This trend is evident in criminal as well as civil cases, in both federal and state jurisdictions (Galanter, 2004). "Vanishing" trials have been replaced not so much by fewer civil lawsuits or criminal prosecutions, but by shifts in litigation practice, such as alternative dispute resolution (ADR) and nontrial adjudication (e.g., summary judgment and dismissal; Galanter, 2004; Hadfield, 2004; Stipanovich, 2004). Thus, one could argue that an exploration of religion's role at trial is relevant to only a very small percentage of cases and therefore cannot teach us much.

We have several responses to this argument. First, even if trial verdicts are a minority of all case dispositions, there are still hundreds of thousands of trials per year (Ostrom et al., 2004). Second, trials, despite being relatively rare, can have a profound impact on business and individual behavior (e.g., Crump, 1998; Galanter & Luban, 1993). Trial outcomes are more public than ADR outcomes, plea bargains, or dismissals, and they thereby enter into the decision-making calculus of those whose behavior might bring them into contact with the civil or criminal justice system. Jury trials are an especially salient and visible expression of the justice system at work. Third, trials influence settlement decisions and negotiations among parties, once they have entered the justice system, by providing a benchmark for possible outcomes. In this sense, trial outcomes cast a "shadow" across the arena of claims and settlements (Galanter, 1990; Gross & Syverud, 1996). Fourth, although some of the issues covered in this book focus more or less exclusively on trial matters (e.g., jury behavior and attorney arguments at trial), other issues go beyond trials and relate to legal practice more broadly. For example, religion is just as likely to influence judges' nontrial adjudications as it is to influence their decision making at trial; and attorneys who wrestle with integrating their spiritual values and their professional work do so in all arenas of practice, and not only when they are trying a case. Thus, much can be learned from a consideration of religion's role at trial and in legal practice more broadly.

In considering these issues, it helps to distinguish between two different perspectives: descriptive and normative. The descriptive perspective addresses the extent to which religion *does* influence legal outcomes. The normative perspective, on the other hand, addresses whether religion *should* influence legal outcomes. The descriptive question is typically easier to answer than the normative one. It seeks to describe whether, the extent to which, and under what circumstances religion actually relates to trial outcomes. As we will show, the descriptive picture in this case is constrained by gaps in the literature, methodological shortcomings, and inconsistent findings; yet it does afford some conclusions. Moreover, since the emphasis is on merely characterizing a state of affairs, the descriptive perspective is relatively value-free. As the following chapters illustrate, religion exerts subtle and, in some instances, overt effects at trial. This is not to say that it is a bigger determinant of trial outcomes than more obvious factors such as legal precedent, statutes, and evidence. Nonetheless, it shows that religion deserves to be considered among the many "extralegal" factors that can influence trial outcomes (for review, see Greene & Bornstein, 2003; Vidmar & Hans, 2007). Research on individual differences in legal decision making has examined the influence of a number of demographic, personality, and attitudinal variables in addition to religion, such as gender, race, age, socioeconomic status, authoritarianism, attitudes toward the legal system, and so on. This research shows that although individual differences generally explain less of the variance in factfinders' decisions than do legal and evidentiary variables, they nonetheless are often significant predictors of judges' and jurors' decisions (Greene & Bornstein, 2003; Vidmar & Hans, 2007). Moreover, they tend to be more predictive in some kinds of cases than in others.

We might expect religion to be associated more strongly with factfinders' decisions than other individual difference variables for a couple of reasons. First, religion is likely to be a more central element of many people's self-concept than some of the other variables, such as age and socioeconomic status. Second, most civil and criminal offenses are neutral with respect to individual difference variables and would therefore not be expected to activate one's sense of group membership. There are, of course, a few notable exceptions. For instance, cases of rape, domestic violence, or sexual harassment could make jurors aware of their gender; racially motivated hate crimes could remind them of their race; and age discrimination allegations could make them aware of their age. But, for most offenses, it should not matter to which group legal decision makers belong. For example, murder, medical malpractice, and breach of contract should not hit closer to home for some demographic groups than others. Religion is arguably different, primarily because of the multifaceted ways that one's religious identification and beliefs color one's entire value system and worldview. As we describe in Chapter 3, religious groups differ in their stance on issues central to the administration of justice, such as the nature and purpose of punishment and forgiveness. Moreover, certain issues that find their way into court, such as reproductive decision making (e.g., abortion), parental autonomy, and the death penalty, are ones on which religious leaders have been particularly outspoken. Thus, from a descriptive perspective, it is reasonable to expect religion to be correlated with trial outcomes.

The normative approach, in contrast to the descriptive one, is very much concerned with values. The question of whether religion should factor into trial outcomes is independent of the question of whether it actually does, and it is harder to answer because it cannot be answered empirically. Values, or norms, reflect legal assumptions and policy considerations. Should the law bar attorneys from excluding prospective jurors on religious grounds, in the same way that it bars them from doing so on racial or gender grounds? Should judges be allowed to rely on scripture in giving sentences? Should a clergyperson found guilty of child sexual abuse be punished more harshly than a layperson who committed exactly the same act? The answers to these and other such questions depend on legal (especially constitutional) considerations, but they also raise deep-seated questions of values.

In many instances, both a yes and a no answer to the question seem reasonable. Consider, for example, the question of whether factfinders' (i.e., judges and jurors) religion predicts their legal decisions. Whether or not it does influence their decisions, should it? On the one hand, it seems that the obvious answer is "No": Factfinders should make their decisions based on the evidence and applicable law, and extraneous factors such as their own background characteristics should be irrelevant. On the other hand, they must rely on their personal experiences in making such common legal judgments as whether a witness is credible or a defendant acted in a reasonable manner. The wealth of an individual's personal history necessarily comes to bear in making such judgments, and if religious values are a part of that history, then it would arguably be inappropriate—not to mention impossible—to exclude them from the equation (e.g., Griffen, 1998; Idleman, 1993, 2005). Perhaps, then, it would be better to get those factors, such as religion, out in the open, where they can be scrutinized.

The same competing approaches color the treatment of religious litigants (see Chapter 9). Should a priest be punished more severely for sexual abuse than a layperson? Should a Jehovah's Witness be punished less severely, or not at all, for withholding medical treatment from her child than members of other religions, simply because it is a cardinal tenet of her religion? Again, one can make arguments either way. In the case of the priest, the letter of the law dictates an emphasis on the defendant's actions, without consideration of his personal characteristics. However, one could reasonably argue that because the priest abused his authority and violated a special kind of trust, his actions are worse than those of a run-of-the-mill pedophile (if such exists) and therefore deserve a harsher punishment. In the case of the Jehovah's Witness withholding medical treatment from her child on religious grounds, constitutional issues regarding religious freedom come into play. One could also reasonably argue that someone who took actions in accord with religious tenets is less culpable than someone who took similar actions for other reasons.

Empirical Considerations

A vast literature exists on topics related to the subject matter of this book. It comes from the multifarious fields of "Religion and X," where X = practically any formal social scientific discipline imaginable—anthropology, law, politics, psychology, sociology. Consequently, the research has been conducted from a variety of perspectives, using methodologies that predominate in a given discipline. The research studies we rely on have variously used qualitative case studies, surveys, experimental and quasi-experimental designs, and archival analyses. It is tempting to draw causal inferences about religion's "influence" from all of these methods, but we can only do that with any degree of confidence in the case of the experimental and quasi-experimental studies (Batson & Ventis, 1982). The other research approaches—which are more common in this area—yield informative data on the association between religion and various outcomes, but they do not afford causal inferences.

These multiple methodologies are nonetheless an advantage, in that we can be more confident in drawing conclusions when the findings from diverse approaches converge. As psychologists (with some legal training as well), we doubtless unintentionally rely more heavily on psychological and legal scholarship than on research from other disciplines; but we have striven to be as inclusive as possible, and research by political scientists and sociologists, in particular, is well represented. Relevant empirical research is published in a number of general journals in each of these disciplines; more specialized journals and book series exist as well.[9] This book is by no means a treatise on the psychology of religion as applied to the legal domain; but we do share one fundamental premise with psychologists of religion, namely, the assumption that the role religion plays in our lives can and should be studied empirically (Batson & Ventis, 1982; Spilka et al., 2003). We therefore rely heavily on scientific research, as well as legal analysis.

Much of the literature on the topic is scattered across disciplinary boundaries, and many of the findings regarding religion come from studies focusing on other or broader topics (e.g., studies of a large number of juror or judge demographic and attitudinal variables), and we have done our best to bring together these disparate threads in a single volume. Throughout the book, our primary emphasis is on empirical research, but we also incorporate theoretical work and sample cases to illustrate key points. In one of the earliest empirical analyses of the legal profession, Smigel (1964) described his book as written on three levels. The first level drew on well-documented evidence, allowing for confident conclusions; the second level relied on material believed to be true, but less well-documented; and the third level used "speculation based more on insight and intuition than on the scientific analysis of the collected data" (Smigel, 1964, p. viii). Over 40 years later, data still do not exist on some of the issues under consideration, so we likewise write on all three levels, but we emphasize levels one and two whenever possible, and we try to be clear about when we are speculating.

Chapter Overview

Just as trial outcomes drive much of what happens in the rest of the justice system, juries drive much of what happens at trial. Juries are very much the face of the American justice system, and because juries are, at least in theory, a representative cross-section of the community, they are the arena where religious diversity is most likely to find expression. Thus, the first section of the book (Chapters 2 through 5) focuses on jurors. Chapter 2 describes common attorney folklore about jurors' religion and how attorneys use those beliefs in jury selection. This chapter also reviews case law on the permissibility of attorneys using religion to exclude potential jurors from serving on a jury, as well as the legality of prospective jurors themselves using their religion as a reason not to serve. Chapters 3 and 4 present data on the critical descriptive question with respect to jurors, namely, whether there is a relationship between jurors' religion and their decisions. Chapter 3 covers jurors' religion in terms of their religious affiliation (e.g., are Jews and Catholics less likely than Protestants to sentence a capital defendant to death?), whereas Chapter 4 does so with respect to various measures of religious expression (i.e., observance and beliefs). Chapter 5 concludes the jury section by reviewing the legal and psychological issues that are raised when jurors introduce religion during their deliberations. This practice has been grounds for appeal in several cases. Defendants' concern is that bringing in an authoritative source such as the Bible—which is, among other things, a legal code—could lead jurors to base their decisions on information other than the evidence and legal instructions presented at trial. It could also lead to undue influence of some jurors over others, if a scripture-quoting juror is viewed as unusually credible or persuasive.

The book's second section (Chapters 6 through 9) covers the role that religion plays in the actions of other courtroom participants: judges, attorneys, and litigants. Specifically, Chapter 6 reviews social scientific research on the relationship between judges' religion and their decisions. It also takes a historical perspective on the role of religion in judicial selection (e.g., Catholic and Jewish seats on the U.S. Supreme Court) and describes cases in which judges have explicitly invoked religion in sentencing. Judges have done this, for example, in sentencing defendants to attend religious services or in quoting religious texts to justify a particular sentence. Chapters 7 and 8 turn to attorneys. In Chapter 7, we consider the role that religion plays in routine legal practice. This matter raises a host of related questions, such as: How religiously diverse is the legal profession in the United States? Does religion have a place in legal education, in either secular or religious law schools? How do religious lawyers reconcile their faith with the sometimes competing demands of their profession (e.g., representing clients who have committed unscrupulous or even evil acts)? A growing "Religious Lawyering Movement" has addressed many of these issues, and we draw on that literature here. Regardless of their own personal religious views, some attorneys might use religion as a trial tactic, as in using religious authority to argue for a particular outcome (e.g., the "eye for an eye" argument again). The courts are split on the admissibility of such religious appeals, with some allowing them, some barring them, and some allowing them only under certain circumstances. Meanwhile, psychological research has investigated whether religious appeals actually affect jurors' verdicts. We review both the legal and psychological aspects of religious appeals in Chapter 8.

Chapter 9 wraps up this section of the book by addressing the role of litigants' religion. Litigants' religion is central to some cases, such as those making a free exercise claim; a substantial factor in others, such as clergy charged with sexual abuse, defendants who introduce their religious conversion to mitigate sentencing, or those who use religion as a defense (e.g., a parent who refused to seek medical treatment for a child on religious grounds); and a peripheral factor in most routine cases. Although a litigant's religion is not relevant in these routine cases, it might nonetheless come up if the person has a religious occupation, and it could also be inferred from a person's surname or dress. In the concluding chapter (Chapter 10), we summarize the major findings, identify some of the key themes running through the book, and discuss future research directions. We also revisit the question raised earlier in this chapter of "why religion at trial matters."

Part I

RELIGION AND THE JURY

2

Religion and the Jury's Composition

> Beware of the Lutherans . . . they are almost always sure to
> convict . . . [a Lutheran] learns about sinning and punishing
> from the preacher, and dares not doubt. A person who disobeys
> must be sent to Hell; he has God's word for that.
> —Famed defense attorney Clarence Darrow, 1936,
> discussing how to select a jury

Many attorneys rely on "folklore" or personal hunches when selecting a jury (Fulero & Penrod, 1990). Others use a more scientific route, taking advice from trial advocacy materials and jury selection books that provide information that is useful for selecting a favorable jury (e.g., Lieberman & Sales, 2006; Lubet, 2004; Mauet, 2002; Posey & Wrightsman, 2005). The decisions attorneys make about which individuals to choose for a jury are often based on potential jurors' demographic characteristics, including their religious characteristics. As such, some attorneys have used their peremptory challenges to exclude potential jurors from jury duty based on their religion. For instance, jurors have been excluded because they are Catholic (*State v. Purcell*, 2001), Islamic (*State v. Hodge*, 2001), served as a missionary (*State v. Fuller*, 2004), or served as a church pastor (*Highler v. State*, 2006). Although many of these trials did not deal directly with religion, there are a variety of cases in which religion could play an especially strong role. For instance, jurors in cases involving alleged child abuse by a priest may be influenced by their personal religious beliefs—perhaps by causing them to be more punitive than they might be if the crime was committed by someone who was not a trusted member of the religious community (see Chapter 9 for further discussion of litigants' religion).

The practice of using peremptory challenges to exclude potential jurors based on their religious characteristics is somewhat controversial. Courts in several jurisdictions have addressed the permissibility of religion-based challenges, with highly inconsistent results (*State v. Fuller*, 2004; *U.S. v. DeJesus*, 2003; for reviews, see Miller, 2006; Miller & Bornstein, 2005; Miller &

Hayward, 2008; Miller, Singer, & Jehle, 2008; Waggoner, 2004). Even legal scholars (Barton, 1995; Kuljol, 2002; Mansfield, 2004) do not agree as to the permissibility of the practice.

In addition to peremptory challenges, legislative acts have affected the religious makeup of juries throughout U.S. history. Laws or legal procedures make it unlikely or impossible for members of some minority religions to be selected for a jury, and this chapter will discuss these exclusions from a historical perspective. In recent decades, legislation has been established that makes it unconstitutional to exclude individuals from jury duty based on their religion. For instance, a Michigan law (MCR 2.511) prohibits "discrimination during voir dire on the basis of race, color, religion, national origin, or sex." Other laws allow some citizens to opt out of jury service on the basis of their religion. For instance, clergy and some religious minorities (e.g., the Amish in Ohio) are exempt from jury duty. Judges also affect the religious composition of the jury, as they make important decisions about whether potential jurors can or should be excused because of their religious beliefs and practices. As a whole, this chapter highlights the legal debate surrounding the exclusion of potential jurors based on their religious characteristics.

The Jury Selection Process

Jury duty is widely recognized as a civil duty that citizens must fulfill in order to protect other individuals' rights—for instance, the right to a jury of one's peers. Getting called for jury duty can evoke a variety of reactions, from curiosity to excitement to dismay. Although some individuals find the opportunity to serve as a juror to be an interesting experience, others find it to be an inconvenient experience they would rather avoid (see Bornstein, Miller, Nemeth, Page, & Musil, 2005). Although many are called, not everyone called is actually selected for jury duty. One purpose of the jury selection process is to determine which of the individuals called would be suitable jurors (i.e., unbiased or impartial).

Historically, individuals called "triors" were given the duty of deciding whether potential jurors were impartial. Lawyers were allowed to "challenge" a potential juror by suggesting to the triors that this potential juror was biased. Some of the first trials to use challenges had religious underpinnings. In 1879, John Miles was a defendant in a bigamy trial in the Utah Territory (*Miles v. United States*, 1880). The prosecutor challenged a potential juror named Oscar Dunn, claiming he was biased because he "believed polygamy to be right that it was ordained of God and that the revelations concerning it were revelations from God . . . [and that] he who acted on them should not be convicted by the law of the land" (p. 306). The triors determined that Dunn was indeed biased, and he was excused (see Vidmar & Hans, 2007).

The process of selecting jurors by using triors has long passed; in modern courts, judges decide whether potential jurors are likely to be impartial (see

Vidmar & Hans, 2007). Potential jurors are questioned by the judge and, in some jurisdictions, also by the lawyers for each party in the trial. How jury selection (more formally called *voir dire*) is conducted varies greatly among states and the federal courts; however, a general review of the process can provide a foundation for understanding how attorneys can use the process to select jurors with favorable characteristics.

When a trial date is approaching, a court issues summonses to citizens, informing them that they have been chosen to perform their civil duties as jurors. Often these citizens are selected from lists of registered voters or people with drivers' licenses. Along with a summons, potential jurors often receive a questionnaire that asks various questions about jurors' lives and beliefs. Questionnaires are most common in controversial or high-publicity cases. Questionnaires can sometimes include questions about a juror's personal religious beliefs and practices. One such example occurred in a 2004 trial in which actor Robert Blake was accused of murdering his wife. Potential jurors completed questionnaires containing questions about their beliefs on many issues, including their views on abortion and religion (Deutsch, 2004). One prospective juror indicated that prayer would help her make a decision in the case, and another wrote that religion would have a "substantial impact" on the trial and that "God stands for justice." Lawyers may have assumed that knowing the strength of potential jurors' religious beliefs would help them choose a favorable jury because the prosecution planned on introducing evidence that Blake had wanted his wife to obtain an abortion. As a result, the defense attorneys sought to eliminate potential jurors who were anti-abortion and/or strongly religious, believing such individuals were likely to be biased against Blake (Deutsch, 2004).

strategy 4 religious contro. evidence

Pretrial questionnaires can also ask jurors their beliefs about religions *other* than their own. Zacarias Moussaoui, also known as the "twentieth hijacker," was facing trial in 2005 for his alleged involvement in the September 11th attacks (Dorf, 2005). Pretrial questionnaires asked potential jurors questions about their familiarity with Islam's history, practices, and followers (Markon, 2005; McNulty, Spencer, Novak, & Raskin, 2005). Other questions asked whether they had strong views against Islam or its members, and whether they thought law enforcement was biased against Islamic people. Such questions presumably guide attorneys' decisions during jury selection.

After completing their questionnaires, potential jurors submit them to the court. Next, potential jurors report to the courthouse on the date and time specified in the summons. These potential jurors comprise the *venire* (i.e., jury pool). All trials starting that day will draw their jurors from this pool. For any particular trial, a subset of the jury pool is chosen; the final jury will be drawn from this subset. During jury selection, potential jurors are questioned by the judge and, in many states, the lawyers. Questions about religion can also occur during the in-person questioning. For example, lawyers asked potential jurors questions about their religious beliefs during jury selection in the recent trial of Victoria Osteen, co-pastor of a large Texas church, who was accused of assaulting a flight attendant ("Mega-preacher's wife sued," 2008; Rogers & Lezon, 2008; we discuss this case further in Chapter 9). The judge and lawyers for each side also view potential jurors' responses to the pre-trial questionnaire.

Responses to the questionnaire or in-person questions can help determine whether a potential juror should be excluded because of a conflict of interest (e.g., knowing one of the parties) or hardship (e.g., financial hardship). The responses also help lawyers determine who would be a "good" juror (i.e., would likely support their side of the case). Trials are adversarial in nature, meaning that the two parties are essentially competing with each other to convince the jury that their side of the story is correct (e.g., the defense attorney tries to convince the jury the defendant is not guilty, while the prosecuting attorney tries to convince the jury the defendant is guilty). Thus, each side is allowed to help select the jury, with each party trying to select favorable jurors. A potential juror can be excluded through *challenges for cause* or *peremptory challenges*. These challenges determine which individuals will be excluded, and which will comprise the final jury.

The notion that some individuals should be excluded because they are not suited to be jurors (at least for a certain trial) dates back centuries (see, e.g., Vidmar & Hans, 2007). In the late 1600s, a sheriff typically had the duty of recruiting jurors. Occasionally, sheriffs had difficulty finding qualified jurors and resorted to recruiting homeless people or reprobates. Sometimes sheriffs were corrupt and sought out jurors who would favor one party to the trial—the party the sheriff himself preferred. Thus, the jury pool often contained individuals who were considered incompetent or partial. To combat this partiality, some courts used "struck" juries; this involved a procedure in which each attorney could remove 12 potential jurors from the pool of 48. Formal recognition of the problem of biased jurors came in 1769, when William Blackstone proposed that there were two types of bias. One form of bias was *manifest prejudice*, which meant that the potential juror was not suitable; for instance, because he had a conflict of interest, could benefit from the outcome of a trial, or knew a party in the case. The other type of bias was *bias on the favor*, which essentially meant that the juror held prejudicial attitudes or beliefs that would make the juror partial (Vidmar & Hans, 2007). These two types of bias are still generally reflected in the modern trial process. The problem of manifest prejudice is addressed through challenges for cause, and bias on the favor is addressed through peremptory challenges.

Challenges for cause are used to exclude jurors who are unlikely to be impartial. For instance, if the potential juror is related to one of the lawyers or parties in the case or otherwise has a close personal connection to the case facts (e.g., a rape victim in a sexual assault case; the spouse of a police officer in a case involving alleged police misconduct). Potential jurors could also be excused for cause if they have financial hardship or would otherwise be unable to attend the trial. During jury selection questioning, a judge could decide independently that a potential juror should be excused. In other instances, one of the attorneys asserts that a potential juror should be excluded for cause. The judge then rules on this challenge and decides if the juror will be excluded.

Lawyers in most jurisdictions can also exercise *peremptory challenges* to remove potential jurors they feel will not be sympathetic to their side of the trial. Attorneys are allowed to remove potential jurors for any reason except the potential juror's race or gender (*Batson v. Kentucky*, 1986; *J.E.B. v. Alabama*, 1994). Lawyers do not have to give reasons for their challenges, unless the opposing lawyer questions a potential juror's removal. If this occurs, the challenging lawyer must give a reason. For instance, a lawyer can question the other side's decision to remove a Black juror if she believes the opposing lawyer removed the potential juror because of the person's race. Because the *Batson* ruling prohibits race-based challenges, the judge will then require the lawyer to give a race-neutral reason for the challenge. If the lawyer can do so (e.g., by stating that the removal of the potential juror was because of the person's occupation), the peremptory challenge is generally allowed. A peremptory challenge can be used to remove a potential juror for any reason imaginable except race or gender—which to some critics is not a very high hurdle. Even if the lawyer did remove potential jurors because of their race, she could lie and give any race-neutral reason, and the challenges would likely be allowed.

ways around the "challenge"

Attorneys have a limited number of peremptory challenges, which is determined by the judge or applicable statute. The number of challenges varies greatly based on factors such as the amount of pretrial publicity the case has received and the severity or nature of the crime. Often, the defense in a criminal trial is allowed more challenges than the prosecution, in an effort to protect the defendant's rights by providing the defendant ample opportunities to remove biased jurors. In federal criminal trials, which have 12-person juries, the prosecution is generally given six challenges and the defense is given ten. In federal capital trials, each side is typically given 20 peremptory challenges. In federal civil trials, which typically have juries of six, each attorney has three challenges (Bartol & Bartol, 2004).

To some degree, the jury selection process both eliminates and selects biased jurors. Although challenges for cause are designed to remove clearly biased individuals (e.g., those who are affiliated with one party in the trial), peremptory challenges are designed to allow lawyers to challenge individuals they feel will be unfavorable. Thus, each lawyer is intentionally trying to create a jury biased in favor of her client or biased against the opponent. This is potentially a trivial issue if one is willing to assume that the efforts of the lawyer on one side counter the efforts of the lawyer on the other side. This is not always a safe assumption, however, because sometimes the two sides do not have equal resources that would allow for sophisticated jury selection decisions. For instance, a prosecutor in a high-profile trial may have the resources to hire trial consultants who can do research and make suggestions about which potential jurors to challenge. Defendants who cannot afford a lawyer are appointed a public defender. It is unlikely that the public defender would be able to hire trial consultants who could give advice on which potential jurors to challenge, nor would a public defender likely have time to do the research personally. This disparity is troublesome to some critics, because it suggests that the party with the most money is more likely to get a favorable jury, and thus more likely to prevail. Some are also concerned that peremptory challenges create juries that are less representative of the community. For instance, if a lawyer challenges all the potential jurors who are Jewish, the final jury will not reflect the general population well because it contains no Jews. As a result of such criticisms, it has been suggested that peremptory challenges should be eliminated or that the number of challenges should be greatly reduced (see, e.g., Ballesteros, 2002). Nevertheless, most jurisdictions still allow the practice.

In sum, the jury selection process is actually a process of *deselecting* some potential jurors. Lawyers attempt to remove unfavorable potential jurors based on their characteristics or attitudes, including those that are religious in nature. The U.S. Supreme Court declined to make a decision as to whether religion-based challenges are permissible (*Davis v. Minnesota*, 1994). Thus, as discussed later in this chapter, lawyers in most jurisdictions can use peremptory challenges to eliminate jurors because of their religious characteristics.

Attorney "Folklore" About Religion and Jury Selection

Attorneys have long believed that the selection of a jury can influence the outcome of a trial. Advocacy guides and the jury selection literature can be helpful for attorneys who want to avoid unfavorable jurors through the use of peremptory challenges (Crocker & Kovera, in press; Fulero & Penrod, 1990; Lieberman & Sales, 2006; Lubet, 2004; Mauet, 2002; Posey & Wrightsman, 2005). In addition, attorneys often base their challenges on their stereotypes or personal biases. For instance, some attorneys have stereotypes about various groups, including men with beards, Scandinavians, Irishmen, left-handed jurors (see Posey & Wrightsman, 2005), jurors who smile (Fulero & Penrod, 1990), and jurors with large mouths (Fulero & Penrod, 1990). Some sources have also included religion as a factor for attorneys to consider in choosing a jury (Appleman, 1952; Darrow, 1936; Goldstein, 1935). For instance, folklore advises against choosing clergymen, as they do not make good jurors for either side because they are accustomed to being sought out for advice; they tend to be too opinionated, will not follow other people's leadership, and will not let go of their own opinions (Appleman, 1952). Jews allegedly make good plaintiff jurors because they have experienced oppression, which makes them more sympathetic to plaintiffs who also have suffered (Harrington & Dempsey, 1969). Other advice is more specific. For instance, Darrow advised defense attorneys to avoid Baptists, Presbyterians, and Lutherans (Darrow, 1936).

Such advice may be well intentioned, but it is likely little more than folklore based on stereotypes or limited experience.

Although attorney folklore has probably been around for centuries, lawyers eventually recognized that science could be used to help select a jury. This brought the possibility of increased accuracy and credibility to the jury selection process. Religion was an integral part of scientific jury selection from the beginning. The trial that is often hailed as the first to use the scientific method to pick a jury was held in 1972 in Harrisburg, Pennsylvania and is now commonly called the trial of the Harrisburg Seven (Hans & Vidmar, 1986; Lieberman & Sales, 2006; Schulman, Shaver, Colman, Emrich, & Christie, 1987). Seven anti-war protesters were accused of conspiring to destroy draft records, conspiring to kidnap Henry Kissinger,[1] and conspiring to bomb heating tunnels in Washington, D.C. Two of the defendants were priests; thus, attorneys believed that jurors' religious beliefs could play an integral part in the trial. Defense attorneys hired social scientists to conduct community surveys and interviews in hopes of identifying the characteristics of those individuals who would be prone to side with the prosecution (Lieberman & Sales, 2006). Researchers asked questions about respondents' religious affiliations and commitments (Vidmar & Hans, 2007), and they found that various religious characteristics were related to attitudes about trial issues. In their final report, researchers recommended that the defense attorneys should ask potential jurors about their religious affiliations and should challenge Episcopalians, Presbyterians, Methodists, and fundamentalists. The report also concluded that the defense should strive to include Catholics, Brethren, and Lutheran jurors (Posey & Wrightsman, 2005; Schulman et al., 1987; Vidmar & Hans, 2007).

It is difficult to say whether this first scientific test was "successful" or not. The jury deliberated for 60 hours over the course of seven days before telling the judge they were deadlocked. The judge declared a mistrial, and the prosecutors declined to retry the defendants. Although the defendants did not receive an acquittal, they ultimately were not convicted. Such an outcome might be considered a trial consulting "success" if one assumes that the selection process resulted in the selection of at least one juror who sided with the defendants and ultimately led the jury to be deadlocked. The Harrisburg Seven trial represented a major innovation in the trial process. The field has since blossomed, such that many lawyers regularly rely on science to select their juries. Since then, more credible jury selection guides have offered attorneys advice that is based on research, rather than folklore (e.g., Crocker & Kovera, in press; Lieberman & Sales, 2006; Posey & Wrightsman, 2005).[2]

How Lawyers Use Religion to Select a Jury

Challenging potential jurors based on their religious characteristics is not an uncommon phenomenon, even in high-profile cases. In several high-profile cases, lawyers have asked potential jurors about their religious affiliation and beliefs, sometimes excluding jurors based on their responses (Miller, Jehle, & Summers, 2007). One such trial was that of Terry Nichols, who was on trial for his role in the bombing of the Alfred P. Murrah building in Oklahoma City in 1995. Lawyers asked potential jurors a variety of questions concerning their religious beliefs (United States District Court for the District of Colorado, 1997). One juror indicated that she had been reared Catholic but had become a Christadelfian. The attorney asked her about the specific beliefs and practices of her religion. After she indicated that her religion teaches that it is not man's place to judge others, the attorney questioned her about her ability to put aside those beliefs in order to perform her civic duty as a juror. Even the judge in this case was concerned about the possible effects of potential jurors' religious beliefs, stating, "We do need to know what influence your religious beliefs might have on your ability to judge as a juror."

In a 2005 trial, a Muslim American named Ali Al-Timimi was convicted of supporting terrorism. During voir dire, jurors were asked almost a dozen questions about their religious preferences, affiliations, and practices (Blum, 2005). Lawyers in the case were using these questions to determine whether a certain potential juror might be predisposed to favor one party to the trial.

Even in lower-profile cases, lawyers can use religion to help select a favorable jury. Spaeth (2008) offers several religious questions lawyers can ask jurors, in addition to their affiliation, such as "Do your family or friends consider you to be a religious person?" or "Do you make major life decisions based on religious principles?" Similarly, Lindsey and colleagues (2008) offer numerous examples of questions that attorneys can use to measure potential jurors' religious beliefs. These include "To what degree do you believe in life after death?" and "Do you believe the Bible to be the literal word of God?" Attorneys can use prospective jurors' answers when deciding whom to challenge. It is impossible to know how often attorneys challenge potential jurors based on their religious characteristics, because they typically are not required to state their reasons for a peremptory challenge; however, there have been many appellate cases in which the defendants claim that the prosecution wrongly excluded potential jurors because of their religious characteristics. These cases indicate that the practice of asking questions about religion, and possibly excluding potential jurors because of their answers, is not a rare event.

This section presents some of the reasons that lawyers have given for their challenges, and then summarizes the case law concerning the use of challenges based on religion. Finally, it reviews some of the legal scholarship discussing the use of peremptory challenges based on potential jurors' religious characteristics.

Reasons Lawyers have Excluded Potential Jurors

A review of appellate cases illustrates that attorneys have excluded potential jurors who were Pentecostal (*Casarez v. State*, 1995), Catholic (*State v. Purcell*, 2001),

Islamic (*State v. Hodge*, 2001), Jehovah's Witness (*Chambers v. State*, 1987; *People v. Martin*, 1998), Jewish (*Joseph v. State*, 1994), a member of the Holiness Church (*Thorson v. State*, 1998), or a member of the Church of Christ (*Chambers v. State*, 1987). Further, potential jurors also have been excluded because they had served as a missionary (*State v. Fuller*, 2004), had strong Christian beliefs (*U.S. v. DeJesus*, 2003), were employed as a pastor (*Highler v. State*, 2006), allowed religion to play a large role in their life (*People v. Malone*, 1991), or wore clothing indicative of being a Muslim (*State v. Fuller*, 2004). Attorneys have also challenged jurors based on behaviors such as carrying a Bible (*State v. Worthy*, 1988) and failing to answer a question about religious beliefs on the jury selection questionnaire (*Grady v. State*, 1987; *Johnson v. State*, 1988). As these examples demonstrate, attorneys have challenged potential jurors for numerous reasons related to religion.

Although the attorneys in the cases above likely made their decisions about whom to challenge on a case-by-case basis, it is also worthy of note that some attorneys regularly challenge potential jurors with certain religious characteristics (e.g., Darrow, 1936). In one particularly well-publicized example, Alameda County California judge Stanley Golde allegedly told prosecutor John R. Quatman that Jews should be excluded from any death penalty case because Jews tend to oppose the death penalty. Although some attorneys dispute this claim, Quatman made a sworn declaration that the conspiracy had occurred, and other attorneys confirmed that it was standard practice (Murphy, 2005). This created quite a stir, because California has the most inmates on death row of any state in the country (640 death row inmates in 2005; Murphy, 2005). Thus, many defendants could have been affected if the judge had shared his advice with many prosecutors, as alleged. As a result of this accusation, some convicted defendants challenged their sentences. One such inmate was Mark Schmeck. In his trial, prosecutors excluded both of the Jewish potential jurors. The judge found that there were other, nonreligious reasons that the individuals could have been challenged, so he determined no harm had occurred. However, Schmeck's attorneys and the Habeas Corpus Resource Center studied the jury selection in 25 death penalty cases from 1984 to 1994 in that county. They found that non-Jews were excluded from jury duty at a rate of 49.97%. Potential jurors who were openly Jewish or had Jewish sounding surnames were excluded at a rate of 93.1% (27 of 29). According to a mathematician hired by Schmeck's attorney, the probability that 27 of the 29 Jews would be challenged is less than 1 in 1.6 million (Murphy, 2005). Thus, there was substantial evidence that Jews were excluded intentionally based on their religious affiliation.

Despite this evidence, the courts have not been convinced that Jews were being removed unfairly. In 2006, the California Supreme Court rejected an appeal in the case of Fred Freeman, finding that there was no conspiracy between the judge and prosecutors (*In re Freeman*, 2006; Kravets, 2006). Nevertheless, it is interesting that some individuals claimed that the prosecutors in the district attorney's office had a blanket rule that called for challenging all

Jewish prospective jurors in any death penalty case due to a belief that Jews were less likely to give the death penalty.[3]

Examples such as those just described indicate that lawyers have attempted to exclude jurors based on various religious characteristics. The following review of case law reveals that the courts often, but not always, allow such exclusions.

Case Law and Legal Scholarship Regarding Religion-based Peremptory Challenges

Soon after the U.S. Supreme Court determined that it was impermissible to exclude jurors based on race (*Batson v. Kentucky*, 1986), various courts were asked to determine the permissibility of using peremptory challenges based on a variety of characteristics—including religious characteristics. The Supreme Court in *Davis v. Minnesota* (1994) was faced with the question of whether religion-based challenges were permissible, but declined to hear the case. As such, states are free to make their own independent rulings on the issue. This freedom has resulted in a variety of rulings (for a more extensive review, see Miller & Bornstein, 2006; Miller & Hayward, 2008; Waggoner, 2004). The existing rules vary in leniency.

The state court ruling in *Minnesota v. Davis* (1993) represents the *most lenient* rule. The Minnesota Supreme Court held that the prohibition on using peremptory challenges for race and gender does not extend to religion for several reasons. First, religious minorities, unlike racial minorities and women, have not experienced the same level of discrimination in jury selection. Furthermore, it would be very demanding on the jury selection process because it would likely increase the number of times attorneys question each other's challenges. Specifically, the court stated, "religious affiliation (or lack thereof) is not as self-evident as race or gender. Consequently, for every peremptory strike, opposing counsel could demand a religion-neutral explanation. This would unduly complicate voir dire" (*Minnesota v. Davis*, 1993, p. 771). Religion-based challenges would also require that the court inquire as to each juror's religious beliefs and affiliation. This would be excessively intrusive. For these reasons, the court determined that it was permissible to challenge a potential juror based on religious characteristics (*Minnesota v. Davis*, 1993).

Another relatively lenient court accepted a challenge of a potential juror who was a member of a Pentecostal church (*Casarez v. State*, 1995). The Texas court declined to extend the *Batson* ruling to cover religion, holding that the state has "sufficiently great" interests that are served by allowing litigants to exclude individuals on the basis of their religious affiliation. Specifically, the court determined that peremptory challenges help the court ensure a fair and impartial jury by providing a mechanism for removing biased jurors.

Although these courts have found no harm in religion-based challenges, others are not as permissive. Some courts have set *moderately restrictive* rules that specify when it is permissible to use a challenge to remove a potential juror based on religious factors; others have only ruled on certain types of religious challenges (e.g., those based on affiliation) and thus leave open the question of the permissibility of challenges based on other religious characteristics (e.g., how often a prospective juror practices his religion). One guideline makes a distinction between religious affiliation and religious devotionalism. The court in *U.S. v. DeJesus* (2003) held that a peremptory challenge was not unconstitutional because the challenge was based on how *often* the potential juror practiced his religion and not because of his membership in a particular religion (i.e., affiliation).

Another popular guideline is the distinction between religious affiliation and religious beliefs. For instance, in *United States v. Stafford* (1998), the Seventh Circuit Court of Appeals determined that it would be improper to challenge a juror on the basis of his particular affiliation (e.g., Catholic or Jewish). On the other hand, it would be proper to challenge jurors because of their religion-based beliefs if these beliefs would impair jurors' ability to make a decision based on the evidence and jury instructions. The court suggested that a peremptory challenge based on religious affiliation might even be unconstitutional, but because various jurisdictions were in disagreement about the issue, it was not an error for the lawyer to make such a challenge. Similarly, the court in *People v. Martin* (1998) stated that, although excluding potential jurors on the basis of their religion may be unconstitutional, it is proper to exclude them based on personal values or beliefs, even if these are based on their religion (see also *Thorson v. State*, 1998). In sum, it would be improper under *Martin* to remove a Jehovah's Witness just because of her religious affiliation, but it would be acceptable to remove her because of her religious belief that people should not judge others.

Another guideline makes a distinction between religious occupation and religious beliefs. An Indiana state court ruling allowed challenges based on religious occupation (e.g., pastor), but it did not allow challenges based on a specific religious affiliation (*Highler v. State*, 2006). Thus, an attorney could challenge a potential juror because he was a religious leader, but she could not challenge the individual because he was a Baptist.

The *most restrictive* position was taken by the New Jersey Supreme Court, which found that attorneys are not allowed to exclude potential jurors for any reason related to religion (*State v. Fuller*, 2004; Bornstein & Miller, 2005). This view has been adopted by other states (*Fields v. People*, 1987; *Joseph v. State*, 1994; *People v. Wheeler*, 1978; *State v. Purcell*, 2001). Courts that forbid the challenges have offered a variety of legal reasons. For instance, attorneys cannot exclude a potential juror based on his particular religious affiliation because it violates the Equal Protection clause of the U.S. Constitution (*State v. Hodge*, 2001) or state constitution (*State v. Fuller*, 2004). Others have found that challenges based on religious affiliation were not allowable because religious groups (in this case, Jews) are cognizable groups (*Joseph v. State*, 1994). The court determined that a potential juror can be identified as being Jewish by surname; similarly, the potential juror could be identified as Jewish if he wears a yarmulke, a six-pointed star, or the traditional attire of Hasidic Jews. Such characteristics make many Jews objectively discernible and thus, they are a cognizable class akin to race- or gender-specific groups (*Joseph v. State*, 1994).

As this brief summary indicates, courts are divided on the issue of the permissibility of religion-based peremptory challenges. Courts also differ as to whether a peremptory challenge based on religion violates the U.S. Supreme Court decision in *Batson v. Kentucky* (1986). This decision prohibits peremptory challenges based on race. Some courts explicitly extend the *Batson* ruling to include challenges based on affiliation (*People v. Martin*, 1998; *State v. Hodge*, 1999; *State v. Purcell*, 2001), whereas others have declined to expand *Batson* to apply to religion (*Casarez v. State*, 1993; *Minnesota v. Davis*, 1993).

Just as courts are far from agreement about the permissibility of religiously based challenges, legal scholars are also sharply divided. Some authors argue that challenges based on religion are unconstitutional because they violate the Equal Protection clause of the Fifth and Fourteenth Amendments and the Free Exercise clause of the First Amendment (Barton, 1995). Some posit that religion-based challenges represent purposeful discrimination by the government (Barton, 1995). Other authors point out that religion-based challenges violate the Sixth Amendment guarantee of an impartial jury (Mansfield, 2004).

In opposition, some authors approve of religion-based challenges (e.g., Kuljol, 2002). These authors reject the finding that peremptory challenges based on religion violate the Equal Protection clause and thus argue that courts should not extend *Batson* to include challenges based on religion. Further, religious groups do not have a history of being discriminated against in jury selection, as do racial groups. Thus, religious groups do not constitute a cognizable class worthy of protection. Finally, because religion does predict a juror's beliefs, it is not an illogical challenge (Kuljol, 2002). Loewy (2000) furthers this argument and supports peremptory challenges in cases in which jurors' religious beliefs are related to their beliefs about the death penalty. Because a challenge that excluded a member of the group "Citizens Against the Death Penalty" would be allowable, it is reasonable to exclude a potential juror who was a member of a church that believes the same thing.

Still other authors agree with the case law that dictates that peremptory challenges based on religious affiliation should not be allowable, but challenges based on religious beliefs should be allowed (Waggoner, 2004). Waggoner proposes that challenges based on affiliation violate the Equal Protection clause because they treat certain classes of people differentially. Further, they erroneously and negatively affect the potential jurors by "insulting their constitutional right to the freedom of religion" (p. 324). Even so, Waggoner posits, challenges based on religious beliefs are not problematic and should be allowed.

As this discussion illustrates, state courts and legal scholars are far from agreement on the issue of religion-based peremptory challenges. Some jurisdictions allow any type of religion-based challenge, whereas others prohibit them entirely. Several courts allow some types of religious challenges but not others. Such challenges, when allowed, affect the jury's composition. Throughout the course of history, legislatures have also taken various steps, described below, that affect the jury's composition.

Legislative Actions That Affect Jury Composition

Up to this point, we have discussed ways in which lawyers have attempted to prevent individuals from serving on juries because of their religious characteristics. As such, lawyers have affected the religious composition of the jury. Legislatures have also affected the jury's religious makeup through various actions that either exclude jurors of certain affiliations from serving on a jury or allow them to opt out.

Intentional Discrimination Against Religious Groups

Because of legislation or jury selection processes, members of some minority religions have historically been barred or discouraged from serving as jurors. Such policies have since been replaced with laws that protect individuals from being excluded because of their religions.

Prior to the 1870s, the Mormon Church (Church of Latter Day Saints) in Utah had even more political power than they currently do; thus, the church could influence the legal process (see, e.g., Jaasma, 1995). As such, the Mormons who were in power could prevent their fellow Mormons from being prosecuted for practicing polygamy. If a Mormon was indicted for polygamy, those in power could control the jury selection process to ensure an adequate number of sympathetic Mormons would serve on the trial. The federal government had banned polygamy, but it was keenly aware that the church was not complying. In 1874, Congress passed the Poland Act, which gave federal judges more power, including the authority to control juror selection in the county courts. The goal was to make sure that juries were comprised of an equal number of Mormons and those who were not associated with the Mormon Church. Thus, the Mormons' control over the trial process was reduced as a result of the Poland Act. Less than a decade later, the Mormon Church's legal power would suffer another, greater blow. In 1887, the Edmunds-Tucker Act authorized legal authorities to require jurors, voters, and officers to take an oath to support anti-polygamy laws (Biber, 2004). The oath effectively prevented Mormons from serving as jurors.

The Mormons are not the only religious group to claim that the legal system essentially barred them from serving as jurors. In 1925, the defendant in *Juarez v. State* (1925) offered evidence that no Roman Catholic had sat on a jury in the jurisdiction for approximately four years, suggesting that the court's procedures were systematically excluding members of this religion. Although no official act of legislation barred Catholics, the court addressed the legality of such hypothetical legislation, stating, "if the Legislature of the state should pass a law saying that hereafter no man holding to the Baptist religious faith, or the Methodist religious faith, or to the Roman Catholic religious faith, should ever be permitted to serve on a . . . jury in this state, and a party adhering to the religious faith so designated should claim that by such legislative act his rights under the Fourteenth Amendment had been violated, the validity of such a law could never be sustained" (p. 1094). The *Juarez* court ultimately determined that a court could not do something that a legislature could not do; thus, the court practice that discriminated against Catholics was impermissible.

Perhaps in recognition of past discrimination, many states have specific statutes that protect groups from being excluded. For example, a Colorado statute (CRS § 13–71–104) entitled "Eligibility for juror service-prohibition of discrimination" states: "(3) (a) No person shall be exempted or excluded from serving as a trial or grand juror because of race, color, religion, sex, national origin, economic status, or occupation." Similarly, a Delaware statute (10 Del. C. § 4502) states that "No person shall be excluded from jury service in this State on account of race, color, religion, sex, national origin or economic status." A Massachusetts law (M.G.L.A. 234A § 3) indicates that "All persons shall serve as jurors when selected and summoned for that purpose except as hereinafter provided. No person shall be exempted or excluded from serving as a grand or trial juror because of race, color, religion, sex, national origin, economic status, or occupation." Statutes such as these presumably imply a ban on using peremptory challenges and any method of developing the jury pool that would affect the composition of those eligible for jury service.

In 1968, Congress addressed this same issue in the Jury Selection and Service Act (28 U.S.C. §§ 1861). This Act establishes that federal litigants have rights to both grand juries and petit juries that are representative of their communities, and forbids jury selection procedures that exclude individuals based on religion or other characteristics. Laws such as these represent efforts by states and the federal government to prevent religious discrimination in jury selection. Other laws, discussed next, allow certain religious groups to voluntarily opt out of jury duty.

Laws Allowing Members of Some Religions to Opt Out

State laws that allow individuals of some religions to decide whether they want to serve as jurors are often passed by lawmakers who recognize that some religions adhere to principles that would make it difficult for their members to serve as jurors (McDonough, 2006). For instance, an Ohio law (OH ST § 2313.16) allows potential jurors who are members of recognized Amish sects to be excused at the individual's request. This law recognizes that the Amish religion forbids its followers from judging others. South Dakota law (SDCL § 16–13–10) allows for a much broader exemption. This statute states that "Any member of a church or religious organization is exempt from jury duty if jury service conflicts with the religious belief of that church or religious organization."[4]

Among the most debated religion-based exemptions are those for clergy or other religious officials. These exemptions have long historical roots. Even in the years preceding the framing of the First Amendment, clergy were given certain accommodations because of their religion. These could include exemption from jury duty and exemption from the requirement that one take an oath (McConnell, 2000). Thus, some exemptions have existed for many decades in one form or another.

Until the late 1990s, many states had statutes that allowed individuals to opt out of jury duty, or specifically did not include some individuals in the jury pool, solely because of their chosen career (Mushlin, 2007). The list of occupations was often quite broad and included professions such as "physicians, dentists, pharmacists, optometrists, psychologists, podiatrists . . . nurses, embalmers, attorneys, police officers, corrections officers, members of fire departments, orthodontists, licensed physical therapists, and all members of the clergy" (Mushlin, 2007, p. 247). It was widely believed that such professionals provided services to the community that were so valuable that the community would be harmed if these services ceased because of jury duty. Clergy were generally excluded because their professional code of ethics forbade them from making judgments about others, as would be required by jury duty. Thus, the incompatibility between the clergy's religious duties and the duties of jury service prompted their exemption (Mushlin, 2007).

Occupational exemptions became so popular that some jurisdictions were excluding a moderate proportion of their citizens. For instance, New York City and surrounding jurisdictions allowed so many occupational exemptions that up to 10% of all individuals were excluded from jury duty (Mushlin, 2007). Times have changed, however, and today few jurisdictions allow occupational exclusions. This change was largely driven by a pair of U.S. Supreme Court cases regarding the exclusion of women from jury duty (see, e.g., Goode, 2003–2004; Mushlin, 2007). A 1975 case, *Taylor v. Louisiana*, involved a local law that excluded all women from becoming jurors. The court held that this categorical exemption was unconstitutional because it prevented the jury from being a fair cross-section of the community. The court determined that a fair cross-section was required as a fundamental part of the right to a jury trial under the Sixth Amendment. Similarly, in *Duren v. Missouri* (1979), the U.S. Supreme Court considered a statute that automatically exempted any woman who asked to be excluded. The Court determined that a group could not be systematically excluded, because it violated the defendant's right to a fair cross-section of the community.

Although neither the *Taylor* nor *Duren* courts specifically addressed occupational exceptions such as those exempting all clergy, they did set a precedent that distinctive groups could not be systematically excluded. This started a movement to examine jury selection processes to ensure that defendants were receiving trials with jurors who represented a fair cross-section of the community. Courts, legislators, and the American Bar Association all appointed various commissions to examine practices and recommend changes (Mushlin, 2007). Thirty years later, few occupational exemptions exist. Half of the states and the District of Columbia have no exemptions for occupation. Seven states have very limited exemptions (e.g., for judicial officers and elected officials or active-duty military), and only a few exempt clergy.

Currently, clergy exemption statutes are in effect in South Dakota, Delaware, and Tennessee (Mushlin, 2007). A South Dakota law (SDCL § 16–13–10) states that "Any member of the clergy, as defined in § 19–13–16, if jury service conflicts with religious belief, is exempt from jury duty." Similarly, a Delaware statute (Superior Court Petit Jury § 8) exempts "active full-time clergy," and Tennessee (T. C. A. § 22–1-103) exempts all clergy.[5]

These examples illustrate that some states have made special accommodations that allow individuals of certain religions, people with certain religious beliefs, or members of a religious profession to opt out of jury duty. Meanwhile, others explicitly state that religion is not an acceptable reason to avoid jury duty or exclude a juror. Such legislation illustrates the range of positions states have taken on the issue of religion-based exemptions.

How Trial Processes Affect Jury Composition

As just reviewed, peremptory challenges and legislative acts can affect the composition of the jury. In addition, certain trial processes can affect the jury. Judges or other court personnel can choose to excuse a juror for many reasons, including hardship related to the individual's occupation, family, or financial situation. Judges may also exclude jurors because of their religious objections to acting as jurors (e.g., Flowers, 1993). The jury selection process itself (e.g., relying on voter registration) can also affect who is called. The following cases illustrate the various opinions state courts have issued regarding these issues.

Under federal statute (28 USC § 1866) and many state laws, individuals must serve as jurors when called; they can face fines and/or imprisonment for noncompliance. But what if an individual's religion forbids him from serving as a juror? This is common, especially among religions such as the Jehovah's Witnesses, who do not believe in serving a government other than that of God. They often cite scripture, such as Exodus 20: 3–5:

> Thou shalt not have strange gods before me. Thou shalt not make
> unto thee any graven image, nor any likeness of anything that is in

heaven above, or that is in the water under the earth; Thou shalt not bow down Thyself to them, nor serve them: for I the Lord thy God am a jealous God, visiting the iniquity of the fathers upon the children unto the third and fourth generation of them that hate me.

They interpret such scripture to mean that they should not participate in any government functions. Thus, they do not vote or serve on juries. When called, they often refuse to serve as jurors, in potential violation of 28 USC § 1866 or similar state law.

Not surprisingly, this issue has been presented to several courts. A trio of cases all agree that jurors can be excused from jury service because of their religion (*In re Jenison III*, 1963; *United States v. Hillyard*, 1943; *West Virginia v. Everly*, 1966; see also Flowers, 1993). In the case of *In re Jenison,*[6] a potential juror named Mrs. Jenison was selected to be a juror, but she declined, claiming that her religious beliefs forbade her from serving as a juror because the New Testament instructs individuals not to judge others. She was found to be in contempt of court, and she appealed her conviction. The Minnesota Supreme Court originally determined that Mrs. Jenison's right to the free exercise of her religion had not been infringed. Further, her refusal to serve infringed on the defendant's right to a jury of his peers and neglected her duty and obligation as a citizen. Ultimately, the court determined that, absent a legislative enactment, jurors cannot be exempted for religious reasons (*In re Jenison I*, 1963). On appeal, the U.S. Supreme Court vacated the judgment and remanded the case back to the state court (*In re Jenison II*, 1963). The Minnesota Supreme Court determined that "unless experience indicated that indiscriminate invoking of the First Amendment poses a serious threat to effective functioning of the jury system, any person whose religious convictions prohibit compulsory jury duty shall be exempted therefrom" (*In re Jenison III*, p. 588). Ultimately, the court determined that the threat to the jury system was not great enough to outweigh Mrs. Jenison's right to free exercise of her religion (*In re Jenison III*, 1963; see also *United States v. Hillyard*, 1943).

Similar case law has established that individuals can also refuse to serve on a grand jury because of their religious beliefs. In *West Virginia v. Everly* (1966), an ordained minister and Jehovah's Witness refused to serve on the grand jury, was held in contempt of court, and was sentenced to serve 10 days in jail. Everly believed that he was a representative of God's Kingdom and thus could not vote or serve jury duty because these actions would indicate that he recognized a worldly government. He asked the court to allow him to opt out of jury duty because it violated his "personal freedom of conscience" to serve (p. 706). The appeals court determined that Everly was within his rights to refuse to serve. Although the state can require individuals to serve as jurors, a judge can excuse a potential juror for any reason that the judge finds to be sufficient. In Everly's case, the court determined that his religious beliefs would be considered a sufficient condition that would allow him to be excused (*West Virginia v. Everly*, 1966).

Case law such as this indicates that individuals can be excused from jury service based on their religious beliefs. Other issues arise when the timing of the trial interferes with religious holidays. For instance, the trial court judge in *Grech v. Wainwright* (1974) was faced with a dilemma because the trial was to begin on Yom Kippur. The judge determined that Jewish individuals could, if requested, be excused from jury duty. The appellate court determined that no harm was done because the exclusion was not a blanket exclusion, but merely an option that Jewish individuals could choose. As such, the judge's decision was not discrimination and did not violate the Constitution.

A similar situation presented itself in the 1998 case of *U.S. v. Myrick*. Knowing that the trial was to take place during Rosh Hashanah, the judge asked potential jurors whether they would feel comfortable serving jury duty. Two potential jurors were excused as a result of this inquiry. The defendant appealed; however, the appeals court determined that the exclusion of these two individuals did not infringe on the defendant's Sixth Amendment rights or violate the Jury Selection and Service Act.

A slightly different set of circumstances initiated a case called *Scott v. Dugger* (1989). In this case, it was not a judge, but a deputy clerk who allowed some potential jurors to be excluded from jury duty. The clerk granted five requests from individuals who requested postponement due to a Jewish holiday. The appellate court found no error because the defendant could not show the jury pool was affected; Jewish individuals were not underrepresented, and thus the defendant's right to a fair cross-section of the community was not affected.

At times, the jury selection process itself comes under fire for how it affects the jury's composition. Some religions are not well represented in jury pools, even though no specific statute forbids their service. This can occur when the court's method of developing a jury pool inadvertently leaves out a religious group, such as Jehovah's Witnesses, because members of this group do not typically vote, and the jury pool is selected from voter registration lists. In *Camp v. U.S.* (1969), the defendant, a Jehovah's Witness, asserted that he did not receive a fair trial because members of his religious group were under-represented in the jury pool from which his jury was drawn. The defendant claimed that the use of voter registration lists for jury selection resulted in the exclusion of all Jehovah's Witnesses from juries. The court determined that the selection process was allowable. Jehovah's Witnesses were not exempted by statute, and "nonvoters" were not a cognizable group; thus, the jury selection procedure did not constitute discrimination.

The *death qualification process* is another trial process that can significantly alter the religious composition of capital juries. During the death qualification phase of jury selection of a capital trial, potential jurors are disqualified if their attitudes toward capital punishment are sufficiently strong so as to prevent them from carrying out their duties fairly (*Wainwright v. Witt*, 1985). For instance, jurors whose attitudes are so strong that they could never give the death penalty would be excluded. The death qualification process has been criticized because it potentially eliminates members of some groups more than others (e.g., Butler, 2007; Fitzgerald & Ellsworth, 1984). In *People v. Hale* (1997), the defendant claimed that the death qualification process violated potential jurors' right to equal protection and freedom of religion. The court recognized that "a juror may not be excluded for . . . expressing conscientious or religious 'scruples' regarding such sentencing" (p. 192, citing *Witherspoon v. Illinois*, 1968), but rather death qualification only should eliminate potential jurors who have opinions so strong that they would "prevent or substantially impair the performance of his duties as a juror in accordance with his instructions and his oath" (p. 192, citing *Adams v. Texas*, 1980). Ultimately, the court rejected the defendant's claim. The court was not concerned about the potential for death qualification to impact the jury's religious composition. Nevertheless, some empirical evidence suggests that death qualification does systematically eliminate individuals with certain religious characteristics (Summers, Hayward, & Miller, in press). Specifically, those scoring higher on a devotionalism scale and Catholics were more likely to be excluded through the death qualification process as compared to their counterparts. In contrast, those participants who subscribed to fundamentalist beliefs or believed the Bible should be translated literally were less likely to be excluded.[7] Thus, there is some concern that the death qualification process alters the jury's religious composition.

As illustrated by the examples above, the process of jury selection affects the interests of the court, the defendant, and potential jurors. Courts must balance these interests in order to determine whether an individual can be excused from jury duty. With the exception of the death qualification process just discussed, the interests of potential jurors often prevail. A decision to allow potential jurors to opt out of jury duty during a religious holiday reflects the court system's willingness to recognize individuals' religious beliefs and practices. The *Camp v. U.S.* (1969) case illustrates how the jury selection process can alter the jury's religious composition. Although the court in this case determined that the procedure was constitutional, a change in the procedure would be unlikely to lead to dramatic changes in a jury's composition. For instance, Jehovah's Witnesses do not vote and thus would not be included in the voter registration list from which the jury pool is drawn. Nevertheless, members of this religious group also do not believe in serving on a jury; thus, even if the jury selection process was altered to include them in the pool, they could be exempted as per cases such as *West Virginia v. Everly* (1966). As long as such individuals are allowed to opt out, the jury pool would be similar under most jury selection schemes. It is important to note, however, that other jury selection procedures could eliminate members of a variety of religions. For example, a procedure drawing prospective jurors from a list of those with driver's licenses would exclude the Amish and other religions whose members do not drive. In sum, these examples illustrate ways in which judges, court personnel, and the entities involved in jury selection can alter the jury's religious composition. Ultimately, it is likely in the court's interest to allow unwilling jurors to be excused, as they may be unable to carry out their duties as jurors or would perform poorly if forced to serve.

Conclusion

Throughout history, legislatures have wavered among several strategies: purposefully excluding members of certain religious groups, allowing them to choose whether or not they want to serve, categorically exempting them, and specifically forbidding their exclusion. Judges have sometimes made exemptions for individuals based on their religious beliefs or practices. Most recently, attorneys have used peremptory challenges to exclude potential jurors based on their religious characteristics. Although some states have restricted an attorney's ability to exclude jurors based on their religion, others have given attorneys total freedom or have implemented less restrictive rules. With such flexibility, there is an increasing trend to exclude jurors based on the potential juror's religion. As such, it is important to understand the relationship between jurors' decisions and the many facets of religious affiliation, practice, and belief. These topics will be covered in the next two chapters.

3

The Relationship Between Jurors' Religious Affiliation and Legal Attitudes

> God of Compassion,
> . . . there is in our land a great cry for vengeance
> as we fill up death rows and kill the killers
> in the name of justice, in the name of peace . . .
>
> Holy Spirit of God,
> You strengthen us in the struggle for justice.
> Help us to work tirelessly
> for the abolition of state-sanctioned death
> and to renew our society in its very heart
> so that violence will be no more. Amen.
>
> —Sister Helen Prejean, "Prayer to Abolish the Death
> Penalty" (www.americancatholic.org/News/
> DeathPenalty/prayer.asp)

The effects of jurors' religious affiliation on their legal attitudes and verdicts have long been the subject of folklore and old wives' tales. Legal experts have suggested that jurors of particular religious affiliations are predisposed to favor either the prosecution/plaintiff or the defense. Clarence Darrow (1936) suggests that a Catholic makes a good defense juror because he "loves music and art; he must be emotional" and thus will side with the defense. Similarly, others have advised lawyers for plaintiffs in civil cases and criminal defendants to seek Jews (among other ethnicities such as Irish, Italian, and French) because these groups will respond most naturally to the sorts of emotional appeals inherent in such trials (e.g., Goldstein, 1935). Such speculation is not confined to generations past, as a lawyer recently made a sworn declaration that a former judge told him to keep Jews off death penalty juries because they are unlikely to give the death penalty (Kravets, 2006; Murphy, 2005). Thus, the folklore remains active (see Chapter 2 for more information about the role of religion in the jury selection process).

This chapter presents empirical research that has investigated whether members of various religious affiliations have different attitudes toward legal issues. Some of these attitudes may come directly from religious mandates; for instance, the Catholic Church has declared its opposition to the death penalty

(Drinan, 2000), which could lead a Catholic juror to be less likely to support capital punishment. Other attitudes may be shaped less directly, through general religious teachings. For example, fundamentalist Protestant churches generally believe that crime is a result of personal sin (as opposed to environmental influences); thus, members of these religiously conservative groups tend to blame and punish the criminal more (Ellison & Sherkat, 1993; Grasmick, Bursik, & Blackwell, 1993). This chapter discusses how religious affiliation is related to one's general worldview, legal attitudes, and attitudes toward civil and criminal sanctions.

How Religious Teachings Affect Individuals' General Worldview

Individuals' religious beliefs and practices can lead them to adopt a variety of attitudes that may shape their perceptions when they serve as jurors. Although religion can affect many beliefs, those about sexual orientation and gender are highlighted here because these topics are controversial and continue to present challenges to the legal system.

One controversial issue that has divided religious groups across the country is whether gays can serve as religious leaders. In August 2007, the Evangelical Lutheran Church in America (ELCA) passed a nationwide resolution that instructed bishops not to discipline gay pastors who were in "faithful committed same-gender relationships." Before this resolution, as recently as July 2007, the ELCA had ordered gay pastors to be fired. The ELCA also created a committee to investigate the issue of sexuality in order to develop a "social statement" about the issue. This social statement will be released in 2009 and will provide guidance for the ELCA's 4.8 million members ("Lutherans to allow pastors in gay relationships," 2007). According to their website (http://www.ELCA.org), social statements are "theological and teaching documents that assist members in forming judgments on social issues [and] set policy for this church." As such, this social statement may be influential in shaping members' general worldviews. These views could, in turn, affect members' legal attitudes.

Other churches have struggled with this issue as well. After Rev. Karen Dammann announced that she was a lesbian, church officials took action. Dammann, who had served as pastor of the First United Methodist Church in Ellensburg, Washington, was put on leave because the church's policy prohibits gays from serving as pastors. The church's *Book of Discipline* indicates that homosexuality is "incompatible" with Christian instruction. Clergy from the United Methodist Church of the Pacific Northwest Conference first voted to allow Dammann to keep her appointment as a pastor; however, the Judicial Council of the Methodist Church reversed that decision. She was then granted a church trial, which was decided by a panel of 13 pastors who eventually decided in her favor ("Church trial acquits gay pastor," 2004).

Other denominations have also been divided by the issue of homosexuality, most notably the Episcopalian Church (Banerjee, 2007), which has lost hundreds of thousands of members since the church consecrated an openly gay bishop in 2003 (Duin, 2008). In the 2008 election, Jewish officials split over the passing of California's Proposition 8, which banned gay marriage in the state. Orthodox Jewish officials supported the measure, but more liberal synagogue leaders were more supportive (Heller, 2008).

Such church actions and policies can influence church members' attitudes about sexuality, and their general beliefs about gays. These beliefs and attitudes can affect how jurors perceive defendants and evidence presented at trial. For instance, jurors who embrace negative beliefs about gays may be less sympathetic toward a gay crime victim or a gay employee who claims employment discrimination, while being more sympathetic toward a defendant accused of anti-gay activities. Beliefs about sexual orientation may affect the fate of Brian Prowel, who claims he was discriminated against in his workplace because he is gay. Prowel sued his employer, Wise Business Forms, because his coworkers called him names such as "Rosebud" and "Princess," left a feathered tiara and a bottle of personal lubricant at his workstation, and wrote things about him on the bathroom walls. Title VII, the federal law prohibiting discrimination based on sex, religion, race, and national origin, forbids discrimination based on *gender stereotyping*. It does not forbid discrimination or harassment based on *sexual orientation*, however. A judge dismissed Prowel's claims, finding that the discrimination was based on sexual orientation—essentially indicating that Prowel did not have a legal cause of action (P.R. Ward, 2008).[1] In such cases, the religious backgrounds of the judge and jurors could influence their decisions. Specifically, someone who was raised in a church that was accepting of gays might be more likely to side with a gay litigant.

Religious affiliation can also shape beliefs about gender. For example, the Southern Baptists banned women from being pastors in 2000 and passed a guideline in 1998 that states that a woman should "submit herself graciously" to her husband (Bell, 2000). Although these attitudes are not related directly to the legal system, they reflect attitudes that could affect members' decisions as jurors. Because these actions communicate expected gender behavior (e.g., a woman cannot be in a position of leadership and should obey her husband), a litigant who does not fit these expectations may be looked down upon in a trial. Jurors with these beliefs might be more likely than their counterparts to have negative attitudes toward a woman who argues she was raped by her husband or a woman business owner suing over a contract dispute.

For instance, members who take this directorate to mean that women cannot be in any position of leadership (rather than believing the directorate only forbids women to be church leaders but allows them to have other leadership roles) may have been more punitive in cases such as the trial of entrepreneur Martha Stewart. In March 2004, a federal jury found Stewart guilty of conspiracy, obstruction of justice, and lying to police investigators

(Steinhaus, 2004). In cases such as Stewart's, jurors with strong religious beliefs that women should not be leaders may be biased against a powerful woman defendant. These gender attitudes may shape the juror's verdict preference. Some jurors would presumably be able to separate their religious beliefs from the legal decision they are making; that is, they may recognize that although they personally feel that a woman should not be in a position of power, the law requires them to be objective and not use their personal opinions as the basis for their verdict. However, many jurors arguably would not be able to make a decision without being influenced by their personal beliefs, whether consciously or not.

Religious affiliation can shape one's attitudes about a variety of legal and social issues. Grasmick, Davenport, Chamlin, and Bursik (1992) reviewed religious differences in beliefs about homosexuality, female politicians, the Equal Rights Amendment, the Pro-Life movement, pornography, and sex education. Table 3.1 lists the official positions of various religious organizations on the death penalty, abortion, and gay marriage.

Differences among religious denominations may partially be due to religious beliefs about attributions of responsibility and forgiveness. For instance, those who are members of fundamentalist churches are more likely to attribute criminal behavior to an individual's character (i.e., dispositional attribution) rather than to environmental factors (i.e., situational attribution; see Ellison & Sherkat, 1993; Grasmick & McGill, 1994). Such individuals tend to be concerned with personal character, because character indicates whether someone will eventually go to heaven. Criminal behavior and other behavior that is counter to the teachings of the Bible are seen as indicative of a negative character. As such, fundamentalists tend to make dispositional attributions, rather than situational attributions. Research confirms this hypothesis: Among White participants, those who held fundamentalist beliefs were more likely to make dispositional attributions (i.e., blaming the offender's bad nature rather than characteristics of the environment) for juvenile crimes. Dispositional attributions were related to more punitive responses toward offenders. Thus, being a member of a fundamentalist church could affect one's attributions, which in turn affect one's punitiveness (Grasmick & McGill, 1994).

Willingness to forgive may also mediate the relationship between religious affiliation and legal attitudes. For instance, the Amish have adopted a culture of forgiveness. This belief was tested on October 2, 2006, when a man opened fire in an Amish schoolhouse, killing five young girls before killing himself. Although many in the country reacted with rage and called for retribution and revenge, the Amish community did not. They expressed their hope that he had met a merciful God, refused to denigrate his memory, and assured his family that they did not blame them. When the Amish families received monetary donations, they shared part of the money with the killer's family. According to Nolt (2007), the Amish believe that forgiving means giving up the need to seek revenge and relinquishing feelings of resentment

All these studies indicate that members of fundamentalist Protestant groups are more punitive than their counterparts.

In contrast, other studies have found no differences in legal attitudes among various religious denominations. For instance, one study found no religious difference among Jews, Protestants, and Catholics in the belief that the courts are too lenient; however, those with no religious affiliation were less likely than the other groups to hold the belief (Flanagan & Jamieson, 1988). Other studies have found no difference between Catholics and Protestants in their likelihood of voting for a candidate who supports more punitive criminal sentences or in their beliefs that police should be stricter (Hindelang, 1974). Nonetheless, it is worthy of note that most of the studies that found no differences among affiliations did not separate Protestants into different groups (e.g., fundamentalist and nonfundamentalist groups). As mentioned earlier, null results may be a result of the cruder way in which denominations were categorized.

In sum, mixed support exists for the notion that religious affiliation is associated with legal attitudes, although the most common theme is that fundamentalist Protestants are more punitive than other groups. As discussed next, the effects of affiliation on individuals' legal attitudes and jurors' decisions may vary based on the type of trial.

Religious Differences in Specific Trial Types

As just discussed, religious affiliation may be related to some *general* legal attitudes. This next section discusses relationships (or lack thereof) between religious affiliation and attitudes/verdicts in *specific* types of trials, including general criminal trials, death penalty trials, child abuse trials, civil trials, and insanity trials.

General Criminal Trials

In addition to the general legal attitudes just discussed, religious affiliation may affect one's verdict preference in a criminal trial. Clarence Darrow (1936) suggested that, based on his experience, Baptists, Presbyterians, and Lutherans are prosecution prone; the defense lawyer should be cautious when accepting jurors who are Methodists, Unitarian, Universalists, and Congregationalists because they are somewhat unpredictable (Darrow, 1936). Meanwhile, Jews and agnostics are good for the defense. Belli (1963) also sought Jews for defense jurors.

These early predictions were "best guesses" based on the lawyer's own experience and the observed successes of other lawyers. Because religion has long been a popular basis for choosing juries, it is no surprise that the earliest attempts at scientific trial consulting investigated the effects of religion (among many other factors). Consultants in the Harrisburg Seven trial (discussed in detail in Chapter 2) found that Episcopalians, Presbyterians, Methodists, and fundamentalists were prone to side with the prosecution. Thus, defense attorneys were advised to remove such individuals from the jury pool. This study confirmed that some basic relationships exist between religious affiliation and preferred verdicts (although not always the same relationships Darrow and Belli predicted).

In a mock juror experiment, Singer and Miller (2008) found that Protestant mock jurors were somewhat more punitive than Catholic mock jurors when judging a theft case, although the difference was not quite statistically significant ($p = .051$). Other studies have found no differences in jurors' verdict preference among various affiliations. For instance, Blumstein and Cohen (1980) found no differences in preferred sentences in criminal trials among Protestants, Jews, and Catholics.[4]

As these few studies indicate, some evidence suggests that religious affiliation is related to preferences about punishment for some criminal acts. Two special categories of criminal trials are those in which the prosecution is seeking the death penalty and child abuse (including corporal punishment) cases. Because capital punishment and corporal punishment are especially controversial social issues on which religions differ (e.g., the Catholic and Southern Baptist churches have taken opposite positions on the death penalty), these two trial types receive special attention in the next two sections.

Death Penalty Trials

Many religious organizations have publicly stated their positions about the death penalty. In 2000, Southern Baptists adopted a resolution supporting the death penalty (Bell, 2000; Drinan, 2000). Reconstruction Christians also have detailed their theological justifications for supporting the death penalty (Cook & Powell, 2003; North & DeMar, 1991). In contrast, most Jewish organizations (with the exception of some Orthodox Jewish organizations) oppose the penalty (Drinan, 2000). The Catholic Church has become more critical of the death penalty in recent years (Drinan, 2000), specifying in the catechism that the death penalty robs the defendant of possible redemption and that the death penalty is not in line with the common good and dignity of humans (Bjarnason & Welch, 2004). The Catholic Church has formed allegiances with mainline Protestant churches on this issue, but it has distanced itself from evangelical churches that read the Bible to support the death penalty (Drinan, 2000). U.S. Supreme Court Justice and devout Catholic Antonin Scalia spoke publicly about his disagreement with his church's position on the death penalty. He suggested that Catholic judges who oppose the death penalty should step down (Lithwick, 2002; "Scalia sticks to his guns," 2002). The next two subsections discuss the research that has investigated the relationship between religious affiliation and (a) attitudes about the death penalty, and (b) jury verdicts in death penalty cases.

Churches dp against

Attitudes About the Death Penalty

When studying differences among affiliations, it is important to consider the time at which the study was conducted because some groups have shifted their stance on the death penalty. As mentioned earlier, the Catholic Church recently began to oppose the death penalty; research indicates that Catholics have adjusted their attitudes accordingly. In 1974, Catholics were more supportive of the death penalty than non-Catholics; however, by 1994, there was no difference between the groups (Bjarnason & Welch, 2004).

Most early studies indicate no relationship between religious affiliation and support for the death penalty (Harris, 1986; Hindelang, 1974; Tyler & Weber, 1982; Vidmar, 1974). Some modern studies also found no difference. Neither Gonzalez-Perez (2001) nor Miller (2006) found any relationship between death penalty attitudes and religious affiliation. It is important to note, however, that neither study included a wide range of affiliations, which limited the comparisons that could be made (e.g., neither study included a sample of Jews). Other studies have failed to find any difference between members of fundamentalist churches and members of other churches (Sandys & McGarrell, 1997; Soss, Langbein, & Metelko, 2003; Unnever & Cullen, 2006).

In contrast, many studies have found that members of fundamentalist churches are more supportive of the death penalty. Barkan and Cohn (1994) found that membership in a fundamentalist church was weakly related to support for the death penalty, although the finding was only marginally significant ($p = .052$). Using the General Social Survey data, Young (1992, 2000) and Stack (2003) also found that belonging to a Christian fundamentalist group was related to support for the death penalty. Similarly, those who are members of evangelical/fundamentalist Protestant churches are more likely to support the death penalty for *adults* than are those who are members of liberal/moderate Protestant churches and those with no affiliation (Grasmick, Cochran et al., 1993). The evangelical/fundamentalist group was also more supportive of the *juvenile* death penalty than were Catholics, although they did not differ from the other groups.

Miller and Hayward (2008) found that Protestants (including both fundamentalists and nonfundamentalists) were more likely to be death penalty supporters than opponents, whereas Catholics were evenly divided between supporters and opponents. This occurred both in a general sample and a sample that had been death qualified.[5] Similarly, Protestants were more supportive of the death penalty than were Catholics, as measured by items such as, "I think the death penalty is necessary" (O'Neil, Patry, & Penrod, 2004). Finally, White Catholics were more opposed to the death penalty than Whites who were members of other religious groups (Soss et al., 2003).

It is worth mentioning, however, that the studies just discussed have investigated attitudes toward the death penalty in general, rather than investigating actual verdicts. For instance, Grasmick, Cochran, and colleagues (1993) measured support by asking participants to rate their agreement with statements such as, "Adults who are convicted of first-degree murder generally deserve the death penalty" and "Sixteen-year-olds who are convicted of first-degree murder generally deserve the death penalty" on a 4-point scale from "strongly agree" to "strongly disagree." Attitudes toward the death penalty do not necessarily translate into *verdicts* in capital cases, however. An individual may generally support the death penalty, but be unwilling to give it in some trials; alternatively, one may generally oppose the death penalty, but be willing to give it in an extreme case. Thus, some researchers have attempted to study actual juror verdicts, as discussed next.

Juror Verdicts in Death Penalty Cases

Several studies have investigated the relationship between religious affiliation and jurors' verdict preferences in death penalty cases. One study asked real death penalty jurors about their "first votes"; that is, whether their initial preference was for a death sentence or for life in prison (Eisenberg, Garvey, & Wells, 2001). Studying first votes allows researchers to understand jurors' personal verdict preferences, independent of any effects that deliberations might have on their verdict preference. The researchers found that nearly 80% of Southern Baptists voted for death on their first vote; in contrast, only 50% of non-Southern Baptist jurors' first votes were for death. This result held even when researchers controlled for race by analyzing only White jurors in both religious groups (Eisenberg et al., 2001). Another study analyzed individual verdict preferences of Catholic and Protestant mock jurors and found that religious affiliation did not predict mock jurors' death penalty verdicts (Miller & Hayward, 2008). Although these two studies may seem contradictory, it is important to note that the studies categorized participants in very different ways. Eisenberg and colleagues divided their group into Southern Baptists (who are fundamentalist Protestants) and non-Southern Baptists (a group that would include nonfundamentalist Protestants, Catholics, etc.). In contrast, Miller and Hayward grouped participants into Catholics and Protestants (a group that would have combined fundamentalist and nonfundamentalist Protestants). The differing findings may very well be because of how the different researchers categorized their participants.

As these studies indicate, there are some differences in attitudes toward the death penalty based on religious affiliation. Commonly, Catholics are less supportive of the death penalty than other groups. These preferences are apparent in the laws that different states enact. Uelmen (2005) reports that "It is not a coincidence that those states which do not utilize the death penalty include the states with the highest proportion of Catholics in their population" (p. 356). In addition, fundamentalist Protestants (e.g., Southern Baptists) tend to favor the death penalty more than other groups. These findings are not that surprising, given that these are the official positions that have been established by these religious groups.

Child Abuse and Corporal Punishment

In addition to the death penalty, child abuse (and corporal punishment) is another topic that deserves special attention because of the controversy that surrounds it—and because a religious divide exists in attitudes about it. In 2007, California and Massachusetts proposed laws that would make it illegal for parents to spank their children. If such laws go into effect, judges and jurors will make important decisions about the future of parents and families. The same religious tenets that make fundamentalist Protestants supportive of legal punishment also lead them to be more supportive of parental punishment (e.g., spanking) and supportive of corporal punishment in schools (Ellison & Sherkat, 1993; Grasmick, Bursik, & Kimpel, 1991; Grasmick, Morgan, & Kennedy, 1992). On the other hand, conservative Protestant parents are less likely to yell at their children, presumably because of a preference for nonemotional punishment (Bartkowski & Wilcox, 2000). These studies, taken together, indicate that fundamentalist Protestants are more likely to support spanking, but less likely to support yelling as a means of disciplining children. This confirms that discipline that is acceptable to members of some religious groups may be less acceptable to members of other religious groups. Thus, judges and jurors who follow the teachings of these fundamentalist Protestant churches may be more lenient in a child abuse case in which spanking was used. That is, they may be less likely to convict a parent for spanking a child, or they may support a more lenient sentence. On the other hand, they may be more punitive toward parents who allegedly abuse their child emotionally (e.g., by yelling). Specific research is needed to support this speculation, however.

The same predictions could be made for legal decisions in the civil child welfare system. Although judges usually make decisions regarding whether a parent's rights should be terminated because of abuse or neglect, a few states allow jurors to make such decisions. Religious beliefs may affect what decision makers consider to be abuse and what they consider to be acceptable parenting practices. Thus, the religious affiliation of the decision maker may affect whether the child is temporarily or permanently removed from the home.

Attitudes Toward Child Abuse and Corporal Punishment

Research generally supports the predictions offered above. Grasmick and colleagues (1991) sampled 394 adults from the 1991 Oklahoma City Survey and found that Protestant fundamentalism was positively related to support for corporal punishment in both the home and in schools. Similar results were found in a sample of adults in Ireland. Irish fundamentalist Protestants were more likely to support physical punishment, to use physical punishment, and to use more severe punishment than either mainstream Protestants or Catholics (Murphy-Cowan & Stringer, 2001). On the other hand, Ellison and Sherkat (1993) did not find that conservative Protestantism was related to support for corporal punishment in a sample drawn from the General Social Survey. Thus, results are somewhat mixed, but generally indicate that members of fundamentalist religious groups are more supportive of corporal punishment—an attitude that could affect their legal decisions if they were asked to serve as jurors.

Jury Verdicts in Child Abuse Cases

Two studies have investigated the relationship between religious affiliation and verdicts in child abuse cases. Mock juror participants with a "Christian-right orientation" (as compared to those without such an orientation) gave more severe punishments in a child molestation case, but only when the defendant had used his religion as a defense (Johnson, 1985). Kerr, Hymes, Anderson, and Weathers (1995) found that Jewish mock jurors were less likely than Christians to convict the defendant in a child molestation case. Importantly, these studies both investigated child sexual abuse cases, rather than physical abuse (e.g., spanking); this is an important distinction to make, because the beliefs that lead one to support spanking a child would not necessarily lead one to be more lenient in a child molestation case.

Civil Trials

Folklore regarding the legal attitudes of people from various religious backgrounds exists also in civil trials. Legal scholars have suggested that Jews make good jurors for civil plaintiffs (Cartwright, 1977; Harrington & Dempsey, 1969), perhaps because they have more empathy (Cartwright, 1977) as a result of having experienced oppression (Fulero & Penrod, 1990). One exception is for medical malpractice trials. Jews are said to be poor plaintiff jurors in such trials because they are believed by some to have a very high admiration of the medical profession (Fulero & Penrod, 1990). Only a small number of studies have investigated the relationship between religious affiliation and legal attitudes or verdicts concerning civil issues.

Attitudes Toward Civil Litigation

Hans and Loftquist (1994) found that Protestants had higher "Litigation Crisis" scale scores than did Catholics, those with "other" religious affiliations, and those who had no religious affiliation. This means that Protestants agreed more strongly that there are too many frivolous lawsuits and that juries' damage awards are generally too high. Protestants may be skeptical of civil plaintiffs; thus, they may be less likely to find a defendant liable or may give lower damage awards. Another study provides support for this proposition. Hans and Lofquist (1992) found a relationship between attitudes about a "Litigation Crisis" and jury awards; specifically, juries made up of more members with a greater belief in a litigation crisis tended to give lower damage awards. Hans and Lofquist (1994) suggest that Protestants have characteristics or historical experiences that lead them to be hostile toward civil litigation (e.g., belief in the "Protestant work ethic").

Jury Verdicts in Civil Litigation Cases

Reed (1965) found no relationship between religious affiliation and the decisions of actual jurors who heard civil trials in Louisiana in 1959. Because there have been so few studies conducted, the connection between religious affiliation and decision making in civil trials has yet to be fully discovered. As in criminal cases, any relationship between religion and juror verdicts is likely to vary depending on the type of case (e.g., personal injury, contract disputes). Clearly, more research is necessary to understand this relationship (or lack thereof) between religious affiliation and civil jury verdicts and attitudes.

Insanity Trials

The insanity defense is essentially a defendant's attempt to convince the jury that he should not be convicted because his mental condition at the time of the crime relieves him of culpability. Thus, the jury has the choice of finding the defendant "guilty," "not guilty," or "not guilty by reason of insanity." Some states also allow jurors to give a "guilty but mentally ill" verdict (Greene, Heilbrun, Fortune, & Nietzel, 2007; Van Voorhis, Braswell, & Lester, 2007). Typically, if a jury finds the defendant not guilty by reason of insanity, he will be committed to a mental institution, whereas a defendant found guilty but mentally ill will receive the same sentence (i.e., a prison sentence) as if he was found guilty. Defendants found not guilty by reason of insanity actually spend a longer time in some form of detention, on average, than defendants found guilty of comparable crimes (Greene et al., 2007).

Attitudes Toward the Insanity Defense

Jurors' religious beliefs might be particularly influential in insanity cases in which the defendant claims that he suffered a hallucination in which God told him to commit the crime. A defendant named Naveed Haq believed God had sent him on a mission when he killed one person and injured five others in the Jewish Federation of Greater Seattle on July 28, 2006 (Singer, 2008).[6] A mistrial was declared because the jury could only agree on a verdict for one of the charges. In cases such as these, jurors must determine whether the defendant was insane as a result of his religious hallucinations. Jurors who belong to religions that are more accepting of the notion of divine prophecy would likely be less inclined to view religious hallucinations as aberrant or a sign of mental illness (and therefore not indicative of insanity), but they might also be more sympathetic toward a defendant who claimed to have had such hallucinations.

"God made me do it"

It is not yet known whether individuals of different religions have different legal attitudes concerning the insanity defense. However, Skeem and Golding (2001) measured participants' "prototypes" of insanity and found some important individual differences. For instance, women and men have different ideas about what constitutes insanity. Some participants viewed mentally insane persons as being unfeeling, manipulative, violent, unpredictable, and having a highly distorted sense of reality; these participants were more likely to be women. In contrast, some participants viewed the mentally insane as someone who is (a) incapable of understanding the harmful nature of one's actions, (b) considered by a credible expert to be insane, and (c) more than just temporarily insane; participants with these views were more likely to be men. The authors suggest that this was, at least in part, due to the different experiences and beliefs of men and women. For instance, women (as compared to men) may be more in tune with the media's portrayal of the mentally ill as psychotics who stalk and victimize women; women (as compared to men) also tend to perceive the mentally ill as more dangerous. This study did not measure individual religious differences; however, the finding that beliefs about insanity vary as a result of some individual differences (e.g., gender) suggests that other individual differences (e.g., religious characteristics) might also affect perceptions of insanity.

Fundamentalists are more likely to believe that someone can be possessed or under the control of the devil or demons. Indeed, one of the questions frequently used to measure fundamentalist or orthodox beliefs is: "I believe there is a supernatural being, the devil, who continually tries to lead men into sin" (Putney & Middleton, 1961). Thus, fundamentalists may be more likely to believe that the defendant did receive commands during a hallucination, although the defendant may be confused and believe the command was from God when in fact it came from the devil. As mentioned earlier in this chapter, fundamentalists are also more likely to attribute blame to the person, as opposed to the situation (Ellison & Sherkat, 1993; Grasmick & McGill, 1994). Thus, a fundamentalist would likely believe that the person suffering the hallucination is responsible for putting himself in a position in which the devil can control his actions, for instance, by using drugs or distancing himself from God. Thus, a fundamentalist juror may be more punitive than a non-fundamentalist juror toward a defendant who had hallucinations about God. Such individuals would be less likely to find the defendant to be insane and would instead find him guilty.

Religious beliefs about insanity may also be affected by an individual's beliefs about mental illness. Followers of the Church of Scientology do not believe in mental illness or psychiatry. Although it has been their official position for decades, this stance was made more public in 2005 when Scientologist and actor Tom Cruise called psychiatry a pseudoscience and chided actress Brooke Shields for using medication to treat her postpartum depression. Scientologists would not likely believe a defendant who claimed he suffered from a mental illness and would thus be unlikely to find him insane or guilty but mentally ill.

Jury Verdicts in Insanity Cases

We could find only one study that investigated the relationship between religious affiliation and jury verdicts. Simon (1967) asked mock jurors to decide whether a defendant was either guilty or not guilty by reason of insanity. Two different cases were used: incest and housebreaking. Simon found no difference in verdict between Protestant, Catholic, and "other or no religion" jurors (Simon, 1967).

Conclusion

Religious affiliation may have an indirect effect on jurors' beliefs; for instance, jurors might have specific beliefs about gender or sexual orientation that can affect their perceptions about female or gay litigants. Religious affiliation can also have a more direct effect if a group's leaders have stated an official position (e.g., the Catholic Church's opposition to the death penalty). Religious teachings can also affect one's beliefs about forgiveness or one's attributional style; these factors could then affect one's legal attitudes and behaviors. Attorneys have long sought to capitalize on these differences; for example, a defense attorney may exclude Catholic potential jurors because he believes that Catholics will be less likely to give the death penalty. Although some decisions made by attorneys are based on science, many are based on hunches or personal experience, both of which can be faulty.

Although attorney intuition and folklore may have visceral appeal, the scientific research has at times brought doubt to the credibility of these hunches. Such speculation highlights the need for scientific research. Although numerous studies exist, this body of research has many limitations. First, existing research in this area is piecemeal. Simply put, no comprehensive study asks participants from a large diversity of religions about their attitudes toward a great number of punishments and crimes. For instance, some studies compare only Catholics and Protestants (e.g., Singer & Miller, 2008) or only compare Christians to Jews (e.g., Kerr et al., 1995); such studies can say nothing about other religious groups. Other studies group all minority religions into the category of "other" religions (e.g., Hans & Lofquist, 1994). Simplistic categorizations ignore major doctrinal differences within that "other" group—this group would presumably include diverse affiliations such as Jews, Mormons, and Buddhists.

It is also important to note that much variation exists even within a certain religious category. Many studies are limited because they do not recognize these potentially important distinctions. There are important differences between fundamentalist Protestants and more liberal Protestants. Similarly, there might be differences between various Jewish denominations (e.g., Orthodox, Conservative Reform, Reconstructionist) and among different groups that consider themselves to be Catholic (e.g., Roman Catholics and Eastern Orthodox), yet no studies we know of make such distinctions. As we observed in Chapter 1, conservative adherents of different religious denominations might be more alike than conservative and liberal adherents within a given denomination. Indeed, the fact that some religious surveys distinguish between evangelical and mainstream religious groups that share the same superordinate label (e.g., Baptist) supports this contention. It reflects the importance of specific attitudes and beliefs, and not mere denominational affiliation (see Chapter 4).

As noted by Smith (1990), there are nearly 1200 different denominations, and the way these groups are categorized, and the specific comparisons made, can affect a study's results. Other studies use a variety of religious affiliations or locations, but study a limited number of crimes (e.g., Young, 1992). This makes it difficult to make generalizations across a variety of criminal and civil judgments. Until there is a comprehensive study using a wide variety of religions and crimes, the overall knowledge about how religious affiliation relates to legal attitudes and jury verdicts will be incomplete.

Despite these limitations, some general conclusions can be drawn. In general, fundamentalist (also called conservative or evangelical) Protestants are more punitive than other religious groups. This makes sense because of the beliefs of fundamentalist groups (e.g., the tendency to attribute crime to the person instead of the situation), but it is also somewhat surprising because another study found that fundamentalists had more forgiving and compassionate beliefs than those belonging to other affiliations (Unnever & Cullen, 2006). It is important to note, however, that the questions Unnever and Cullen used to measure forgiveness were not related to forgiving criminals. The questions involved how often participants' religious beliefs led to forgiving themselves, forgiving others who hurt them, and knowing that God forgives them. It is possible that the study would find that fundamentalists (who tend to be more punitive toward criminals) were not as forgiving toward *criminals*.

Some studies may find that one religious group is more punitive than other groups, yet another study will fail to replicate this finding. There are a few reasons for the inconsistent findings across studies. First, as discussed earlier, there might be important differences in how studies measured affiliation. Second, these studies measured affiliation, but they did not take into account "how religious" individuals are (see Unnever & Cullen, 2006). Just because someone is a member of a certain religious group does not necessarily mean that he subscribes to the tenets of that group. Thus, the influence of the religious affiliation may not be strong enough to influence his legal decisions. A study that had participants who were "less religious" might not find significant differences, whereas a study that had participants who were "more religious" might find significant differences among affiliations. Third, the differences might be due to different stimuli—for instance, various civil claims and criminal offenses. Members of various religious affiliations might differ in their beliefs about some types of crimes and punishments, but not about other crimes or punishments. Thus, some studies may have found differences (or not) because of the type of civil offense, crime, or punishment that was under investigation. Similarly, different studies measured legal attitudes in different ways (e.g., by asking participants to rate their support in general, or by asking them to make a verdict as a mock juror). As mentioned earlier, attitudes do not always translate directly into action; thus, having a particular attitude or belief does not mean one will act on it in a particular trial. Thus, a study investigating attitudes may be inconsistent with a study investigating verdicts. Such differences in methodology contribute to the inconsistency in findings among studies.

Nevertheless, many studies have found that religious affiliation is related to legal attitudes and jury decision making. In addition to differences in religious affiliation, some studies have investigated differences in religious characteristics. Individuals' religious traits are discussed in the next chapter.

4

The Relationship Between Jurors' Religious Characteristics and Their Legal Attitudes and Decisions

> [There is] a standard already [written] down in the Bible as to what the rules should be. Therefore those should be the rules we live by . . . a perfect law . . . God has distinctly put in different places within the scriptures that this is worthy of the death and [that] is worthy of death.
>
> —Participant in study conducted by Cook and Powell (2003)

Chapter 3 discussed the relationship between legal attitudes and religious affiliation; however, "religiosity" is a complex construct that has been conceptualized in a variety of different ways in different studies (e.g., Evans & Adams, 2003; Howard & Redfering, 1983; Leiber & Woodrick, 1997; Miller & Hayward, 2008; Vogel, 2003; Young, 1992). This chapter will review empirical literature on the extent to which individuals' degree of observance (e.g., frequency of church attendance), specific religious beliefs or attitudes (e.g., evangelism, literal interpretism), and other measures of religiosity affect their legal attitudes and decision making. Where specific research is lacking, anecdotal evidence is discussed.

Individuals' Religious Beliefs and Characteristics

A variety of religious beliefs and characteristics have the potential to affect jury decisions and other legal attitudes. Such characteristics include evangelism, evangelicalism, fundamentalism, literal interpretism, and devotionalism. We also discuss other less-studied characteristics and beliefs (e.g., belief in a harsh God) to give a more complete picture of how individuals' religious characteristics and beliefs might relate to their legal attitudes.

Evangelism

Evangelism is generally defined as the desire to convert others to Christianity through proselytizing (Young, 1992).[1] Evangelism has been measured in a variety of ways. Young (1992) used a single-item measure (a yes/no response to the question "have you ever tried to encourage someone to believe in Jesus Christ or to accept Jesus Christ as his or her savior?"), while others have used a 6-item scale (Miller & Hayward, 2008; Putney & Middleton, 1961), including questions such as "It is important to help others become enlightened about religion."

Because of their desire to help others find salvation in Jesus Christ, people who evangelize may reject the death penalty because it ensures that the defendant will not find Jesus (Young, 1992). Further, such individuals may display greater compassion and willingness to forgive than other individuals, giving the defendant a second chance to find Jesus. Some research has supported these notions, finding that those who evangelize were less supportive of the death penalty (Young, 1992). Borg (1998) studied both individuals who had and who had not experienced the homicide of a loved one. Among both groups, evangelism was related to lower support for the death penalty. Even though evangelism may affect attitudes toward the death penalty in general, it may not affect actual trial verdicts. Specifically, scores on an evangelism scale did not predict verdicts in mock jury death penalty trials (Miller, 2006; Miller & Hayward, 2008). Thus, the few studies that have been conducted found that those who believe in evangelizing are less punitive or equally punitive than their counterparts—importantly, we could find no study that reported that those who evangelize are more punitive.

Evangelicalism

Evangelicalism refers to a specific set of beliefs that includes believing in the importance of proselytizing, in Christ as the only way to attain eternal life/salvation, in the divinity of Christ, and in an inerrant Bible (Kellstedt, 1989). Further, evangelicalism is quite diverse and includes groups from across the political spectrum (i.e., liberal-conservative).

We could find only one study (Finamore & Carlson, 1987) that investigated how "evangelicalism" (as an individual difference) relates to jurors' legal attitudes.[2] Finamore and Carlson call their scale an "evangelicalism" scale; however, the one item they list from their scale measures personal "born-again" experience—something that others (e.g., Kellstedt, 1989; Smidt, 1989) specifically say is not a requirement of evangelicalism. Specifically, the example item they list was, "I would call myself a born-again Christian because I personally had a conversion experience related to Jesus Christ." Thus, there is some question about how well this scale measured evangelicalism. These researchers found that evangelicalism was related to *more* punitive legal attitudes on a 6-item scale of punitiveness (e.g., "Judges should punish criminals more severely").

Fundamentalist Beliefs

A third religious characteristic that has often been studied is fundamentalism. This term is sometimes called *religious orthodoxy* or *conservatism*, and it is sometimes contrasted with liberalism (Applegate, Cullen, Fisher, & Vander Ven, 2000; Putney & Middleton, 1961; Smith, 1990). Commonly, it is a characteristic that varies among Protestant groups, but it is hard to define (see Young, 1992). Generally, fundamentalism is a set of traditional beliefs about religion. Fundamentalism promotes the idea that individuals have free will, yet have a sinful nature. In the fundamentalist view, crime and immorality result from this human weakness and sin, which should be punished in order to make individuals take responsibility for their behavior (Applegate et al., 2000; Ellison & Sherkat, 1993; Grasmick, Bursik, & Blackwell, 1993; Young, 1992). For fundamentalists, the Bible is the authority given by a punitive God and religion is a "blueprint" for good living (Grasmick, Bursik, & Blackwell, 1993). In addition, fundamentalists generally believe that immoral behaviors (e.g., divorce, abortion) are sins against God, and they tend to attribute behavior to one's character instead of situational factors (Grasmick & McGill, 1994). These beliefs lead fundamentalists to believe that breaking laws, which are secular representations of divine laws, is sinful and must be punished.

Whereas religious liberals allow the scriptures to be interpreted in light of current cultural and social issues, fundamentalists tend to believe in a stricter reading of the Bible (Grasmick, Bursik, & Blackwell, 1993). Thus, fundamentalists generally believe that the Bible should be interpreted literally. For instance, they subscribe to the notion that crime should be repaid an "eye for an eye," and thus tend to promote a retributive punishment philosophy. In general, fundamentalists believe that offenders should receive payback, even if the punishment does not rehabilitate criminals or deter crime (Grasmick, Davenport et al., 1992). As a result of these beliefs, they tend to be more supportive of interpersonal violence (Ellison, 1991) and corporal punishment (Grasmick, Bursik, & Kimpel, 1991) than are nonfundamentalists. This group also generally holds more conservative and traditional views on social and political issues such as homosexuality, sexual behavior, abortion, and environmental protection (Applegate et al., 2000; Pew Forum on Religion and Public Life, 2008).

Like many other religious characteristics, fundamentalism is hard to measure. Sometimes it is combined with evangelicalism, sometimes it is treated as an affiliation (e.g., comparing individuals who are members of a "fundamentalist Protestant church" with individuals who are members of other religious groups), and sometimes it is treated as a personal characteristic that is independent of affiliation (e.g., measuring an individual's level of agreement with fundamentalist beliefs). The studies that treat fundamentalism as a personal characteristic are reported in this chapter (studies that measure it as an affiliation were discussed in Chapter 3). Researchers have used a variety of measurements, including a 5-item scale (e.g., Britt, 1998) or 6-item scale (Miller, 2006; Putney & Middleton, 1961), containing items such as "I believe there is a supernatural being, the Devil, who continually tries to lead men into sin." Other researchers have analyzed individual items taken from established scales (e.g., Howard & Redfering, 1983).

As discussed in Chapter 3, being a member of a fundamentalist Protestant church is associated with more punitive beliefs, verdicts, and sentences. Similarly, when measured as an individual difference (rather than as an affiliation), fundamentalism is related to beliefs about punishment. For instance, supporters of the death penalty tend to have more fundamental/conservative beliefs, whereas opponents tend to have more liberal or moderate religious beliefs (Vogel, 2003). Similarly, individuals who score higher on a scale of fundamentalism tend to be more supportive of the death penalty than those who score lower on the scale (Miller & Hayward, 2008); and mock jurors who subscribed to fundamentalist beliefs were more likely to favor a death sentence rather than a sentence of life in prison (Miller & Hayward, 2008).

Other studies, however, have failed to replicate the relationship between fundamentalism and punitiveness (Britt, 1998; Leiber & Woodrick, 1997), including one study that investigated the relationship between fundamentalism and juror verdict (Miller, 2006). Nevertheless, it is interesting to note that no study (that we know of) has found that fundamentalists were *less* punitive than nonfundamentalists.

Literal Interpretism

As mentioned earlier, fundamentalists tend to be biblical literalists who believe that "the Bible is the actual word of God and is to be taken literally, word for word" (Young, 1992, p. 82); thus, many studies have used literal interpretism as a proxy for fundamentalism. Even so, concepts of fundamentalism and literal interpretism are not one and the same, as one could believe in a literal interpretation of the Bible, but not subscribe to the other tenets to which fundamentalists adhere. Because many researchers have treated these as separate characteristics, we will do the same in this chapter.

The defining belief of literalists is that the Bible should be interpreted literally. As such, the death penalty is justified and mandated because of various biblical passages such as the "eye for an eye" doctrine (Ellison & Sherkat, 1993). Literal interpretism has been measured in a variety of ways, including scales with four items (Grasmick, Cochran et al., 1993), one item (Miller & Bornstein, 2006; Young, 1992), and three items (Leiber & Woodrick, 1997). For instance, Leiber and Woodrick's three questions measure a belief in the literalness of the Bible, the devil, and the resurrection of Jesus. Researchers have investigated the relationships between this characteristic and attitudes toward punishment in general, the death penalty, and treatment of juvenile offenders.

Literalists tend to be more supportive of punishment in general (Applegate et al., 2000; Leiber & Woodrick, 1997), and more supportive of punitive sentences imposed by the courts (Grasmick, Cochran et al., 1993). Similarly, literalists are more likely to endorse a retributive punishment philosophy (Grasmick, Davenport et al., 1992), and are less likely to support prison rehabilitation or treatment for prisoners (Applegate et al., 2000). In contrast, literalism was not related to support for harsher courts (Applegate et al., 2000).

Other studies have investigated literal interpretism as it relates to the death penalty, finding that literalists were more supportive of the penalty than nonliteralists (Grasmick, Bursik, & Blackwell, 1993; Grasmick, Cochran et al., 1993; Leiber & Woodrick, 1997; Young, 1992). This effect was found in a sample of 264 juvenile justice personnel (Leiber & Woodrick, 1997), a sample of 395 Oklahoma community members (Grasmick, Cochran et al., 1993), a sample of 998 mostly Nebraska community members (Miller & Hayward, 2008), and a sample of 1228 participants from the 1988 General Social Survey (Young, 1992). The effect was found for both a death-qualified sample[3] and a sample of the general population (Miller & Hayward, 2008).

Just as literalists are more supportive of the death penalty for adults, they are more supportive of the death penalty for juveniles (Grasmick, Bursik, & Blackwell, 1993; Grasmick, Cochran et al., 1993; Leiber & Woodrick, 1997; Leiber, Woodrick, & Rhoudebush, 1995).[4] Literalists are also more punitive toward juvenile offenders, as measured by items such as "juvenile offenders should be harshly punished to pay them back for the crimes they have committed" (Grasmick & McGill, 1994). Similarly, literalists are more supportive of a stricter juvenile court system (Leiber & Woodrick, 1997) and stricter sentences for juveniles (Leiber et al., 1995). Mock jury studies suggest that literal interpretism may even affect sentences. Specifically, mock jurors who were literalists (as compared to nonliteralists) were more likely to give the death penalty rather than life in prison (Miller, 2006; Miller & Hayward, 2008).

In other studies, however, literalism was not related to support of capital punishment (Applegate et al., 2000; Sandys & McGarrell, 1997; Unnever & Cullen, 2006). This discrepancy might be due to differences in methodology and samples among studies. Applegate and colleagues used a statewide survey of Ohio residents, and Sandys and McGarrell conducted a statewide survey of Indiana residents. As noted by Sandys and McGarrell, a distinct possibility exists that Grasmick and colleagues found a relationship between fundamentalism in their Oklahoma population largely because of their location in the "Bible Belt," and other studies would not find the relationship because of the location of their respective samples.

Even some studies that used similar methodologies found divergent results. Like Young (1992), Unnever and Cullen used a sample from the General Social Survey. Even though Young (who did find a relationship between literalism and death penalty support) and Unnever and Cullen (who did not find this relationship) both used the same survey questions, they used different analytic strategies and used data from different years, 10 years apart (1988 and 1998, respectively). Perhaps these methodological differences explain the inconsistent findings.

Overall, although most studies have found that literalists are more punitive, a few found no difference between literalists and nonliteralists. Importantly, no study that we know of has found that literalists are less punitive than nonliteralists.

Devotionalism

Devotionalism essentially means "how religious" someone is. This characteristic is sometimes called by other names such as "religious salience" (Applegate et al., 2000; Evans & Adams, 2003; Leiber & Woodrick, 1997), "religious importance" (Putney & Middleton, 1961), "personal religiosity" (Grasmick et al., 1991), "religious participation," and "religious identity salience" (Grasmick, Bursik, & Blackwell, 1993).

Devotionalism has been measured in a variety of ways. Various researchers have measured devotionalism by asking how often the participant attends religious services, prays, and/or reads the Bible (Bjarnason & Welch, 2004; Grasmick, Bursik, & Blackwell, 1993; Young, 1992). Others have measured it by asking participants whether they consider themselves to be religious and whether religion is a basis for their day-to-day decisions (Grasmick, Bursik, & Blackwell, 1993). A 2-item scale used by Evans and Adams (2003) measured agreement with variables such as "Religion is a very important part of my life," and various researchers have used a 6-item scale, including items such as "My ideas about religion are one of the most important parts of my philosophy of life" (Miller & Bornstein, 2006; Miller & Hayward, 2008; Putney & Middleton, 1961). Some researchers have analyzed only a few items taken from established scales, rather than using the whole scale (e.g., Howard & Redfering, 1983). Devotionalism has been studied in regard to its relationship to attitudes toward punishment in general and attitudes toward the death penalty.

Beliefs About Punishment

Some studies have found a relationship between devotionalism and general attitudes toward punishment. Grasmick, Davenport, and colleagues (1992) found a negative relationship between "religious identity salience" (i.e., the importance of religion and how religious participants perceive themselves to be) and support of retribution, although this effect only occurred when controlling for biblical literalism. Greer and colleagues (2005) found that people who were "extrinsically" devotional (e.g., consistently donated to their church) were more supportive of retaliation, whereas those who were "intrinsically" devotional (e.g., those who frequently attended church) were less supportive of retaliation. In addition, O'Neil and associates (2004) found that individuals high in "religiousness" (i.e., higher frequency of religious services) were more likely to believe that the death penalty has a deterrent effect.

Other studies did not find relationships between various measures of devotionalism and beliefs about punishment. Applegate and colleagues (2000) found no relationship between religious salience and either support for harsher courts or support for punitive treatment of criminals. Similarly, support for rehabilitation was not related to frequency of participation in religious activities or a scale measuring religious salience (Evans & Adams, 2003). As a whole, these studies paint a somewhat complicated picture of the relationship between devotionalism and beliefs about punishment.

Jury Verdicts

Some mock jury studies have investigated the relationship between devotion-alism and specific crimes or penalties. In a child abuse case, mock jurors who attended church often or a moderate amount gave more punitive verdicts and sentences than those who attended less often (Johnson, 1985). However, Hepburn (1980) measured religious attendance (i.e., whether the participant attended religious services at least once weekly), and did not find an effect in a mock murder trial. Similarly, a 6-item devotionalism scale did not predict mock jurors' decisions in death penalty sentencing trials (Miller, 2006; Miller & Hayward, 2008).

Attitudes Toward the Death Penalty

As with the other religious characteristics, devotionalism is most commonly studied in relation to the death penalty. A somewhat complicated relationship exists between one's level of devotionalism and one's beliefs about this par-ticular form of punishment. Most studies have found that the more devo-tional a person is, the less punitive he is (e.g., less supportive of the death penalty). For instance, people who prayed, read the Bible, or attended reli-gious services more frequently (Young, 1992); reported having "stronger" religious practices (Unnever & Cullen, 2006); or attended church more regu-larly (Baumer, Messner, & Rosenfeld, 2003) were less supportive of the death penalty. Similarly, among Catholics, those who self-reported more attach-ment to their parish, volunteered more time to the parish, had more frequent contact with their priest, or reported having a greater individual spiritual con-nection with God were less supportive of the death penalty (Bjarnason & Welch, 2004). Evans and Adams (2003) asked participants to indicate the age at which a criminal should be eligible for the death penalty. Individuals who scored high on the religious salience scale (e.g., high agreement with variables such as "Religion is a very important part of my life") recommended higher ages. This suggests that more devoted individuals are less supportive of the death penalty for younger criminals.

In contrast, some studies have found no relationship between various measures of devotionalism and support for the death penalty. Evans and Adams (2003) measured the number of religious activities individuals participated in per week; this measure was not related to attitudes about the age at which someone should receive the death penalty. Similarly, Vidmar (1974) and Stack (2003) both measured frequency of church attendance but did not find any relationship with death penalty attitudes. Applegate and colleagues (2000) did not find any relationship between religious salience and death penalty in a sample taken from the General Social Survey. Similarly, neither of the two measures of devotionalism (i.e., "religious participation" and "religious identity salience") was related to attitudes toward the death penalty for either adults or juveniles (Grasmick, Bursik, & Blackwell, 1993).

Other researchers found a more nuanced relationship between death penalty attitudes and devotionalism. Gonzalez-Perez (2001) conducted a survey of jurors in two parishes in Louisiana. Researchers found that 9% of those who never or only once a year attended church supported the death penalty, whereas 15% of those who attended monthly or weekly opposed the penalty. Even so, the researchers found a different pattern of results among those with the strongest beliefs about the death penalty. Specifically, 92% of "strong death penalty advocates" attended church weekly or more. Meanwhile, those who had the least support for the death penalty never attended church. Thus, Gonzalez-Perez found that the relationship between devotionalism and church attendance depended on how the variables were analyzed—and that the relationship between the two variables was not linear.

We could find only one study that found that people who were more devotional were more punitive (Skovron, Scott, & Cullen, 1989). Telephone surveys in two Ohio cities found that those who were "more religious"[5] were more supportive of the death penalty for juveniles. This effect was only significant in the Columbus sample and not in the Cincinnati sample, however. The authors note that the Columbus sample had more Protestants and fewer Catholics, and was overall more religious than the Cincinnati sample; this may have affected the outcome, considering that Protestants are more supportive of the juvenile death penalty than are Catholics (e.g., Grasmick, Cochran et al., 1993).

The relationship between devotionalism and support for the death penalty is likely affected by the various religious affiliations of those being studied. For some religions, greater attendance/religiosity should *increase* support for the death penalty; for other religions, increased attendance/religiosity should *decrease* support for the death penalty. This is because, as discussed in Chapter 3, many religious affiliations have an official stance on the death penalty. Thus, a highly pious Catholic is likely to be more opposed to the death penalty than a less devoted Catholic. On the other hand, a highly devotional Southern Baptist is likely to be more supportive of the death penalty than one who is less strongly affiliated with the church. Thus, devotionalism would be best studied in tandem with affiliation.

As with the other religious characteristics, there is some variability in findings, which could be due to different measurements used across studies. Contradicting studies often used different measures of devotionalism and asked about attitudes toward punishment in different ways; this variation in measurement could explain the differences in findings.

Other Beliefs and Experiences

There are several other general categories of beliefs, and some miscellaneous beliefs, that have also been investigated. One characteristic is the belief that one is "born again." One study found that personally having been born again did not relate to death penalty support (Young, 1992). Yet another study found that personally being born again was positively related to support for the adult death penalty, but not the juvenile death penalty (Grasmick, Bursik, & Blackwell, 1993).

A second belief that predicts some legal attitudes is a belief in a punitive God. Those who believe in a punitive God (e.g., agreement with statements such as "After I do something wrong I fear God's punishment") indicated younger ages at which individuals should be eligible for the death penalty (Evans & Adams, 2003). This confirms earlier findings that belief in a punitive God was related to support for the juvenile death penalty (Grasmick, Bursik, & Blackwell, 1993). Grasmick, Bursik, and Blackwell used a scale that asked participants to rate how much eight adjectives (punishing, vengeful, forceful, angry, helping, loving, sympathetic, and friendly) described their personal image of God. Similarly, Unnever and Cullen (2006) found that a belief in a "harsh God" was related to greater support for the death penalty. Finally, the perception that God is punitive is positively related to support for punitive treatment for prisoners (Applegate et al., 2000). More broadly, cultures that believe in an aggressive and harsh God are more likely to use punitive child rearing practices (Lambert, Triandis, & Wolf, 1959).[6] Belief in a punitive God, however, was not related to beliefs about rehabilitation (Evans & Adams, 2003).

Another set of religious beliefs involves one's perception of God's attitudes toward punishment. One study asked participants whether they believed that God supports the death penalty for murderers (Miller & Hayward, 2008). Participants who believed that God is a supporter of the death penalty were also more supportive of the death penalty in general, and they were more likely to give a death sentence when asked to serve as mock jurors. The same study investigated whether participants based their attitudes toward the death penalty on their religious beliefs. Participants who did so were more opposed to the death penalty in general, and they were less likely to give the death penalty when acting as a mock juror.[7]

A few other "miscellaneous" beliefs have been the subject of study. Support for religious-based tenets of forgiveness was negatively related to support for the death penalty, belief that local courts were too lenient, and support for punitive treatment of criminals (Applegate et al., 2000). Another study found that real jurors who served on a variety of criminal trials were more likely to vote guilty if they also believed in life after death, believed that a divine plan/purpose exists for everyone, and believed that the world would be a better place if more people shared their religious views (Howard & Redfering, 1983). Studies such as these illustrate the many, sometimes complicated relationships between religious beliefs and legal attitudes and beliefs.

Relationships Among Religious Characteristics

Although we discuss these religious characteristics separately, it is important to note that many are intertwined. In one notable study, researchers combined "fundamentalists" and "evangelicals" because both groups put an "emphasis on interpreting the Bible literally" (Grasmick, Cochran et al., 1993); this clearly indicates the interconnectedness of these variables. Further, fundamentalists believe in evangelizing, indicating an overlap with the variable "evangelism,"[8] and those with "Christian-Right" orientations (which could be interpreted as being fundamentalist) tend to have more frequent church attendance (a common measure of devotionalism; see Johnson, 1985). Another study also found that fundamentalists tend to have stronger personal religious beliefs (i.e., devotionalism), believe in a punitive God (Grasmick, Bursik, & Blackwell, 1993), and believe in a literal biblical interpretation (Unnever & Cullen, 2006). As these examples illustrate, many of these religious variables overlap. To complicate the picture further, some studies have indicated that, in order to find effects for one variable, researchers had to take one or more of the other factors into account, for instance by statistically controlling for the factor (Grasmick, Davenport et al., 1992; Leiber & Woodrick, 1997; Young, 1992).

Finally, some authors point out the complications inherent in defining these variables (McFarland, 1989). For example, "devotionalism" or "religiosity" can mean different things to different people. Some meanings are relatively objective (e.g., frequency of attending religious services), but others, such as the sincerity with which one holds core religious beliefs, are not. To further complicate things, these religious characteristics are not used consistently across studies. Although two characteristics might be highly correlated and use similar scale items, they may be considered "different" concepts (e.g., different researchers may give them different names). At other times, two scales purportedly measure the same characteristic but use different items to do so. Thus, the relationships between characteristics have made it somewhat complicated to measure and test their relationship to each other, and to legal attitudes.

Conclusion

As the research presented in this chapter suggests, religious characteristics and beliefs are related to a variety of legal attitudes. In general, individuals who are high in evangelism or devotionalism are less punitive, whereas those high in fundamentalism or literal interpretism are more punitive. However, not all studies found these patterns, which is likely because of different measures of these characteristics and different measures of the legal attitude in question. This does not explain all the inconsistencies, however.

Trial consultants and authors have speculated (e.g., Kressel & Kressel, 2002; Lieberman & Sales, 2006), and some research has confirmed (Miller & Hayward, 2008), that religious characteristics influence jurors' decisions. Even though the research is not completely consistent, the generalizations that can be drawn can inform trial consultants and lawyers. As discussed in Chapter 2, lawyers in many jurisdictions are allowed to exclude potential jurors based on their religious characteristics. As such, prosecutors may wish to exclude those high in evangelism and devotionalism, whereas defense attorneys will try to exclude those high in fundamentalism and literal interpretism.

It is important to note, however, that most of these results are not robust. As with the research presented in Chapter 3, the effect sizes are fairly small, indicating that religious characteristics are only a small part of what affects one's legal attitudes.[9] Further, few of the studies, especially those in this chapter, measured jurors' verdicts, as opposed to their attitudes, and even fewer measured verdicts of *real* jurors or juries. Thus, the utility of this research for jury selection purposes is modest.

More comprehensive research is needed to fully understand the relationships between religious characteristics and legal attitudes or verdicts. Future research should utilize more religious variables and a greater variety of legal attitudes (e.g., more types of punishment and more types of cases). A juror's religious characteristics may play a role in some types of cases, such as death penalty trials, but may play a very small part in other types of trials. More research will determine the full range of relationships between religious characteristics and legal attitudes.

5

Religion in Jury Deliberation

> That jurors may consider their religious beliefs during penalty
> deliberations is also to be expected. . . . Given the collective
> nature of jury deliberations, we do not find it unusual, much less
> improper, that jurors here may have shared their beliefs with
> other jurors either through conversations or prayers.
> —*People v. Lewis* (2001, p. 73)

The research discussed in Chapters 3 and 4 indicates that religious affiliation
and a variety of religious beliefs can affect legal attitudes and behavior, such as
juror decision making. Chapter 2 highlighted the ways in which lawyers can
use this information during jury selection. It is important to note, however,
that the vast majority of these studies only investigate the effects of religious
characteristics on individual *juror* verdicts. There is no research that we know
of concerning how an individual juror's religious characteristics can affect
jury decisions. It is possible that the group discussion process may neutralize
the effects of any particular juror's beliefs, such that religious beliefs influence
a juror's individual judgment, but not the jury's final verdict. Nevertheless,
there is concern that religion will alter the deliberation process. For instance,
jurors may mention their religious beliefs, cite scripture during deliberation,
pray, or consult with pastors. Courts are divided about whether it is appropriate for jurors to do these religious activities and whether such jury behavior
constitutes misconduct that necessitates a new trial. This chapter will consider
the role of jurors' religion in their deliberations, an issue that has been
raised in numerous recent cases (e.g., *Oliver v. Quarterman*, 2008; *People v.
Harlan*, 2005).

Jurors' Reliance on Their Religious Beliefs

Even though much research indicates that religious affiliation and characteristics are related to legal attitudes and juror verdicts, this leaves a question

unanswered: Do jurors *consciously* rely on their religious beliefs when making a decision? Some recent trials provide anecdotal evidence that at least some jurors do look toward their religion for guidance. Not surprisingly, most of these cases (at least those that make it to the appellate courts) are death penalty cases. Because of the extremity of the life or death decision, jurors may experience more psychological difficulty deciding on a verdict in death penalty trials as compared to other trials. This may lead them to rely on religious sources for comfort. Jurors in death penalty cases may also rely on religious texts because the texts offer what appear to be explicit instructions about the death penalty (e.g., the Bible's "eye for an eye" verse), whereas the texts do not offer such clear advice about other crimes or trial types.[1]

The courts are divided as to whether it is permissible for jurors to consult religious sources during deliberation. In August 2008, the 5th Circuit Court of Appeals heard an appeal by a defendant named Khristian Oliver, who claimed that his Sixth and Eighth Amendment rights were infringed when jurors in his death penalty sentencing trial consulted biblical scripture. According to jurors' post-trial statements, one juror read biblical verses aloud to a few other jurors while in the jury room. Additionally, a female juror mentioned to a male juror that the Bible has instructions about who deserves the death penalty—he then asked her to read those verses to him. She read the passages, which she had highlighted. Two other jurors read the Bible to themselves during deliberations. The verses they read included a verse from the Book of Numbers (35:16): "And if he smite him with an instrument of iron, so that he die, he is a murderer: the murderer shall surely be put to death." Jurors testified that there were approximately four Bibles in the jury room because many members of the jury went to Bible study at night. The court determined that the jurors' behavior was improper, but there was not enough evidence to indicate that the use of the Bible actually influenced the jury's decision (i.e., they held that it was harmless error). Thus, the court declined to overturn Oliver's conviction (*Oliver v. Quarterman*, 2008; see also "Court: Bible in jury room," 2008).

Just two months later, in October 2008, the U.S. Supreme Court decided not to hear a case involving a similar issue (Richey, 2008). During deliberations in the 2005 death penalty sentencing trial of Jimmie Urbano Lucero, the foreman of the jury took out his personal Bible and read several biblical verses that urged people to submit to governing authorities, who are God's servants and are entitled to punish offenders. Several hours later, the jury voted to give Lucero the death penalty. On appeal, Lucero's attorney argued that the Bible-quoting juror's actions had violated the defendant's right to a fair trial. Although this case would have been an ideal opportunity to settle the divide on this issue among state and federal courts, the U.S. Supreme Court declined to grant certiorari in the case (*Lucero v. Texas*, 2008).

As these examples illustrate, some jurors use their religious beliefs to guide their decision making or to convince other jurors. Courts recognize that jurors will draw on their religious beliefs. For instance, one judge said, "the court in no way means to suggest that jurors cannot rely on their personal faith and deeply held beliefs when facing the awesome decision of whether to impose the sentence of death on a fellow citizen" (*Jones v. Kemp*, 1989, p. 1560). Another judge wrote, "Prayer is almost certainly a part of the personal decision-making process of many people, a process that is employed when serving on a jury" (*State v. DeMille*, 1988); another stated that:

> We do not find it surprising that "conscientious people who are faced with a life and death decision resort to their religious scruples in reaching such a decision. Such deep introspection neither violates principles of justice nor prejudices the defendant." (*Young v. State*, 2000, pp. 48–49, quoting *Bieghler v. State*, 1997, p. 203)

Anecdotal evidence suggests that some jurors rely on their religious beliefs and biblical authority in making decisions. Some judges expect that jurors will rely on their religious beliefs in making their decisions; however, there are limits to the degree to which jurors can use religious materials or partake in religious activities. For example, some controversy exists over whether religious texts can be used in deliberation. The next section presents numerous appellate cases in which the courts have had to decide whether praying, using a Bible, having a discussion about religion, and consulting with pastors are improper juror behaviors.

Case Law About Jurors' Religious Activities

As the *Oliver* case discussed earlier (*Oliver v. Quarterman*, 2008) illustrates, some courts have determined that a jury's use of the Bible is improper because it constitutes extraneous evidence or law. In the next section, we discuss the laws, such as the prohibition on "extraneous material," that underlie these cases, then we discuss some of the major and recent cases in which courts have considered whether religious material and activities are proper or prejudicial.

What Is "Extraneous Material"?

To understand why relying on the Bible might be considered improper, it is important to understand the reasoning behind the "extraneous material" rule in general. In *Remmer v. United States* (1954), the U.S. Supreme Court determined that any type of communication, contact, or tampering with a juror was presumed to be prejudicial. For instance, if an outside party persuades one of the jurors to favor one of the litigants, this act brings unfair bias into the trial. This case recognized that it was improper for jurors to receive any information from any source outside the trial.

Later, the U.S. Supreme Court in *Smith v. Phillips* (1982) determined that a defendant does not automatically get a new trial if a juror had received information from an outside source. Instead, the court determined that a trial court should conduct an investigation and have a hearing to determine whether the juror's exposure to extraneous information or influence resulted in bias. Even if the jury did have contact with extraneous material, the prosecutor can argue that it did not affect the ultimate outcome of the trial. Specifically, if the defense presents evidence that a juror had contact with an external source, the prosecution has to prove that the contact was "harmless error." For example, the prosecutor may try to convince the judge that the evidence against the defendant was so strong that the extraneous material was harmless and jurors would have convicted the defendant even without the extraneous material. Although neither of these cases dealt with religious activities, they set the foundation for future courts that were faced with that issue.[2]

In some cases, it is obvious when an outside party has unfairly tampered with the jury (e.g., someone pays jurors to acquit the defendant). In such a case, it seems clear that the judge should be able to question jurors about this extraneous influence. But it is not so clear whether a court can make inquiries into the jury deliberation process if it comes to light that the jurors might have relied on the Bible or other religious activity (e.g., prayer). Typically, the jury deliberation process is considered to be a secretive process that represents the jurors' autonomy. They do not have to give reasons for their verdicts or tell anyone what went on during deliberation. However, if there is an accusation of misconduct, the judge can investigate. This investigation is limited by Rule 606(b) of the Federal Rules of Evidence and similar state codes. A judge cannot inquire as to a juror's emotional reactions or mental impressions regarding the trial. However, the judge can inquire as to whether the juror encountered extraneous information, material, or influences. So, for example, a judge cannot ask a juror whether she might have had an emotional reaction to the evidence, but a judge can ask the juror whether she read the Bible or another religious text.

In deciding whether judges can ask jurors about their religious activities during trial, courts have had to determine whether prayers, Bible readings, religious discussions, and consultations with pastors constitute "extraneous material." If a court decides that such religious materials or activities constitute extraneous material, the court next decides whether this affected the defendant's Sixth Amendment right to a fair trial. These cases, discussed next, remain controversial.

Jury Prayers

In *State v. Graham* (1982), the trial judge determined that a defense attorney was not entitled to question jurors about their religious activity during the trial. The jury foreman, who was also a minister, had held daily prayer services. The defendant wanted to question the jurors about this after the trial, but the Supreme Court of Louisiana determined that the jury's privilege of confidentiality outweighed any possibility that the defendant's constitutional rights might have been compromised by the jurors' participation in religious services during the trial.

A juror in the case of *State v. DeMille* (1988) prayed for a "sign" that would indicate whether DeMille was guilty. She then had a "revelation" from which she knew that if the defense attorney did not make eye contact with her during closing arguments, then the defendant was guilty. The attorney did not make eye contact, and the juror voted to convict the defendant, explaining to other jurors her reasons for doing so. After the conviction, in post-trial affidavits, the juror revealed that she had relied on her revelation to decide how to vote. The defendant argued that this constituted an "outside influence" (i.e., extraneous material) that was inappropriate. The defense attorney asked for a new trial because of the juror's misconduct. The judge determined that the juror's affidavit was inadmissible under the state version of Rule of Evidence 606(b) and refused to grant the defendant a new trial. Essentially, the trial judge decided that he was not at liberty to question the juror about the prayer because prayers are essentially emotional reactions. The case was appealed to the Utah Supreme Court.

In front of the Utah Supreme Court, the defendant argued that the prayer, and its answer, were an "outside influence" that prejudiced the jury's verdict. The court disagreed and affirmed the conviction. This decision was made, in part, because of the court's opinion that considering prayer to be extraneous material would imply that a juror can never rely on prayer in decision making. Such a ban would infringe on a juror's religious freedom. Thus, DeMille did not get a new trial, despite the fact that a juror based her verdict preference on a divine revelation and a lawyer's behavior.[3]

Similarly, an Ohio Court of Appeals ruled in 2005 that a defendant was not entitled to a new trial, even though the jurors had prayed together. During the murder trial of Robert Williams, Jr., the jurors were sequestered after the first day of deliberating. The next morning, the bailiff came to the jury's hotel to get them. Before leaving the hotel, a juror asked the bailiff if they could pray, and she said it was not her decision. The jurors then all prayed together. They then went back to the courthouse and decided on a death sentence an hour later. The court could find no precedent that allowed a defendant to get a new trial based on the Establishment clause, the Free Exercise clause, due process, or the Eighth Amendment's prohibition of cruel and unusual punishment. Further, the court determined that the prayer was not improper extraneous material, did not interfere with the judge's instructions to jurors, and did not lead any of the jurors to change their opinions (*State v. Williams*, 2005; see also "Jury prayer didn't violate killers rights," 2004).

In the California case of *People v. Lewis* (2001), jurors held hands and said a prayer before deliberations. The court found that this did not amount to juror misconduct; rather it was normal and expected that jurors deciding whether they should give the defendant the death penalty would rely on their religious beliefs. Thus, the defendant was not given a new trial. Another court approved of deliberation prayers because they were "strictly for support in arriving at a decision and for a proper decision" and did not ultimately affect jurors' final decisions (*Holladay v. State*, 1992, p. 678). Cases such as these illustrate the courts' general agreement that jury prayers are not grounds for granting the defendant a new trial.

Jurors' Reading of Biblical Scripture

The court cases just described have generally established that prayer was not extraneous material or was not prejudicial; however, the courts are divided as to whether reliance on the Bible is extraneous material, and whether it violates the defendant's rights. The cases below describe the vastly different rulings courts have issued (see also Miller et al., 2008).

In 2006, a jury in a death penalty sentencing case asked the court bailiff (who also happened to be a minister) if they could borrow his Bible while they deliberated. After the defendant, Kristi Leigh Fulgham, was sentenced to death, the defendant's attorney learned the jury had requested a Bible. Immediately, he requested a new trial and claimed that, "The death penalty can only . . . result from the deliberation of aggravating and mitigating evidence, and the Holy Bible cannot be cited" (Descant, 2006). This case is pending, but it may succeed based on precedent set by the following cases.

Two jurors in the case of *People v. Harlan* (2005) consulted a Bible during a nightly recess, after one juror's parents brought her personal Bible to the hotel where the jury was sequestered. The next day, the jurors brought a Bible into the jury room, along with the notes they had made from the previous night. The jurors read the passages aloud during deliberations. Among the passages was Romans 13:1, which states "Let every soul be subject unto the higher powers. For there is no power but of God: The powers that be are ordained of God." This verse is sometimes said to mean that jurors should obey and trust the law of the government, which is ordained by God. Another passage was Leviticus 24: 20–21, which states "Breach for breach, eye for eye, tooth for tooth: as he hath caused a blemish in a man, so shall it be done to him again. And he that killeth a beast he shall restore it: and he that killeth a man, he shall be put to death." The defendant was sentenced to death. After learning that the jurors had quoted scripture during deliberations, the court conducted an evidentiary hearing and ordered a new sentencing trial. The court determined that the biblical scripture reading had improperly encouraged jurors to give the death penalty and did not allow jurors to exercise discretion in their decision and thus violated Colorado law. Ultimately, the appellate court overturned Harlan's death sentence, and the Colorado Supreme Court upheld the appellate court's ruling (*People v. Harlan*, 2005). In 2005, the U.S. Supreme Court declined to hear the case (*Colorado v. Harlan*, 2005).

Similarly, an appellate court in Georgia reversed a death sentence because jurors used a Bible in deliberations (*Jones v. Kemp*, 1989). The court ruled that the Bible qualifies as an "extrajudicial" source that is not allowed in deliberations. The court found that the jurors' use of the Bible could have influenced their verdict. This would have prejudiced the jurors in violation of the Sixth Amendment right to a fair trial. Additionally, the jurors' use of the Bible violated the Eight Amendment prohibition on cruel and unusual punishment. The court noted that a state must create a death penalty sentencing scheme that gives jurors guidance and avoids capricious or arbitrary juror decisions. The court found that a sentence based on biblical guidance is arbitrary because biblical law does not help jurors distinguish between cases in which the death penalty should be given and cases in which it should not.[4]

In contrast to these cases, some courts have declined to give the defendant a new trial even though the jurors consulted a Bible during deliberations. In the California trial of Bob Russell Williams, Jr. (not to be confused with the defendant named Robert Williams, Jr. in the Ohio prayer case described earlier), a juror brought several pages that were copied from a Bible into the jury room (*People v. Williams*, 2006). He read the biblical passage aloud in an attempt to convince another juror who had not yet decided how to vote in the death penalty case. Among the many passages recited were passages from 1 Corinthians (5:5): "to deliver [one] unto Satan for the destruction of the flesh, that the spirit may be saved in the day of the Lord Jesus" and Romans (13:1–3):

> Let every soul be subject unto the higher powers. For there is no power but of God . . . Whosoever therefore resisteth the power, resisteth the ordinance of God: and they that resist shall receive to themselves damnation. For rulers are not a terror to good works, but to the evil. Wilt thou then be afraid of the power? Do that which is good and thou shalt have praise of the same.

Further, one juror told the others not to consider the Bible when making their decision. Williams was sentenced to death and appealed his sentence because of the Bible-quoting juror's actions.

In 2006, the appellate court in California decided that the Biblical scripture did not propose alternate rules for deciding when to apply the death penalty; they "merely counseled deference to governmental authority and affirmed validity of sitting in judgment of one's fellow human beings according to law" (*People v. Williams*, 2006, p. 80). Thus, it is apparently acceptable for jurors to hear scripture urging people (e.g., jurors) to follow their rulers (or face damnation for disobeying), as long as the scripture does not suggest following rules other than those the government provides for deciding whether to sentence the defendant to death. Further, the court presumed that jurors took the advice of the juror who told them not to rely on biblical scripture. Finally, the court determined that the Bible must not have influenced them because the jury was still split 10 (for death) to 2 (for life in prison) after the Bible verses were read (even though it had been 9 to 3 before the discussion of biblical verses). Ultimately, the court determined that the reading of the Bible *was* juror misconduct because the Bible is an improper external source, but this action was not prejudicial because it did not affect the jurors' decisions (*People v. Williams*, 2006).

In another California case, the defendant argued that he should get a new trial because of juror misconduct (*People v. Danks*, 2004). During deliberations, a juror shared several biblical verses, which she had highlighted, in order to comfort other jurors who expressed their concern about imposing the death penalty. The discussion became so focused on religion that another juror had to remind the rest that religious beliefs should not affect their verdict (two jurors also consulted their pastors about what the Bible says about the death penalty; this is discussed later in this chapter).The Supreme Court of California declined to give the defendant a new trial, reasoning that it was unlikely that this had swayed the other jurors.

In *Fields v. Brown* (2007), the defendant argued that his Sixth Amendment right to a fair trial was violated because the foreperson consulted a Bible and made notes of passages that were "for" and "against" the death penalty. He brought his list to the deliberation room the next day and read the relevant passages to the other jurors. The jurors deliberated most of the day and sentenced the defendant to death. On appeal, the court refused to give the defendant a new trial. The court reasoned that it was impossible to determine whether the passages "for" the death penalty had an effect on the verdict, because the juror had also read passages that were "against" the death penalty. In addition, the jury must have considered more than just the biblical passages, since the deliberations took almost all day. The court also determined that the biblical passages were "common knowledge" and thus were not extrinsic material. Thus, the court found that there was no error.

As this review demonstrates, the courts are divided, with some finding the use of the Bible harmless, some finding it entitles the defendant to a new trial, and some finding it improper but that there was not enough evidence that it affected the jurors. The courts even disagree as to whether it is "extraneous material" or not; that is, it is not extraneous material if it is simply common knowledge. In general, virtually all courts have determined that the jury's use of the Bible is improper; they mainly disagree as to whether this error entitles the defendant to a new trial.

Jurors' Religious Discussion

Although the courts are divided as to whether it is improper to use a Bible or other religious text during deliberation, they are less divided in cases in which religious discussion occurs among jurors. In the *People v. Danks* (2004) case just discussed, jurors discussed their "Christian beliefs" during deliberations. The court did not find this to be adequate reason to give the defendant a new trial; to the contrary, the court determined that it is normal for jurors to rely on their religious beliefs in making a decision.

In *Young v. State* (2000), the defendant was convicted and sentenced to death. After the trial, the defendant requested an evidentiary hearing because the defense attorney learned that a juror had read from a Bible during deliberations. The juror later changed her story; thus, there was some controversy over whether there had been a Bible in the deliberation room. As a result, the court refused to give the defendant a new trial. The defense attorney appealed, claiming that, even though there was no actual Bible, any discussion of a religious nature violated the defendant's right to a fair trial. The appellate court disagreed and determined that it was appropriate for individuals to rely on their religious "scruples" in making their decision. Thus, religious discussion is not extraneous material, and the defendant was not awarded a new trial.

Similarly, the court in *People v. Harlan* (2005), discussed earlier, differentiated between jurors' reliance on a Bible (which was found to be impermissible), and mere discussion of the "religious upbringing, education, and beliefs" (p. 632) of deliberating jurors. The court determined that discussions are permissible, as long as no religious text is involved. The judge in the case of *People v. Lewis* (2001) came to a similar conclusion. During deliberations, one juror hesitated to give the death penalty. The foreperson told her "he did not know if it would help her, but what had helped him make his decision was that [the defendant] had been exposed to Jesus Christ and if that was in fact true [the defendant] would have 'everlasting life' regardless of what happened to him" (p. 71). The appellate court found this behavior to be acceptable and declined to give the defendant a new trial. In general, these courts have found that it is acceptable to discuss religion, especially if no Bible is involved.

Discussing Biblical Scripture Outside of Deliberations

The final way in which religion can potentially affect deliberations concerns jurors' consultation with religious authorities outside of deliberations.[5] In *People v. Danks* (2004), discussed earlier, two jurors discussed biblical scripture about the death penalty with others outside of the jury. One juror talked with her husband about her hesitation to give the death penalty. Her husband advised her to read scripture from the Bible, including verses that seemingly approve of the death penalty (e.g., "the murderer shall be put to death"). Her husband told her it would be permissible to talk to her pastor about it because the pastor is a "higher authority." The juror and her husband talked to her pastor after services one evening during the trial. When the pastor learned that she was a juror in the *Danks* case, he mentioned that these scriptures supporting the death penalty were "good scriptures" and that he believed that the defendant should receive the death penalty. The juror said she was comforted by these actions, and the next day, she shared the passages with other jurors who were reluctant to give the death penalty. Another juror also consulted her pastor, who told her that he thought he knew what case the juror was involved in, and if he was a juror in that case, he would not be reluctant to give the death penalty. Even so, the court declined to give the defendant a new trial, finding that the counsel from the husband was not misconduct, and although the counsel from pastors was misconduct, it was unlikely to have influenced the jurors' verdict and was therefore not prejudicial.

Legal Analysis Concerning Jurors' Use of Religious Activity and Materials

Various legal scholars have analyzed this issue, with many determining that religious texts, religious discussion, or prayer should not be allowed in deliberations. For instance, Egland (2004) argues that religious texts, including the Bible, are not consistent and are subject to varying interpretations. Thus, two jurors could support opposite verdicts, both claiming to be relying on the Bible. Further, if courts allow religious texts, they would also have to allow other philosophical arguments, such as Gandhi's theory of nonviolence. Allowing such materials would reduce the deliberations to a religious and philosophical debate, rather than a debate about the evidence and the law (see also Miller, 2006). Similarly, Ashley (2002) posits that such material should not be allowed because it prevents the jurors from following the law. Instead of carefully weighing aggravating factors and mitigating factors as they are supposed to (see Chapter 8), they may be relying on biblical instructions.

Egland (2004) also discusses the possibility that sentences based on religious texts violate the Sixth Amendment right to a fair and impartial jury, the Eighth Amendment right to be free from cruel and unusual punishment, and the First Amendment Establishment Clause. Egland agrees with courts that have found that the Bible and other religious sources are prejudicial to the defendant's right to a fair trial because they bias jurors and encourage them to rely on sources other than the law and evidence. Egland also argues that a verdict based on religion is arbitrary and thus violates a defendant's right to be free from cruel and unusual punishment as stated in the Eighth Amendment.

Both Egland (2004) and Simson and Garvey (2001) suggest that verdicts influenced by religion violate the First Amendment's Establishment clause, which forbids the government from showing preference for a particular religion. Under *Lynch v. Donnelly* (1984), a government act is unconstitutional if it advances or inhibits religion or creates an "entanglement" of religion with government. Egland argues that a verdict based on religion essentially allows the jury to pass on their burden as factfinder to a higher power, namely, God. By allowing a verdict to be determined by biblical law, the government endorses religion. Simson and Garvey (2001) also point out that the use of religion in the deliberation room does not have a "unique history" that would provide an exemption to the First Amendment. In contrast, the legislature is allowed to pray before every session because this practice has a long-established history and is thus exempt. A First Amendment Establishment clause challenge is difficult, however. Among other things, a defendant would have to convince a judge to consider the jury to be an actor of the government. Thus, First Amendment challenges are unlikely to be as successful as challenges based on other grounds.

Some authors have made suggestions that could reduce the likelihood of encountering such constitutional difficulties. A few scholars suggest that the courts provide the jury with instructions that specifically forbid using religious materials, praying, quoting religious scripture, or making any religious-based arguments during deliberations of death penalty trials (Ashley, 2002; Spiller, 2005).

Spiller (2005) also argues that protecting the defendant's right to a fair trial should outweigh the jury's provision of privacy that is found in Federal Rule of Evidence 606(b) and similar state statutes. In a somewhat controversial suggestion, the author recommends that Rule 606 (b) be amended (at least at the state level) to allow the court to record and review the jury's deliberations in death penalty cases. This would assure that the deliberations were free from bias that can result from the jury's use of religious material or activities. As a result, whenever a question of misconduct arises, the court could review the recording to ensure that the defendant received a fair trial.

Shively (2008) suggests a modified test to determine whether the trial has been prejudiced by the use of religious materials or activities. The modified test would provide extra protection for defendants in death penalty trials and prevent Sixth Amendment violations. When applying the new test, courts would first ask: Was the use of the religious material inherently prejudicial? If not, is it prejudicial under a "totality of circumstances" rule? That is, taking into consideration all the circumstances of the trial and deliberation, did the jury's behavior affect the outcome of the trial? Shively finds that the approach is flexible and avoids the extremes that other decision rules produce. Authors such as these recognize the issues surrounding the use of religious activities and have offered suggestions for limiting any constitutional violations that could result.

Research Concerning Jurors' Use of Religious Activity and Materials

Although there has been some legal analysis concerning the issue of religious activities during deliberation, empirical research is largely lacking. A few studies support judges' suspicions, finding that some jurors do rely on their religious beliefs in decision making, and may also use their religiosity as a coping mechanism. In one study, jurors were asked to keep journals about their experience as death penalty jurors (Sundby, 2005). Some jurors' decisions and decision-making processes were influenced by their religious beliefs. One juror wrote, "I can't tell you how much I've prayed over this [during the trial], for the wisdom to do the right thing" (Sundby, 2005, p. 73). The juror also wondered:

> Which is worse, spending thirty, forty, or even fifty years behind bars, or living in Paradise where there is no worry, no fear, only great joy and happiness? . . . I can't help but wonder if we wouldn't be doing him a favor by choosing death (Sundby, 2005, p. 74).

The jury decided on a verdict of life in prison, however. This juror later had a religious experience that provided comfort that she had made the right decision. She wrote in her journal, "last night I attended choir practice for the first time [since the trial]. Call it coincidence, call it an omen, but I call it the answer to a prayer: the first song we rehearsed was entitled 'We Choose Life'" (p. 73). There was also evidence that the trial affected at least one juror's own religiosity, as one wrote, "my own faith in God has certainly been strengthened by this experience" (p. 74).

Miller (2006) asked mock jurors how much they relied on their personal religious beliefs when reaching their death penalty sentencing verdict. Responses ranged from 2.62 to 3.46 (depending on the experimental condition) on a 7-point scale. The same study asked mock jurors how much they relied on biblical authority while making their decision. Responses ranged from 2.49 to 3.67 (depending on the condition) on a 7-point scale. This indicates that jurors rely on religion a low to moderate amount. These responses could be underestimates, however, as participants were instructed to make the verdict based only on the law and the evidence.[6] As such, many jurors might be hesitant to admit that they relied on the Bible and their religious beliefs as well. The study also found that participants who heard the defense attorney quote scripture as a way of encouraging jurors to show mercy reported relying on both personal religious beliefs and biblical authority more than participants who did not hear the attorney quote scripture.[7] Thus, the attorney's words could prime jurors to rely on their religious beliefs. Chapters 3 and 4 indicate that a person's religious characteristics and beliefs *do* affect his attitudes and beliefs. Priming these beliefs (e.g., when a juror reads the Bible or the jury prays) could lead jurors to act on them even more.

In addition, being exposed to religious activities could raise jurors' emotions—leading them to make decisions based on emotion rather than on legal factors. Much research (e.g., Epstein, 1990, 1994) indicates that individuals make different decisions when they are feeling emotional than when they are not. Thus, emotional jurors could come to different verdicts compared to less emotional jurors. For instance, jurors exposed to emotional evidence and testimony typically favor harsher sentences (see Miller, Greene, Dietrich, Chamberlain, & Singer, 2008 for review).

Research has yet to investigate directly the effects of religious activities on a jury's verdict. A few studies (Miller, 2006; Miller & Bornstein, 2006) have found that biblical arguments coming from *attorneys* are generally ineffective (see Chapter 8) at affecting verdicts. Even so, are biblical arguments from *other jurors* effective? No research that we know of has addressed this question. The anecdotal cases discussed earlier indicate that jurors sometimes try to use religious materials to persuade others. Whether other jurors are persuaded may depend on their own religious beliefs; for instance, a moderately or highly religious juror may be more persuaded than an atheist or a less religious juror.

Whether jurors are influenced by religious arguments may also depend on the identity of the messenger. In some of the cases described earlier, the person providing the religious information was a jury foreman (*Fields v. Brown*, 2007; *People v. Lewis*, 2001; *State v. Graham*, 1982) or pastor (*People v. Danks*, 2004). Such individuals could be seen as authority figures and thus might be more influential than other individuals. Research has indicated that the leader of a group is often the most influential on the group's decision (Dembo & McAuliffe, 1987). More specifically, jury forepersons were seen as more influential by other jurors than were non-forepersons (Foley & Pigott, 1997). Another study found that Baptist ministers and Catholic priests intentionally use their authority to influence the actions of members of their congregation (Falbo, New, & Gaines, 1987). Some of these strategies may include intentionally reminding their followers that religious leaders are God's servants, behaving a certain way when in public, or educating followers about biblical principles. Such strategies are believed to encourage church members to follow the guidance of the priest or pastor. Assuming these strategies are effective, religious leaders could be quite influential. Leaders or authority figures could be even more influential on others in stressful situations (Klein, 1976). Because research indicates that some jurors experience stress during the trial process (e.g., Bornstein et al., 2005; Miller & Bornstein, 2005), it remains a distinct possibility that jury foremen and pastors could have a pronounced influence on the jury's decisions. Thus, the assumption that some courts have made that jurors are not influenced by others is in question.

Another questionable assumption courts sometimes make is that jurors who are told by other jurors not to rely on the Bible would actually follow that advice (e.g., *People v. Williams*, 2006). For instance, the court in *Williams* said, "[the juror's] remark after the Bible reading that jurors were not to consider such verses in arriving at a verdict reinforced the limited manner in which the biblical verses were used. The fact that the jurors did not discuss the verses is an indication that they took [the] admonition to heart" (p. 80). Research on the "reactance effect" has found that jurors may reject an argument if they feel they are given no choice (i.e., because scripture demands a particular verdict); such a strong argument may actually backfire. This may be the reason that Miller and Bornstein (2006) found that a defense attorney who quoted scripture (in an attempt to secure a lighter sentence for the defendant) actually resulted in jurors giving a *more* severe sentence. Further, even if people try not to let something they have heard influence their decision, they may be unable to do so. Research has shown that an instruction to ignore inadmissible evidence tends to be ineffective (e.g., Greene & Dodge, 1995; Steblay, Hosch, Culhane, & McWethy, 2006). For instance, exposure to pre-trial news articles about the defendant and the crime can affect mock jurors' verdicts and perceptions, even when the judge specifically instructed them not to rely on the pre-trial information (see Kramer, Kerr, & Carroll, 1990).

One reason that judicial instructions to ignore inadmissible evidence are ineffective is because jurors may not even be aware that they are being influenced (Kramer et al., 1990). Research suggests that individuals are often unaware that they have been influenced by certain stimuli (Nisbett & Wilson, 1977); as such, they may not have the "cognitive control" to prevent their being influenced (Kahneman, Slovic, & Tversky, 1982; Nisbett & Wilson, 1977). Thus, jurors may not be able to eliminate the effects of biblical appeals on their verdicts, in part because they are not aware that they are being influenced.

Conclusion

Because the jury process is largely secretive, and is somewhat protected by laws such as Federal Rule of Evidence 606(b), it is difficult to know how often jurors rely on religious texts, discussion, or prayer. Typically, the court does not find out unless a juror speaks up; thus, religious activities are likely much more common than the number of cases in which it has been an issue would indicate (Simson & Garvey, 2001). Previous chapters (3 and 4) provided evidence that individuals' religious affiliation and characteristics are related to some legal attitudes, including verdict preference in some types of trials. But individual jurors do not decide cases; *juries* decide cases. Although some research has confirmed that religious beliefs can affect jurors' decisions, little is known about how religion can affect the jury deliberation process.

Defendants commonly argue that their First, Fifth, Sixth, Eighth, or Fourteenth Amendment rights are violated by the use of religious material or religious activities in deliberation. Such claims have achieved mixed success. Some courts find that the jurors did not do anything improper; others find that jurors' behavior was improper and give the defendant a new trial. Others recognize the legal impropriety of jurors' religious activities during deliberations, but they refute the possibility that these acts could have influenced jurors (i.e., they hold that the behavior was harmless error).

From a psychological standpoint, the assumptions courts make are questionable, such as jurors being able to ignore a scripture-spouting fellow juror. In addition to these psychological concerns, legal concerns exist about a slippery slope that allowing religious material or activity could introduce. Although some courts have allowed jurors to use Judeo-Christian Bibles during deliberations (*People v. Danks*, 2004; *People v. Williams*, 2006), they do not often set boundaries as to where this permission ends. Would a court allow jurors to consult a Koran or other religious texts? What if two different texts were used in deliberation? What about nonreligious, philosophical texts? Should jurors be able to quote from Gandhi's writings, which urged forgiveness and peace? These questions are largely unanswered, but they are ones that courts may someday have to answer.

Even if judges can keep religious texts out of the jury room, it may be impossible to remove the influence of religion entirely. Jurors who are not allowed to read or discuss religion may use their religious beliefs when deciding on a verdict anyway. In fact, religion may be such a fundamental part of some people's worldview that they would not even be aware that their religious beliefs were influencing their decision making. Thus, it may be impossible to remove religion totally from the deliberation process (see Miller et al., 2008). Even so, courts would be wise to discourage or even forbid jurors from using the Bible or other religious materials to convince other jurors, to protect the rights and interests of defendants and other jurors.

Part II

RELIGION AND JUDGES, ATTORNEYS, AND
LITIGANTS

6

Judges' Religion

You shall also seek out from among all the people capable men
who fear God, trustworthy men who spurn ill-gotten gain. Set
these over them as chiefs of thousands, hundreds, fifties, and
tens, and let them judge the people at all times.
—Exodus 18:21–22

Like other Americans, many judges have deep-seated religious convictions.
In most cases, there is no reason to suspect that their religious beliefs interfere
with their job performance, which those beliefs might even enhance. Judges'
religion can become problematic, however, when they are unusually vocal
about it—in either their public comments or official written decisions—which
arouses concerns that they would be unable to discharge their duties impar-
tially (Idleman, 2005). The one does not necessarily imply the other, of course,
but it is enough to create a suspicion that can cost them their job. The most
prominent recent example is Alabama Supreme Court Chief Justice Roy
Moore, who was removed from office in 2003 after he placed a 5300-pound
Ten Commandments monument in the rotunda of the state judicial building
and refused to remove it after being ordered to do so. He installed the monument "in order to remind all Alabama citizens of, among other things, his
belief in the sovereignty of the Judeo-Christian God over both the state and
the church" (*Glassroth v. Moore*, 2003, p. 1284).

Just as with jurors, there has been extensive commentary on the role that
judges' religion does and should play in their decisions (e.g., Collett, 2000;
Conkle, 1998b; Songer & Tabrizi, 1999; Wiehl, 2000), and its implications
for judicial selection (Ebrahim, 2006; Shuman & Champagne, 1997). For
example, religion may be included on questionnaires submitted to judges as
part of the election or appointment process, an increasingly popular and
controversial practice (Coyle, 2006; Ebrahim, 2006). U.S. Supreme Court
nominations are a prominent example of religious considerations in
judicial appointments, as in the supposed existence of designated positions

for members of certain religious persuasions on the Court (i.e., "Catholic and Jewish seats").

Arguably, judges' religion might matter more in countries where they are deciding matters of religious law, as in some countries where Islam is the official state religion, than in countries such as the United States, where judges' religion and other social background variables are ostensibly irrelevant. However, we limit our analysis of judges' religion to American courts, for several reasons. First, with very few exceptions (e.g., Tate & Sittiwong, 1989), empirical research on the question has focused almost exclusively on American judges, especially at the appellate court level. This Americocentrism likely reflects the second important factor, which is that it is impossible to study religion's influence on judicial decision making unless there is religious diversity on the bench. If all, or nearly all, of a country's judges adhere to a single religion—as they presumably do in several Muslim countries, Israel, and possibly Ireland—then religion might influence their decisions, but without being able to compare the decisions of judges from different religious backgrounds, there is no way to tell. Third, an effect of the decision maker's religion on matters of religious law would hardly be surprising; indeed, it could hardly be otherwise. All major religions have learned clergy who act as judges in certain types of cases. For example, a rabbinical court known as a *beit din* makes decisions for divorcing couples who want their marriage dissolved according to the precepts of Jewish law, and not merely according to state law.[1] The situation in countries that have an official state religion is somewhat trickier, for there devout judges decide both religious and secular matters; but again, because all judges are themselves adherents of the official religion, it is impossible to tease apart religious from other influences. Thus, our concern here is with religiously diverse judges' decisions on secular legal matters—although, as we shall see, some of the legal matters that come before judges in secular courts either explicitly (e.g., in questions about separation of church and state) or implicitly (e.g., in questions about reproductive rights and responsibilities) touch on religion.

An emphasis on religion in choosing judges naturally presupposes the existence of a relationship between the particular religion a judge practices and the judge's decisions. One aspect of this issue parallels that for jurors; for example, will Jewish judges be more lenient toward criminal defendants than Protestant judges? Will evangelical judges favor the death penalty? On the one hand, one might expect judges, as professionals deciding case after case after case, to be able to ignore extralegal factors such as their religious beliefs; yet other aspects of judges' religion suggest that it is a larger concern for judges than for jurors. First, judges are solitary decision makers, so any influence of a judge's religion would not be diluted by countervailing religious (or nonreligious) influences, as it would be for one juror among many.[2] Second, judges rule on matters of law, as well as determining factual matters. This opens up a new arena for possible religious influence, as the legal questions might themselves contain explicit or implicit religious elements (e.g., separation of church and state, freedom of religious expression, a woman's right to an abortion).

A final issue relating to judges is the extent to which judges invoke religious texts in their rulings. Judges have virtually unfettered discretion in fashioning their opinions, which some have taken as an opportunity to advance a personal or political agenda, including an expression of religious views (e.g., *State v. Arnett*, 2000; see Barringer, 1996; Mathis, 2004). Some judges have gone so far as to impose attendance at religious services or meetings of quasi-religious organizations, such as Alcoholics Anonymous, as a condition of sentencing. Thus, the major sections of this chapter will be (a) religion as a factor in judicial selection and elections, including religion among Supreme Court justices; (b) the relationship between judges' religion and their decisions; and (c) judges' explicit use of religion in their decision making.

Religion in Judicial Selection

The manner of selecting judges varies depending on the jurisdiction (Murphy, Pritchett, Epstein, & Knight, 2006). In the federal courts, the president nominates judges for vacancies at all levels—district court, court of appeals, and Supreme Court. The Senate then advises and consents—or not—to the appointment. Federal judges have lifetime tenure. With the exception of the Supreme Court (discussed later), religion has not been a prominent issue in federal judicial appointments, at least not in recent years (Goldman, 1997)—although it can, and does, still come up, as in questioning federal judgeship nominees about their views on abortion. Historically, Democratic administrations appointed more Catholics and Jews to the federal bench than did Republican administrations, but that has not been the case since President Reagan (Goldman, 1997). Although some court-watchers were concerned that President Kennedy, the nation's first Catholic president, would favor Catholic judges, only 15% of his appointees were Catholic, less than those of both Franklin Roosevelt and Lyndon Johnson (25% and 23%, respectively), and approximately equal to Eisenhower's 13% (Perry, 1991; Wilkey, 1973). Eisenhower, Kennedy, and Johnson appointed an equal number of Jewish judges—8% (Wilkey, 1973). Thus, the majority of federal judges, like the majority of the American population, are Protestant.

Judicial selection in the states differs from the federal process, and states also differ from one another. Most states provide for some sort of electoral component in the selection of its judges (Murphy et al., 2006). Only six states appoint judges serving on their courts of last resort (by the legislature in two states and by the governor in four states). The remaining states are roughly evenly split between election (38% by partisan, and 62% by nonpartisan ballot) and the "merit" or "Missouri" plan, which is a compromise between the election and appointment methods (Murphy et al., 2006). Under this system, a screening committee nominates several candidates for an opening, and the governor selects one. The judge is then periodically on the ballot to determine if he should be retained. Overall, 87% of the nation's 11,000 state judges face voters in some type of election (Ebrahim, 2006).

Religious Groups' Involvement in Judicial Campaigns

Historically, judges have rarely been voted out of office in retention votes. However, the prospects for judicial nonretention, as well as defeat in an initial election campaign for lower state court judgeships, are increasing. The increase is due largely to the growing involvement of special-interest groups in judicial selection. These groups, many of which are (or have ties to) conservative Christian, "pro-family" organizations, such as Phyllis Schlafly's Eagle Forum or James Dobson's Focus on the Family, administer questionnaires to judicial candidates and then seek to influence the election's outcome by supporting candidates who agree with their positions or by opposing candidates who disagree (Ebrahim, 2006; Eisenberg et al., 2005). They seem to be taking the biblical command to select as judges "men who fear God" (from the epigraph that opened this chapter) quite literally. Coyle (2006) quotes Cynthia Gray, director of the American Judicature Society's Center for Judicial Ethics, as saying "My impression is that there are more questionnaires and most are coming from what would be considered religious right groups." The groups are especially interested in candidates' positions on controversial issues with religious overtones, such as abortion, the death penalty, same-sex marriage, and evolution. Most initiatives to oust judges who have run afoul of the Religious Right have failed, but at considerable cost to the judges. In addition to the emotional and financial toll on judges—who have been forced to do more campaigning and fundraising than previously—there is the more insidious effect on how, and when, they decide cases. For example, Iowa District Judge Jeffrey Neary survived a campaign by a conservative Christian group to defeat his retention bid because of his decision dissolving a same-sex civil union. Afterward, he admitted that in the future, "I will think a little bit about timing. I will sit on decisions around retention time" (Ebrahim, 2006, p. 56). Such behavior has obvious, and ominous, implications for the impartial administration of justice.

Judges do not have to respond to the questionnaires or requests for position statements, but they cannot rely on a judicial canon of ethics for that decision. Such ethical canons were struck down by the U.S. Supreme Court on First Amendment free speech grounds (*Republican Party of Minnesota v. White*, 2002; see Coyle, 2006; Ebrahim, 2006), and one could argue, moreover, that a legal rule or ethical standard that precludes a judge from openly espousing and utilizing religious values in his decision making "dehumanizes" religiously devout judges (Conkle, 1998b; Griffen, 1998). Judicial candidates can expect to be taken to task by the organization sponsoring the questionnaire if they decline for other reasons.

Some religious organizations have gone beyond merely surveying judicial candidates and expressing support or opposition based on their responses and have actively recruited candidates. For example, in 2004, the Alabama League of Christian Voters recruited an entire slate of conservative Christian attorneys to run for open judgeships (Ebrahim, 2006). One of their charges against the sitting state Supreme Court justices was that they had failed to support former Chief Justice Roy Moore in his Ten Commandments dispute, and Moore himself helped them pick candidates. Two of the three candidates whom the League backed for the Supreme Court won.

Thus, it seems clear that, in early 21st-century America, judges, or those who aspire to become judges, can expect their religion (or at least their religious beliefs) to become an issue in any debate over their professional qualifications for the position. Ebrahim (2006, p. 57) concludes that "In the future, such confrontations promise to become more systematic, as religious conservatives across the country examine judges and smite the ones who don't obey God's law, as they see it, or fail to agree with their interpretation of the Constitution." Because federal judges are appointed, rather than elected, such confrontations are somewhat muted, but religion can be an issue there as well; the nation's highest federal court, the Supreme Court, is a case in point.

Religious Seats on the U.S. Supreme Court

Many Supreme Court justices have been personally devout or involved in organized religion (Berg & Ross, 1998), to the extent that three justices (Joseph Story, Samuel Miller, and Harold Burton) served as national president of the Unitarian Church (Hitchcock, 2004, Vol. 2). Among current justices, Antonin Scalia and Clarence Thomas are the most vocal about their faith[3]; but generally speaking, the justices themselves have not made a big issue out of their religion (although others occasionally have), and they have been careful to disavow religious influences during their confirmation hearings. The "most religiously zealous of any justice in the Court's history" was William Strong (Associate Justice, 1870–1880), a Presbyterian who was president of the American Sunday School Union and headed an organization that sought to amend the Constitution to make the United States an officially Christian nation (Hitchcock, 2004, Vol. 2, p. 81; see also Berg & Ross, 1998). Even in Strong's case, however, his religious views did not find direct expression in his written opinions. This is in contrast to Justice David Brewer (1889–1910), who referred to the United States in *Holy Trinity Church v. United States* (1892) as a "Christian nation"; he apparently meant it not merely in a historical sense but in an official, legal sense (Berg & Ross, 1998; Hitchcock, 2004).

Supreme Court justices have belonged to a variety of religions.[4] Twelve different religious denominations have been represented on the Court, with Episcopalians having the greatest number (35; see Table 6.1).[5] Notably, the only non-Christian Justices have been the Court's seven Jews; there have been no Muslim, Hindu, Buddhist, or atheist Justices, nor have there been any

Table 6.1 Religious Affiliation of U.S. Supreme Court Justices (through 2008)

Affiliation	# Justices	% Justices	Affiliation	# of Justices	% Justices
Episcopalian	33	30.0	Congregationalist	2	1.8
Presbyterian	19	17.3	Disciples of Christ	2	1.8
Catholic	13	11.8	Lutheran	1	0.9
Unitarian	9	8.2	Quaker	1	0.9
Jewish	7	6.4	Huguenot	1	0.9
Methodist	5	4.5	Undefined Protestant	13	11.8
Baptist	3	2.7	None*	1	0.9

*Justice David Davis (1862–1877) was not a member of any church, but this should not be taken to mean that he was an atheist. No avowed atheist has ever served on the U.S. Supreme Court.

Jehovah's Witness, Seventh Day Adventist, or Mormon (Church of Latter Day Saints) justices.[6] On the one hand, religion might not seem to be much of an issue for the Supreme Court, considering the unprecedented number of Catholics (five: Roberts, Alito, Scalia, Kennedy, and Thomas) and Jews (two: Ginsburg and Breyer) currently on the Court; on the other hand, religion was an issue in President George W. Bush's recent nominations to the Supreme Court of John Roberts (confirmed in 2005, and presently Chief Justice), Harriet Myers (2005, withdrawn), and Samuel Alito (confirmed in 2006). Religious concerns in Supreme Court nominations have existed since the late 19th and early 20th centuries. Although Supreme Court justices cannot be disqualified for religious reasons—Article VI of the Constitution forbids any religious test for federal office—they can and have been chosen, at least in part, on account of their religion.

A variety of factors go into the presidential selection of Supreme Court nominees: political and ideological compatibility, objective merit, personal friendship, and representativeness (Abraham, 1992; Davis, 2005; Wrightsman, 2006; Yalof, 1999). As described in the following section, religion can influence a judge's ideology, but it is most prominently a factor in terms of representativeness—that is, in selecting a justice who is representative of a particular population demographic. In the early years of the republic, representativeness was manifested almost solely in terms of geography; a Supreme Court vacancy was usually filled with someone from the same state, or at least the same region (Perry, 1991). The influence of geography waned in the post-Civil War era, as advocates of states' rights and regionalism lost their battle with nationalism, sectional economic differences declined, and circuit riding for members of the Court (i.e., traveling throughout a specified geographic area to hear cases) ended in 1891 (Perry, 1991). At the same time, American society was becoming more diverse, thanks largely to immigration, and as previously disenfranchised groups (racial, ethnic, and religious minorities, and women) gained the right to vote and gradually acquired some degree of electoral clout.

Consequently, it behooved presidents to appeal to these groups of voters, and one way in which they did that was by considering members of these groups for judicial (including Supreme Court) vacancies. Unlike geography, characteristics like religion, race, and gender involve "passive representativeness," because there is generally no assumption that members of these groups, if appointed, will actively represent group concerns (Perry, 1991).

Representativeness has almost certainly not been the paramount consideration in any Supreme Court nomination—as opposed to, say, merit or ideology—but it has nonetheless been a significant factor in a number of nominations over the last 100 years. The evidence suggests that this is likely to continue, due to the increased public nature of the process and the involvement of the media and special interest groups (Davis, 2005; Silverstein, 1994; Yalof, 1999). As Davis observes, "The Court increasingly has been viewed as a body that should represent the greater diversity in the American populace. This expectation makes representativeness a potent force in presidential selection" (p. 81). After geography, the first representativeness factor to play a role in Supreme Court nominations was religion.

For many years, there were presumed Catholic and Jewish seats on the Supreme Court. The common wisdom is that such seats reflected a quota system, with the appointments meant as recognition of newly politically viable religious groups (Perry, 1991); but another view is that they were, in effect, reverse quota systems, designed to limit religious minorities' presence on the Court to a single representative (Knee, 1993). Regardless of the rationale, there are clear threads of religious considerations in Supreme Court appointments.

Catholics on the Supreme Court

The first Catholic Justice was Roger B. Taney, whom President Andrew Jackson appointed Chief Justice in 1836; but according to Barbara Perry's (1991) analysis of representativeness in Supreme Court appointments, the "Catholic seat" did not really start until Edward White's appointment in 1894 (see also Chase, Green, & Mollan, 1960). Although Taney's nomination received criticism on grounds of his Catholicism, the anti-Catholic opposition was relatively muted. There was not another Catholic justice for three decades after Taney's death in 1864. In the intervening period, a large wave of Catholic immigration occurred, mainly from Ireland, and American Catholics had become a political force. Catholicism thus became a "plus" factor in the nominations of White (by President Cleveland) and Joseph McKenna (by President McKinley, in 1897). As Catholic electoral support became even more important in the ensuing years, so too did a prospective nominee's religion, until "with [Pierce] Butler's selection [in 1922], religion moved beyond its previous status as an 'over-the-top' factor: it had now become one of the primary considerations in choosing a Supreme Court justice" (Perry, 1991, p. 33). Franklin Roosevelt, who had strong Catholic electoral support, averaged an unprecedented one Catholic for every four judicial appointments while president (Perry, 1991), including Frank Murphy's appointment to the Supreme Court in 1940 (replacing Butler).

After Murphy's death in 1949, President Truman ignored calls to maintain the "Catholic seat" and instead nominated his close friend, Attorney General Tom Clark, who was Presbyterian. He sought to assuage Catholic dissatisfaction with this decision by simultaneously nominating J. Howard McGrath, a Catholic, to replace Clark as Attorney General (Yalof, 1999). When asked by reporters about breaking the Catholic seat tradition, Truman replied, "If he is qualified, I wouldn't care what his faith is, whether it's Catholic, Baptist, or Jewish" (Yalof, 1999, p. 37).

According to Perry (1991), as Catholics became increasingly assimilated into American politics after World War II, the justification and motivation for offering representation on the Court to Catholics as a group diminished. President Eisenhower declined to name a Catholic to replace Robert Jackson in 1954, despite "increasingly furious lobbying" to do so (Yalof, 1999, p. 54); he did, however, delay announcing the nomination of John Marshall Harlan II until after the midterm election, so as not to antagonize the Catholic electorate (Yalof, 1999). William Brennan's Catholicism was not a major factor in his appointment by President Eisenhower in 1956 (Perry, 1991), but it was nonetheless a significant one, as Eisenhower sought to appeal to Catholic voters in his reelection campaign (Yalof, 1999). And indeed, Eisenhower's share of the Catholic vote increased by 5%, compared to the 1952 election (Davis, 2005).

After Brennan, another Catholic was not appointed to the Court until Antonin Scalia in 1986. There is no evidence that President Reagan considered religion in nominating either Scalia or Anthony Kennedy (1988), or that President George H.W. Bush considered Clarence Thomas's (1991) Catholicism; nor did their religion garner much media attention. In Thomas's case, much greater emphasis was placed on issues of race and gender. Race was an issue because he replaced Thurgood Marshall, the only other African-American justice, and gender was an issue because of allegations against him of sexual harassment. To a large extent, the same lack of attention to nominees' religion is true of the most recent Catholic additions to the Supreme Court, John Roberts (2005) and Samuel Alito (2006). These nominees did, however, have to answer questions about the role their religion would and should play in their decisions about specific issues, such as abortion (Levinson, 2006).[7] Catholics have clearly arrived on the Supreme Court, currently constituting a majority of the Court's membership. Of the Court's 17 Chief Justices over the past 220 years, three have been Catholics (including Roberts, the current Chief Justice), second only to the seven Episcopalians who have served as Chief Justice.

Jews on the Supreme Court

The supposed "Jewish seat" was established with President Wilson's appointment to the Court of Louis Brandeis in 1916, although there are rumors that

President Fillmore might have offered a seat to Senator Judah P. Benjamin (who later held several high Confederate offices during the Civil War, including secretary of war and secretary of state) in 1852 or 1853 (Burt, 1988; Perry, 1991). Much like the early Catholic nominations, Brandeis's appointment was seen as an appeal to Jewish voters, whose numbers had increased greatly due to recent immigration. Although Brandeis was not a practicing Jew, he never denied his Jewish identity, and he became an ardent Zionist and leader in the American Zionist movement, not long before his nomination (Auerbach, 1990; Burt, 1988; Karfunkel & Ryley, 1978; Urofsky, 1994).[8] Wilson was aware of Brandeis's faith, but the evidence suggests that he made the choice on account of Brandeis's legal qualifications and progressive political views, much more so than on account of his religion (Perry, 1991). Although Wilson did capture a majority of the Jewish vote in his 1916 reelection bid, it was only 55%, probably not enough to have influenced the outcome (Perry, 1991).[9]

More so than with Taney's nomination, Brandeis's religion made headlines. "Virtually all press accounts of Brandeis's selection referred to the fact that he was the first member of his religion to be chosen for the Supreme Court" (Perry, 1991, p. 64). Brandeis's confirmation process was protracted (lasting five months), divisive (he was confirmed by a vote of 47–22), and characterized by considerable attention to his religion and no small amount of anti-Semitic rhetoric (Perry, 1991). This rhetoric was occasionally overt but more often reflected subtle stereotypes. Because of his work as the "people's lawyer," representing consumer interests and the "little man" in a variety of causes, Brandeis was portrayed as a clever, crafty, but crooked lawyer who lacked the "judicial temperament" to serve on the Supreme Court (Burt, 1988; Karfunkel & Ryley, 1978). According to Silverstein (1994, p. 3), "[b]eneath the surface of the debate over political and judicial philosophy lay a virulent strain of anti-Semitism."

Nor did the anti-Semitism die down after Brandeis took his seat on the Court. James McReynolds, a pious member of the Disciples of Christ (Hitchcock, 2004, Vol. 2) and one of Brandeis's colleagues on the Court, was a virulent anti-Semite (and racist) who openly expressed his disgust for his junior Associate Justice. He refused to speak to Brandeis for Brandeis's first three years on the bench, he often left the justices' conference room when Brandeis spoke, and he refused to sit next to Brandeis for the Court's annual picture (Abraham, 1992). McReynolds even refused to sign the customary testimonial to Brandeis upon Brandeis's retirement (Abraham, 1992; Karfunkel & Ryley, 1978).[10]

Unlike Wilson's nomination of Brandeis, little evidence exists to suggest that President Hoover's 1932 nomination of Benjamin Cardozo (to replace Oliver Wendell Holmes, Jr.) was an appeal to Jewish voters in his reelection campaign that year. At that point in history, Republican efforts to attract Jewish voters were largely an exercise in futility; Franklin Roosevelt received 82% of the Jewish vote in 1932 (Perry, 1991). On the contrary, Hoover was sensitive to concerns about having *too many* Jews—two—on the Supreme Court at the same time (Karfunkel & Ryley, 1978; Silverstein, 1994). Although Cardozo had a more religious upbringing than Brandeis and maintained a lifelong synagogue membership, he still was not particularly observant (Kaufman, 1994). More importantly, his legal qualifications were so impeccable that his nomination received little opposition on religious (or any other) grounds, and he was confirmed quickly and unanimously (Abraham, 1992; Silverstein, 1994).

Like Brandeis, Cardozo was a victim of his colleague McReynold's anti-Semitism. He read a newspaper during Cardozo's swearing-in ceremony while muttering "another one," and one of McReynold's law clerks claims that he never even spoke to Cardozo (Abraham, 1992). Cardozo served on the Court for only six years, dying suddenly in 1938. President Roosevelt wanted to appoint Felix Frankfurter, his close friend and adviser and also a Jew, to replace Cardozo; but he vacillated because of the widespread perception that Brandeis's chair was the true, and sole, "Jewish seat." According to Perry (1991), he essentially had to overlook Frankfurter's religion in order to appoint him as Cardozo's replacement, which he did in 1939. The appointment was fitting in the sense that Cardozo and Frankfurter had been personal friends, to the point that Cardozo performed the Frankfurters' marriage ceremony while he was on the New York Court of Appeals (Parrish, 1994).

Brandeis retired just one month after Frankfurter's appointment, effectively transferring the Jewish seat to Frankfurter, which he held for 23 years. Like Brandeis, Frankfurter had a reputation for public advocacy and siding with the oppressed prior to coming to the Court (Burt, 1988). He acted on these views by hiring the Supreme Court's first African-American law clerk (William T. Coleman, Jr., in 1948) and promoting the careers of other African-American lawyers (Parrish, 1994). He also resembled Brandeis religiously: nonobservant (even describing himself as a "reverent agnostic"), although never denying his religion; involved in the Zionist movement (partly at Brandeis's instigation); and sensitive to his outsider status in both the legal profession and larger American society (Auerbach, 1990; Burt, 1988; Parrish, 1994).

President Kennedy preserved the Jewish seat by nominating Arthur Goldberg, his Secretary of Labor, to replace Frankfurter upon his retirement in 1962. Because by this time overt anti-Semitism was on the decline in the United States, Jews were increasingly assimilated into American life, and the trail had already been blazed, Goldberg's religion was not much of a factor in either his nomination or his confirmation hearings (Perry, 1991). By the same token, Goldberg's appointment indicated that religion *did* matter, in the sense of there now being an implicit—and in the media, an explicit—acknowledgment that one seat on the Court was reserved for a Jewish justice (Perry, 1991). Goldberg left the Court in 1965 to become U.S. Ambassador to the United Nations, in which capacity he worked hard to further human rights. His commitment to human rights reflected a decidedly Jewish perspective, as evidenced by his co-founding (in 1969) of the International Association of Jewish Lawyers and Jurists, an organization dedicated to advancing human rights (see Chapter 7).

The Jewish seat tradition held when Abe Fortas replaced Goldberg, but there were no Jewish justices between Fortas's resignation in 1969 and Ruth Bader Ginsburg's appointment in 1993. President Nixon apparently did consider religion in choosing Fortas's replacement, asking his attorney general, "Is Rehnquist Jewish? He looks Jewish" (Wrightsman, 2006). Although William Rehnquist, the Court's only Lutheran, was not appointed at that time (the seat went to Harry Blackmun instead), he was appointed in 1972 and served for 33 years, the last 19 as Chief Justice.

There was one nomination of a Jew in the interim, President Reagan's nomination of Douglas Ginsburg in 1987. Although his religion was a consideration in Ginsburg's selection (Roberts, 1987), it did not play a factor in the nomination's eventual withdrawal.[11] Ruth Bader Ginsburg's nomination by President Clinton was hailed by some as a reclamation of the Jewish seat (Knee, 1993), but by that time Jewish representation in politics and the legal profession was sufficiently widespread that, as with recent Catholic Supreme Court appointments, her religion had little bearing on her selection and was a trivial issue during the confirmation process (Davis, 2005). The same was true for Associate Justice Stephen Breyer, appointed by President Clinton in 1994. Interestingly, Breyer had clerked for Justice Goldberg prior to Breyer's own appointment to the Court.

Religion's Current Role in Supreme Court Appointments

Barbara Perry's (1991) review of religion's role in Supreme Court appointments leads her to conclude that it displays a parabolic function, reflecting a religious constituency's electoral influence and assimilation into American society: Initially, it is a trivial or nonexistent factor, then a plus factor, then an important consideration; after this peak, it diminishes to a plus factor again, then a trivial consideration. Perhaps not coincidentally, the first Catholic and Jewish Justices (Taney and Brandeis) consistently make the lists of "great" Justices (Abraham, 1992, pp. 412–414), suggesting that their legal qualifications and abilities far outweighed representativeness in their selection. The idea of religious representativeness on the Court has now become sufficiently well entrenched that a prospective nominee's religion is doubtless considered during the selection process, but only after first attending to the more important criteria of merit and political/ideological compatibility. In this way, presidents "could have their cake and eat it too by appointing otherwise acceptable justices, who were members of the 'right' religious faith" (Perry, 1991, p. 79).

The religious composition of the court has changed dramatically in the two-plus centuries of its existence, going from an all-Protestant body until Taney's appointment in 1836 to a 2008 Court with a majority of

Catholics, two Jews, one Episcopalian (David Souter), and one Protestant without a formal religious affiliation (John Paul Stevens). Although some commentators argue that religious representativeness on the Court has been superseded by other kinds of representativeness, such as gender, race, and ethnicity (Davis, 2005; Perry, 1991), it is interesting to consider the most recent unsuccessful Supreme Court nomination—President George W. Bush's nomination of Harriet Miers in 2005—in light of Perry's thesis. Much was made by both media commentators and the President himself of Miers's conservative Christian credentials (Scheiber, 2005). Evangelical Christians had not previously been represented on the Court, even though they had become a strong political and electoral force from the 1980s onward and were an important core part of Bush's political base. Further evidence of evangelicals' interest in the Supreme Court's religious composition comes from conservative religious figures like Pat Robertson, who called on God to take an active role in the selection process. He announced "Operation Supreme Court Freedom" in July 2003, a "prayer offensive" whose purpose it was for God to induce three justices to retire whom Robertson deemed too liberal ("Robertson asks God to oust liberal justices," 2003).[12]

The opposition to Miers—which ultimately led to the withdrawal of her nomination—did refer to her religious beliefs, in a manner reminiscent of some of the anti-Catholic and anti-Semitic reactions to the first Catholic and Jewish nominees. However, the bulk of the opposition focused on her unimpressive legal qualifications (Scheiber, 2005). Bush's mistake was in elevating her religion beyond a mere plus factor to a major consideration, despite questions about her objective qualifications. In other words, the President focused more on her religious than on her legal credentials (Scheiber, 2005). A better-qualified evangelical nominee would likely have been confirmed, thereby extending religious representativeness on the Supreme Court in a new direction.

The Relationship Between Judges' Religion and Their Decisions

There is a growing consensus that attitudes and opinions on matters of public policy are important predictors of appellate judges' decisions (Champagne & Nagel, 1982; Greene & Wrightsman, 2003; Pritchett, 1941; Segal & Spaeth, 1993[13]). This *attitudinal model* holds that an appellate court, such as the U.S. Supreme Court, "decides disputes in light of the facts of the case vis-à-vis the ideological attitudes and values of the justices" (Segal & Spaeth, 1993, p. 65). It is frequently contrasted with the *legal model* of judicial decision making, whereby the court decides disputes "in light of the facts of the case vis-à-vis precedent, the plain meaning of the Constitution and statutes, the intent of the framers, and a balancing of societal versus constitutional interests" (Segal & Spaeth, 1993, p. 64). The attitudinal model is related to the *social background model* of judicial decision-making, which posits a relationship between demographic and experiential variables (e.g., sex, race, employment prior to becoming a judge, seniority) and judges' decisions (e.g., Tate, 1981; Ulmer, 1970, 1973, 1986). It is also closely related to what some scholars refer to as the *extralegal model*, which subsumes attitudinal and background variables in addition to factors relating to characteristics of the parties, the larger political environment, institutional arrangements, and so forth (George & Epstein, 1992; Hall & Brace, 1992). Some evidence suggests that these extralegal variables are becoming more important over time (at least with respect to Supreme Court decisions; see Ulmer, 1986), and they can influence the outcome of judicial decisions, as well as the judicial reasoning that undergirds those decisions (Sisk, Heise, & Morriss, 2004).

Although the majority of these studies have not looked specifically at judges' religious affiliation or beliefs, it stands to reason that religion would be one important factor—albeit one of many social background characteristics—influencing judges' attitudes, values, personality, and ideology (Champagne & Nagel, 1982; Feldman, 2006; Greenawalt, 1995; Songer & Tabrizi, 1999; Ulmer, 1973). The common assumption is that members of religious minorities, especially Catholics and Jews, would be socialized to favor the "underdog" in legal disputes—that is, the member of the less privileged economic or social group—by virtue of their historical and perhaps personal experience as outsiders in American society (Burt, 1988; Goldman, 1975). With respect to specific issues, the most obvious example is probably the Catholic Church's stance on abortion, but religion doubtless influences case-relevant attitudes in much more subtle ways as well.[14]

To be sure, several difficulties arise when attempting to use judges' religious identification as a predictor of their decisions (George, 2001). As we discussed in previous chapters, adherents of any religion vary widely in their degree of observance and particular beliefs, often going against their religion's official doctrine (e.g., many American Catholics' pro-choice stance on abortion); and religious groups' status and perspective change over time (e.g., the Catholic Church's evolving stance on capital punishment; see Chapter 3). George cites the example of American Catholics, as a group, being more politically conservative now than they were 50 years ago. If anything, this high within-religion variability would make findings of any religious differences in judicial decision making all the more notable.

A few studies have included judges' religion as a possible predictor of their decisions, and those studies are described next. Information on judges' religious affiliation is available from a variety of sources, such as judicial and legal directories, and is even more widely available than previously due to the increasing popularity of questionnaires for judicial candidates (see earlier discussion). As the task engaged in by trial and appellate judges is fundamentally different—that is, deciding primarily matters of fact versus matters of law (see generally Murphy et al., 2006)—we treat these two classes of judges separately.

Trial Judges

Studies of individual differences in trial judges' decision making date to the early 20th century (see Schubert, 1964, for review). For example, Everson (1919) analyzed the sentencing records of 42 New York City magistrates for the year 1914, covering the disposition of 153,000 cases. He found marked variations in sentencing, presumably due to differences in temperament, personality, and education. Other studies, using different samples of judges and different databases of verdicts, have likewise found considerable variability in sentencing for comparable cases (e.g., Gaudet, 1938/1964), leading to the conclusion that judges' attitudes and ideology are significant determinants of their decisions (Green, 1964).

A few of these archival studies of judicial decisions have included religion among the personality and social background variables studied, and they have found that judges' religion appears to matter more in some types of cases than others. For example, judges have occasionally recused themselves from cases when they felt that they could not be impartial due to their religious beliefs, such as Catholic judges who routinely recuse themselves from abortion hearings (e.g., those in which a minor has requested judicial permission in lieu of parental consent; see Barringer, 1996; Osborn, 2006). Vines (1964) examined 37 federal district judges' decisions in race relations cases in the Southern United States following *Brown v. Board of Education* (1954). Based on the percentage of cases in which they decided in favor of Black litigants, judges were classified as Segregationist, Moderate, or Integrationist. There were relatively few Catholic judges, but they were all Integrationists.

A subsequent study by Giles and Walker (1975) investigated 42 Southern federal district judges' decisions in a single kind of race relations cases—public school desegregation—for the year 1970. In addition to focusing on a single type of case and a single year, the study differed from Vines' study in two other important respects: the primary dependent measure was not a judge's decision but the degree of segregation that existed in the school district under the judge's supervision; and they classified the judges' religion as "Fundamentalist Protestant" (operationalized as Southern Baptist or Methodist) or "other."[15] There was no correlation between a judge's religion and the degree of segregation present in the district's schools.

The difference between Giles and Walker's findings and those of Vines could reflect the passage of time between the two studies, the different religious classification systems, or the fact that judges in the Giles and Walker study had less direct control over the study's outcome measure—that is, segregation in the schools—than they had over the legal decisions assessed by Vines (Champagne & Nagel, 1982). Nevertheless, the discrepancy makes it hard to conclude with confidence that trial judges of different religious backgrounds vary in how they treat cases involving matters of race. Trial judges' religion also appears to matter little in the outcome of federal civil rights cases (Ashenfelter, Eisenberg, & Schwab, 1995).

Appellate Judges

More research has focused on appellate court than on trial court decision making. Some appellate judges have acknowledged using a religious rationale in their opinions. For example, Raul Gonzalez (1996, p. 1148), a Texas Supreme Court justice, acknowledges making a number of decisions that were "directly impacted" by his Catholic beliefs, such as those involving children's (including unborn children's) rights. Notably, Justice Gonzalez did not quote biblical passages in his opinions, but he nonetheless relied on his religious convictions in interpreting and applying the relevant law (for discussion of more explicit religious references in judicial opinions, see the last section of this chapter). The distinction is subtle yet important (Greenawalt, 1995). Like all decision makers, judges have value systems that are a complex product of their background and experiences, are often informed by religious beliefs, and which cannot simply be set aside on demand. As Justice Gonzalez observed, "One's views on how the world began, sin, forgiveness, and redemption influences our attitudes, behavior, and everything that we do" (Gonzalez, 1996, p. 1157).

Several quantitative analyses of Supreme Court decisions likewise provide support for the attitudinal model (e.g., Pritchett, 1964; Schubert, 1974; Segal & Spaeth, 1993; Wrightsman, 2006). For example, Schubert (1974) analyzed U.S. Supreme Court decisions from 1946–1969, covering the Vinson and Warren Courts. The justices clustered together into three groups: one that was liberal on both political (e.g., civil liberties, criminal procedure) and economic (e.g., governmental regulation of business) issues; one that was economically conservative but politically neutral; and one that was politically conservative but economically neutral. These ideological positions were "remarkably stable" over time (Schubert, 1974, p. 144). Attitudes are important not only in determining the disposition of cases, but also in the selection of cases (i.e., granting of certiorari) and assignment of majority-opinion writing duties (Segal & Spaeth, 1993).

Attitudes do not always come into play, but they are especially likely to matter in certain types of cases or ones in which the appellate court is closely divided (Pritchett, 1964; Wrightsman, 2006). For example, Wrightsman found that ideology (i.e., liberalism vs. conservatism) predicted Supreme Court justices' votes better in cases involving criminal defendants' or prisoners' rights than in other kinds of cases.

Nagel (1964; see also Nagel, 1969) conducted a study of judicial decisions as a function of judges' religion (among other social background variables), using as a sample 313 judges of state and federal supreme courts for the year 1955. There were too few Jewish judges in the sample for comparison purposes, limiting the comparison to Protestant (mostly Methodist, 19% of the sample; Presbyterian, 15%; Episcopalian, 15%; and Baptist, 11%) versus Catholic judges. Using as a baseline the judges' own respective courts, he found that Catholic judges were significantly more likely than Protestant judges to show a liberal voting pattern in nonunanimous cases for four (of 15 total) types of cases: those involving criminal matters, business regulation, divorce settlement, and employee injury ("more liberal" was operationalized as voting for the criminal defendant, the administrative agency, the wife, and the employee, respectively). Protestant judges were more liberal in none of the case types.

Goldman (1975; see also Goldman, 1966) likewise compared Catholic and Protestant appellate judges, using as a database all nonunanimous decisions by U.S. Courts of Appeals from 1965 through 1971. Although he categorized the legal issues somewhat differently from Nagel, the results were generally consistent: Catholic judges were more liberal in certain types of cases, in the sense of being more likely to side with injured persons and to vote for the economic underdog. These religious differences were especially true for Democratic judges (the author notes that there were very few—only four—Republican Catholic judges in the entire sample). Protestant judges were never more liberal, and religion exerted no influence in a number of types of cases (e.g., criminal procedure, civil liberties). There were too few Jewish judges ($n = 13$) to include in the statistical analyses, but their median scores were more liberal than both Catholics and Protestants for virtually all kinds of cases.

Studies focusing on a narrower spectrum of cases likewise show that judges' religion matters. Pinello (2003) analyzed all published appellate court decisions (state and federal; $N = 468$) from 1981 to 2000 that dealt with issues falling under the rubric of "gay rights": lesbian/gay family matters (including same-sex marriage), sexual orientation discrimination, gays in the military, consensual sodomy and solicitation laws, and free speech/association of gays and lesbians. He classified 393 of the cases as "essential" to gay and lesbian rights, and he obtained background data on 84% ($N = 849$) of the judges who decided those cases. The findings varied somewhat depending on the legal issue and type of court (e.g., intermediate appellate court vs. court of last resort), but overall, Jewish judges were relatively liberal, whereas Catholic judges were relatively conservative. "*Jewish judges had a probability of voting in favor of gay rights by .15 more than Protestants, and by .26 more than Catholics*" (Pinello, 2003, p. 87; italics in original). The pattern of findings was robust for both Jewish and Catholic judges, but especially for the former. Minority and women judges were also comparatively liberal, leading Pinello to conclude that belonging to a historically powerless group makes judges empathize more with other disenfranchised groups.[16] He notes Catholics' history of discrimination as well, but argues that any empathetic effects of that discrimination would be countered by the successful assimilation of Catholics into American society over time, in general, and by antihomosexual church dogma, in particular.

The previous studies aggregated a number of different appellate courts, drawing data from both federal courts and the states. A single federal appellate court, the U.S. Supreme Court, receives special scrutiny in many respects, and the relationship between judges' personal attributes and their decisions is no exception. At a superficial level, there seems to be little evidence that Supreme Court justices' religion is directly associated with their decisions. Catholic justices have ranged from very conservative (e.g., Butler, Scalia) to very liberal (e.g., Murphy, Brennan), and Perry (1991, p. 46) maintains that "Catholics on the Court have exhibited an exaggerated degree of religious impartiality." For example, Frank Murphy, perhaps the most devout of the 19th- and early 20th-century Catholic justices, upheld the doctrine of church–state separation even when it went against Church doctrine and was a passionate defender of Jehovah's Witnesses' right to freedom of expression (Berg & Ross, 1998; Chase et al., 1960; Hitchcock, 2004, Vol. 2).

However, empirical studies that have focused on specific issues suggest the existence of a relationship between judges' religion and case outcomes. For example, Ulmer (1973) analyzed the voting behavior of the 14 justices who sat on the U.S. Supreme Court from 1947–1956. He found that the three background variables of age at appointment, federal administrative experience, and religious affiliation (Protestant vs. non-Protestant) accounted for 70% of the variance in the rate at which they supported the government in criminal cases. Religion was the weakest of the three predictors but still improved the amount of variance explained by 21% over and above the other two factors. The non-Protestant justices were less likely than Protestant justices to support the government (means of 28% and 48%, respectively).[7] Catholic Supreme Court justices are also more likely to dissent than their Protestant brethren (Ulmer, 1970).

This pattern of findings has been replicated cross-nationally. Tate and Sittiwong (1989) analyzed the nonunanimous decisions of Canadian Supreme Court justices in civil rights or economics cases ($N = 606$) from 1949 to 1985. Catholic justices were more liberal than non-Catholic justices in both types of cases, with non-Catholic judges coming from outside Quebec the most liberal of all (Quebecois origin exerted a conservative influence, independent of religion).

Nagel (1964) explored possible differences among judges belonging to different Protestant denominations by grouping together denominations associated with relatively high economic status (Congregationalist, Episcopalian, Presbyterian, and Unitarian) and those associated with lower economic status (Baptist, Lutheran, and Methodist). Although there was a tendency for judges belonging to low-status denominations to vote in the liberal direction for certain case types more often than judges belonging to high-status denominations—again, compared to their court average—the difference was not statistically significant.

However, a more recent study by Songer and Tabrizi (1999) did find differences among Protestant judges. They examined votes of state supreme court justices on three issues—death penalty (a sample of 3909 votes), gender discrimination (437 votes), and obscenity (2023 votes)—from 1970 to 1993. They classified judges as evangelical Christian, mainline Protestant, Catholic, or Jewish.

Evangelicals were defined by membership in a religious denomination, so that some of the evangelical classifications included entire Protestant churches (e.g., Southern Baptists, Church of the Nazarene), whereas other Protestant faiths could be classified as either mainline or evangelical, depending on a judge's particular church affiliation (e.g., the mainline Evangelical Lutheran Church in America vs. Missouri Synod or Wisconsin Synod Lutherans; the mainline United Methodist Church vs. the Free Methodist Church; the mainline Presbyterian Church USA vs. Orthodox Presbyterians). Even after controlling for a number of other variables, such as party affiliation, prosecutorial experience, changing U.S. Supreme Court policy, and case facts relevant to each issue, judges' religion was strongly associated with their voting behavior. Evangelical judges were significantly more conservative than judges from other religious backgrounds in all three types of cases—that is, they more often voted to uphold the death penalty, maintain the gender gap, and restrict free speech in obscenity cases. Jewish judges were consistently the most liberal; mainline Protestant judges were liberal on the death penalty and obscenity, but less so on gender discrimination (although they were still more liberal than evangelical judges). Of the various groups, Catholic judges' behavior varied the most depending on the issue: They were liberal on gender discrimination, in the middle on the death penalty, and nearly as conservative as the evangelical judges on obscenity. Songer and Tabrizi interpret their results as demonstrating support for the attitudinal model of judicial decision making, in light of survey data showing the strong conservative attitudes of the Religious Right on public policies related to the legal questions raised by these particular kinds of cases.

Judges' Religion and Religious Freedom Cases

The empirical studies just described suggest that judges' religion matters in some types of cases but not others. One might reasonably expect it to matter most in cases that are directly concerned with religion, the most prominent examples of which are cases that raise issues of religious liberties, and which therefore deal with the Free Exercise and Establishment Clauses of the First Amendment. Free exercise cases, which are often referred to as *accommodation* cases, typically involve a claimant seeking an exemption, or special accommodation, from some law that burdens the exercise of her religion (Feldman, 2006; Sisk et al., 2004). Establishment cases raise questions of church–state relationships, or *separation*, such as prayer in public schools (Sorauf, 1976).[18] Because of the constitutional issues involved, these cases frequently reach appellate courts, but they are initially litigated at the trial level, in both state and federal courts. Several studies of judicial decisions in religious liberties cases have addressed, among other factors, the role played by judges' own religion.

In what is perhaps the earliest such study, Sorauf (1976) analyzed 67 separation cases decided by high appellate courts (both state and federal) from

1951–1971. Judges in several cases recused themselves for religious reasons; for example, some judges in cases about government aid to parochial schools recused themselves if they had children who attended Catholic schools (note that these judges were presumably Catholic themselves, which would reduce the number of Catholic judges hearing such cases). Sorauf found that judges' religion was strongly associated with their behavior in these cases: "Nothing explains the behavior of the judges in these church–state cases as frequently as do their own personal religious histories and affiliations. Jewish judges vote heavily separationist, Catholics vote heavily accommodationist, and Protestants divide" (p. 220). The pattern was strongest in nonunanimous appellate cases, in which Jewish judges voted for separation 82.4% of the time, compared to 56.1% for conservative Protestants (e.g., Baptist, Methodist), 48.7% for liberal Protestants (e.g., Episcopalians, Presbyterians), and 15.6% for Catholics; but the trend was present in unanimous appellate cases and for trial court judges as well. Among Protestant judges, those who belonged to the more involved and committed Masonic organizations—such as the Shrine and Scottish Rite—were strongly separationist, reflecting the Masons' traditional separationist values (e.g., their longstanding ties to separationist organizations such as Americans United for Separation of Church and State; see Sorauf, 1976).

Yarnold (2000) examined all cases in the federal circuit courts from 1970–1990 that concerned religious liberties ($N = 1356$); that is, cases about the Free Exercise and Establishment Clauses of the First Amendment. Judges represented a wide range of religions, including Catholicism, Judaism, and a number of Protestant denominations; some judges were nonreligious. The dependent variable was whether the decision was beneficial to religion, in the sense of promoting litigants'—regardless of which side they were on—ability to practice their faith. Yarnold (2000) found that, except for Lutherans, all judges (including the nonreligious ones) generally adopted a pro-religion position. Lutheran judges' tendency to take an anti-religion position in deciding these cases was not statistically significant; however, Catholic and Baptist judges were significantly more likely than other groups to rule in a pro-religion fashion. Yarnold also examined the relationship between judges' religion and the religion of parties involved in the case. Religious similarity did not improve litigants' chances of winning, but it did make a pro-religion decision more likely.

Sisk and colleagues (2004) partially confirmed these findings in a similar, more recent study that examined all published decisions ($N = 729$) in religious liberties cases in the federal courts (district courts and Courts of Appeals) from 1986–1995. They categorized judges as Catholic, mainline Protestant (e.g., Presbyterian, Episcopalian, Methodist), Baptist, Other Christian (most of whom identified themselves simply as Protestant), Jewish, Other (e.g., Unitarian, Mormon), or having no religious affiliation. In addition to coding judges' religion, they also coded claimants' religion and the religious demographics of the community where the judge maintained chambers (specifically, the Catholic and Jewish percentages in the community, the total rate of adherence to any religious group, and a score for the community's religious homogeneity).

They concluded that "the single most prominent, salient, and consistent influence on judicial decision making was religion—religion in terms of affiliation of the claimant, the background of the judge, and the demographics of the community" (Sisk et al., 2004, p. 614).[19] Specifically, Jewish judges and judges from "non-mainstream" Christian denominations (i.e., neither Catholic nor mainline Protestant) were significantly more likely to approve of accommodation requests in free exercise cases. Jewish judges were also significantly more likely to uphold claims challenging governmental acknowledgment of religion under the Establishment Clause. Moreover, they found that

> this distinctly Jewish attitude toward constitutional questions of Church and State exists independent of party affiliation or ideology, appearing to motivate Jewish judges regardless of whether they otherwise may be labeled as conservative or liberal on other legal or political issues. In sum, our study suggests that something about the Jewish experience or perspective moves a Jewish judge toward this particular approach to religious freedom issues, even when controlling for other background or attitudinal variables (Sisk et al., 2004, p. 582).

The behavior of Catholic judges was less straightforward. Catholic judges did differ from mainline Protestant judges, but only in cases raising certain kinds of issues. Specifically, they were more receptive to free exercise claimants in school cases in which parents or students sought exemption or accommodation on religious grounds, whereas they were less likely to sustain Establishment Clause claims that challenged affirmative acknowledgment of religion in a public school setting or government aid to private religious schools.

With respect to the community variables, Sisk and colleagues (2004) found that judges living in more religious communities were more liberal, in the sense of voting for claimants in both free exercise and establishment cases (i.e., supporting accommodation in the former and separation in the latter). Judges were also more liberal as the percentage of Jews in their community increased. Because the authors' analysis of these variables controlled for judges' own religion, the findings suggest that "the religious environment or culture of a community may have an influence even upon those judges in that community who do not share a religious perspective" (p. 590).

In her study of religious freedom cases, Yarnold (2000) concluded that most judges (except for Baptists and Catholics) were able to overcome their own predilections in deciding cases on religion. She suggests that the reason for Baptists' and Catholics' tendency to be more supportive of religious liberties is their history of minority status in terms of popular acceptance, compared to mainline Protestant denominations, which would explain Sisk and colleagues' (2004) findings regarding Jewish judges as well. To be sure, all of these groups have experienced past discrimination in the United States, but such an interpretation seems questionable when one considers that Baptists and Catholics currently constitute roughly 15% and 24%, respectively, of the U.S. population,[20] and Baptists, Catholics, and Jews have all been well-integrated elements of the American populace for several generations. She proposes that some other social background variable that is correlated with judges' religion, such as socioeconomic status, might also explain the result. It is also possible that some groups, such as Jews, are socialized to be especially sympathetic to individuals' civil liberties (Sorauf, 1976).

Although judges' decisions in religious freedom cases will rarely have a direct effect on judges' own religious group—only three of 48 nongovernmental plaintiffs in Sorauf's study were Jewish, and only two were Catholic—the cases would nonetheless have indirect implications, and judges belonging to religious minorities might be more sensitive to those implications. It is therefore not surprising that the issue is less salient for Protestants, who comprise the majority. Whatever the explanation, the findings are intriguing, especially in light of concerns that Catholic appellate judges would have a hard time keeping church and state separate (Chase et al., 1960; "John the Evangelist?" 2005; Lithwick, 2002). Some of Supreme Court Justice Antonin Scalia's comments appear to lend credence to such concerns (Levinson, 2006; "Scalia escalates attacks," 2005), but another Catholic justice, William Brennan, is regarded as a strict separationist (Hitchcock, 2004, Vol. 2).[21]

On the whole, despite some claims that judges' religion matters little (e.g., George, 2001), there do appear to be systematic differences in judges' decision making as a function of their religion. Jewish judges, on average, are consistently more liberal, arguably because of their stronger identification with the downtrodden and disenfranchised, owing to their own outsider status (Burt, 1988; Ginsburg, 1994). Catholic judges' liberalism varies more as a function of the individual (compare, e.g., Brennan vs. Scalia) and the issue, with Catholic judges being more liberal than non-Catholics on some issues (e.g., school desegregation, economics cases) but more conservative on others (e.g., gay rights). One explanation of this pattern is that the Catholic Church has taken an explicit position on many social policy issues, to which the majority of pious Catholics adhere. On the other hand, there is no "official Jewish position" on these same issues, or at least not one with which the majority of American Jews are familiar or to which they likely feel bound, thus freeing them to side with the underdog across a range of different types of cases.

Judges' Explicit Use of Religion in Decision Making

There are significant concerns about judges explicitly relying on their religious beliefs; most of these concerns revolve around the perception of possible bias (Barringer, 1996). Expressly religious judicial behavior is regulated by Canon 3(b)(5) of the American Bar Association (ABA) Model Code of Judicial Conduct, which states that judges shall perform their duties without bias, including (but not limited to) bias on the grounds of religion (Barringer, 1996; Osborn, 2006).[22] Statutes specifying the circumstances under which judges should recuse themselves do not mention religion, but they do include "personal bias or prejudice" as a basis for disqualification, which would include religious bias (Collett, 2000; Osborn, 2006).

Litigants have asked judges to recuse themselves on religious grounds in a variety of cases: Catholics on abortion, Mormons on gender equality, Jews on Islamist terrorism, and Baptists on religious discrimination against Jews (Collett, 2000; Lithwick, 2002). Other recusal motions have been based merely on judges sharing a religion with one of the parties, such as a Catholic judge in a priest sexual abuse case or a Mormon judge in a case involving a Mormon church-controlled newspaper (Lithwick, 2002; MacLean, 2005). Most of these motions for recusal are unsuccessful, because of the difficulty in demonstrating that a judge's religious affiliation would necessarily produce bias against a particular party (Collett, 2000). The assumption is that judges would be able to set aside their personal beliefs, religious or otherwise, and decide a case based on the facts and the law. As Idleman (1993, p. 433) notes, "It is virtually axiomatic today that judges should not advert to religious values when deciding cases, unless those cases explicitly involve religion." Despite the assumption of religious neutrality, research suggests that judges cannot so easily ignore their religious belief system, and some judges have even extolled the contributions of religious belief to their judicial decision making (Gonzalez, 1996; Merz, 2004).

Idleman (1993) presents a case for "why certain religious values can and even should enter into the judicial decision-making process" (p. 434; see also Idleman, 1998, 2005). Specifically, he sets forth historical, philosophical, utilitarian, and empirical reasons for religion's role in judicial decision making. For example, he argues that because religious values have informed American jurisprudence since the nation's birth, they have an implicit role that is impossible to exclude. Evidence that religion already *does* influence judicial reasoning, as reviewed earlier, should lead us to acknowledge religion's role, in order to foster a higher degree of accountability. This argument in and of itself is unpersuasive—that is, "we might not like it, but we can't avoid it, so we might as well make the best of it"—but combined with Idleman's philosophical and utilitarian perspectives, it demands serious consideration. The open use of religious values in judicial decision making, as a source of moral knowledge, can enrich the decision-making process and thereby contribute to society by improving the administration of justice (Carter, 1989; Collett, 2000; Griffen, 1998; Modak-Truran, 2004). A reliance on religion, especially as it informs judges' understanding of "natural law," can enable judges to "stand sentinel over our Constitution" (Cascarelli, 2000, p. 315).

Of course, any expected benefit depends, in part, on the nature and content of a particular judge's religious understanding (Conkle, 1998b).

If a Mormon fundamentalist judge favored polygamy, or a radical Muslim judge supported jihad, we, as a society, probably would not want those religious beliefs—which may or may not correspond to religious "values"—to influence their legal rulings.

This problem can be circumvented, to some extent, by arguing that judges should rely on their religious beliefs only in rare, circumscribed situations—such as hard cases in which legal precedent is conflicting or indecisive, or the law itself is so abominable as to warrant subversion (e.g., laws permitting slavery; see Greenawalt, 1995; Mathis, 2004; Modak-Truran, 2004). In such cases, if the judge's religious beliefs also reflect community standards of morality, then relying on religion is much less objectionable. It does, however, raise the subsequent problem—not so easily surmounted—of determining what is "abominable" and identifying the relevant community standards.

In the final analysis, there is no easy answer to the question about whether religion should influence judges' decisions for, as Idleman (1993, p. 487) concludes, "a debate about the role of religious values in judicial decision making is necessarily part of the ongoing debate about the role of religion in public life." Nonetheless, if religiously informed decisions would lead to better, more just, or more humane outcomes, then although judges should generally exercise restraint in relying on their religious beliefs, there might be a role for religion in judicial decision making after all, at least in some instances (Greenawalt, 1995, 1998).[23]

Thus, considerable debate exists about the extent to which judges' religious values and beliefs should influence their decisions. A related, although separate, question is whether it is proper for judges to invoke religion explicitly in their written opinions. Religion can become an explicit factor in judicial decisions in two main ways: by judges incorporating religion into an unconventional sentence, and by their using religious precepts as a justification for deciding on a conventional sentencing outcome (e.g., citing the biblical maxim "an eye for an eye" in sentencing a defendant to death). As an example of the former, in 1993, Judge Thomas Quirk of Lake Charles, Louisiana gave Gregory Thompson, a 23-year-old bricklayer who pleaded no contest to a charge of driving while intoxicated, a choice between going to jail or attending church once a week for a year ("A.C.L.U. sues judge," 1994; Barringer, 1996). The American Civil Liberties Union (ACLU) sued on Thompson's behalf, alleging that the sentence violated the separation of church and state. The suit was dismissed after Thompson's probation expired, and Judge Quirk continued to include church attendance as a sentencing alternative, to the point where, by his own estimation, roughly 1500 offenders in his court had chosen the option (Barringer, 1996).[24] Comprehensive figures on the practice do not exist, but Judge Quirk is not alone ("Judge gives offenders option," 2005).

The separation issues involved in sentencing criminal defendants to attend worship services may be fairly apparent, but they can come up in more subtle ways as well. An interesting area of First Amendment jurisprudence in which this has occurred is when judges have sentenced defendants—usually convicted of driving under the influence or a related charge—to attend Alcoholics Anonymous (AA) as a condition of their probation. AA is probably the most popular intervention for alcohol-related problems in the United States and possibly the world, and it is reasonably successful for those who complete its 12-step program. However, it also has religious, or at least "spiritual" overtones, and some evidence suggests that embracing the religious element improves participants' odds of success (Jenkins, Moore, Lambert, & Clarke, 2005).

Although AA does not have a formal institutional religious affiliation, it was originally based upon Christian principles, and five of the 12 steps mention God by name, while another refers to "a Power greater than ourselves."[25] The 12th step refers to "a spiritual awakening," and many participants liken becoming sober to a born-again conversion. Houses of worship are leading sponsors of AA and locales for meetings. Thus, a number of courts have held that sentencing defendants to mandatory AA participation, without a realistic secular alternative, violates the Free Exercise and/or Establishment Clauses mandating separation between church and state (Honeymar, 1997; Jenkins et al., 2005; Sherbine, 2006). The counterargument is that these cases require a balancing of the state's and individual's interests, and the state's interest in promoting public safety outweighs any infringement on a drunk driver's rights that may be occasioned by mandatory attendance at AA. As is true of any legal balancing test, some courts and commentators think that the scale tips in favor of allowing mandatory AA attendance (e.g., Jenkins et al., 2005; *O'Connor v. California*, 1994), whereas others (probably a majority) think that the scale favors prohibiting it (e.g., Honeymar, 1997; Sherbine, 2006; *Warner v. Orange County Department of Probation*, 1996). As with sentencing defendants to attend worship services, the objections to including AA as a condition of probation are vastly reduced if a nonreligious support program alternative is available (Honeymar, 1997).

In assigning more conventional sentences, judges have nearly unfettered freedom in what they write to justify them. Of course, most judges rely on legal precedent, sentencing guidelines, and case facts most of the time; but they have occasionally been known to inject into the record a little social commentary, value judgment, or literary flair. Given the wide latitude judges have in writing their opinions, it should not be surprising that they sometimes make religious references. As discussed earlier in this chapter, religious values even have the potential to enhance the decision-making process; but it is problematic when judges overtly express their religious convictions in their written opinions, as it raises concerns about bias and church–state separation (Greenawalt, 1995; Mathis, 2004; Modak-Truran, 2004). Just how problematic it is depends on the manner in which they cite religious sources. If they merely survey religious positions on some issue (e.g., assisted suicide) but do not adopt one of those views as a justification for the law, then there is little cause for concern (Modak-Truran, 2004). However, if they do use religion as a justification for their decision—especially if they appear to use it as the main or sole justification—then they are flirting with disaster (which, in judicial terms, typically means reversal by a higher court).

Roy Moore, former Chief Justice of the Alabama Supreme Court, provides an illustrative example.[26] In a custody dispute in which the majority ruled against the lesbian mother (on grounds other than her sexual orientation), Chief Justice Moore wrote a concurrence in which he condemned homosexuality on biblical grounds (*Ex parte H.H.*, 2002). He stated that "Homosexual conduct is, and has been, considered abhorrent, immoral, detestable, a crime against nature, and a violation of the laws of nature and of nature's God upon which this Nation and our laws are predicated" (*Ex parte H.H.*, p. 26). He also cited the apparent biblical prohibition of homosexuality in Leviticus (20:13), and he quoted the 6th-century Roman legal code *Corpus Juris Civilis* as stating that "Sodomy is high treason against the King of Heaven" (p. 34).[27] Because the majority reached its decision on nonreligious grounds, Moore's opinion was not binding law and was, in fact, little more than a soapbox oration; but it elicited a critical response in the academic literature for having nonetheless crossed the line of allowable religious references (see, e.g., Mathis, 2004; Modak-Truran, 2004).

Judges have drawn on the New Testament as well. For example, in sentencing a convicted child rapist to a term of 51 years, a trial judge in Ohio quoted from the book of Matthew (18:6): "Whoso shall offend one of these little ones which believe in me, it were better for him that a millstone were hanged about his neck, and that he were drowned in the depth of the sea" (*State v. Arnett*, 2000, p. 796). The defendant appealed, on grounds that the judge's religious beliefs were an irrelevant sentencing factor and indicated a lack of impartiality, therefore violating his due process rights; he also alleged that the explicit religious references violated the First Amendment's Establishment Clause (*State v. Arnett*, 2000; Wiehl, 2000). The Ohio Court of Appeals agreed, but the Ohio Supreme Court reinstated the trial court's sentence, holding that it is not inadmissible per se for a judge to cite a religious text during sentencing (although it may be inadmissible under some circumstances).

How far can judges go in expressing their religious convictions? Quite far, apparently. In *United States v. Bakker* (1991), the Fourth Circuit Court of Appeals overturned the trial court's sentence of televangelist Jim Bakker after convictions for wire and mail fraud. The appellate court found that the trial judge's sentencing decision was based on personal religious principles because he stated that "those of us who do have a religion are ridiculed as being saps from money-grubbing preachers or priests" (pp. 740–741). Despite this repudiation of a sentencing judge's religious comments, most appellate courts—such as the Ohio Supreme Court in *Arnett*—have declined to vacate sentences in which judges explicitly invoked religion (Wiehl, 2000). Religious texts are allowed to provide *a* reason for sentencing, as long as they do not provide *the sole* reason (Wiehl, 2000), and the latter is virtually impossible to prove.

Wiehl (2000) argues that the same standard should apply to judges and juries. If it would bias jurors to use the Bible in their decision making or hear biblical references in court (see Chapters 5 and 8), then judges should not be allowed to make biblical references in sentencing. Wiehl's logic is a little bit murky. When jurors or lawyers make religious references, they are introducing potentially biasing information, the targets of which are the factfinders—namely, the jurors (unless it is a matter of attorney argument in a bench trial, in which case the target is the judge); but when judges make religious references, they are both the introducers and the targets of the potentially biasing information. Thus, the two situations are not totally comparable; however, Wiehl is correct that bias could result in both cases.

Modak-Truran (2004) makes a more compelling argument for prohibiting explicit religious references, which is that they raise serious practical problems in addition to the legal issues (i.e., those related to church–state separation). He points out that if Moore had spoken for the majority in *Ex parte H.H.* (2002), his religious convictions would have become an official precedent needing to be either embraced or refuted in future litigation. Subsequent cases on the issue (here, homosexuals' fitness to be parents) would involve litigating the facts, the law, and the judge's religious reasoning. Consequently, "lawyers would find themselves arguing issues of jurisprudence, theology, philosophy of religion, biblical hermeneutics, and the proper role of judges in a pluralistic democratic society in addition to arguing the facts and the law" (p. 791).

If nothing else, barring judges from using the Bible in reaching a sentencing decision would avoid the *appearance* of unfairness, even if no unfairness actually occurred. That would clearly be a desirable outcome, but when weighed against judges' free speech rights, as well as the argument that they should be able to draw on their religion just like any other experiences or values, Wiehl's (2000) proposition is likely to be a losing one. Like it or not, judges will probably continue to be able to make religious references in their decisions.

Conclusion

Judging, as a profession, is often portrayed as a dispassionate exercise based on facts and legal precedent; but empirical scholarship on judges shows that psychological, attitudinal, and background factors exert considerable influence over the process. Religion influences judges' work in a number of respects. At a very basic level, religious affiliation and beliefs are a consideration in who becomes a judge in the first place, whether by election or appointment. Some evidence suggests that the importance of judges' religion in some sort of quota system, especially in Supreme Court appointments, is declining. On the other hand, the growing involvement in judicial elections of faith-based groups, coupled with the ever-expanding dialogue about religion's role in both private life and public policy, is likely to increase the level of scrutiny paid to judges' religious beliefs.

In light of the documented relationship between judges' religion and their decision making, it is hard to argue that discussion of judges' religion—both before and after they don the black robe—should be off limits. Studies of different types of judges in various kinds of cases show, on the whole, that Jewish judges tend to adopt relatively liberal positions. Catholic judges also tend to be relatively liberal, although less consistently so. Evangelical judges, on the other hand, are relatively conservative. Mainline Protestants, who serve as the reference group in the majority of studies, are harder to characterize as a group, which is not surprising, given the high diversity of denominations and beliefs within such a broad classification. This pattern characterizes both cases in which religion is explicitly at issue, as in religious freedom cases, and cases in which religion is totally irrelevant.

Finally, a minority of judges rely on religion in their decision making. One could claim, of course, that anyone's religious beliefs would implicitly influence her decisions, in the same way as any other personal value system would; yet some judges have been much more overt in acknowledging religion's role. They have done so in a number of ways, such as by admitting that they draw on their faith for guidance, citing religious sources in rendering a verdict, and giving what amounts to a religious sentence (e.g., attendance at worship services). These practices, which highlight questions about exactly how judges *should* be making their decisions, raise important legal and ethical issues. They cannot be easily solved, but neither should they be ignored.

7

Attorneys' Religion

The intellect of man is forced to choose
Perfection of the life, or of the work,
And if it take the second must refuse
A heavenly mansion, raging in the dark.
When all that story's finished, what's the news?
In luck or out the toil has left its mark:
That old perplexity an empty purse,
Or the day's vanity, the night's remorse.
—William Butler Yeats, *The Choice*, 1933/1962[1]

Religion touches on attorneys' lives in many ways. Like all secular professions in the United States, the legal profession is open to anyone, regardless of religious background (although as we describe later in this chapter, such openness has not always been the case). And indeed, attorneys profess as large a variety of religious beliefs as Americans in general. Nevertheless, attorneys' religion is not simply a microcosm of Americans' religion; some religious groups are better represented in the legal profession than others. Organized religions have also taken an active role in legal education and in pursuing legal issues that are compatible with their beliefs. In the words of the noted theologian Martin Marty, beneath the explicit legal separation of church and state there lies a complex subculture of "Christian and 'Judeo-Christian' law schools, legal aid societies, filers of amicus curiae briefs" (Marty, 2007, p. viii). Finally, many religious attorneys wrestle with the challenge of leading a successful professional life and a successful spiritual life at the same time.

This chapter reviews research on how attorneys' religion influences their practice. Relevant topics include the extent to which the legal profession is (and has been) religiously diverse, the role of religion in legal education, and the tensions that can arise between religious beliefs and legal practice. But first we need to ask: What does it mean to consider someone (or oneself) a religious attorney? This typically (although not necessarily) entails identification with a particular denomination; hence, one might be a Jewish attorney, a Catholic attorney, a Muslim attorney, and so on. This is one manifestation of what Levinson (1993/2003, p. 9) calls "adjectival lawyering," in the sense that one can also be referred to as a woman attorney, a liberal attorney, a Black attorney, ad infinitum; but, he argues, religion is not precisely like these other attributes, because the major religions (unlike, say, sex or race) mandate certain ways of acting that are applicable to the practice of law. According to Levinson, then, the critical question is: To what extent does the modifying religious adjective convey important information about the kind of attorney one is?

To answer this question, Levinson (1993/2003) proposes five possible models for identifying the Jewish lawyer. For purposes of greater generality, we characterize the models in terms of the "religious" lawyer (i.e., a lawyer having any particular religious identity). The first model simply looks at the intersection of sets: Jewish lawyers are people who happen to be both Jews (however that is defined) and lawyers (however that is defined), Presbyterian lawyers are people who happen to be both Presbyterians and lawyers, and so forth. Second, one can consider the extent to which a lawyer's legal practice draws on, and expresses solidarity with, the relevant religious community. A lawyer might draw her client base from a given religious community, or she might feel a duty to defend co-religionists. The third model, which is essentially a subset of the first model, identifies only those lawyers who are religiously observant. The lawyers' observance would influence *when* they do their legal work (e.g., not practicing on the Sabbath and religious holidays), but it would not necessarily influence *how* they do their legal work.[2]

The last two models, in contrast, do influence the very nature of a lawyer's legal practice. The fourth model encompasses attorneys who practice a specific brand of religious law, as in representing clients before religious courts. Judaism, Islam, and Catholicism all have such courts, with their own legal codes and procedures, and some other religions do as well.[3] Finally, religious lawyers might find that the way they practice secular law is significantly affected by their religious beliefs. In this fifth approach, one's religion is brought to bear on issues such as where one practices, the kind of law one practices, the clients one works for, and how one represents those clients. As Levinson (1993/2003) notes, the models are not exclusive, and some will apply better to some religious lawyers than to others. Because the fifth model offers the richest set of issues and identifies the greatest source of potential conflicts that religious lawyers are likely to encounter, it is the approach taken in most of the literature on the topic; but it is instructive to keep the other models in mind as well.

Religious Diversity in the Legal Profession

In looking simply at religious diversity in the legal profession, it makes the most sense to adopt Levinson's (1993/2003) first model and ask: How many practicing attorneys belong to various religious groups, especially religious minorities? Jewish lawyers are an interesting case in point. Jews are so well represented in the legal profession nowadays that Jewish lawyers are a widely held stereotype. Although we could find no national data on the religious demographics of the legal profession, the local data described here suggest that the number of Jewish lawyers is indeed disproportionate to their numbers in the American population at large (e.g., roughly 25–30% of Chicago-area lawyers are Jewish, compared to less than 2% of the general U.S. population; Heinz & Laumann, 1982; Kosmin, Mayer, & Keysar, 2001). There are a number of possible reasons for the large number of Jewish lawyers. For religious Jews, it is a duty (as well as a joy) to study religious law, which is found in the Torah (i.e., the first five books of the Bible) and subsequent written and oral commentary. Rabbis are lawyers, in a sense, in that they are learned legal scholars and interpreters of the law.[4]

Jewish law and other writings, especially the books of the prophets, are suffused with a concern for justice, and they command all Jews to pursue justice and to fight against injustice.[5] Their concern with social justice, along with their people's history as victims of discrimination, probably underlies Jewish lawyers' disproportionate contributions to the public-interest sector of legal practice (Galanter, 1999). Given the highly similar "legalistic" skills necessary for the study and application of religious and secular law, it makes sense for Jews to gravitate toward law as a secular profession (Galanter, 1999; Michaelson, 2006).

The attraction of law as a career for Jews was facilitated by several other factors as well, such as historic restrictions on Jews' entrance into other occupations (e.g., prohibitions on owning land) and the legal profession's relatively high prestige and earning potential. Over time, as Jews became more integrated into the dominant cultures of the countries where they lived, secular law came to supplant religious law. In the United States, in particular, American Jews' emancipation, enlightenment, and assimilation in the late 19th and early 20th centuries were accompanied by a "transfer of allegiance from a sacred to a secular legal system" (Auerbach, 1990, p. 94). The significant number of Jewish lawyers is somewhat ironic, considering that the Jewish legal system functioned under an inquisitorial model of justice and is actually hostile to the client-centered advocacy used in an adversarial model like the American legal system (Levine, 2006; Levinson, 1993/2003). In traditional Jewish courts, parties generally represented themselves (Levinson, 1993/2003). In the remainder of this section, we consider religious discrimination in the American bar against Jews and other groups and the representation of various religious groups in different subspecialties of legal practice.

Religious Discrimination in the American Bar

Despite the widely accepted contemporary notion of the "Jewish lawyer," the American Bar Association (ABA), the country's largest professional organization of lawyers, largely excluded Jews (as well as African Americans and women) from membership as late as World War II (Murphy, Pritchett, Epstein & Knight, 2006). In recent decades, the ABA has become much more open, even electing several Jews as president (Margolick, 1994; Murphy et al., 2006).[6] Jews (as well as racial minorities and women) were also largely excluded from jobs in big, corporate, or "white shoe" law firms until the World War II era and into the 1960s (Auerbach, 1976; Galanter & Palay, 1991; Lin, 2005; Smigel, 1964). Although much (and possibly most) of the discrimination was due to the established bar members' own prejudices (Auerbach, 1976), at least some of it reflected the (perceived) prejudices of clients, some of whom refused to work with a Jewish lawyer (Smigel, 1964). This exclusion of Jews from the elite corporate firms led to the formation of "Jewish firms," which date back to the late 1800s (Auerbach, 1990) but began to proliferate after World War II, as top law schools relaxed their religious quotas, the economy boomed, and young Jewish lawyers gained experience working for New Deal government agencies (Auerbach, 1976; Lin, 2005; Smigel, 1964). The Jewish firms were similar to the elite Christian firms in terms of their organization and structure, but they typically had fewer attorneys than the large non-Jewish firms (Smigel, 1964), had smaller clients (e.g., individuals or small businesses as opposed to large corporations; see Galanter & Palay, 1991; Smigel, 1964), and often specialized in work that the elite firms deemed undignified, such as litigation, bankruptcy, and real estate (Lin, 2005). The clients were often mostly (but not all) Jewish, as social and business ties within the local religious community influenced client relationships and recruitment (Auerbach, 1976, 1990; Nelson, 1988; Smigel, 1964).

During the same period, there were likewise few Catholics in the larger, more prestigious firms, which led to the formation of Catholic firms analogous to the Jewish firms (Lin, 2005). Anti-Catholic discrimination in hiring is ironic in light of the fact that many of the first American law schools, established in the latter part of the 19th century, had a Catholic affiliation and did not themselves discriminate in admission (White, 1995). Discrimination in hiring was based less on Catholic lawyers' religion than on their ethnicity—that is, "their 'lower-class' origins, their foreign-born parents, and their lack of 'proper' education" (Smigel, 1964, p. 45). The growing numbers of Catholics at large firms reflected a growing tendency for those firms to hire graduates of lower-status (especially regional and local) law schools, as opposed to the elite law schools from which they had traditionally recruited. In his study of four large Chicago law firms, Nelson (1988) found that Catholic lawyers in those firms were more than twice as likely to have attended a regional or local law school as any other religious group, with 48.1% having done so. Jewish lawyers in these firms, on the other hand, had "duplicate[ed] the high-status social origins and high-status law school credentials of the Protestant and nonidentifying groups" (Nelson, 1988, p. 134). Thus, both Jewish and Catholic lawyers gradually integrated the large, elite law firms, but they did so by different routes.

Once Jews and Catholics started being hired, many firms were concerned about having too many on their roster, creating a de facto quota system (Smigel, 1964). Such concerns appear to have largely dissipated. Nowadays, the American bar is religiously quite diverse. Writing in 1991, Galanter and Palay concluded that as of the late 1980s, "[b]arriers against Catholics, Jews, women, and Blacks have been swept away. The social exclusiveness in hiring that was still a feature of the world of elite law practice in 1960 has receded into insignificance" (p. 57). Supporting this conclusion, a survey by Heinz and Laumann (1982) of 777 Chicago attorneys working in diverse kinds of practices found that in 1975 (when they conducted the interviews), 30.4% were Catholic, 32.5% were Jewish, and 25.2% were Protestant (the remainder reported no religious affiliation).[7] In a follow-up study of 787 Chicago attorneys, for which the data were collected 20 years later, Heinz and colleagues found that little had changed in the interim (Heinz, Nelson, Sandefur, & Laumann, 2005).[8] Specifically, 32% of the sample were Catholic, 25% were Jewish, and 26% were Protestant. Heinz and colleagues attribute the drop in the number of Jewish lawyers to the rapid growth of the bar overall between the 1970s and 1990s, which would make it hard to maintain the overrepresentation of Jews, given their relatively small numbers in the population. They also observe that the considerable growth in the total number of attorneys would still mean there were more Jewish lawyers in 1995 than in 1975.

Today, other than the smallest firms, religiously homogeneous law firms are essentially extinct, as the old Jewish (and Catholic) firms have themselves hired lawyers from other faiths (Lin, 2005; Smigel, 1964). Beyond the mere sweeping away of barriers, religious diversity—just like diversity in gender, race/ethnicity, etc.—can even be a significant plus. As American society becomes more pluralistic, diversity among its practitioners can help a law firm market itself to a broader clientele (McMurry, 1998). Law firms struggling with racial and gender diversity can learn valuable lessons from the course of religious integration over the last half century, such as how to attain the benefits of diversity without giving the appearance of tokenism (Lin, 2005).

Perhaps not surprisingly, in light of their history of discrimination, both Jewish and Catholic lawyers have formed their own professional societies. The International Association of Jewish Lawyers and Jurists was founded in 1969:

> To advance human rights everywhere, including the prevention of war crimes, the punishment of war criminals, the prohibition of weapons of mass destruction, and international co-operation based on the rule of law and the fair implementation of international covenants and conventions. The Association is especially committed to issues that are on the agenda of the Jewish people, and works to combat racism, xenophobia, anti-Semitism, Holocaust denial and negation of the State of Israel. . . . Membership is open to lawyers and jurists of all creeds who share our aims.[9]

There is a Jewish Lawyers Guild in New York City (www.jewishlawyers-guild.org), and Catholic lawyers have also formed organizations offering a sense of community to co-religionists (e.g., Catholic Lawyers Guilds and St. Thomas More Societies). For example, the Catholic Lawyers Guild of Chicago "supports Catholic lawyers, seeks to promote the highest ethical standards in the practice of law and encourages service in society."[10] Other religions can lay similar claims to their lawyer adherents' pursuit of justice (e.g., the National Association of Muslim Lawyers and KARAMAH: Muslim Women Lawyers for Human Rights; see generally Failinger et al., 1999; Pearce & Uelmen, 2004).

The largest faith-based organization of lawyers is probably the evangelical Christian Legal Society (CLS), founded in 1961, whose mission is "to inspire, encourage, and equip Christian lawyers and law students, both individually and in community, to proclaim, love and serve Jesus Christ through the study and practice of law, the provision of legal assistance to the poor and needy, and the defense of religious freedom and the sanctity of human life."[11] Some faith-based lawyer organizations pursue overt religious aims more actively than others, with the CLS probably the most active in that regard (e.g., Failinger et al., 1999; Gerdy, 2006). For example, the CLS has a Center for Law & Religious Freedom, and it has recently been actively involved in suits against law schools over the conflict between freedom of association and the schools' nondiscrimination policies (see, e.g., Gerdy, 2006; Russo & Thro, 2007; Visser, 2007).

Religion Across Fields of Practice

Despite this religious diversity in the profession as a whole, religious representation across different areas of legal practice varies considerably. Until relatively recently, Jewish and Catholic lawyers were much more likely to work in small firms or as solo practitioners, where they typically earned less than Protestant attorneys; whereas large firms, especially elite firms, were disproportionately Protestant (Auerbach, 1976; Dinovitzer, 2006; Lena, Roach, & Warkov, 1993; Lin, 2005). Heinz and colleagues found that, in 1995, Jewish male lawyers were more likely to work in large firms than they had been in 1975, and they were just as likely as their Protestant colleagues to be in the top income quartile; but they were still less likely than White males in the higher-status Protestant category (Episcopalians, Presbyterians, and Congregationalists) to be a partner in a large firm by the mean age of 43 (11% vs. 26%; Heinz et al., 2005). Other Christian males (Catholics and lower-status Protestants) were likewise less likely than high-status Protestants to be a partner in a large firm (predicted probability of 13%).

The particular field of law that one specializes in may also differ according to one's religion. Figure 7.1 shows the distribution of attorneys of different religions across selected fields, in the two Heinz studies. In 1975 (Fig. 7.1, top panel), Protestant attorneys were overrepresented (compared to their numbers in the total sample; see the far right bar of the figure) in corporate securities and banking, whereas no Protestants specialized in divorce, and

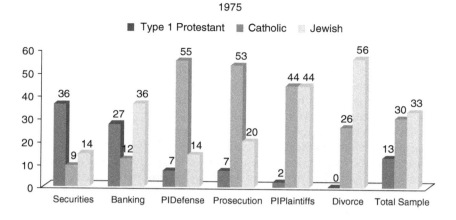

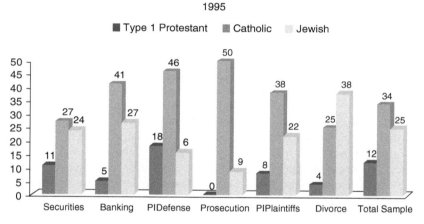

Figure 7.1. Religious differentiation among selected fields, 1975 and 1995 (percentages)

Data are from Heinz et al. (2005). The "Type I Protestants" in the figure are their higher-status category of Episcopalians, Presbyterians, and Congregationalists. PI refers to Personal Injury.

only 2% of personal-injury plaintiffs' attorneys were Protestant.[12] Catholic lawyers were most likely to do personal-injury work (for either plaintiffs or defendants) or criminal prosecution. Jews were overrepresented among divorce lawyers, but underrepresented in the fields of securities, personal-injury defense, and prosecution. In the authors' follow-up survey conducted 20 years later, the field of practice differences had diminished but not disappeared altogether (Heinz et al., 2005; see Fig. 7.1, bottom panel). Some fields more closely mirrored the religious demographics of the total sample (e.g., securities, banking), but Catholic lawyers were still overrepresented in personal-injury work (especially on the defense side) and criminal prosecution, and Jewish lawyers were still disproportionately involved in divorce work.

Jews are also well represented among franchise lawyers—a relatively new development on the legal practice scene, in which national law corporations open cookie-cutter franchises, often in strip malls—but Protestants (at least White Protestants) are not (van Hoy, 1997).[13] There is a perception that law school faculties are disproportionately Jewish, especially in certain areas, such as constitutional law (Michaelson, 2006).[14] There is some evidence that these religious disparities within the legal profession continue to diminish over time (Dinovitzer, 2006; Heinz et al., 2005).

This pattern is not peculiar to the American bar. Hagan and colleagues (Hagan, Huxter, & Parker, 1988) surveyed over 1000 lawyers in Toronto, Canada and found that, just as in the United States, Jewish lawyers (and to some extent Catholic lawyers as well) were underrepresented, whereas Protestant lawyers were overrepresented, in elite corporate firms. Also consistent with American data, they found that more Jews were finding employment with large firms than had been true in the past. In a more recent Canadian study, Dinovitzer (2006) found that Jewish lawyers in Toronto were more likely to be in solo practice than non-Jewish lawyers, due in part to greater embeddedness within their ethnic community, and they also reported lower levels of job satisfaction.[15]

Heinz and colleagues' (Heinz & Laumann, 1982; Heinz et al., 2005) main conclusion is that the legal profession consists of two distinct "hemispheres": lawyers (either members of large firms or "in house") who represent large organizations, and those who work for individuals or small businesses owned by individuals.[16] Despite some balancing out over time, it is still the case that Protestant lawyers disproportionately occupy the former, "corporate" sector, whereas lawyers from other religious backgrounds disproportionately occupy the latter, "personal client" sector. Religious minorities may be entering the legal profession in greater numbers than ever before, but a finer-grained analysis shows that attorneys' career paths differ depending on their religious background. In this respect, then, there is still room for improvement in the legal profession's religious diversity.

Religion and Legal Education

In light of the commitment of the major religions and the law to the pursuit of justice, it seems that it should follow naturally that religion and legal training are compatible. And indeed, the law has been compared to a religion, and legal training has been likened to a process of religious indoctrination, with the law as a temple and the lawyers as priests (Elkins, 1987; Fred, 1998; Huff, 1986; Shaffer, 1987, 1998). Nonetheless, except for coursework that covers topics such as religious freedom and religious discrimination, and the existence of religious student organizations like the CLS, religion and law do not mix much in the majority of American law schools. As Gaffney (1986, p. 64) observes, "it would understate the matter to suggest that American legal education tends to ignore the relationship between law and religion generally, let alone the more particular questions about the shaping of American law by the biblical traditions. Very few American law schools attend to these questions at all." Gaffney cites several reasons for this practice, such as a desire to avoid "extraneous" material when covering the basics (i.e., contracts, property, torts, crimes, and legal processes and procedures), the assumption that religion is a personal and not a public matter, the emphasis in contemporary jurisprudence on rationality, and most law professors' lack of formal training in religion.

Those who favor incorporating religion into legal education perceive educators at nonreligious law schools as viewing religious influence to be detrimental to legal education (e.g., Gaffney, 1986; Lee, 1995; Schutt, 2007). There appears to be some validity to this perception: Stewart and Tolley (2004) found that the divergence between legal academics' (law school deans and faculty) and nonacademics' (judges and practicing lawyers) ratings of religious law schools' academic quality (for the *U.S. News & World Report* rankings) was greater than the divergence for secular law schools. In other words, legal academics gave harsher evaluations of religious law schools than of nonreligious law schools, a difference that covaried as a function of the schools' perceived conservatism (Stewart & Tolley, 2004). In the remainder of this section, we explore religious law schools further, by considering three issues: what constitutes a "religious law school," how these schools incorporate religion into the curriculum, and how successful they are.

The Class of Religiously Affiliated Law Schools

A number of law schools are part of universities having some sort of religious affiliation, and these schools explicitly do, to varying degrees, incorporate religion into legal education. In addition, the late 20th century saw Christian colleges that had previously emphasized undergraduate education move increasingly into graduate training, including law. Depending on how one classifies religious universities, as many as one-third of ABA-approved law schools have some sort of religious affiliation (White, 1995). The question arises: Why would a religious institution of higher learning *want* a law school? There are several answers. First, given the close and longstanding connection among religion, morality, and law, a logical connection exists between secular legal processes and religion. Second, the addition of graduate schools, especially professional schools such as law and medicine, can enhance any institution's prestige, as well as its financial health. Third, religious law schools can help fulfill a religion's mission, as in providing vertical mobility to members of the faith or in serving the community (Shaffer, 1993, 1995). Fourth, and perhaps most importantly, religious law schools provide a setting for the discussion of those complex issues near and dear to the hearts of many religious denominations, such as church–state separation and pressing social issues like abortion, capital punishment, same-sex marriage, and so on (Buzzard, 1995;

Fitzgerald, 2001). This setting provides what Shaffer (1995, p. 402) calls "a spiritually cordial atmosphere for believers who study law." Moreover, the schools provide a forum for training lawyers who will represent the denomination's interests in these matters (Rice, 1999).

At present, ABA-accredited law schools exist at universities affiliated with a variety of mainline and evangelical Protestant denominations, the Roman Catholic and Mormon (Church of Latter Day Saints) churches, and Judaism. These universities belong to a number of denomination-specific consortia, such as the Association of Catholic Colleges and Universities; the International Association of Methodist-related Schools, Colleges and Universities; and the Lutheran Educational Conference of North America. The closest thing to an umbrella organization is the Association of Religiously Affiliated Law Schools (RALS), formed in 1994 by a number of Christian law schools to share resources and host a biennial conference (Eisenberg, 1998–1999).[17] Table 7.1 lists 59 American law schools having some sort of religious affiliation.

Perhaps the greatest challenge in evaluating "religious" or "religiously affiliated" law schools is in identifying which schools belong to their number. The difficulty arises because of the varying degrees of secularization among American institutions of higher education. Nearly all American colleges originally had some sort of church affiliation; some retain very close denominational ties, while others do not, except in a historical sense (Burtchaell, 1998; Ringenberg, 2006). Some require a profession of faith (which, depending on the institution, could mean a belief in God, belief in Christ, or membership in a particular denomination) from students and/or faculty, whereas others are adamantly pluralist. Some provide a religious atmosphere both inside and outside the classroom (including behavior codes), whereas others scrupulously avoid any sort of religious overtones in both academic and extracurricular life. In 21st-century America, "some church-related colleges wish to be known as Christian, some do not, while still others prefer a partial identity" (Ringenberg, 2006, p. 259). Thus, it is more meaningful to categorize them according to the centrality of the Christian worldview in the college's intellectual program, or how "serious" they are about their faith, rather than in terms of their denominational connection (Riley, 2005; Ringenberg, 2006); the former, however, is considerably more difficult to accomplish. Although there is a tendency to perceive religiously affiliated law schools as a "monolithic block," they differ significantly on theological, moral, political, and social issues (Barkan, 1995, p. 247).

The most rapid growth in religious higher education in the United States has been among evangelical colleges and universities (Riley, 2005; Ringenberg, 2006). Legal training has not been exempt from this trend, as evidenced by the growing enrollment and public impact of the country's two evangelical law schools, at Regent University (in Virginia Beach, Virginia, founded 1986) and Liberty University (in Lynchburg, Virginia, founded 2004).[18] New Catholic law schools have also been founded in the last 25 years: St. Thomas University School of Law in Miami, Florida, was founded in 1984; Ave Maria School of

Table 7.1. Outcome Data on ABA-Accredited Religiously Affiliated Law Schools

Law School	Affiliation	BarPass	StateAvg	Difference	Employment
Ave Maria (MI)	Catholic	96.3	89	7.3	73.3
Boston College (MA)	Catholic	95.2	86	9.2	97.6
Catholic (DC)	Catholic	79.6	77	2.6	93.7
Creighton (NE)	Catholic	75	83	−8	97.3
Dayton (OH)	Catholic	78	84	−6	88.1
DePaul (IL)	Catholic	87.2	87	0.2	90.3
Detroit Mercy (MI)	Catholic	92	89	3	86.0
Duquesne (PA)	Catholic	87.5	83	4.5	86.1
Fordham (NY)	Catholic	89	77	12	94.7
Georgetown (DC)	Catholic	91	77	14	97.8
Gonzaga (WA)	Catholic	84.3	82	2.3	92.6
Loyola Marymount (CA)	Catholic	74.9	65	9.9	96.9
Loyola (IL)	Catholic	89.5	87	2.5	89.2
Loyola (LA)	Catholic	79.7	75	4.7	95.3
Marquette (WI)	Catholic	100	89	11	95.7
Notre Dame (IN)	Catholic	89.5	83	6.5	97.3
Pontifical (PR)	Catholic	n/a	n/a	n/a	n/a
St. John's (NY)	Catholic	88.8	77	11.8	88.7
St. Louis (MO)	Catholic	85.6	86	−0.4	93.0
St. Mary's (TX)	Catholic	82.6	82	0.6	81.9
St. Thomas (FL)	Catholic	64.5	74	−9.5	83.0
St. Thomas (MN)	Catholic	91.2	91	0.2	94.9
San Diego (CA)	Catholic	75.5	65	10.5	87.9
San Francisco (CA)	Catholic	73.3	65	8.3	92.7
Santa Clara (CA)	Catholic	77.3	65	12.3	92.5
Seattle (WA)	Catholic	81.9	82	−0.1	98.5
Seton Hall (NJ)	Catholic	85.4	79	6.4	98.3
Villanova (PA)	Catholic	86.2	83	3.2	94.3
American (DC)	Methodist	81.4	77	4.4	95.8
Boston University (MA)	Methodist	95	86	9	98.7
Denver (CO)	Methodist	65.7	76	−10.3	95.9
Duke (NC)	Methodist	97	74	23	98.2
Emory (GA)	Methodist	95	85	10	98.3
Hamline (MN)	Methodist	85.8	91	−5.2	91.5
Oklahoma City (OK)	Methodist	89.8	92	−2.2	84.4
Pacific (CA)	Methodist	72.7	65	7.7	94.4

(Continued)

Table 7.1. Outcome Data on ABA-Accredited Religiously Affiliated Law Schools

Law School	Affiliation	BarPass	StateAvg	Difference	Employment
Southern Methodist (TX)	Methodist	90.4	82	8.4	94.7
Syracuse (NY)	Methodist	79.6	77	2.6	92.6
Texas Wesleyan (TX)	Methodist	85.8	82	3.8	82.7
Vanderbilt (TN)	Methodist	97.8	78	19.8	98.3
Willamette (OR)	Methodist	83.7	82	1.7	87.8
Baylor (TX)	Baptist	98.5	82	16.5	96.4
Campbell (SC)	Baptist	96.5	74	22.5	93.9
Mercer (GA)	Baptist	88	85	3	94.4
Mississippi College (MS)	Baptist	83	88	−5	86.7
Samford (AL)	Baptist	89.7	79	10.7	90.1
Stetson (FL)	Baptist	81.5	74	7.5	97.7
Wake Forest (NC)	Baptist	87.5	74	13.5	95.0
Liberty (VA)	Evangelical	n/a	n/a	n/a	n/a
Regent (VA)	Evangelical	73.7	74	−0.3	82.5
Capital (OH)	Lutheran	84.3	84	0.3	82.1
Valparaiso (IN)	Lutheran	82.5	83	−0.5	88.1
Touro College (NY)	Jewish	78.4	77	1.4	74.4
Yeshiva (NY)	Jewish	88.8	77	11.8	95.4
Howard (DC)	Congregationalist	61.5	77	−15.5	94.1
Faulkner (AL)	Churches of Christ	n/a	n/a	n/a	n/a
Pepperdine (CA)	Churches of Christ	82.8	65	17.8	95.0
Tulsa (OK)	Presbyterian	88.2	92	−3.8	90.5
Brigham Young (UT)	Mormon	96.2	87	9.2	91.2

In defining "religiously affiliated law schools," we have striven to be maximally inclusive, but we have omitted universities that are now completely independent of their sectarian origins (e.g., Ivy League universities). Some law schools have their own names (e.g., Cardozo at Yeshiva, Cumberland at Samford), but we list the better-known names of the universities with which they are affiliated. No American law schools are affiliated with non-Judeo-Christian religions, such as Buddhism, Hinduism, or Islam. This table was compiled by cross-referencing a number of online and printed sources, as well as the individual schools' websites. Especially helpful were websites of the Law School Admissions Council, http://officialguide.lsac.org; Association of Catholic Colleges and Universities, http://www.accunet.org; International Association of Methodist-related Schools, Colleges, and Universities, http://www.gbhem.org/iamscu; Internet Legal Research Group (which collects bar passage and employment data), http://www.ilrg.com; and lists provided by Ringenberg (2006) and Stewart and Tolley (2004).

BarPass is a school's bar passage rate for first-time test takers in Summer 2006/Winter 2007. *StateAvg* is the average passage rate for the state in which the law school is located, except for the four D.C. law schools (American, Catholic, Georgetown, and Howard), which are for the state where the most graduates of the school took the exam. *Difference* is the difference between *BarPass* and *StateAvg*. *Employment* is the employment rate, reported by the school, for 2006 full-time graduates 9 months after graduation. The table is accurate and complete to the best of our knowledge.

Law in Ann Arbor, Michigan (relocating to southwest Florida in 2009), was founded in 2000; and the University of St. Thomas School of Law in Minneapolis, Minnesota, reopened in 2001 (after being closed since 1933; see, generally, Fitzgerald, 2001; Schiltz, 2004). Faulkner University, affiliated with the Churches of Christ, acquired the Thomas Goode Jones School of Law (in Montgomery, Alabama) in 1983. These developments are a clear indication that religious legal education is on the rise.

Religion in the Religious Law School Curriculum

The heterogeneity in the centrality of religiously affiliated law schools' "religious worldview" means that there is considerable variability in the extent to which religion is incorporated into the law school culture and curriculum (Buzzard, 1995; Eisenberg, 1998–1999; Fitzgerald, 2001; Gerdy, 2006; Shaffer, 1993). Indeed, the majority of religiously affiliated law schools have no more religious content than their secular counterparts (Shaffer, 1993). Shaffer (1993, p. 1878) argues that such schools have failed in an important respect, because:

> A religiously affiliated law school cannot account for itself theologically by being or aspiring to be like law schools maintained by the state or by nonreligious private sponsors. It cannot be faithful to itself and also be secular. To the extent that a religiously affiliated law school is content with being secular, it denies its heritage and its purpose. . . . It is hard to know why their religious sponsors continue to maintain them.

Even at universities where religion is fairly central, law schools are often isolated from the rest of the university, with the result that "in most instances the law school and the law school faculty are not as committed to the religious mission of the university as other units and other faculty" (Eisenberg, 1998–1999, p. 9). One can distinguish between institutions whose religious affiliation is primarily historical and no longer a living, breathing part of the university's mission and those at which religious commitment and instruction are core elements of the university's identification and mission.[19] Examples of the latter category can be drawn from every denomination listed in Table 7.1. Educators at these law schools believe that "a combination of learning both by study and faith can add a new dimension to the training of lawyers, resulting in a better end product" (Lee, 1995, p. 255).[20] Thus, they "act as advocates of Christian perspectives" (Buzzard, 1995, p. 273) and make a concerted effort to integrate religion and secular legal training. This integration both provides a religious perspective on substantive topics and nurtures a positive value system in the lawyers-to-be.

Gaffney (1986) argues that the teaching and understanding of secular law in core areas can be enriched by an exploration of biblical law. For example, bankruptcy laws and mortgage moratorium acts are modern descendants of biblical property laws prohibiting interest on loans and abusive debt collection; and biblical tort law treats extensively of liability for injuries to persons or their goods, specifying compensation and/or punishment. Gaffney (p. 95) concludes that an exploration of these connections between biblical and secular law can "serve us greatly in our task of redefining substantive and procedural norms in our own culture" (see also Scarlato & Kohm, 1998–1999; Wolfe, 1995).

Consider, for example, the self-described missions of several of these law schools. Ave Maria School of Law describes itself as offering:

> An outstanding legal education in fidelity to the Catholic Faith as expressed through Sacred Tradition, Sacred Scripture, and the teaching authority of the Church. . . . Ave Maria School of Law affirms Catholic legal education's traditional emphasis on the only secure foundation for human freedom—the natural law written on the heart of every human being.[21]

Law schools affiliated with other denominations use similar language: Baylor Law School seeks "to educate men and women by integrating academic excellence and Christian commitment within a caring community,"[22] Regent University School of Law "thoroughly integrate[s] a Christian perspective in the classroom,"[23] and the purpose of legal education at Brigham Young University "is to teach students the laws of men in the light of the laws of God."[24]

The religious element of several other religiously affiliated law schools, especially those at Jesuit and Jewish universities, is less prominent but still present. For example, the Fuchsberg Law Center at Touro College is closed on the Jewish Sabbath and serves kosher food in its cafeteria—despite the fact that only about 30% of the students are Jewish, of whom only a small percentage are religiously observant (Glickstein, 1995). Cardozo Law School at Yeshiva University takes pains to keep its secular legal training separate from religion, although it, like Touro, offers classes on Jewish law (Glickstein, 1995; Riley, 2005). The Dean of Touro Law School stated that "it is not necessary, we think, or desirable, or even possible in a pluralistic society that each and every person be religiously engaged, so long as some significant representation of the religious point of view takes place" (Glickstein, 1995, p. 483). It seems unlikely that the dean of an evangelical Christian law school would make such a statement, considering that "religious engagement" is a core tenet of evangelicalism (Kellstedt, 1989; see Chapters 1 and 4).

How do religious law schools integrate religion and law? A few of the more outwardly religious ones heed Gaffney's (1986) call to incorporate religion into substantive coursework at every opportunity. For instance, the Ave Maria courses on property and labor law cover relevant papal encyclicals, as well as material from the Gospels and major Catholic theologians such as Thomas Aquinas (Dobranski, 2002; Riley, 2005); and Liberty students discuss whether judicial decisions contravene biblical principles or natural law (Liptak, 2004). Touro strives to incorporate a Jewish approach to ethics "in all aspects of the curriculum," including both core topics (e.g., property, family law) and professional responsibility (Glickstein, 1995, p. 482). A variety of techniques are used to accomplish this integration, such as requiring students to connect course issues with their faith as a formal part of the class, using the Bible as a text, and including prayerful devotion or spiritual exercises in class (Scarlato & Kohm, 1998–1999; Uelmen, 2004). Some of these techniques—such as encouraging students to reflect on their religious beliefs and even using the Bible as an ancient legal text—seem relatively unobjectionable and might even work in a secular environment, but the more radical proposals would raise serious church–state separation concerns at secular public institutions.

The main way in which religious law schools have worked religion into their curriculum is in coursework on legal ethics. All ABA-accredited law schools have a course on ethics, usually entitled "legal ethics" or "professional responsibility." At secular law schools, these courses typically focus on the state bar–approved codes of conduct (which vary somewhat depending on jurisdiction) regulating attorneys' professional behavior.[25] They cover abstract statements of principles that are taught using the standard casebook method; moreover, they tend to emphasize relatively mundane regulatory matters. The regulations raise concrete, practical concerns that practicing attorneys are likely to encounter, such as attorney–client confidentiality and conflict of interest; but they (and the courses in which they arise) typically fail to grapple with big, moral questions, such as how to lead a meaningful, ethical life while also practicing law (Bost & Perrin, 2005; Kelly, 2007; Litowitz, 2006; Rice, 1999; Schiltz, 1998, 2004; Shaffer, 1987). The sort of neutral and detached professionalism that the regulations dictate tends to "bleach out" individuating aspects of the self, such as one's religion (Levinson, 1993/2003).

As a result, "what [the legal profession] calls ethics are traffic regulations that make professional intercourse efficient and keep professional practice at least (and often at most) within the boundaries set by the criminal law. The nationally organized legal profession in the United States has lately and clearly dropped even the attempt at moral admonition for its younger members" (Shaffer, 1987, p. 131). This development is somewhat ironic, for a couple of reasons. First, "the development of American professional ethics took place in a culture of religious belief" (Shaffer, 1987, p. 40). Religion—especially mainstream Judeo-Christian beliefs—influenced the development of legal codes of professional responsibility, but in a subtle way in which the Bible was not mentioned explicitly. Second, the teaching of abstract ethical principles leaves many law school graduates feeling that they did not really learn anything about ethics—in the larger sense of the word—at all (Kelly, 2007; Schiltz, 1998). Including religion as part of law students' ethical training can provide yet another source of wisdom in teaching and thinking about ethics—namely, religious wisdom (Allegretti, 1998a).

These shortcomings of the traditional legal ethics curriculum have led even some nonreligious law schools to reenvision how they approach the topic (e.g., Kelly, 2007). Religious law schools have taken the lead in this, because they tend to agree that codes of professional responsibility merely "establish the ethical bottom-line below which a lawyer cannot fall without risking professional sanction" and do not do much to assist lawyers in aspiring to the highest ethical standards (Allegretti, 1996, p. 110). On the contrary, they agree with White (1995, p. 373) that "those schools with a religious affiliation have a special opportunity to instill a sense of ethics by utilizing their religious foundations." Thus, legal ethics has special importance in religious law schools (Schiltz, 2004; Wolfe, 1995), and their teaching of ethics and professional responsibility has a decidedly religious bent. Some religious law schools even have specialized seminars in "religious lawyering," which draw on relevant concepts in both legal ethics and jurisprudence (Uelmen, 2004), and a few have established institutes for the study of law, religion, and ethics.[26] An emphasis on religiously informed morality and ethics, rather than on mere rules, allows teachers and students to "focus on the forest rather than the trees" (Allegretti, 2001b, p. 269).

Measures of Religious Law Schools' Success

By several indices, religious law schools have successfully become a part of the mainstream legal establishment. First is the issue of ABA accreditation. Among other things, accreditation is beneficial in terms of students receiving governmental financial aid, employment opportunities, admission to the bar, and prestige. As Table 7.1 shows, a large number of religious law schools—some with a quite explicit religious mission—have been accredited and thereby, to a significant degree, attained acceptance by the American bar (two of the schools listed, Faulkner and Liberty, have only provisional accreditation). The more overtly religious law schools have Oral Roberts University to thank for their status. In 1981, an ABA accreditation committee recommended against accrediting the Oral Roberts Law School, largely because the school required students and faculty to make a profession of (Christian) faith (Ringenberg, 2006). The university sued and won, forcing the ABA to amend its accreditation standards. Henceforth, religious law schools could discriminate in admitting students and hiring faculty, as long as their policies were clearly advertised (Casson & Curran, 1984; Ringenberg, 2006). Oral Roberts subsequently shut down its law school and sent its library to Regent University, which founded its law school in 1986 (Savage, 2007).

A second measure of these schools' acceptance by the larger legal community is their reputation. There are numerous ways of measuring an academic institution's reputation, all of them imperfect. One highly publicized metric is the annual rankings published by *U.S. News & World Report*. Without arguing for the superiority of this method over any other, it is instructive to consider where religious law schools fall on the list. In the 2008 rankings, eight law schools with a religious affiliation were in the top 30: Duke (#12), Georgetown (#14), Vanderbilt (#15), Boston University (#21), Emory (#22), Notre Dame (#22), Boston College (#26), and Fordham (#27). Although the religious affiliation at some of these universities is of an almost entirely historical nature (e.g., Duke, Vanderbilt), it is very much present at several others (e.g., Georgetown, Notre Dame). Despite the widely acknowledged limitations of the *U.S. News & World Report* methodology, the rankings are highly similar to those produced by other, more qualitative methods.[27] This is not to say, however, that all religious law schools fare well in the rankings. The 2008 *U.S. News & World Report* rankings have a number of them, from across the denominational spectrum, in the lowest tier (e.g., Ave Maria, Campbell, Duquesne, Touro, Valparaiso). If anything, the wide range of rankings of religious law schools suggests that religion is not a factor and that the schools rise or fall according to the same secular criteria as other law schools. It also suggests that having a religious mission does not hinder a law school's chances for success, at least in terms of the peer assessments and quantitative criteria (e.g., bar passage rate, LSAT scores) used in the *U.S. News & World Report* rankings.

A third indication of a law school's quality is the success of its graduates. One could compare different law schools on their bar exam pass rate, job placement, number of graduates who obtain judicial clerkships, starting salary, and so forth. Based on data compiled by the Internet Legal Research Group, we could find no indication that graduates of religious law schools are disadvantaged.[28] As seen in Table 7.1, most religious schools' most recent bar passage rate surpassed the state average, in some cases quite substantially (e.g., Campbell exceeded its state average by 22.5%, Baylor by 16.5%, and Santa Clara by 12.3%).[29] Ave Maria's first graduating class in 2003 had a higher bar exam passage rate than any school in Michigan (including the University of Michigan, a perennial top 10 law school; see Dobranski, 2002; Riley, 2005), and its 2006 passage rate was 96.3%. Faulkner Law School graduates had the highest passage rate in the state of Alabama on the February 2008 bar exam.[30]

The evangelical law schools got off to a rocky start but have improved substantially. For example, Regent Law School's initial graduating classes performed poorly on the bar exam, but the school responded by raising the minimum LSAT score required for admission (Riley, 2005), and by 2006 the passage rate was up to 73.7%, which is roughly equal to the state average of 74% for first-time test takers. Regent students have also won national ABA competitions in recent years. Regent has accomplished this by investing heavily in recruiting better-qualified law students and doing a better job of training them, and there are signs that the investment is paying off (Savage, 2007). They are obtaining better jobs—especially, but not limited to, in the government—and the legal community has noticed an improvement in the quality of Regent graduates (Savage, 2007).

One area in which religious law school graduates appear to be doing especially well is in hiring by the government, especially the U.S. Justice

Department (Savage, 2007). The George W. Bush administration shifted the focus of the Department's Civil Rights Division from racial and sex discrimination to religious discrimination, which created new opportunities for religious law school graduates (Lewis, 2007). There was a significant increase in hires from religious law schools for these highly competitive positions between 2003 and 2006, leading some to accuse the Justice Department of pursuing a religious political agenda (Lewis, 2007). The increase followed the Bush administration's appointment in 2001 of Kay Coles James, dean of Regent University's government school, to be the director of the Office of Personnel Management, which manages human resources for the executive branch (Savage, 2007).

The Justice Department's higher religious profile has not come without cost, however. Monica Goodling, a 1999 graduate of Regent University School of Law and former top aide to U.S. Attorney General Alberto Gonzales, was at the center of the firestorm over the Justice Department's firing of U.S. attorneys in 2006. Goodling—who, like Gonzales, was forced by the controversy to resign—oversaw the firings despite having only scant prosecutorial experience herself; she also testified that she had improperly used political considerations in hiring federal prosecutors (Lewis, 2007; Lichtblau, 2008; Savage, 2007). Goodling's role in the controversy called attention to Regent's less than stellar reputation in the legal education community and raised concerns that the Bush administration was subordinating academic qualifications to politics in making hiring decisions (Lewis, 2007; Lichtblau, 2008; Savage, 2007).[31]

Religious Beliefs and Legal Practice: Convergence or Conflict?

Law is seemingly a profession noted for the disgruntlement and dissatisfaction of its practitioners. For example, most lawyers say that they would choose another career in hindsight and would not want their children to become lawyers (Daicoff, 2004; Linowitz & Mayer, 1994; Litowitz, 2006; Rhode, 2000). A series of quality-of-life surveys by the ABA's Young Lawyers Division has found that although most attorneys are satisfied with their current position, there is significant career dissatisfaction among attorneys, along with evidence that it is increasing (McNeil, 1996; Rhode, 2000).[32] Some lawyers are more dissatisfied than others, with attorneys in large firms and those working for franchise firms less satisfied than their solo and small-firm counterparts (McNeil, 1996; Schiltz, 1999; van Hoy, 1997). A major source of dissatisfaction is the difficulty many lawyers experience in striking a balance between their work and personal lives (ABA Young Lawyers Division, 2000; Daicoff, 2004; Linowitz & Mayer, 1994; Litowitz, 2006; McNeil, 1996; Rhode, 2000; Schiltz, 1999).

Although the ABA surveys have not specifically addressed attorneys' religious, or spiritual, lives, there is no reason to expect that attorneys would be an exception to the need many people feel for some sort of spiritual connection in their lives. In Yeats's terms (from the poem that opened this chapter), many people feel "forced to choose perfection of the life, or of the work." However, one might expect this choice to be felt even more keenly by attorneys than by those with many other types of occupations, given the weighty and morally ambiguous matters that attorneys often deal with; the demanding and often frustrating nature of legal work; the profession's seductiveness in terms of money, power, and prestige; the knowledge that others' well-being may depend directly on their efforts; and the close connection between morality and law. According to Joseph Allegretti, one of the more prolific writers on the relationship between religion and legal practice, these pressures have created "a spiritual crisis" in the legal profession (e.g., Allegretti, 1996, p. 3). Evidence that attorneys' involvement in religious organizations is increasing (Conkle, 1998a; Heinz, Schnorr, Laumann, & Nelson, 2001) might be one response to that crisis. The very existence of such a crisis (or the perception that it exists) implicates Levinson's (1993/2003) fifth model of lawyers' religious identification, inasmuch as it emphasizes the potential conflicts and points of convergence between a lawyer's faith and profession.

A sizeable literature exists on how one can be a successful attorney as well as a successful believer, and can even have career and religion complement one another. This approach has even become prevalent enough that some have referred to a "Religious Lawyering Movement" (e.g., Pearce, 1998, 2001; Pearce & Uelmen, 2004, 2005–2006), which has produced a substantial amount of academic discourse (see Pearce & Uelmen, 2005–2006, for review). Considering that most American lawyers, like most Americans, are Christian, it is not surprising that the focus of most such works is on being a good Christian and a good lawyer. Books on the topic carry such titles as *On Being a Christian and a Lawyer: Law for the Innocent* (Shaffer, 1981), *The Lawyer's Calling: Christian Faith and Legal Practice* (Allegretti, 1996), *Can a Good Christian Be a Good Lawyer?* (Baker & Floyd, 1998), and *Redeeming Law: Christian Calling and the Legal Profession* (Schutt, 2007). Nonetheless, as many of these authors note, the same issues, concerns, and possible solutions apply by and large to devout adherents of any faith, and several works have been written from other religious perspectives, such as Judaism (see, e.g., Levine, 1996; Levinson, 1993/2003; Pearce, 1996), Hinduism (Nanda, 1996), Islam (al-Hibri, 1996), and Baha'i (Nelson, 1996).

Religion and Lawyering: Sources of Conflict

Often, a client's interests and ethical behavior (whether or not it is grounded in religion) are at odds. Rhode (2000, p. 15) observes that an "undivided fidelity to client objectives is often difficult to square with commonly accepted ethical principles," listing as examples cases in which third-party interests (health, safety, or financial) are at risk from the client's (perfectly legal) behavior. Tension can also arise when a client's own best interests are at odds with his stated goals (Allegretti, 1996; Edwards, 1998; Shaffer, 1989).[33] At the extreme end of the continuum, because anyone accused of a crime is entitled to competent legal representation, attorneys might also find themselves working on behalf of unsavory clients who have been charged with, and in some cases have admittedly performed, reprehensible acts. Codes of professional responsibility governing legal practice view lawyers as neutral partisans of their clients, who zealously advocate their clients' interests without passing moral judgment (Allegretti, 1996, 1998a). This would enable them to engage in activities that some might deem immoral, such as defending the guilty, helping clients skirt the law (e.g., avoiding paying taxes or following environmental regulations), or making a truthful witness appear dishonest (Allegretti, 1996; Shaffer, 1989).

In both a legal and a moral sense, these individuals are entitled to competent representation and advocacy on their behalf; nonetheless, many attorneys find it difficult to reconcile such work with their religious beliefs, which could view it as abetting the person's wrongdoing (Levinson, 1993/2003). Levinson uses the example of a client who states his intention to embezzle or commit other economic crimes. Ethical rules governing attorney–client confidentiality allow an attorney to disclose a client's secret in order to prevent a criminal act "likely to result in imminent death or substantial bodily harm" (Model Rule 1.6(b)(1)), but the exception would not apply in this case, where the potential harm is economic. The religious lawyer's understanding of her moral obligations might dictate disclosure, creating a conflict requiring her to decide which community—the professional or the religious—she identifies with more closely (Levinson, 1993/2003).

In some cases, the client's behavior is legal, but the attorney might nevertheless object on religious grounds. Pearce (2001; see also Miller, 1999; Pearce & Uelmen, 2004) gives the example of a devout Catholic lawyer, opposed to abortion, who was appointed by the court to represent minors seeking waivers of parental consent for abortion. Should the lawyer be allowed to counsel them about alternatives or decline the appointment? In the opinion of the Tennessee Supreme Court's Board of Professional Responsibility, the answer to both questions is "no." One might wonder, however, how capably the attorney could represent the clients' interests, given his fundamental opposition to their legal claim; indeed, a concern that his beliefs would impair his professional judgment was the main reason he sought recusal. Doctors who are opposed to abortion are not forced to perform them, even as part of their medical training; so it is reasonable to ask why lawyers should be required to further clients' actions to which they are morally opposed. Presumably, courts making such appointments would take the attorney's religious objection into account, but they are not obligated to do so.

A common source of difficulty for religious lawyers is the potential conflict between the law of the state and a "higher" law, that is, natural law or the law of God. Such conflicts can arise in a variety of legal contexts, such as family law (e.g., parental rights, surrogacy, same-sex marriage/civil unions), privacy rights (e.g., abortion, assisted suicide), bioethics (e.g., removal of life support, palliative care), and criminal law (e.g., capital punishment). Although members of the bar have sworn to uphold the state's laws, "that Divine Law is superior to secular law is virtually an axiom of theistic religion, religion's own version of the Supremacy Clause" (Carter, 1998, p. 6). According to this view, faith does not need to be reconciled with something else, because it trumps everything else (Breen, 2006; Schutt, 2007; Shaffer, 1998). Cascarelli (2000; pp. 309–310) argues that Catholic legal professionals have "the obligation of creating and nourishing an atmosphere that is receptive to natural law as a recognized, legitimate body of law," even when it conflicts with positive law. Some commentators have gone even further and have encouraged young religious lawyers to "recognize the nature of the pagan culture in which we live" and "resolve to become a warrior, not a spectator, in the religious and cultural war" through active evangelization (Rice, 1999).[34]

All of the books on the topic emphasize the conflict between personal fulfillment and making time for oneself and one's family, and productivity, especially in terms of generating billable hours and income. According to this view, the economic motive in and of itself does not distort the personal side of legal work, but it can easily do so if it becomes too much of an end in itself and the sole definition of "success" (Droel, 1989).

It is tempting for many lawyers to deal with these conflicts by compartmentalizing their professional and personal lives, but that compartmentalization is precisely the sort of thing that can create dissatisfaction and a sense of meaninglessness and purposelessness in the long run (Allegretti, 1996; Bost & Perrin, 2005; Droel, 1989; Hall, 2005; Pearce, 2001; Schiltz, 1999; Schutt, 2007). As Hall (2005, p. 8) expresses it:

> The law creates an artificial illusion that we can neatly separate
> and compartmentalize various parts of our human selves. Though
> we can to a certain extent, our spiritual realities will and should seep
> into other parts of our lives, including our professional work. . . .
> Our reluctance to embrace this part of our reality only limits
> our power and ability to enhance our lives and enrich the
> profession of law.

Religion and Lawyering: Finding Convergence

Thus, there are numerous ways in which one's legal practice and religious beliefs can come into conflict, but there are also ways in which one's religion can enrich one's legal work. As described in Chapter 6, some judges feel that their religion has enhanced their performance on the bench (e.g., Gonzalez, 1996; Merz, 2004). Many attorneys report the same thing. Dan Edwards, an attorney and Episcopalian priest, even argues that the conflicts are beneficial because they make both work and faith stronger:

> Law and Christianity are both said to be "practiced." We say someone is a "practicing" lawyer or a "practicing" Christian. This terminology suggests that Christianity and law are enterprises which are done. The word practice may even imply that law and Christianity are done repeatedly in the hope of developing proficiency at them. . . . The practices of law and Christianity are not perfectly compatible, not comfortably complementary. Just as there are opportunities to practice Christianity in the midst of practicing law, so there are opportunities to betray either practice in the interest of the other. But it may well be the opportunities, even the temptations of betrayal, which make each practice helpful to the other. . . . The practice of law is an opportunity to meaningfully practice faith precisely because it is simultaneously an opportunity to betray faith. (Edwards, 1998, pp. 22–25)

Thomas Shaffer, whom many regard as "the 'father' of the religious lawyering movement" (Pearce & Uelmen, 2004, p. 129), seems to mean much the same thing when he says that "faith among Christians is nothing until it can be allowed to mess up American democratic, constitutional, legal, professional commitment" (Shaffer, 1998, pp. 195–196; see also Shaffer, 1981, 1987).

Allegretti (1996, p. 24) observes that "the word profession comes from the Latin 'to profess,' to take a vow or make a public declaration." This etymology reflects the historical connection between the profession of faith and the profession of work, wherein professionals (i.e., doctors and lawyers) were individuals who had also taken religious vows and whose work had a strong religious component (see also Conkle, 1998a; Shaffer, 1987). Most of the works written for lawyers on resolving the conflicts between work and faith emphasize reestablishing this ancient connection by finding a place for the sacred in their secular activities and developing a "spirituality of work" (e.g., Allegretti, 1996; 1998b; DiSalvo & Droel, 1998; Droel, 1989; Hall, 2005; Pearce, 1996; Shaffer, 1987; Schutt, 2007).[35] For example, Droel (1989, p. 11) writes that:

> Lawyers who would be good Christians must not allow the harsh environment of law to hide the link between the sacred and the secular. In fact, they must find a way for that harshness and the disturbance they experience under it to reveal the connections between faith and work. They must also try to see a sacred dimension in the secular language and values of their trade—in the excellence, good work, solidarity, competence, and teamwork of the practice of law.

Similarly, Allegretti (1996, 1998b) encourages attorneys to think of their work not as a curse but as both calling and creation. Legal practice can be a calling, or vocation, because "[a]ny job can be a calling if we approach it as an avenue of loving service to our God and our neighbor. Our calling is to serve God *in and through our work* no less than the rest of life" (Allegretti, 1998b, p. 149; italics in original). Viewing the law as a vocation, rather than merely a job that exists apart from one's personal life, is a common theme in the religious lawyering literature (e.g., Dobranski, 2002; Lee, 1998–1999; Lesnick, 2003; Osler, 2005; Schutt, 2007). By working at their chosen calling competently and diligently, attorneys can collaborate in God's ongoing plan for creation.

The attempt to discern God's will in one's professional, as well as in one's personal, life is not peculiar to legal practice or to any particular faith; rather, it characterizes most religious believers (Carter, 1998). Yet, because of the particular nature of the challenges and conflicts faced by lawyers, some of the techniques for resolving those conflicts are tailored specifically to legal practice. What, then, can lawyers do to achieve the goal of integrating personal, religious values with their public, professional lives?

Some of the recommendations, such as working competently, responsibly, and diligently in the pursuit of justice, are part and parcel of simply being a good lawyer and do not necessarily contain a religious element. Other recommendations do emphasize religion, particularly in terms of finding a spiritual component to one's work. To do this, lawyers are advised to overcome the inclination to think of God as relegated to the Sabbath, the house of prayer, or specific religious occasions, and instead be aware of God's presence in all areas of one's life (Allegretti, 1996, 1998b; Droel, 1989; Edwards, 1998; Osler, 2005; Rice, 1999; Schutt, 2007). It can be hard for lawyers to "do justice" unless they know it in their own lives (Chopko, 1998). Such awareness can create what Allegretti (1998b, p. 151) calls a "spirituality of the ordinary" and open one up to opportunities to minister to others in the course of everyday legal practice (see also Allegretti, 1996). They can do this by forming a *covenant* with their clients, which involves taking clients' concerns seriously, valuing them as persons, collaborating with them on decision making, and pursuing reconciliation and a fair resolution for all parties to a dispute, as opposed to merely seeking victory for one's client (Allegretti, 1998a, 2002; see also Conkle, 1998a; Lee, 1998–1999).

These activities sound like perfectly reasonable and worthy goals, but they can be hard to put into practice. Taking clients' concerns seriously often requires taking more time to listen to those concerns, which is not easy to do for attorneys who are working on multiple cases simultaneously, have jam-packed schedules, and are trying to meet a high billable hours quota. Valuing clients as persons can be difficult when they have been accused of (and might have admitted to) committing bad acts, such as criminal or tort defendants, or when the clients themselves are faceless corporations. And bringing religious values to legal practice has the potential to result in paternalistic attitudes toward clients. In the case of representing unsavory clients, reconciliation is possible if one considers not only the traditional justifications for defending the guilty (e.g., protecting the individual against the unbridled power of the state), but also the religious justifications for doing so. Defending the guilty allows the religious lawyer to act as a companion and minister to the guilty, and thereby to serve this category of society's outcast and downtrodden (Allegretti, 1996, 1998a; Shaffer, 1981, 1989). An additional payoff is that it can give lawyers a stronger connection to their clients, which can benefit both of them as persons, and which can also benefit the work itself (Allegretti, 1998a).[36]

A particularly thorny issue is the conflict that can arise between seeking "justice for all" (i.e., justice in its largest sense) and the best possible outcome for one's client. Striving for an optimal resolution for all parties is fundamentally at odds with the adversarial system. Many attorneys would argue that "merely seeking victory" is precisely what their clients hire them to do, and that acting otherwise would mean shirking their professional obligations. Nonetheless, there are ways to make it work. One strategy is to encourage clients to use Alternative Dispute Resolution (ADR) instead of litigation (Allegretti, 1996; 2001a). ADR processes such as mediation and arbitration encourage forgiveness and compromise; they are therefore more likely to produce outcomes in which both parties get something, which foster peace and reconciliation, as opposed to the "I-win-you-lose" outcomes that characterize most litigation (Allegretti, 2001a).

One can also bring spirituality to one's work by approaching it with patience, reflection, compassion, and humility (Droel, 1989; Schutt, 2007), and by recognizing that, although work is important, it is not what gives one's life ultimate meaning (Allegretti, 1996, 1998b). To be sure, these are virtues in the legal profession as in so many other areas of life, but, one could argue, only in moderation. A lawyer who is too patient and reflective might not be as productive; one who is too compassionate might lose objectivity; one who is too humble might not represent clients as tenaciously; and one who makes work less of a priority might be perceived as lacking the commitment and drive to deserve partnership in the firm. Resolving this conflict might entail leaving a demanding, stressful practice for one in which the mix of cases would be more personally fulfilling and would leave one time to "have a life."

Much of the advice on reconciling a legal career with religious beliefs emphasizes the importance of faith—in one's clients, in the system (both the religious system and the legal system), and in oneself (e.g., Matheny, 1998). Faith can help one realize that seemingly insurmountable conflicts are temporary, and faith can help resolve those conflicts (Matheny, 1998). This strategy—of relying on faith—often seems naïve and facile to those who do not have it, but there are numerous testimonials to its success as a strategy for overcoming obstacles, both in legal practice (e.g., Baker & Floyd, 1998) and in life more generally (e.g., Batson & Ventis, 1982; James, 1902). It is easier to make these connections between work and faith if one takes time occasionally to get away from work, to recharge and reflect (Allegretti, 1998b). Most attorneys work long hours, have constant deadlines, and deal with a demanding populace (clients, senior associates/partners, court personnel), making it easy to become so immersed in the job that everything else fades into the background. Stepping back periodically to think about one's life and work, and the role of religion in both, can bring the religious lawyer greater fulfillment in both arenas (Allegretti, 1996, 1998b; Schutt, 2007). Becoming involved in socially concerned civic organizations can accomplish the same goal. Research shows that attorneys who identify with a particular religious denomination—regardless of which one it is—are more likely than nonreligious attorneys to participate in voluntary associations of both a religious and secular kind (Heinz et al., 2001).

To deal with situations in which one has moral objections to a client's (planned or performed) behavior:

> A lawyer does not do her client a disservice when she provides the client an opportunity to think about these matters. Further, a lawyer who has religious objections to a client's cause need not keep silent about her misgivings, but should feel free to raise them in an appropriate, non-paternalistic manner. (Allegretti, 2002, p. 29; see also Breen, 2006; Conkle, 1998a)

This is not an easy course to take, but it is one that balances the attorney's moral duty to herself with her professional obligations to her client. And the attorney must recognize that the ultimate decision is the client's, even if the attorney disagrees with the decision. In that situation, attorneys should feel comfortable invoking their right of "conscientious objection" and not pursuing the client's interest, even if that might entail losing the client's business or incurring the court's wrath (Allegretti, 1998a, 2002; Shaffer, 1981). According to this viewpoint, religious attorneys must occasionally be willing to say "no" and challenge a client who pushes the boundaries too far, as when the attorney suspects the client of perjury (Allegretti, 1996, 1998a; Breen, 2006). The Model Rules of Professional Conduct permit a lawyer to withdraw from a case, subject to court approval, if "a client insists upon pursuing an objective that the lawyer considers repugnant or imprudent" (Rule 1.16(b)(3); see Allegretti, 2002). They also allow lawyers to refer to "other considerations, such as moral, economic, social and political factors, that may be relevant to the client's situation" (Rule 2.1). These rules clearly imply that "lawyers need not shed their religious values in order to practice law" (Allegretti, 2002, p. 31). Although some states have gone so far as to propose or adopt statutes forbidding discrimination by lawyers on the basis of race, age, sex, religion, and the like, such statutes arguably run afoul of the lawyers' own freedom to exercise their religion (Miller, 1999).

The answer to whether a devoutly religious person can be an attorney while remaining true to her religious values is not a simple one, nor is it a problem to be solved and set aside; rather, it is an ongoing challenge (Osler, 2005). Allegretti depicts the complexities well:

> Some answer with a resounding "no." . . . Others answer the question with a defensive how-dare-you "yes." . . . Both extremes fail to take the question seriously, so they have little to contribute to those of us who want to bring together our life as a Christian and our life as a lawyer. . . . Our challenge, then, is one of balance, of integration. It is a matter of *religion*, for the original meaning of the word is to tie or bind together. Religion is what ties our life together, gives it backbone, substance, meaning. The question is whether we will allow our deepest values and commitments to really influence our daily life . . . faith and work belong together, [and] cross-fertilization is better than rigid separation . . . the question whether we can be a Christian and a lawyer can only be answered if it remains open-ended, unresolved. . . . We will never succeed completely. There will always be an irreducible tension between our faith and our work. There will always be a gap between what we profess and what we do. But that is no reason not to begin.
> (Allegretti, 1996, pp. 125–127; italics in original)

Putting Religion into Practice

One way of reconciling one's religious beliefs with one's legal practice is to pursue legal work that explicitly furthers those beliefs. This approach is taken by attorneys who represent religious organizations or who defend clients' religious liberties in First Amendment cases (e.g., Ball, 1998; Horrigan, 2002), as well as by those who work for religiously oriented legal advocacy groups.[37] For example, William Ball, a Catholic practicing First Amendment law, found representing clients from diverse religious backgrounds "deeply satisfying" because he shared with them a common sense of purpose (Ball, 1998, p. 43). His particular area of legal practice provided him with personal and professional satisfactions, while simultaneously helping others in need and serving a cause that he believed in.

In his analysis of church–state separation cases decided in American appellate courts between 1951 and 1971, Sorauf (1976) found that over half of the plaintiffs' attorneys were Protestant, whereas only 6% were Catholic. Eighteen percent of the attorneys were Jewish, owing largely to their involvement with organizations frequently involved in church–state litigation, such as the American Civil Liberties Union and the American Jewish Congress, that often attract Jewish attorneys. The religion clauses of the First Amendment raise enough issues and enough competing perspectives (e.g., representing accommodationist vs. separationist interests) that there is something at the table for any religious attorney who wants to work in the area, regardless of his particular religious affiliation.

Some religious attorneys consider representing co-religionists a form of service to the faith, whether the representation involves religious matters or more mundane ones (Conkle, 1998a; S.F. Ward, 2008). Some large firms have also established religious organization practices, which do work for religious organization clients in a number of substantive law areas. Horrigan (2002) describes the efforts of Valerie Munson, a partner at the Pittsburgh-based firm of Eckert Seamans Cherin & Mellott, to create such a practice in her firm. The 15-lawyer interdisciplinary practice group includes attorneys from the firm's litigation, tax, trusts and estates, corporate, and real estate sections. In addition to representing clients on religious liberty issues, the practice deals with a variety of corporate, tax, labor, property, civil, and even criminal matters (e.g., clergy sexual abuse allegations, covered in Chapter 9) involving religious organizations. Many issues (e.g., a property dispute) are wholly nontheological but still benefit from a familiarity with church policies and practices. Both the lawyers and their clients are from different faiths. For Munson, the founder of the practice group, it has been a rewarding way to combine her interests in faith and the law. Other religious attorneys are more outspoken about advertising their religion, thereby using it as a marketing tool to attract those clients who will see it as a plus (S.F. Ward, 2008).

Religious advocacy groups are a legally specialized subset of "parachurch" organizations, which are voluntary, nonprofit associations of Christians working outside denominational control to achieve a specific ministry or social aim (Moore, 2007).[38] Historically, parachurch groups have not typically concentrated on legal activities, but they have gravitated toward the courts as conservative Protestants in the mid to late 20th century increasingly perceived themselves as displaced from the center of American culture, due to American society's becoming both religiously more pluralistic and more secular (Moore, 2007). The legal activism was also a response to what the groups viewed as "defeats" in several important church–state cases, such as those relating to school prayer and school curricula (i.e., teaching of evolution vs. creationism).

A number of such advocacy groups have arisen in recent decades (Heinz, Paik, & Southworth, 2003; Moore, 2007): the Christian Law Association (founded in 1969), the Christian Legal Foundation's Center for Law and Religious Freedom (1976), the Rutherford Institute (1982), the National Legal Foundation (1985), the Christian Coalition of America (1989), the Liberty Counsel (1989), the American Center for Law and Justice (1992), the Becket Fund (1994), and the Alliance Defense Fund (1994). They were founded originally to support people who felt that their religious liberties were being threatened, but several have gradually expanded their scope to other, nonreligious areas in which government has threatened individual liberties or about which religious groups are especially passionate (e.g., abortion).[39] Thus, some of the groups have relatively broad political and social agendas, whereas others are fairly narrow (Heinz et al., 2003). Conservative Christian legal advocacy groups have had some successes, especially in their zealous promotion of individuals' free exercise claims; but Moore (2007) argues that their legal activism has also had unintended consequences, such as "inadvertently feeding the bureaucratic monster they sought to fight" (p. 34). So many groups are pursuing so much litigation on both sides of the religious freedom debate that it has "hindered the ability of conservative Christian voices to be heard above the din" (Moore, 2007, p. 197). Nonetheless, such work would seem to provide a ready way for a religiously devout attorney's practice to inform and complement her spiritual life, and vice versa.

Of course, religious attorneys can pursue religious values in their work without necessarily serving overt institutional interests. A lawyer might make a conscious effort to fulfill religious precepts by representing indigent clients, doing civil rights work, protecting the environment, and so forth (Droel, 1989; Uelmen, 2004); in other words, by working on behalf of the poor and oppressed (Levine, 2006; Power, 2009; Shaffer, 1998) and performing a "prophetic ministry" (Allegretti, 1996; see also Schutt, 2007).[40] For example, being a legal aid lawyer can be a religious act in that it enables one to "do justice" and act on important religious values (Cromartie, 1998; Wiltshire, 1998). One can also practice religious values through criminal prosecution, in the process restoring order to society and making the community safe (Levine, 1996). Such activities enable one to display character and contribute to the larger community (Rice, 1999; Shaffer, 1987). In the process, one can reconnect (or strengthen the connection) with one's religious beliefs and religious denomination. This goal can also be accomplished by engaging regularly in pro bono work, not simply as a matter of charity, but because it is what God (and justice) demands (Allegretti, 1996, 2001b).

Conclusion

"Religion and law make for odd talk. And we are going to have to live with that oddness, think about it, worry about it, and let the oddness confuse us and inform us about our fears" (Elkins, 1987, p. 527). In other words, we ignore the role of religion in attorney's lives at our peril. The legal profession in early 21st-century America is more diverse than at any time in history; yet it is still not a proportional reflection of the U.S. religious demographic, and significant variation exists across subareas of legal practice. It seems clear that attorneys, like many other individuals, struggle with reconciling their career with their faith. There are strategies that they can engage in on an individual level, and they can also join denominational professional societies for fellowship and support.

Religious law schools are also increasingly filling the void, by incorporating religion and morality in law students' ethical training. By doing so, they provide new lawyers with an understanding of the rules of professional responsibility, an appreciation of the complex moral dilemmas that can occur in legal practice, and, ideally, with strategies for dealing with them if and when they occur. The legal profession itself has been slower to respond, but as concerns about declining professionalism and rising lawyer burnout mount, it will eventually be forced to reexamine traditional practices, including the relationship (or lack thereof) between legal practitioners' work and their faith. Meanwhile, there are expanding opportunities for attorneys to "practice what they preach," either by specializing in religious issues or by applying religious principles through work on behalf of the needy and disenfranchised.

Despite these developments, what is missing from the discussion about religion and legal practice is data. We do not know, for example, the real extent to which the work–spirituality conflict is a source of dissatisfaction for lawyers, and whether lawyers from some religious backgrounds are more likely to experience it than others. We do not know whether religiously devout attorneys are more or less satisfied with their careers. And despite the sense that a "Religious Lawyering Movement" is under way, we do not know the size and scope of the movement, nor its impacts. An abundance of materials is available on how to imbue one's legal work with a sense of spirituality, as well as anecdotal evidence on attorneys' efforts to combine religion with their work lives, but we do not know how many lawyers are following this advice nor the consequences—for the lawyers themselves and for the profession as a whole—of their doing so.

Lawyer dissatisfaction and burnout are significant problems. There are tantalizing suggestions that forging a closer connection between religion and legal practice is a possible means of addressing those problems, but we need answers to these and related questions before we can make more concrete recommendations. Nonetheless, we agree with Russell Pearce (2001, p. 281) that "as long as professionalism continues to fail to provide meaning to most lawyers, interest in the Religious Lawyering Movement will grow." The movement's hardest work still lies ahead, for it must now "move beyond the question of *whether* lawyers should bring religious values to bear on their work, toward the difficult issues of *how* this should be done" (Pearce & Uelmen, 2005–2006, p. 270; italics in original). Religious lawyers have their work cut out for them, but the potential rewards, both to themselves and to the legal profession generally, are great.

8

Attorneys' Use of Biblical Appeals

> In the book of Exodus . . . it says: He that smiteth a man, so that
> he die, shall be surely put to death. . . . And in Numbers, chapter
> 35, verse 18, it states: Or if he smite him with a hand weapon . . .
> and he die, he is a murderer: the murderer shall surely be put to
> death. . . . Whoever killeth any person, the murderer shall be put
> to death by the mouth of the witnesses. And moreover, you shall
> take no satisfaction for the life of a murderer which he is guilty of
> death but he shall surely be put to death. Ladies and gentlemen . . .
> That's what this Bible—what this good book says.
> —*State v. Williams*, 1999, p. 642–643

Religion has long been a part of the trial process. Witnesses once had to swear
on the Bible, although they are no longer required to do so (Brooks, 1999).
Osler (2007) notes many similarities between the current criminal process
and that which led to Jesus's execution. Even the traditional number of jurors
on a jury is thought to be biblical, as many believe the number 12 was chosen
because Jesus had 12 apostles (*People v. Gajadhar*, 2007). More recently, religion has found its way into trial through the arguments that some lawyers
have offered in their closing statements. Specifically, lawyers have used biblical appeals, such as the chapter's opening quote, at trial (e.g., *Fahy v. Horn*,
2008; *People v. Zambrano*, 2007). Courts are inconsistent in their stance on
the admissibility of such arguments, and the reasons offered for disallowing
religious arguments are varied (for extensive review, see Chavez & Miller, in
press). In essence, courts that forbid biblical appeals are concerned about
their impact on jury decision making. Empirical research on the question has
yielded somewhat conflicting findings (Miller, 2006; Miller & Bornstein,
2006). This chapter discusses the use of biblical appeals, highlighting the court
opinions, legal analyses, and research findings.

Types of Biblical Appeals

In attempts to convince a jury to give a certain verdict, lawyers often utilize a
variety of persuasive tactics. One such technique involves the use of a biblical
appeal (i.e., argument) to convince the jury that God, the Bible, or religious

teachings in general support a certain trial verdict or sentence. Both the prosecution and the defense have used such appeals. Biblical appeals come in a variety of forms. Some are short biblical quotes, often only one or two sentences. Others are detailed accounts of biblical stories involving a death sentence that was or was not carried out.

Although biblical appeals are most often used in opening or closing arguments of death penalty cases, they could be used in any type of case. Blume and Johnson (2000) discuss a variety of case types that could bring about religious appeals, including "abortion, gay rights, euthanasia, divorce, welfare, segregation, or war" (p. 61). These and other hotly debated social issues could provoke supporters and/or opponents to use religion to further their arguments. Even so, religious arguments are infrequent in cases other than death penalty trials, perhaps because the death penalty is the ultimate punishment, or perhaps because the Bible makes so many references to the death penalty.

It is difficult to report exactly how often biblical appeals are used in trial courts. Databases such as Westlaw and Lexis-Nexis typically report only appellate court cases and exclude trial cases. Thus, only cases in which defendants are convicted and appeal their convictions and/or sentences are reported in these databases. If the defendant is found not guilty, there is no appeal. If the defendant does not appeal the case based on the biblical appeal, then there is no record of the biblical argument. As such, the sample of appellate cases involving biblical appeals is necessarily much smaller than the number of trials in which they are actually used. Chavez and Miller (in press) conducted a thorough search of death penalty cases in which defendants were appealing their death sentences, at least in part because biblical appeals were used during their trials. They collected 99 cases that were decided since the 1970s (see Fig. 8.1).

As the illustration demonstrates, there were few cases in the early 1980s, which may be, in part, because the databases are incomplete. After that period, the number of cases increased until it reached a peak in the mid-1990s, after which time the number of cases remained fairly steady. This increase could be due to an increase in the use of biblical appeals or an increase in attorneys using biblical materials as grounds to appeal their case. The subsequent leveling off is likely a result of many jurisdictions having "settled" the issue, so that those jurisdictions no longer have to dispute the issue. Even though it is difficult to tell whether the frequency of appeals has increased, decreased, or remained steady, legal scholars and researchers have paid considerable attention to the topic in recent years (Blume & Johnson, 2000; Chavez & Miller, in press; Echols, 2005; Henson, 2001; Loewy, 2000; Miller, 2006; Miller & Bornstein, 2005; Miller, Singer et al., 2008; Simons, 2004; Walker, 2003).

Although both prosecutors and defense attorneys use biblical appeals, it is harder to research those used by the defense. Biblical appeals offered by the defense attorney rarely appear in appellate cases. If an appeal offered by the defense attorney is successful, the defendant is not convicted or does not get

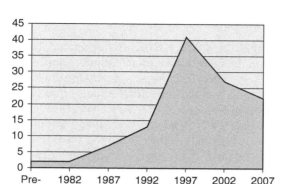

Figure 8.1. Number of appellate cases involving a religious appeal.

Adapted from Chavez & Miller, in press; each point represents the number of cases in the previous 5-year period.

the death penalty. The Fifth Amendment's Double Jeopardy clause forbids prosecutors from trying again to get a conviction; prosecutors are therefore not in a position to challenge the defense's use of the biblical argument, and there is no appeal. Defense appeals are discussed in cases in which a defense attorney *wanted* to make a biblical appeal, but the judge forbade him from doing so, and that is the basis for the appeal (e.g., *State v. Patterson*, 1996). Other defendants argue that they received ineffective counsel because their defense attorneys did not offer religious evidence, because they offered religious appeals that were improper, or because the only argument they made was a brief religious appeal (e.g., *State v. Messiah*, 1988; *Ward v. Dretke*, 2005). Finally, biblical appeals offered by the defense are discussed in appellate cases in which both the prosecutor and defense attorney used appeals (e.g., *Call v. Polk*, 2006). Even though there are fewer cases discussing appeals made by defense attorneys, there exists a wide variety of appeals, just as there is a variety of appeals made by prosecutors.

Several legal scholars have analyzed these appeals (e.g., Blume & Johnson, 2000; Echols, 2005; Miller & Bornstein, 2005), and some have created general categories of appeals. For instance, Miller (2006) and Miller and Bornstein (2005) suggest three types of appeals that have been used by prosecutors: retributive commands, claims of divine authority, and comparisons to biblical stories and characters. They also identified two types of defense appeals: biblical commands for mercy and comparisons to biblical stories. Chavez and Miller (in press) used this same typology and found that each type of appeal was used frequently. They also found two more categories not listed in previous typologies: "God/the Bible endorses the death penalty" and "God/the Bible does not endorse the death penalty." We discuss each of these types of appeals below.

Prosecution Appeals: Retributive Commands

The first type of appeal is called a *retributive command*. Lawyers essentially quote passages from the Bible that seemingly support retribution or the death penalty itself (*People v. Viera*, 2005; *People v. Zambrano*, 2007; *State v. Williams*, 1999). One of the most popular retributive appeal types is grounded in the "eye for an eye" biblical passage (e.g., *Greene v. State*, 1996; *Hammond v. State*, 1995; *People v. Hughes*, 2002; *People v. Wash*, 1993). Popular quotes include these or similar excerpts from the Bible: "Whoever sheds the blood of man, by man shall his blood be shed" (*Carruthers v. State*, 2000; *Coe v. Bell*, 1998; *Doss v. State*, 1996; *People v. Samuels*, 2005; *State v. Middlebrooks*, 1999), and "He who fatally strikes a man shall be put to death" (*People v. Mahaffey*, 1995; *People v. Samuels*, 2005; *People v. Wash*, 1993; *State v. Williams*, 1999). Such passages seemingly require the death penalty for murderers.

A similar approach is for prosecutors to tell the jurors that defendants must "reap what [they] sow" (*State v. Cribbs*, 1998), or "eat the fruits of their doings" (*United States v. Kirk*, 1994). Although these appeals are more vague, they suggest that the Bible has precepts for what should happen to people who violate the law; specifically, that they must pay for their crimes.

Lawyers choose some quotes because they apply directly to the defendant's crimes. For instance, in cases involving a child murder, prosecutors have quoted or paraphrased from Luke 17:2: "It were better for him that a millstone were hanged about his neck, and he were cast into the sea, than that he should offend one of these little ones" to demonstrate that child murderers should receive the death penalty[1] (e.g., *Commonwealth v. Brown*, 1998; *State v. Holden*, 1997; *State v. Sidden*, 1997; *State v. Walters*, 2003; *Ward v. Dretke*, 2005). In another case, a lawyer in *Bussard v. Lockhart* (1994) drew on a biblical quote when talking about a defendant who had escaped from police custody and had avoided capture for four years. The prosecutor stated, "Proverbs 28:1 fits . . . just as clear as it can be, 'the guilty flee when no man pursueth while the righteous stand bold as a lion.' . . . [defendant] fled to avoid coming to trial; that shows guilt."

All of these biblical quotes promote retribution, a doctrine that has been the basis of the justice system of society for centuries (Simmonds, 2004). As such, it is not surprising that biblical appeals supporting "an eye for an eye" or similar retributive messages appear often in modern courtrooms.

Prosecution Appeals: Claims of Divine Authority

The second type of appeal used by the prosecution involves making the claim that humans—jurors, the prosecutor, or the state in general—have been empowered by God to punish the defendant (e.g., *Bennett v. Angelone*, 1996; *People v. Samuels*, 2005; *People v. Viera*, 2005). Some appeals in this category are direct quotes, but others are statements made by lawyers that are not direct quotes. Some prosecutors have argued that God has given humans, in general, the power to execute wrongdoers. One prosecutor told jurors that several biblical passages "all repeat the same basic message: 'Whoever sheds the blood of man, by man shall his blood be shed, for in his image did God make man.' . . . in [the book of] Romans, Paul calls for capital punishment by saying, 'The ruler bears not the sword in vain for he is the minister [of] God, a revenger to execute wrath upon him that doeth evil'" (*People v. Samuels,* 2005). This argument informs jurors that God has given man the power to carry out God's will and execute murderers (see also, *People v. Slaughter,* 2002; *People v. Zambrano,* 2007).

Other prosecutors have assured the jury that the government has the right to try the defendant and administer the death penalty (e.g., *Bennett v. Angelone,* 1996; *Buttrum v. Black,* 1989; *Ex parte Waldrop,* 1984; *McNair v. State,* 1992; *People v. Rohn,* 1980; *State v. Moose,* 1984). For instance, one prosecutor told the jury, "Our governments are ordained by our creator, and a duly constituted body like this has the authority . . . [and] the duty to impose the proper and just punishment" (*Branch v. State,* 2004). Similarly, the prosecutor in *Wilcher v. State* (2003) told the jurors that when God first established a worldly government, he gave man the death penalty as an important tool to carry out justice and to protect humans. Prosecutors have sometimes offered specific details as to how God gave the state the authority to execute wrongdoers; for instance, by saying that God "handed the sword of Justice to Noah," one prosecutor insinuated that God had given the state the power to carry out justice on Earth (*Bennett v. Angelone,* 1996). Another prosecutor proclaimed that he was "the servant of God to execute His wrath on the wrongdoer" (*Buttrum v. Black,* 1989). According to some prosecutors, the state capital punishment statutes are also directed by God. At least two prosecutors have argued that the state's statute is "a statute of judgment . . . whoso killeth any person, the murderer shall be put to death by the mouth of witnesses" (*State v. Artis,* 1989; *State v. Haselden,* 2003), equating the power given by the state statute with power prescribed by the Bible.

Some prosecutors have sought further to encourage jurors to support the death penalty by telling them that jurors have to obey police and prosecutors, who are representatives of God. According to these prosecutors, disobedience toward these officials is essentially disobedience to God. These prosecutors cite Romans 13:2, "whosoever therefore resisteth the power, resisteth the ordinance of God; and they that resist shall receive to themselves damnation" (e.g., *Miller v. State,* 1978; *Sandoval v. Calderon,* 2000, *State v. Moose,* 1984). This threat of damnation is intended to encourage jurors to obey the prosecutor and give a death sentence.

Many prosecutors have anticipated that some jurors might question their personal roles in deciding whether the defendant should die. One prosecutor reassured the jurors by telling them that the jury is the "tool of the Lord," insinuating that they are properly acting under God's authority

(*State v. Middlebrooks*, 1999). Another prosecutor tried to preempt the defense attorney's use of religion by arguing that:

> I suspect that at least one of [the defense attorney's] arguments is going to be that the death sentence is contrary to the Good Book. It's contrary to our Christian ethics . . . and say, thou shalt not kill. If you're up on the Good Book . . . [you know] it means that you and I shalt not kill. It doesn't mean that you shouldn't do it pursuant to the statutes . . . just a few verses below that, right after that thou shalt not kill . . . it says he that smiteth a man so that he die shall surely be put to death. . . . I suggest to you that that is biblical authority for the death sentence. Not a mandate that you do it in any one case, but it is the authority for those of you [who] worry about that. (*State v. Haselden*, 2003)

Another attempt to ease jurors' fears was issued by the prosecutor in *Sandoval v. Calderon* (2000). "You are not playing God. You are doing what God says." The attorney in *Coe v. Bell* (1998) went further, reminding the jurors that God supports the death penalty and suggesting that they be "true to God" and sentence the defendant to death. Arguments such as these are attempts to convince jurors that they have the authority, or even the duty, to implement the death penalty. Further, they are attempts to persuade them that prosecutors, police, state statutes, government, or humans in general are called on by God to give the death penalty.

Prosecution Appeals: Comparison to Biblical Characters or Stories

The third type of prosecution appeal involves making comparisons between the defendant and various characters or stories in the Bible (e.g., *Bussard v. Lockhart*, 1994; *Commonwealth v. Henry*, 1990; *Cunningham v. Zant*, 1991; *Fahy v. Horn*, 2008; *Farina v. State*, 2006; *People v. Jackson*, 1996; *People v. Lewis*, 2006; *Shell v. State*, 1989; *State v. Holden*, 1997). Some appeals in this category are direct biblical quotes, whereas others are biblical stories that prosecutors interpret to mean that the Bible supports the death penalty.

Some religious appeals compare defendants or their actions to biblical characters such as Satan (*Commonwealth v. Henry*, 1990; *Commonwealth v. Whitney*, 1986; *State v. Cauthern*, 1996; *Fahy v. Horn*, 2008), Judas Iscariot (*Cunningham v. Zant*, 1991; *State v. Phillips*, 1997), false prophets (*State v. Lundgren*, 1995), or Cain, who killed his brother Abel (*People v. Jackson*, 1996). Such appeals include the one by a lawyer who stated, "if there is a reprobate, profligate, and a representative of Satan who committed this act, the evidence in this case indicates that the representative of Satan in this case is seated right over there" and then motioned toward the defendant (*Fahy v. Horn*, 2008); another lawyer said, "How do you know that if you let him go this time it won't be done again? You know, Judas Iscariot was a good person, the most trusted of them all and you all know what he did" (*Cunningham v. Zant*, 1991). Such appeals compare the defendants to notorious biblical villains, suggesting that jurors should feel similarly toward the defendant as they do toward these infamous biblical characters.

The defendant or his crimes have been analogized, compared to, or contrasted with biblical figures and stories, such as Cain and Abel (*People v. Jackson*, 1996; *Shell v. State*, 1989), David and Goliath (*State v. Gentry*, 1995),[2] and the Apostle Peter (*United States v. Giry*, 1987).[3] One attorney told the jury the story about Jesus and the thieves:

> When Christ was crucified there were two thieves on each side of
> Christ, and they asked forgiveness. They asked what they should do,
> and he told them how . . . they could get forgiveness. They did that . . .
> and Christ said, 'You're forgiven.' And I think that [the defendant]
> can and probably has been forgiven. But Christ didn't take the thief
> off the tree. Christ let the thief pay for the crime that he committed,
> and I think that's important. (*Ward v. Dretke*, 2005, p. 494)

Similarly, the prosecutor in *State v. Haselden* (2003) used the same story to indicate that even Jesus supports the death penalty. He told the jurors that, when Jesus and two thieves were on their crosses, Jesus chose to let them die for their crimes, stating that "he had the power to take himself away from justice and get down off that cross. He had the power to take those two criminals down and put them on the ground and let them walk away, but he didn't did he? . . . he didn't take justice away from man. He didn't take them down off the cross." Such metaphors and comparisons to biblical characters inform jurors that the Bible supports capital punishment for individuals such as those in the Bible, and, by comparison, for the defendant.

Prosecutor Appeals: God Generally Supports the Death Penalty

Chavez and Miller (in press) also found another category of prosecutor appeal. This category includes a set of appeals that are not direct biblical quotes, but are statements suggesting that God sanctions or approves of the death penalty (e.g., *Manning v. State*, 2006). Such appeals include: "Nowhere between the first book of the Bible and the last book of the Bible is there any language against capital punishment, because that is a tool that God gave man in order to protect the public and give safety to the people in this world" (*Wilcher v. State*, 2003); "the Bible and the scriptures themselves are replete with those circumstances where capital punishment has been applied. It's applied in reference to both the Old Testament and the New Testament" (*Coe v. Bell*, 1998); and "they had the death penalty way back then. Also the death penalty isn't just an Old Testament or a New Testament [sic]. Both the Old Testament and New Testament are not against the death penalty. They do support it" (*People v. Bradford*, 1997). Although these examples do not use direct biblical quotes, they generally suggest that God or the Bible supports the death penalty.

Prosecution Appeals: Miscellaneous Arguments

Many prosecutors have offered biblical appeals that do not clearly fit into the categories just discussed (e.g., *Call v. Polk*, 2006; *State v. Roache*, 2004). Prosecutors have implied that jurors will someday have to answer to a higher power, implying that God may punish them if they do not give the death sentence (*Call v. Polk*, 2006); another told jurors to thank the Lord for their safety, their families' safety, and for the knowledge that they made the right decision by giving the death penalty (*State v. Roache*, 2004).

Some appeals have mentioned the religious implications of the jurors' verdicts or the religious implications for the victim of the crime. One such prosecutor suggested that jurors may help the defendant receive salvation by giving him a death sentence (*People v. Wrest*, 1992; *Sandoval v. Calderon*, 2000),[4] and others have argued that the victim was not allowed to reconcile with God or become all that God had planned because of the defendant's crime (*Commonwealth v. Brown*, 1998; *Eldred v. Commonwealth*, 1994).

Prosecutors often question whether the defendant's religious beliefs or religious conversion is sincere (*Commonwealth v. Cook*, 1996; *People v. Payton*, 1992; *Todd v. State*, 1991). One argument suggests to jurors that the defendant, who was the son of a pastor, should be held to a higher standard than the average person because he should have a good understanding of the Fifth Commandment, "thou shalt not kill" (*People v. Eckles*, 1980; *State v. Wangberg*, 1965). In such cases, the prosecutors use the defendants' religiosity against them. Similarly, the religious defendant in *Heglemeier v. State* (1994) brought a Bible to court. The prosecutor suggested to the jury that this act was merely a ploy to convince the jury he was a good Christian.[5]

Prosecutors deliver messages such as those discussed in this section to assure jurors that they are not offending God by sentencing the defendant to death. By using biblical analogies, quotes, or generalizations, prosecutors intend to increase the chances of securing a death penalty. Appeals are not limited to the prosecution, however; the next sections review various appeals used by defense attorneys.

Defense Appeals: Biblical Commands Forbidding the Death Penalty

Although prosecutors have utilized a variety of biblical appeals, so too have defense attorneys (e.g., *Commonwealth v. Cooper*, 2007; *Dycus v. State*, 2004; *Minor v. State*, 2004; *State v. Messiah*, 1988). Researchers have analyzed these appeals, creating several categories (e.g., Miller & Bornstein, 2006; Chavez & Miller, in press). The first category consists of direct biblical quotes that seemingly call for mercy or prohibit retribution.

One common biblical appeal offered by defense attorneys is given in response to the prosecutor's use of the "eye for an eye" argument. Defense attorneys counter with a quote from Jesus: "You have heard that it has been said 'an eye for an eye and a tooth for a tooth;' but I say to you, do not resist an evil doer. But if someone strikes you on the right cheek, turn the other also." The quote is said to be a command from Jesus to promote forgiveness and not retribution (e.g., *Bennett v. Angelone*, 1996; *Dycus v. State*, 2004; *State v. Messiah*, 1988). Other attorneys try to convince the jurors that life and death decisions belong to God, not to man, for instance, by quoting biblical passages such as "Vengeance is mine, thus sayeth the Lord" (e.g., *Bennett v. Angelone*, 1996; *Manning v. State*, 2004; *State v. Middlebrooks*, 1999).

Defense Appeals: Comparison to Biblical Characters or Stories

Like some prosecutors discussed earlier, some defense attorneys use appeals that rely on biblical characters or stories to illustrate their point (e.g., *Bennett v. Angelone*, 1996; *State v. Patterson*, 1996; *State v. Shafer*, 2000; *Wilcher v. State*, 2003). For instance, some prosecutors give examples of biblical characters who committed wrongdoings but were spared from death by God. The defense attorney in *Wilcher v. State* (2003) listed many such characters in this quotation:

> Adam and Eve in the Garden of Eden were told one thing not to do by God, one thing. In other words, the only crime they could have committed was to eat the forbidden fruit, and they did it. . . . What did God do? He didn't kill them. He didn't sentence them to die. He banished them. . . . King David [was] a murderer. . . . What did God do to King David? He subjected him to punishment of tribulations and inflictions, but he didn't kill him. Moses . . . What did God do to Moses? He didn't kill him. Paul, who formerly was Saul, a persecutor and killer of Christians, what did God do to Paul? He didn't kill him for what he did. He turned his life into the greatest missionary that the world has since known. (*Wilcher v. State*, 2003)

Some attorneys have told the biblical story of the brothers Cain and Abel to illustrate God's mercy. Although Cain killed Abel, God did not put him to death. Defense attorneys tell this story in an attempt to convince jurors to show the defendant mercy as God showed Cain mercy (*Commonwealth v. Daniels*, 1994; *People v. Bradford*, 1997; *People v. Zambrano*, 2007). Another story comes from the New Testament book of John, Chapter 8, which describes a woman who committed adultery. Instead of allowing her persecutors to execute her for her wrongdoing (which is the biblically mandated punishment), Jesus tells them, "He that is without sin among you, let him cast the first stone." This story illustrates that jurors should not execute the defendant for his wrongdoing, because all men have committed transgressions (e.g., *State v. Patterson*, 1996[6]; *State v. Shafer*, 2000). Other attorneys have told jurors the story of the crucifixion of Jesus, and then quote Jesus when he said, "Forgive them Father for they know not what they do." This story illustrates that Jesus promoted forgiveness for his killers, instead of asking God to condemn the men to death (e.g., *Bennett v. Angleone,* 1996; *Minor v. State,* 2004; *State v. Messiah,* 1988). Such examples and stories encourage jurors to be merciful, as are God and Jesus.

Defense Appeals: God Dislikes the Death Penalty

Chavez and Miller's (in press) analysis found another category of defense appeal. This category includes biblical appeals that are not direct quotes from the Bible but are general arguments that communicate to jurors that God, Jesus, or the Bible promote mercy or forbid retribution. The defense attorney in *Minor v. State* (2004) stated, "all of you are Christian and the thing about Christ is love. It's love. It's mercy. The highest standard there is, the highest level you can go to, the most Christ-like is mercy." By emphasizing that Jesus promotes mercy, and reminding jurors that they are followers of Jesus, he encourages them to show the defendant mercy.

Another defense attorney told jurors, "lots of people in the Bible disobeyed God and he punished [them] but not by death. . . . In every situation, God punished; but, not by death. Don't get me wrong. If [the prosecutor] comes up here and says I'm comparing [the defendant] to any of those people, I'm not. I am merely showing you by example what the greatest of all judges has done through history to people who have killed" (*Wilcher v. State,* 2003). Such statements are clearly aimed at persuading the jurors to spare the defendant by implying that God is merciful.

Finally, defense attorneys can try to convince jurors that God does not want people to show vengeance. One lawyer stated, "We do not apologize for asking for mercy, asking for leniency or sympathy. . . . Our life is given by our creator, and it is not to be taken lightly by man or our government using the guise of due process and the judicial system as a thinly veiled guise for vengeance" (*State v. Middlebrooks,* 1999). Suggestions such as these clearly suggest to jurors that they should show mercy because God generally disfavors the death penalty and vengeance.

Defense Appeals: Miscellaneous Arguments

In addition to these just described categories, there are some miscellaneous arguments defense attorneys have used. One popular tactic is to appeal to the jurors' own religiosity. One defense attorney encouraged jurors to seek Jesus in sinners (i.e., to see the goodness of a person as separate from her criminal act) as God and Jesus do, by stating, "I was trying to pick a jury of 12 Christs because I think all [of us] seek . . . to meet the Christ in other people" (*Melson v. State,* 1999). Taking a different approach, the defense attorney in *McNair v. State* (1992) told jurors that capital punishment violated Christian beliefs and warned jurors that they would suffer after their deaths if they imposed the death penalty.

Other attorneys utilize quasi-religious or philosophical arguments that appeal to jurors' good nature. Such quotes include, "[e]very philosophical tenet of faith that I'm familiar with, Christianity, Judaism, Buddhism, almost says the same thing. To err is human, to forgive divine. Man without mercy is not man at all" (*People v. Zambrano*, 2007). More specific arguments try to appeal to jurors' sense of responsibility or ethics by using statements such as "love your neighbor as yourself" (e.g., *State v. Daniels*, 1994) and "Judge not that ye be not judged" (*People v. Freeman*, 1994). Such statements come from the Bible generally, but they are also common phrases used in our culture and may not be universally thought of as biblical. Appeals can also communicate that religious authorities, such as the Pope, oppose capital punishment (*People v. Freeman*, 1994; *People v. Wash*, 1993); other appeals lead jurors to question their authority to give the death penalty. One defense attorney told jurors that they would be playing God if they chose the death penalty (*People v. Sandoval*, 1992).

As a whole, biblical appeals delivered both by the prosecution and the defense are intended to persuade the jury. It is interesting that both sides can provide quotes, stories, or other evidence to support their position. Even the same story (e.g., Jesus and the thieves on the cross) can be told to further either the prosecution's argument or the defense attorney's argument. It is therefore not surprising that biblical appeals have aroused much controversy; these debates are settled in the appellate court decisions discussed next.

Case Law Concerning Biblical Appeals

Since 1978, courts in 16 jurisdictions have issued rulings about the use of biblical appeals in closing arguments (Chavez & Miller, in press), including courts in 13 states, two circuit courts, and Puerto Rico. Some jurisdictions (e.g., Florida, Mississippi, Ohio) have consistently approved of biblical appeals, whereas a handful of others (e.g., Illinois, Texas) have consistently disapproved of biblical appeals. The majority of jurisdictions have issued both rulings that approve of, and rulings that disapprove of biblical appeals. Courts are clearly not in agreement about the permissibility of biblical appeals. This is often due to the large variety of appeals and the circumstances surrounding the appeal. For example, a court may approve of an appeal that it interprets as "weak" but disapprove of a "stronger" appeal; a court may also disapprove of a prosecutor's appeal unless the defense had also used an appeal. We summarize the various rulings here (see also Blume & Johnson, 2000; Chavez & Miller, in press; Duffy, 1997; Henson, 2001; Miller & Bornstein, 2005; Walker, 2003).

Court Rulings Regarding Religious Appeals by Prosecutors

Various courts have disapproved of prosecutors' biblical appeals (*Bennett v. Angelone*, 1996; *Commonwealth v. Brown*, 1998; *Commonwealth v. Cooper*, 2007;

People v. Wash, 1993; *State v. Cribbs*, 1998), making determinations such as, "[biblical] statements, worthy of the profoundest respect in proper contexts, have no place in our non-ecclesiastical courts and may not be tolerated there" (*Bennett v. Angelone*, 1996, p. 1346). On the other hand, some courts allow prosecutors to discuss issues that are not part of the evidence at trial if the discussion is "common knowledge or are illustrations drawn from common experience, history, or literature" (*People v. Sandoval*, 1992, p. 883). Although prosecutors are generally limited to discussing the evidence, the *Sandoval* court decided that it was allowable for a prosecutor to talk about religion even if it is not part of the evidence in the trial. As these examples illustrate, wide variation occurs in court rulings regarding the acceptability of appeals.

At one extreme, some courts are quite permissive, generally allowing any type of appeal. These courts have determined that biblical appeals are part of a prosecutor's "poetic license" or are generally within the allowable bounds of attorney arguments (*Bussard v. Lockhart*, 1994; *Commonwealth v. Henry*, 1990; *Commonwealth v. Whitney*, 1986; *People v. Lewis*, 2006; *United States v. Mitchell*, 2007). One court eloquently specified that:

> Counsel may draw upon literature, history, science, religion, and philosophy for material for his argument. He may navigate all rivers of modern literature or sail the seas of ancient learning; he may explore all the shores of thought and experience; he may, if he will, take the wings of the morning and fly not only to the uttermost parts of the sea but the uttermost limits of space in search of illustrations, similes, and metaphors. (*Shell v. State*, 1989, p. 899)

Another court agreed, further stating that "counsel are allowed wide latitude in arguing hotly contested cases" (*State v. Artis*, 1989, p. 496).

Some courts are not so permissive and only allow biblical appeals that follow certain guidelines. According to such courts, appeals must not be excessive or grossly improper (*People v. Lewis*, 2006; *State v. Debler*, 1993; *State v. Phillips*, 1997; *State v. Roache*, 2004); they must apply only to the character of the defendant (*Commonwealth v. Daniels*, 1994; *State v. Cauthern*, 1996); they must not evoke jurors' prejudice (*Cunningham v. Zant*, 1991); and they must not offend jurors so much that it leads to an unfair trial (*State v. Ramsey*, 1993).

At the other end of the spectrum, a few courts have forbidden all biblical appeals (e.g., *Commonwealth v. Cook*, 1996; *Commonwealth v. Cooper*, 2007; *Commonwealth v. Daniels*, 1994; *Sandoval v. Calderon*, 2000). For instance, in 1991, the Pennsylvania Supreme Court ruled that an appellate court could reverse any death sentence if the prosecutor quotes a religious teaching, stating that "reliance in any manner upon the Bible or any other religious writing in support of the imposition of a penalty of death is reversible error per se" (*Commonwealth v. Chambers*, 1991, p. 644).

Court Rulings Regarding Religious Appeals by Defense Attorneys

Even though not nearly as many rulings are made concerning the defense's use of religious appeals as are made for prosecution appeals (see Chavez & Miller, in press), a few courts have disapproved of defense appeals. The court in *Ice v. Commonwealth* (1984) determined that defense appeals make it likely that the jurors will follow biblical law rather than state law (see also *Commonwealth v. Daniels*, 1994). Reliance on biblical law that forbids the death penalty is problematic, because the state allows the penalty. Specifically, the *Ice* court said that "[t]he law specifies when the death penalty is appropriate . . . the defense counsel should [not] be permitted to adduce evidence as to how this case should be decided on religious grounds" (p. 676). The court further determined that defense appeals are not allowable because they distract jurors and prevent them from considering the evidence and following the law. In another case, the court determined that defense attorneys in some circumstances could present biblical appeals as mitigation evidence, but drew the line at "religious canons as a factor weighing against the death penalty" (*People v. Sandoval*, 1992).

As the previous two sections demonstrate, some controversy exists over the permissibility of biblical appeals. Along with the variety of rulings comes a number of reasons for these rulings, as discussed next.

Reasons Biblical Appeals Are Impermissible

A few courts have found that biblical appeals violate the Constitution, for instance, because they violate the Due Process clause of the Fifth and Fourteenth Amendments (e.g., *Bennett v. Angelone*, 1996), or the Eighth Amendment's prohibition on cruel and unusual punishment (e.g., *Sandoval v. Calderon*, 2000). The defendant in *Bennett v. Angelone* (1996) argued that the religious appeals were so inflammatory and irrelevant that they unfairly prejudiced the jury; thus, they violated the defendant's due process. The appellate court disagreed.

More frequently, courts rule that biblical appeals violate the Eighth Amendment. They commonly offer one of two (or sometimes both) explanations. The first way in which an appeal violates the Eighth Amendment (according to some courts) is by not allowing jurors to consider mitigating factors, as required by case law. Specifically, a state's sentencing rules must provide jurors with "channeled discretion" that will help them make the life or death decision (*Furman v. Georgia*, 1972; *Gregg v. Georgia*, 1976). Such rules prevent arbitrary and capricious death penalty sentencing verdicts. For instance, jurors should be given a list of aggravating factors and mitigating factors that they must "weigh" in their decision. Many biblical appeals do not encourage consideration of mitigating factors; for instance, the "eye for an eye" appeal suggests that *all* murderers must receive the death penalty.

As such, the appeal discourages consideration of mitigating factors and does not provide channeled discretion (*Carruthers v. State*, 2000; *Sandoval v. Calderon*, 2000; *State v. Barden*, 2002; *State v. Gell*, 2000).

The second way in which a biblical appeal potentially violates the Eighth Amendment is by diminishing jurors' sense of self-responsibility (e.g., *Carruthers v. State*, 2000; *People v. Wash*, 1993; *Sandoval v. Calderon*, 2000). Biblical appeals that seemingly require a certain verdict could lead jurors to believe that God or the Bible is responsible for the sentence. This is not allowable, according to Supreme Court case law (*Caldwell v. Mississippi*, 1985); jurors must realize that the responsibility for the death sentence is theirs alone.

In addition to these Eighth Amendment violations, biblical appeals are forbidden in some jurisdictions because they lead jurors to follow a law other than the state's law (*People v. Roldan*, 2005; *State v. Walters*, 2003; *Ward v. Dretke*, 2005), or they are impermissibly prejudicial or inflammatory (*Commonwealth v. Whitney*, 1986; *Todd v. State*, 1991; *Ward v. Dretke*, 2005). The court in *Jones v. Kemp* (1989) stated that biblical arguments "come from a source which would likely carry weight with laymen and influence their decision," and that "the effect may be highly prejudicial to the defendant . . . [and as a result] the confidence in the reliability of the jury's decision . . . may be undermined" (p. 1560).

In some circumstances, a court may find that the appeal used was improper, but ultimately did not affect the outcome of the trial. As a result, the court does not reverse the verdict or sentence (see Chavez & Miller, in press). Courts have allowed appeals for a variety of reasons, even though they were used improperly. First, an improper appeal by a prosecutor is often allowed if the defense also used a biblical appeal (e.g., *Boyd v. French*, 1998; *Call v. Polk*, 2006; *McNair v. State*, 1997; *People v. Hill*, 1992; *Thompson v. State*, 1991; *United States v. Mitchell*, 2007). One court stated that a prosecutor is "allowed to make comments in rebuttal that would otherwise be improper" (*People v. Sandoval*, 1992).

Second, some appellate courts have determined that certain biblical appeals are erroneous, but are ultimately allowed because they are "harmless error" (e.g., *People v. Sandoval*, 1992). According to *United States v. Hasting* (1983), it is the duty of the appellate court to consider the trial record and overlook any trial court errors that are harmless and did not result in a miscarriage of justice. As such, if the defendant cannot prove that the sentence he received resulted in prejudice, the judge will ignore the misdeed by the attorney. This decision making has come to be known as the "harmless error" test. In some cases, the court has determined that the weight of evidence against the defendant was so strong that the jury would most likely have come to the same decision even absent the appeal; thus, the appeal was "harmless error" (e.g., *Fahy v. Horn*, 2008; *People v. Lewis*, 2006; *People v. Viera*, 2005; *People v. Zambrano*, 2007).

Third, some improper appeals are allowed because the judge offered a curative instruction that directed the jurors to ignore the appeal (*Boyd v. State*, 2003; *People v. Wrest*, 1992). For instance, the appellate court in *Daniels v. State* (1994) determined that no harm was done because the trial judge "gave prompt curative instructions, thus removing any basis for a mistrial" (p. 557). Such courts assume that jurors who are instructed to ignore biblical appeals can and will do so; this presumably negates the improper impact of the appeal.

Fourth, some courts have determined that the length of the proceedings or the attorney arguments could dilute the effect of an erroneous appeal. In one case, a prosecutor gave a biblical appeal and then gave a "lengthy and detailed argument devoted exclusively to the evidence in aggravation" (*People v. Wash*, 1993, p. 1136). In this case, the appellate court determined that the appeal, even though it was improper, likely had little or no effect because the brief appeal was only a small portion of the full trial.

Fifth, an appeal is often allowed if the defendant did not object to its use at the time of trial. As a result, the defendant cannot object to the attorney's statement on appeal (e.g., *Hodges v. State*, 2005; *People v. Zambrano*, 2007; *State v. Berry*, 2004; *State v. Roache*, 2004). The appellate court in *People v. Lewis* (2006) determined that "Defendants did not object to the foregoing remarks on any ground at trial. Hence, they have forfeited their misconduct claims on appeal" (p. 842). Essentially, the appeal is allowed because of a technicality; thus, even if the appeal was improper, the court will allow it.

As these cases illustrate, even erroneous appeals are sometimes allowed. Thus, attorneys who make impermissible religious appeals often prevail, and the defendant rarely receives a new trial (Chavez & Miller, in press). Except in a few jurisdictions (e.g., *Sandoval v. Calderon*, 2000), typically no sanction is placed on the use of biblical appeals (Duffy, 1997; e.g., *Bennett v. Angelone*, 1996). One major exception is in Pennsylvania, where the courts have adopted a "per se reversible" rule (*Commonwealth v. Chambers*, 1991). Under this rule, all biblical appeals are forbidden, and attorneys who use biblical appeals may face disciplinary action. Other courts are more lenient and allow lawyers to use appeals with little threat of sanctions. Still other courts have not yet ruled on the permissibility of appeals, or else the case law in the jurisdiction is mixed. Lawyers in these jurisdictions cannot be certain whether they can use appeals or not. Nevertheless, no uniformity exists among judicial decisions.

Legal Scholarship Concerning Biblical Appeals

Several legal scholars have argued that appeals should be allowed, at least under some circumstances. Loewy (2000) proposes that both the prosecution and defense should be allowed to offer religious appeals during the death penalty phase, providing that the appeals are accompanied by judicial commentaries that the Bible is not the law. Blume and Johnson (2000) propose that religious comments by prosecutors should be limited, but defense counsel should be given wider latitude to address subject matter related to religion. This protects the defendant's rights by allowing him more freedom to present mitigating evidence. Such rules would consider the rights conferred by the Eighth Amendment's Cruel and Unusual Punishment Clause.

Brooks (1999) suggests that judges should be reluctant to restrict both prosecutors' and defense attorneys' remarks to juries just because those statements might reference or paraphrase theological ideology or because an illustration is drawn from a religious text. He claims that invoking a per se reversible error rule for all arguments that make reference to religious concepts is neither feasible nor proper use of a judge's authority. The author sets forth guidelines for determining which arguments should be permissible and which arguments should be considered prosecutorial misconduct. He proposes that determination of the propriety of religious statements should not be based on the religious origins of the argument, but instead, judges should compare religious arguments to other improper arguments to see if they rise to the same level of impropriety.

Scholars such as these are more permissive than others, who offer stricter rules concerning the admissibility of religious appeals. Some critics advocate the adoption of a reversible error rule, such as Pennsylvania's (Duffy, 1997; Walker, 2003). These scholars argue that the religious appeals violate the defendant's right to due process and the Establishment clause (Walker, 2003). To avoid prejudice and unfair trials, they argue that biblical appeals should be forbidden.

Other authors urge researchers to study the effects of appeals more thoroughly (Chavez & Miller, in press; Miller & Bornstein, 2006). Chavez and Miller investigated the frequency with which judges make decisions that are based on assumptions about jury decision making. For example, some appellate judges have found religious appeals to be improper, but still allow them because the judge issued a curative instruction that instructed jurors to ignore the appeal. Such judges assume that jurors can and will ignore the appeal. Chavez and Miller suggest that this may be an erroneous assumption because psychological research and theory suggest that jurors may be unable or unwilling to ignore this information and may actually pay more attention to forbidden information (e.g., Greene & Dodge, 1995; Steblay et al., 2006). The authors conclude that judges should consider psychological research when making such assumptions.

As this review indicates, courts and legal scholars are divided in their opinions about whether biblical appeals are allowable. Both judges and scholars make assumptions about the effects of biblical appeals, with many assuming that appeals will affect jurors' decisions.[7] Only limited research has investigated the impact of religious appeals on jurors' perceptions and verdicts.

Empirical Research Concerning Religious Appeals

Some research has investigated how individuals use the Bible to support their attitudes toward the death penalty (Cook & Powell, 2003). The earlier review of various types of religious appeals may make it seem as if the Bible gives sharply contrasting commands. In one breath, it tells people to give an "eye for an eye" but in the next breath to "turn the other cheek." Thus, a lawyer (or juror) could rely on the Bible either to support or oppose a death sentence. Cook and Powell (2003) interviewed 30 adults about their attitudes toward punishment. They identified four distinct "mentalities." The first was an anti-punitive mentality. These individuals subscribed to anti-government attitudes and did not believe in punishment because it is often unfairly meted out. The second was a nonpunitive mentality. These individuals typically advocated alternatives such as prevention, rehabilitation, or restitution. The third was a retributive mentality; such people viewed punishment as justice and sought equal harm for harm. The final mentality was a vengeful mentality, which supported magnification of punishment.

Participants in every mentality category relied on the Bible or their religious beliefs to support their attitude. Those with anti-punitive mentalities felt that religion was intruding on politics. Individuals with nonpunitive mentalities generally stated that God is forgiving and offers unconditional love. Further, forgiveness trumps retribution and vengeance. All six people with retributive mentalities quoted the "eye for an eye" doctrine. Those with vengeful mentalities tended to believe that all law should be based on a conservative interpretation of Christian scripture and that punishment should be harsh and swift. Thus, Cook and Powell found that all categories of punitive mentalities gave biblical or religious support for their positions. This research indicates that individuals do look to the Bible to support their attitudes toward punishment; thus, jurors might be influenced by biblical quotations. For instance, jurors with retributive mentalities would likely be swayed by a prosecutor who quoted the Bible.

Other research provides a more direct test of the effects of biblical appeals on jurors' decisions (Miller, 2006; Miller & Bornstein, 2006). Two mock juror experiments presented participants with trial summaries that included arguments made by the attorneys. Both studies used a condition in which participants read that the prosecutor quoted the Bible, for instance, telling jurors they should punish "an eye for an eye." Participants in the other conditions did not receive a biblical appeal from the prosecutor. Both studies revealed that appeals did not affect jurors' sentencing verdicts. The Miller and Bornstein (2006) experiment also manipulated whether the defense attorney used a biblical appeal for mercy. Interestingly, the defense attorney appeal seemed to backfire. Specifically, participants were most punitive when the defense attorney gave a biblical appeal. This was particularly true when participants were reading about a case with multiple mitigating factors present. Miller (2006) found that defense attorney appeals for mercy did not affect mock jurors' sentencing verdicts. As such, these two studies indicate that defense attorney appeals for mercy are ineffective and may even backfire; this may depend on the case facts, crime type, or type of appeal.

In addition to the concern over how appeals might affect verdicts, concern also exists that appeals might affect the jurors' ability to weigh aggravators and mitigators properly (e.g., *State v. Barden*, 2002). As noted earlier, jurors must be given "channeled discretion" when making their sentencing verdict in capital trials. One common practice is for the state to develop a statute that contains a list of aggravating factors and mitigating factors, which jurors must weigh. If the aggravators outweigh the mitigators (and are generally strong enough to warrant the death penalty), then jurors are to give the death sentence. Concern arises when an argument, such as a biblical appeal, interferes with the proper weighing of aggravators and mitigators. Miller and Bornstein (2006) found that some types of appeals did, in fact, make it difficult for participants to weigh aggravators and mitigators. Theoretically, mock jurors who read a trial with many aggravators and few mitigators should be more likely to give the death sentence, whereas mock jurors who read a trial with many mitigators and few aggravators should be more likely to give a life in prison sentence. This pattern was found for the control condition (i.e., the condition that contained no biblical appeal), but when the defense attorney quoted biblical scripture promoting mercy, participants did not weigh aggravators and mitigators properly. As such, some types of biblical appeals can affect the process of jury decision making, and to a lesser extent, affect jurors' verdicts.

Further, biblical appeals may encourage jurors to rely on religion in their decision making. There is mixed evidence for this. Miller (2006) conducted two studies (discussed earlier): One investigated the effects of religious appeals given by the prosecutor, and one investigated the effects of appeals given by the defense attorney. Mock jurors who read a trial containing a prosecutor's appeal did not rely on the Bible in reaching a verdict more than did those who did not receive an appeal. In contrast, the other study found that mock jurors who read a defense attorney's religious appeal did rely more on their personal religious beliefs and biblical authority, as compared to those who did not receive an appeal. Thus, some types of appeals may encourage jurors to rely on religious factors when making a decision.

Finally, the concern exists that appeals reduce the jurors' sense of personal responsibility (e.g., *Carruthers v. State*, 2000); however, there is no empirical support for this notion (Miller, 2006). Mock juror participants who heard biblical appeals did not have a reduced sense of responsibility as compared to those who did not hear an appeal.

Conclusion

As this discussion highlights, both prosecuting and defense attorneys have used biblical appeals. Some courts have accepted the use of appeals, whereas others have strictly limited or placed restrictions on their use. Some courts that forbid their use have determined that they violate the defendants' constitutional rights; other courts that allow their use have determined that they are as harmless as using references from literature. Clearly, no consensus exists among courts as to the permissibility of biblical appeals. Some scholars find that fact troublesome in and of itself. Montz (2001) proposed that state and federal courts need to unify their position regarding what is allowed and not allowed during closing arguments.

Legal scholars also do not agree on whether biblical appeals should be admissible. Studies that have investigated the use of biblical appeals have generally found that they are ineffective or may even backfire. Nevertheless, some appeals interfere with the *process* of decision making, which could affect the jurors' ability to make legally proper decisions. As this review of case law, legal scholarship, and research illustrates, biblical appeals are quite controversial and could negatively affect jurors' decisions.

9

Religious Figures and Institutions As Litigants

It was the seventh deadly sin. My children weren't righteous.
They stumbled because I was evil. The way I was raising them
they could never be saved. They were doomed to perish in the
fires of hell.

> —Andrea Yates, explaining why she drowned her five
> children (Roche, 2002)

When Nebraska state senator Ernie Chambers sued God (see Chapter 1), God did not appear in court. Nonetheless, religious figures and institutions do often find themselves in court, as regular media watchers can attest: "Omaha nun sentenced to prison" (2008), "Court: Exorcism is protected by law" (2008), "Texas evangelist cleared of assault" (2008), "Antigay church revels in trial publicity" (Hotakainen, 2007). These are just a few of the numerous recent headlines about court cases involving religious figures and institutions, and they omit the most widely publicized cases, namely, the Catholic Church sexual abuse scandal, which has resulted in thousands of lawsuits against priests. All of these cases involve different individuals or institutions, who (at least allegedly) committed very different offenses. What do trials of religious figures have in common?

We can divide legal disputes involving religious entities into four categories: First, there are cases in which religion is the central issue raised by a civil plaintiff. The legal issues in these cases typically revolve around First Amendment jurisprudence, as when a plaintiff alleges that government action has infringed upon her free exercise of religion (e.g., a prisoner suing for certain privileges in order to be able to practice his religion while incarcerated), or when a plaintiff alleges that the government is endorsing religion (e.g., in providing state aid to parochial schools). These cases involve the First Amendment's Free Exercise Clause, the Establishment Clause, or both.

In the second category of cases, the ultimate legal issue is a secular one, but the defendant raises religion as a defense. For example, a defendant charged with child neglect, for not allowing her sick child to receive medical care, might argue that her religious views preclude doing so. In such cases, even though the ultimate issue is not a religious one (e.g., did the defendant commit the crime of child neglect?), religion becomes a major, and often the primary, issue in the case.

In the third category of cases, religion likewise does not directly inform the central legal issue; in these cases, no "religious defense" is raised, but there are "religious overtones" in the sense that it is difficult, if not impossible, to consider the case without reference to a party's religious identity. This is the case in instances of alleged sexual abuse by clergy. One could argue that this sort of crime is particularly egregious when committed by clergy, and that the harm to victims is thereby greater, by virtue of the trust placed in them by their congregants; legally speaking, however, an abuse defendant's occupation is tangential to a determination of whether the alleged abuse actually occurred. Nonetheless, it is hard to imagine that the religious element would not be featured prominently at trial.

The fourth category includes cases in which a litigant's religious identity is largely, if not entirely, peripheral. Consider, for example, a rabbi who owns a few rental properties and goes to court to evict a troublesome tenant; a minister who runs a stop sign and hits another vehicle while driving home from work (or is hit by another car in a similar scenario); or a church sued because someone slips and falls on its allegedly inadequately maintained sidewalk. The list of these kinds of scenarios is endless, but the key point is that, although the religious element might make a litigant more or less sympathetic, likeable, or easy to identify with, it is utterly tangential to the facts of the case and is unlikely even to come up at trial.

The central question that this chapter addresses is whether litigants are treated differently by virtue of their religious identity. This necessarily entails a comparison of litigants in similar kinds of cases as a function of their religion (e.g., Catholics vs. Protestants, clergy vs. laypeople, etc.). Some, although not much, research has explicitly made such comparisons; where directly relevant research is lacking, we review other studies with implications for the question, such as research addressing legal defendants' occupation, status, or character.

The categories just described are not perfectly discrete and blur somewhat at the edges. Nonetheless, the categories provide a useful heuristic for discussing cases with religious litigants. So as not to become bogged down in First Amendment jurisprudence, we will largely avoid the first category of cases, in which the relationship between civil authority and an individual litigant's or institution's religious status is directly at issue. We make an exception to this rule in reviewing several studies that address how plaintiffs of various religious backgrounds fare when making free exercise claims. This chapter's primary focus is on the remaining three categories of cases. Thus, we explore whether religious figures are treated differently at trial from nonreligious figures in secular cases. For example, is religion a defense to charges of civil or criminal liability? Is a cult member accused of kidnapping treated differently from a non-cult kidnapper? Are harsher penalties imposed for embezzling from a church than for embezzling from a secular employer? Is a church involved in a property dispute treated differently from a secular corporation? Is a priest charged with sexual abuse treated differently from a layperson? How about a priest accused of vehicular negligence or battery in a bar fight? As litigants' religion is likely to interact with jurors' religion, we revisit some of the issues covered in Chapters 3 and 4 on the relationship between jurors' religion and their verdicts, and we conclude the chapter with a brief consideration of the role played by the victim's religion.

Litigants' Religion and Religious Liberties Cases

The earliest study to address the role of litigants' religion in First Amendment cases was done by Sorauf (1976).[1] In Sorauf's sample of church–state separation cases decided in American appellate courts between 1951 and 1971, half of the 48 nongovernmental plaintiffs were Protestant, and a large number of those were from traditionalist and fundamentalist denominations. Of the remainder, the largest number (22.9%) were atheists, nonbelievers, or unaffiliated. There were few Catholic (4.2%) or Jewish (6.3%) plaintiffs (the remaining cases had multiple plaintiffs of diverse religions or a secular corporate plaintiff). The large number of "unchurched" plaintiffs reflects the fact that "at the root of some of this litigation is a suspicion of or hostility to organized religion" (Sorauf, p. 145). In Sorauf's view, the large number of fundamentalist Protestants and scarcity of Catholics in the plaintiff sample reflects the general tendency toward separationism (i.e., supporting the separation between church and state) among the former and toward accommodationism (i.e., supporting limited government sanction of religion, as long as it does not favor one religion over others) among the latter. The low number of Jewish plaintiffs is somewhat surprising, given American Jewry's generally separationist views and the substantial role of Jewish attorneys in the cases (e.g., legal representation by the American Jewish Congress; see Chapter 7).

The defendant in these cases was almost always a governmental entity. Nonetheless, religious organizations became involved in many of the cases as *intervenor defendants* by convincing the court that their interests were unrepresented and would be directly affected by the outcome of the case (Sorauf, 1976). Intervenor defendants participate in the proceedings in several ways, such as by offering evidence and making motions. They also have the right of appeal, even if the principal defendant chooses not to appeal. More than half of the intervenors, and nearly all of those with a religious connection, were Catholic (e.g., parents of parochial school pupils). Just as with the small number of Catholic plaintiffs, Sorauf argues that Catholics' substantial involvement as intervenor defendants reflects American Catholics' propensity for accommodationism.

The course of the litigation differed somewhat depending on the plaintiff's religious background. For example, plaintiffs who originated the litigation tended to be less conventionally religious (i.e., fundamentalist Protestant or unchurched), whereas plaintiffs who were recruited after the decision to bring suit was made were more conventionally religious (i.e., high-status Protestant, Jewish, or Catholic). Perhaps the most important question, of course, is whether the outcome of the cases differed depending on plaintiffs' religion. Sorauf (1976) concluded that the final outcomes were not related to the nature of the parties, but he did not present specific data with regard to the parties' religion. Subsequent studies have addressed the outcome question, with some intriguing results.

For example, Way and Burt (1983) examined the universe of all reported state and federal cases involving the Free Exercise Clause from 1946 to 1956 ($N = 66$) and 1970 to 1980 ($N = 384$).[2] To explore case outcome as a function of religion, they categorized litigants as members of "marginal" versus "mainline" or "established" religions. Marginal religions were those that emphasized doctrinal purity and included groups such as Pentecostals, Jehovah's Witnesses, Seventh Day Adventists, and Muslims. For marginal religions:

> More than 50% of the litigation involving its members concerned:
> 1. Conflicts with authorities over public evangelism and proselytizing activities; 2. Challenges to secular laws or regulations based on religious beliefs, such as prohibition against war, blood transfusions, and Sabbath activity; work-related activity; dietary constraints; religious admonitions to engage in certain worship activities, such as the handling of snakes or use of sacramental drugs; and proscriptions and prescriptions concerning secular education. (Way & Burt, 1983, p. 654)

Approximately half of litigants (49%) who specified a religion were members of marginal faiths. As this figure is substantially higher than their proportion in the U.S. population at large, it suggests that marginal religious groups are especially zealous in pursuing religious liberty claims. Established religions, on the other hand, were the more highly acculturated, "mainline" Protestant churches (i.e., Methodists, Episcopalians, Baptists, Unitarians, Lutherans, and Presbyterians; they also included Mormons [members of the Church of Latter Day Saints] in this category), Catholicism, and Judaism.

Way and Burt found that the percentage of successfully litigated claims increased from the first (12.1%) to the second period (36.9%) and, more relevant to the present discussion, that some religious groups were more successful than others. For the more populous 1970–1980 period, claimants from marginal faiths won 55% of the cases decided on the merits, compared to a success rate of 41% for Jewish claimants and 33–34% for mainline Protestants and Roman Catholics. Their explanation of these findings is that the very characteristics of marginal religions—namely, an emphasis on doctrinal purity and strict codes of behavior—predispose them to successful free exercise claims. Those characteristics make it relatively easy for claimants to demonstrate that a challenged law or regulation imposes a significant burden on their religion. Such a demonstration is necessarily more difficult for members of more established and acculturated religions, who would have a harder time demonstrating such a burden by virtue of their acculturation.

Subsequent studies have replicated Way and Burt's (1983) findings. For example, Ignagni (1993) conducted a more intensive analysis of U.S. Supreme Court jurisprudence in free exercise cases and likewise found that the Court sided more often with claimants from marginal religious groups. Conversely, in their study of federal judges' decision making in religious freedom cases, Sisk and colleagues (2004) found that Catholic and Baptist free exercise claimants were significantly *less* likely than other groups to succeed.[3] This result essentially mirrors Way and Burt's (1993) major finding: Claimants from marginal religions have an advantage in free exercise litigation, whereas claimants from widespread, mainstream denominations—such as Catholics and Baptists—are at a comparative disadvantage. Sisk and colleagues echo Way and Burt's conclusion in arguing that it is harder for religious groups that are acculturated into American society to prove that a law is burdensome; and they propose further that the relatively poor showing by Catholic and Baptist claimants might reflect a general distrust by courts of groups adhering to traditional or conservative social values and moral principles. Consistent with this interpretation, they also found weak evidence—manifest in some analyses but not others—that Muslim claimants fared poorly in free exercise cases.[4]

Finally, some evidence suggests that marginal religious status matters in both Free Exercise and Establishment Clause cases (e.g., Ignagni, 1993). There are numerous cases of claimants from marginal religions who have prevailed on establishment grounds, such as the Wiccan plaintiff who objected to her Missouri town's use of a fish symbol, commonly associated with Christianity, on the city seal (Paxton, 2004). Overall, then, it appears that for the first category of cases—those that are explicitly about religion and that invoke the First Amendment's religion clauses—litigants from mainstream religions fare relatively poorly, whereas members of religions on the periphery of the religious spectrum tend to do better than average.

Religion As a Defense

In the second category of cases, a civil or criminal defendant uses religion as a defense against some allegation. Religious individuals and institutions often raise church–state separation as a defense against an ordinary civil action. For example, a church might dispute liability for injuries incurred during a worship service or sanctioned church activity, or resulting from church-decreed "shunning"[5]; or an individual might resist compelled medical treatment on religious grounds. On the criminal side, individuals may use religion as a defense to prevent conviction or to mitigate punishment if they are convicted. In all instances in which religion is used as a defense, the case necessarily becomes "about" a defendant's religion, at least to some extent. Consequently, these cases can also (but do not necessarily) have constitutional elements.

Civil Cases

Exorcism, Shunning, and Funeral Protests: Religious Organizations As Tort Defendants

In a variety of tort cases, religious figures and institutions have invoked their religious status as a defense against liability for damages. For example, in a recent Texas case, a 17-year-old girl named Laura Schubert sought compensation for injuries suffered in an exorcism conducted during a church youth group meeting (*Pleasant Glade Assembly of God v. Schubert*, 2008; see also "Court: Exorcism is protected by law," 2008). The girl testified that she was cut and bruised during the exorcism, which caused subsequent psychological problems, including a suicide attempt. She and her parents sued the church, the senior pastor, the youth minister, and several church members. They alleged negligence, intentional infliction of emotional distress, child abuse, assault, and false imprisonment, of which only the claims of assault and false imprisonment went to trial. A jury awarded her $300,000 for her pain and suffering, lost earning capacity, and medical expenses, but the Texas Court of Appeals reduced the award to $188,000 (eliminating the damages for lost earning capacity), and the Texas Supreme Court threw out the award altogether. In doing so, the court relied on the First Amendment's Free Exercise Clause. The Texas Supreme Court held, in essence, that the church's free exercise of religion precluded its being held liable for the plaintiff's emotional injuries.[6] Exorcism is, by definition, a religious activity; but abuse, false imprisonment, and intentional infliction of emotional distress are not. Religion was not a critical issue at trial, but it was in the Texas Supreme Court's review of the case ("Court: Exorcism is protected by law," 2008). That court dismissed the case because it "presents an ecclesiastical dispute over religious conduct that would unconstitutionally entangle the court in matters of church doctrine" (*Pleasant Glade v. Schubert*, 2008, p. 1).

Tort claims have also been filed against churches for injuries due to shunning, a practice engaged in by a number of American religious denominations, such as the Reformed Mennonite Church, the Amish, and Jehovah's Witnesses (Merkin, 2001). Shunning can cause plaintiffs a variety of noneconomic (e.g., emotional distress, loss of consortium) as well as economic (e.g., lost business earnings) injuries. Churches sued for shunning-related injuries typically invoke the Free Exercise Clause as a shield against liability; some courts have accepted this argument, but others have not (Merkin, 2001).

In another recent and highly publicized case, the family of Matthew Snyder, a U.S. Marine who was killed in Iraq, sued the family of Fred Phelps and the Phelps-led Westboro Baptist Church. The antigay church picketed Snyder's funeral as a means of airing its message that soldiers' deaths are divine retribution for America's tolerance of homosexuality. The church claims to have staged thousands of such protests, with signs carrying messages such as "Thank God for Dead Soldiers," "No Fags in Heaven," and "God Hates Fags," at funerals of soldiers, gays, and even child murder and accident victims.[7] The Snyder lawsuit, the first to be brought against the group for its funeral protests, sought damages for invasion of privacy and intentional infliction of emotional distress. Phelps' defense relied on his rights to free expression of his religion and free speech. In October 2007, a federal jury in Baltimore, Maryland ordered the defendants to pay $2.9 million in compensatory damages and $8 million in punitive damages. The judge subsequently reduced the punitive award to $2.1 million, for a total award of $5 million; Phelps and the church have filed an appeal.

Withholding Medical Treatment on Religious Grounds

Probably the best-known, and most frequently litigated, exemplar of these "religious defense" cases are those involving adherents of certain religions, such as Jehovah's Witnesses or Christian Scientists, who have relied on the Free Exercise Clause in withholding medical treatment from their children.[8] These cases span both civil and criminal law, as government agencies have sought to mandate treatment against the parents' wishes, and the parents have been prosecuted under child neglect and related statutes, and even for manslaughter (Bullis, 1991; Merrick, 1994; Richardson & DeWitt, 1992). In these kinds of civil cases, the reasonableness of a person's conduct (whether plaintiff or defendant) could be viewed differently depending on the person's religion (e.g., Jehovah's Witnesses). Members of minority religions would arguably be disadvantaged at trial when judged according to the reasonableness standards of the majority.

The First Amendment's right to the free exercise of religion is not absolute and can be overridden to protect a child (Bullis, 1991; Merrick, 1994; Richardson & DeWitt, 1992). For example, in *State v. Norman* (1991), a father refused traditional medical treatment for his son's diabetes in favor of spiritual healing. The court held that the father's religious liberty rights did not allow him to put his child's life in danger. On the other hand, some courts have found that parents have immunity from criminal prosecution if their refusal is based on religious beliefs (*Bradley v. State*, 1920; *In Re Hudson*, 1942; *State v. Lockhart*, 1983). In such cases, the state's compelling interest in the health and welfare of its children is weighed against the parents' religious rights. The trend nationally, through both legislation and case law, is toward limiting the spiritual healing exemption (Bullis, 1991).

The issue can arise even before the child is born. There are a number of cases in which women have refused to undergo cesarean sections (C-sections) based on their religious beliefs, even though, in medical experts' judgment, a C-section would be better for the fetus. Typically, courts weigh the rights of the mother against those of the fetus or the state. The outcomes of such cases vary. Some courts have accepted a religious justification for refusal of a C-section to save a fetus, even if it results in harm to the fetus (e.g., *In re Baby Boy Doe*, 1994), but others have not (e.g., *In re Jamaica Hospital*, 1985; *Jefferson v. Griffin Spalding County Hospital*, 1981; *State v. Norman*, 1991), effectively compelling the women to have the procedure against their wishes and without their consent. In the latter cases, courts have held that the state had a compelling interest in a fetus and that the fetus's right to life outweighed the mother's wishes (e.g., *Jefferson v. Griffin Spalding County Hospital*, 1981).

Other prenatal cases involve blood transfusions. For example, Darlene Brown was undergoing a medical procedure unrelated to her pregnancy. During the procedure, she lost more blood than anticipated, and doctors asked her to permit a blood transfusion, which she refused because she was a Jehovah's Witness. Doctors continued surgery without the transfusion, but later they requested one again because of the life-threatening risk to Brown and her fetus (medical opinion was that they both had only a 5% chance of surviving without a transfusion). The court appointed the hospital administrator as temporary custodian of the fetus, giving the administrator the right to consent to a transfusion. Brown had the transfusion, still without her consent, and gave birth to a healthy baby (*In re Brown*, 1997).

Jehovah's Witnesses' reluctance to use conventional medical treatments can affect their standing as civil plaintiffs, and not just as defendants (Parobek, 2006–2007; Ramsay, 2007). Consider, for example, an automobile accident in which the non-negligent driver receives injuries that are treatable but require a blood transfusion. The driver refuses the transfusion on religious grounds and dies; her family then sues the negligent driver for damages. Should the defendant be liable for all of the injuries that ultimately ensued, or only for those that would have resulted under the "best-case" scenario (i.e., if the plaintiff had availed herself of the best possible treatment)?

Ordinarily, plaintiffs can recover damages if a pre-existing condition makes them particularly vulnerable to injury. For example, if the automobile driver had a pre-existing heart condition before the accident, and the wreck precipitated a fatal heart attack, then she could recover damages for the heart attack, even though the accident would not have caused a heart attack in most drivers (this is known colloquially as the "eggshell" or "thin-skull" doctrine). Courts typically consider pre-existing conditions to be physical maladies, but they can be mental conditions as well (e.g., schizophrenia, posttraumatic stress disorder, depression; Parobek, 2006–2007). Nonetheless, plaintiffs are required to do what they can to minimize an injury's effects: "One injured by the tort of another is not entitled to recover damages for any harm that he could have avoided by the use of reasonable effort or expenditure after the commission of the tort" (Restatement [Second] of Torts § 918; American

Law Institute, 2000). The premise underlying this "mitigation of damages" doctrine is that it prevents waste, in the form of unnecessary and superfluous injury (Parobek, 2006–2007). A plaintiff is required to act "reasonably" in mitigating damages, and judges and jurors—especially those from different religious backgrounds—might find a Jehovah's Witness's refusal to accept a blood transfusion unreasonable.

Indeed, the evidence suggests that they do. Courts have generally been reluctant to apply the pre-existing condition doctrine to a plaintiff's religious beliefs (Parobek, 2006–2007). Parobek argues, however, that courts should apply the doctrine of pre-existing conditions to religious beliefs (see Ramsay, 2007, for a similar analysis based on Canadian law). The rationale for this argument is that an injured plaintiff in this kind of case is not purposefully failing to receive medical treatment just to reap a larger damage award, but is merely exercising a sincere religious belief that constitutes her "prior state," in the same way that a physical ailment or predisposition would. The plaintiff cannot be made whole—restored to her pre-accident state—if doing so would force her to relinquish part of what made her whole in the first place (i.e., her religious beliefs). Our injured car driver is in the untenable position of having to choose between knowing that she has violated her religious beliefs or dying because of those beliefs (Parobek, 2006–2007), placing her in a more difficult position than a routine tort plaintiff.

Criminal Cases

In criminal cases, a religious defense can take different forms. In some cases, defendants invoke the First Amendment's Free Exercise Clause in arguing that their religion entitles them to engage in some action, such as drug use, that the state deems criminal. In other cases, defendants argue that their religious beliefs diminish their culpability because the beliefs justify or excuse their criminal behavior.

Drugs and Devils: The Free Exercise Defense to Criminal Charges

Just as with civil offenses, some defendants have used the First Amendment's Free Exercise Clause as a defense to crimes. The most recognized example is drug use or possession, especially the religious use of peyote (other cases have involved marijuana use). Peyote is a cactus found in the southwestern United States and Mexico that can be harvested and used as a psychedelic drug. Some Native American tribes have used it in ceremonial rituals for thousands of years, but because it is considered a controlled substance, individuals have been prosecuted for its religious use. Defendants have challenged such prosecutions on free exercise grounds, but the U.S. Supreme Court has ruled that the religious use of peyote by Native Americans is not constitutionally protected (*Employment Division v. Smith*, 1990).[9] Congress subsequently passed a law (42 USC §1996a) protecting the possession and use of peyote as part of a Native American religious ceremony. Many states have similar laws that provide exemptions for religious use.

Members of other religions have, in some cases, also been allowed to claim a religious exemption for drug use. In *United States v. Bauer* (1996), the defendants were Rastafarians who were arrested for marijuana use. The trial court did not allow the defendants to use their religion as a defense. The Ninth Circuit Court of Appeals indicated that Rastafarianism is a recognized religion that started in Jamaica in the 19th century and has some followers in the United States. Thus, the defendants were given another trial and were allowed to use their religion as a defense, although they would have to prove that they were, in fact, Rastafarians.

Defendants adhering to other religions have not fared so well. In 2005, Daniel Hardesty was arrested for possession of marijuana. He claimed he was a member of the Church of Cognizance (coc.enlightener.net), which uses marijuana as an essential part of its practices. He was convicted and, on appeal, argued that he had the right to use the drug under the First Amendment's Free Exercise Clause. The Arizona Court of Appeals determined that there is no religious right to possess marijuana. The court held, further, that the First Amendment provides the right to hold religious beliefs, but it does not provide the right to practice those beliefs. Because the drug poses a threat to public health and safety, the government had the right to ban the drug completely (*Arizona v. Hardesty*, 2008; Fischer, 2008). The court accepted that Hardesty's religious beliefs were sincere; however, it is still noteworthy that he did not belong to an established, mainstream religion (even compared to Native American religions and Rastafarianism). Thus, the success of the free exercise defense in drug cases might depend on both the defendant's religion and the drug involved (i.e., peyote vs. marijuana).

Failed exorcisms have resulted in criminal charges as well as civil actions like the one discussed earlier.[10] For example, Ray Hemphill, pastor of the Faith Temple Church of the Apostolic Faith in Milwaukee, was tried for child abuse in the death of 8-year-old Terrance Cottrell Jr., who died after Hemphill sat on his chest, for hours at a time, while performing an exorcism (Reynolds, 2004). In such cases, the defense is typically that the defendant was performing a religious ritual, as guaranteed by the First Amendment, and that any harm was inadvertent (the lack of intent is why Hemphill was charged with child abuse, rather than murder, and sentenced to only 2½ years in prison; Reynolds, 2004). Similarly, polygamists have invoked First Amendment protection against prosecution for multiple marriage or related offenses.[11] Courts have generally not allowed religion as an exculpatory defense against criminal charges for exorcism injuries or polygamy (e.g., Hamilton, 2004), but the relatively light sentences incurred by many perpetrators suggest that judges and juries might nonetheless be taking the religious element into account.[12]

Causing Harm in God's Name: Religion As Justification or Excuse

Defendants in several high-profile cases have used a slightly different religious defense, arguing essentially that "God told me to do it." In addition to religious freedom as guaranteed by the First Amendment, the criminal defenses most relevant to religion are justifications and excuses (see, generally, Dressler, 2007; Fukuno & Ohbuchi, 1998; Gonzales, Haugen, & Manning, 1994; Schopp, 1993). People who offer justifications admit to engaging in conduct that fulfills the material elements of a criminal defense, but they redefine the behavior as acceptable under the circumstances because it prevents an even greater harm (Schopp, 1993). For example, one might be justified in shooting an armed robber to prevent him from harming others. Thus, justification involves an acceptance of responsibility for the behavior but refutes its negativity. Individuals who have killed doctors who performed abortions, or who have destroyed abortion clinics, have used this kind of reasoning. In one such case, Reverend Paul Hill, in 1994, murdered Dr. John Britton, an abortion provider, and his bodyguard. Hill said that he had committed the crime to prevent an even greater harm, namely, the future deaths of the unborn (Dawkins, 2006).[13]

Excuses also admit commission of the wrongful act, but not in furtherance of some greater good; moreover, they minimize accountability because of some uncontrollable, unanticipated, or external cause. Excuses exempt the defendant from punishment due to some disability, but they do not designate the defendant's conduct as acceptable under the circumstances (Schopp, 1993). Excuses involve admitting that the behavior is inappropriate, bad, or wrong, but the actor denies full responsibility for the behavior, and hence culpability, as when the behavior results from mental impairment.

There are a couple of additional ways in which justifications and excuses usually differ. First, a justification would apply to anyone who performed the same conduct in the same circumstances. Excuses, in contrast, are specific to individual defendants because they exculpate these individuals for their criminal conduct due to particular disabilities they have, such as psychological disorder (Schopp, 1993). Second, and relatedly, a justification is based on an individual's *acts*, whereas an excuse is based on some characteristic of the *actor*. Although these factors generally distinguish between the two categories of defenses, the line blurs in some cases.

Consider, for example, someone like Andrea Yates, who drowned her five children because she believed that Satan was inside her. She killed the children to save them from hell, and to punish herself for being a bad mother ("Yates found guilty," 2002; Roche, 2002; Russell, 2004). In her mind, the killings were justified, because they prevented an even greater harm and served a higher, divine purpose; but because the circumstances of the crimes lacked an objective basis and would not justify someone else's killing Yates' children, her mental state comes into question, leading to the excuse of insanity, which was her main defense.[14] In 2002, Yates was unsuccessful at convincing a jury that she was insane. She obtained a retrial in 2006, on grounds unrelated to her religious excuse defense, and was found not guilty by reason of insanity ("Jury finds Yates not guilty," 2006).

The case of Ron and Dan Lafferty is similar. The Laffertys were Mormon fundamentalists who brutally stabbed to death their sister-in-law and her child. They testified that they committed the crimes because Ron had received a "removal revelation" in which God commanded him to "remove" the victims (as well as two others, who fortuitously escaped). They therefore argued that their actions were justified because they were doing God's will; but because of the irrationality of their beliefs, they raised an insanity defense as well (Krakauer, 2003; *State v. Lafferty*, 2001). Neither the justification nor the excuse succeeded, and they were both convicted (in Ron's case, in two separate trials). More recently, an adult education student in Michigan was charged with assault and battery after he tossed liquid on a teacher. He believed she was a witch in need of purification, and he intended to burn her ("Police: Teacher attacked over witch claim," 2008). Several other defendants have recently claimed that they committed their crime because they experienced hallucinations involving instructions from God. In these cases, the justification component is the argument that the harm—to the perpetrator, the victim, or society at large—from disobeying God's command would outweigh the harm from committing the crime, so that the crime was the right or sensible thing to do.

The excuse component, which is more common and on stronger legal ground, is the argument that the defendant's mental state—experiencing divine hallucinations—makes him not responsible for his deed. In such cases, religion can be offered as evidence that a defendant was insane or is mentally incompetent. A unique legal challenge occurs when the mentally ill defendant knows what he did was wrong (or illegal) but asserts that he did it anyway, because God commanded him to commit the act. In these instances, the religious excuse can be used as an exception to the legal insanity rule, which in most jurisdictions requires (often among other criteria) that defendants not appreciate the wrongfulness of their actions. Under the *deific decree* defense, "a defendant may be adjudicated insane *even if the defendant knew that the act was illegal* . . . but, due to a mental disease or defect, believed that God had ordained the act" (*People v. Serravo*, 1992, p. 130; italics added). Thus, the excuse can work, even though it does not technically satisfy insanity criteria.

As the Yates and Lafferty cases illustrate, the "religious excuse" defense has had mixed success. In January 2007, Lashuan Harris was convicted of assault (but found not guilty by reason of insanity on the three second-degree murder charges) after she threw her three children into the San Francisco Bay ("Oakland mother convicted," 2007). Harris claimed she was obeying God's command to make a human sacrifice and was sending her children to heaven (Burt, 2006). In contrast, Deanna Laney was successful in convincing the jury that she was insane when she followed God's orders to stone her sons to death in 2003 (Springer, 2004). The next year, Dena Schlosser cut off her daughter's arms in an attempt to "give her child to God." Schlosser was found incompetent to stand trial ("Severed-arm baby mom," 2005). Brian David Mitchell was also found mentally incompetent to stand trial, in his case for the kidnapping of Elizabeth Smart ("Smart's accused kidnapper ruled incompetent," 2005). During several hearings in 2005, Mitchell was removed from the courtroom because he continually sang hymns and yelled religious proclamations such as "Awaken, arise Israel. Come forth, Babylon. Repent, repent for the kingdom."[15]

As these cases suggest, juries do not invariably buy into religious excuses. A recent study by Miller and Dolson (in press) supports this skeptical view. They found that whether a defendant is considered to be insane may depend on the type of hallucination; specifically, it might depend on the entity that orders the defendant to commit the crime. Participants rated the likelihood that a criminal was insane based on whether God, the president, or a dog commanded him to perform the crime (Miller & Dolson, in press). Within-participant analyses demonstrated that a criminal who committed a killing spree or robbed a bank was more likely to be considered sane when he followed orders from either God or the president (as compared to a dog). However, an individual who vandalized a church was more likely to be deemed sane when he followed orders from God as compared to either the president or a dog. Thus, hallucinations containing orders from God are less likely to indicate insanity, despite the deific decree exception.

Religious Conversion As a Mitigating Factor

In some cases, a criminal defendant introduces evidence of religiosity or a religious conversion as mitigating evidence at trial, especially during the sentencing phase (for review, see Loewy, 2000; Miller et al., 2007). Although factors that can aggravate (i.e., enhance) a sentence are limited by statute, courts generally allow unlimited evidence of mitigation.[16] Defendants introduce religion as a mitigating factor either through their own testimony or through other witnesses (e.g., prison ministers, inmates, family, or prison employees) who testify as to their religious character or religious activities, such as establishing a prison ministry or writing Christian books (*Brown v. Payton*, 2005; *Miniel v. Cockrell*, 2003).[17] Such evidence is designed to suggest to jurors that the defendants are, or have become (post-conviction), religious and moral individuals who deserve mercy (*Boyd v. French*, 1998; *Brown v. Payton*, 2005; *Commonwealth v. Cook*, 1996; *Commonwealth v. Daniels*, 1994; *Crowe v. State*, 1995; *Ice v. Commonwealth*, 1984; *People v. Clark*, 1993; *People v. Payton*, 1992; *Robinson v. State*, 1995; see generally Skaf, 2008).

Such religious evidence is generally allowed by courts as evidence of the defendant's character (*Commonwealth v. Daniels*, 1994), in keeping with the Supreme Court's ruling that the defendant has a right to introduce evidence of his character that could be considered mitigating evidence (*Lockett v. Ohio*, 1978; Skaf, 2008). For example, Justice Sandra Day O'Connor stated that the defendant's "religious devotion might demonstrate positive character traits that might mitigate against the death penalty" (concurring, *Franklin v. Lynaugh*, 1988, p. 186). The Federal Death Penalty Act has been understood not to allow religion per se to be offered as a mitigator, but the effects and experiences of religion on a defendant's character, such as the effects of religious discrimination, would be admissible (18 U.S.C. §§ 3591–3598; see, e.g., *United States v. Gooch*, 2006; *United States v. Webster*, 1998).

Perhaps the best-known religious conversion case is that of Oklahoma City bombing accomplice Terry Nichols. During the sentencing phase of Nichols' trial, the jury became aware, through others' testimony and his attorney's oral argument, that Nichols had converted to Christianity while in prison. During deliberation, the jury deadlocked; some of the jurors indicated that they were unwilling to give the death penalty because they felt his conversion was evidence that he did not deserve to be put to death ("Juror: Sympathy spared Nichols," 2004). Defendants who convert are not always spared, however. Carla Faye Tucker was on death row for 14 years in Texas. Many religious figures appealed on her behalf, arguing that she not be executed because of her religious conversion while in prison. Courts, the Texas Board of Pardons and Parole, and then-Governor George W. Bush were unsympathetic—perhaps because they doubted the sincerity of her death row conversion—and she was executed on February 3, 1998.

An experiment conducted by Miller and Bornstein (2006) found that mock jurors were less punitive (i.e., less likely to sentence a capital defendant to death) toward a defendant who had converted to Christianity than toward a defendant who did not convert.[18] This study provides some evidence that a religious conversion can lead to more lenient verdicts in death penalty cases. Much like the Terry Nichols jurors, the mock jurors in this experiment might have felt that the conversion showed the defendant had changed his evil ways and was now able to be a better member of society (albeit prison society). In contrast, evidence that the defendant had "always been a Christian" did not lead jurors to be as lenient (Miller & Bornstein, 2006). Perhaps mock jurors felt that a lifelong Christian would have refrained from killing in the first place.

A jailhouse conversion can become evidence not only at trial, but also at a convict's parole board hearing. Are born-again convicts more likely to be released on parole? Miller, Lindsey, and Shamblin (2008) found that parole board members and mock (student) parole board members were not more lenient toward born-again Christian prisoners. Participants read that, while in prison, the prisoner had experienced no change (control condition), had converted to Christianity, had converted to Islam, or had read self-help books (a nonreligious life change). Results indicated that the person who had experienced a nonreligious life change was significantly more likely to be paroled than any of the other groups, which did not differ from one another. Further, the nonreligious life change was seen as more believable than the other conversion types. Perhaps these participants were skeptical and believed that the prisoner was only claiming to have adopted a religion in order to be released from prison. The results suggest that the influence of a religious conversion varies depending on the nature of the decision (i.e., a jury choosing between different sentences versus a parole board choosing between parole and continued incarceration).

Evidence of a defendant's religiosity can also be brought to bear less directly, in the defendant's public statements or behavior. For example, a defendant might display his religious devotion by bringing a Bible to court every day (*Heglemeier v. State*, 1994). Jayson Williams, a former National Basketball Association player who was tried on multiple charges, including reckless manslaughter and witness tampering (Ryan, 2004), wore a cross on his suit jacket while in court. Williams was acquitted of the most serious charges, and jurors deadlocked on the reckless manslaughter charge.

Defendants in several highly publicized cases have bruited their newfound religion in the media, presumably (at least according to cynics) in an attempt to lessen their punishment. Michael Vick, the Atlanta Falcons football player who pleaded guilty in 2007 to dogfighting charges, stated "I'm upset with myself, and, you know, through this situation I found Jesus and asked him for forgiveness and turned my life over to God" (Capehart, 2007). Some skeptics believed it was a ploy to keep fans and to receive a lighter sentence (Capehart, 2007). His sentence was in the mid-range of federal sentencing guidelines. In 2005, Richard Scrushy was accused of a $2.7 million conspiracy to defraud a chain of hospitals he founded decades before. In the months before his trial, Scrushy began visiting and donating money to local churches, and he appeared on his own Christian television program. Skeptics saw his sudden interest in religion as a tactic to sway potential jurors (Romero, 2005). If so, the tactic apparently worked, as Scrushy was acquitted.

The key question in these "religious mitigation" cases (apart from the question of whether it works) is: What message are defendants trying to send? What do they hope jurors will infer? There seem to be several possibilities: (a) My newfound religion makes my previous actions (from before I found God) less bad, and therefore less deserving of punishment; (b) My newfound religion makes me appear (at present) less bad, more sincerely remorseful, and so on, and therefore less deserving of punishment; (c) Punish me less so that I can do something good with my life (e.g., prison ministry, charitable works); (d) Like me better and take it easy on me (the cynical alternative). The first message would change factfinders' inferences about the nature of the defendant's prior (criminal) behavior, whereas the other three would produce inferences about the defendant's present and future situation. Any of these interpretations could make a defendant advocating religious mitigation appear more sympathetic, especially compared to someone who claimed to be religious all along—for if that person was so religious, then why did he commit the crime in the first place?

Thus, letting the public (prior to trial) or courtroom decision makers (judge or jury) know you are religious can encourage a diminished perception of the defendant's culpability, leading to greater mercy. Although anecdotal evidence suggests that presenting religious evidence such as one's religious convictions or conversion may help get an acquittal or lighter sentence in some cases, there is just as much evidence, if not more, that it fails to have the desired effect (Skaf, 2008).

Moreover, religiosity of the defendant is not always a positive thing, depending on the type of religion the defendant practices. If he is or has become Christian, jurors—most of whom are probably Christian themselves—may be more lenient, believing that he is less deserving of punishment.[19] However, if he has converted to a religion that jurors disapprove of, jurors may react negatively and be more likely to convict or give harsher sentences. Skaf (2008) concluded that using a defendant's Christian beliefs as mitigation might be generally unsuccessful, but using a defendant's Muslim conversion is even more so.

Religion As a Negative Factor

Depending on the religion, prosecutors might also use a defendant's religion to impute negative character traits to the defendant and to convince the jury or judge that the defendant is guilty or deserving of a more severe sentence (Ogletree, 1987; Skaf, 2008). For example, in *Commonwealth v. Mahdi* (1983), the prosecutor told the jury that the defendant, who was on trial for murder in the first degree, assault with intent to murder by means of a dangerous weapon, and robbery, was Islamic. The Massachusetts Supreme Court reversed the conviction, finding that such information would not allow jurors to decide the case fairly: "We conclude that the references by the district attorney . . . to the racial origins and religious beliefs of the defendant, present a substantial risk of a miscarriage of justice and thus require reversal of the convictions" (p. 706). In general, such evidence is not allowed: Federal Rule of Evidence 610, which contains the sole reference to religion in the federal rules, explicitly prohibits lawyers from using witnesses' religious beliefs or opinions to undermine their credibility (Ariens, 1992). As discussed earlier, some aspects of a defendant's religion (although not religion per se) can be used as a mitigating factor relevant to character in capital sentencing, but it cannot be used conversely to demonstrate negative character—that is, as an aggravating factor (*Flanagan v. State*, 1993; *United States v. Lemon*, 1983). This rule applies even to extremely non-mainstream religions, such as Satanism and the Black Hebrews, the rationale being that participation in any religion is protected by the First Amendment (*Flanagan v. State*, 1993; Ogletree, 1987).[20]

However, the rule against using religious beliefs or behaviors against the defendant is not a hard and fast rule. In 2007, a California court heard a case in which the prosecutor told the jury that the defendant had turned his back on his religious heritage (*United States v. Mitchell*, 2007). The court found that this comment was proper because the prosecutor was making this religious-based argument in rebuttal of the defense attorney's statement that the defendant's Navajo religion teaches adherents to value life and does not allow taking a life out of vengeance. Because the defense attorney had used a religious argument first, the prosecution was allowed to do so. Other courts have similarly held that prosecutors can introduce evidence of a defendant's religiosity (or supposed lack thereof) when the defense offers religion-based mitigation evidence, such as a post-conviction conversion (*Todd v. State*, 1991).

In sum, religious evidence has been used as a defense in several different respects. Despite assumptions by attorneys and criminal defendants about the likely effects of such evidence, very limited research has been conducted to determine whether such evidence is influential. Some evidence suggests that evidence of a religious conversion can mitigate punishment, but other religious defenses—such as a free exercise claim, or using religion as a justification or excuse—have only mixed success, at best.

Religious Figures in Secular Cases with Religious Overtones

In the third category of cases in which religion is relevant, religion does not directly inform the central legal issue, nor is a litigant's religion proffered as evidence. Nonetheless, there are "religious overtones" in the sense that it is difficult, if not impossible, to consider the case without a party's religious identity coloring the case. For example, Sister Barbara Markey, a nun in Omaha, Nebraska, pleaded guilty to embezzling more than $250,000 from the local archdiocese, which she used to fund vacations, homes, and a gambling addiction.[21] The judge sentenced Markey to 3–5 years in prison, which some observers (including the defendant) deemed inordinately harsh and led her to attempt to withdraw her guilty plea. Unlike the church–state separation cases discussed earlier, embezzlement deals with the theft of money, not religion. But the case raises several interesting questions: Would her sentence have been lighter if she had stolen from a local homeless shelter instead of the church? Would a layperson, working for either the archdiocese or a secular organization, have received a comparable sentence? To address these questions, it is necessary to consider the relationship between a litigant's religion and trial outcomes in routine civil and criminal cases.

In this category of cases, the legal issues themselves are not religious, but the cases have what we refer to as religious overtones, because litigants' religion necessarily comes up and is part and parcel of their alleged offense (e.g., an embezzling nun). Other examples of these kinds of cases include clergy accused of sexual abuse, religiously motivated terrorists, and cult members charged with false imprisonment. In some of these cases (e.g., those involving a clergy defendant), a litigant's occupation can serve as a proxy for her religion; a religious occupation might also create character judgments or behavioral expectations in the minds of jurors, leading them to treat religious defendants differently from other defendants charged with similar acts.

Little research has specifically addressed the question of whether religious figures are treated differently at trial (an exception is the study by Pfeifer, 1999, described later). Doing so would require comparing—by either archival or experimental research methods—trials for the same offense involving religious litigants to those involving nonreligious litigants. There is, however, research relevant to this question, which looks at the role of defendants' status and character.

Defendants' Status

Although it is extraneous to legal issues such as determining whether a crime has actually been committed, defendants' status is not ignored. In newspaper stories about crimes, stories about defendants with professional (e.g., politicians, physicians) or criminal-justice occupations (e.g., police officers, attorneys) are longer than stories involving blue-collar defendants (Chermak & Chapman, 2007). This suggests that people (at least those in the media) are sensitive to defendants' occupation and pay greater scrutiny to some defendants than others, depending on their status and occupation.

Other than the studies investigating religion as a defense (discussed earlier), we do not know of any studies that have specifically compared trial outcomes in secular cases for religious versus nonreligious litigants. However, several studies that have looked at the role of defendants' status can inform this question. Different researchers have operationalized "status" in various ways, typically by manipulating an individual's education, occupation, wealth/income, or socioeconomic background, either singly or in combination. A meta-analysis by Mazzella and Feingold (1994) of criminal defendants' status found that, although there was some variability across studies, overall, relatively low-status defendants were more likely to be found guilty and to receive greater punishment than relatively high-status defendants. Inasmuch as clergy have relatively high status, by virtue of being well-educated and well-paid members of a respected profession, one might therefore expect clergy defendants to receive lenient treatment in the courts. However, the magnitude of these effects was small ($d = .15$ for both guilt and punishment) and varied somewhat across crime type; and several subsequent studies have failed to find an effect of defendant status on verdicts or sentencing (e.g., Chamberlain, Miller, & Jehle, 2006; Loeffler & Lawson, 2002; McGraw & Foley, 2000; Skolnick & Shaw, 1997). This pattern of findings suggests that a defendant's status or occupation might matter only in close cases (Dane & Wrightsman, 1982), or might help in some circumstances but hurt in others, depending on the presence/absence of other variables. Indeed, as we describe next, other research has found that to be the case.

Researchers have explored several possible moderators of the defendant status effect. According to Rosoff (1989), the effect of defendant status might depend on the magnitude of the crime. Thus, high-status defendants (such as clergy) might be treated more leniently for minor crimes, but more harshly for major crimes. Consistent with this hypothesis, Rosoff found that mock jurors treated a high-status defendant (a surgeon) more harshly than a lower-status defendant (a dermatologist) when the charge was murder, but the pattern was reversed when the crime was insurance fraud.[22] We might expect, therefore, that clergy would fare well when charged with a crime such as shoplifting, compared to lower-status defendants, but would fare poorly when charged with a crime such as child sexual abuse.

Even considering crimes of comparable severity, religious defendants might be treated differently from nonreligious defendants depending on the context in which the crime took place. Skolnick and Shaw (1994) extended Rosoff's (1989) findings by investigating the role of a crime's professional relatedness. Their study varied crime severity (rape vs. insurance fraud), offender status (licensed clinical psychologist vs. graduate student), and professional relatedness of the crime. The professionally related crime involved a client during her therapy session (for rape) or overbilling of an insurance company for therapeutic services (for insurance fraud); whereas the professionally unrelated crime involved a neighbor (for rape) or overbilling of an insurance company for storm damage (for insurance fraud). The mock jurors were told that the defendant had already been found guilty, and they were asked to rate the defendant's degree of responsibility and recommend the deserved length of incarceration and professional penalties (both ranging from none at all to the maximum allowed). There was a "status shield" effect for professionally unrelated crimes, such that the high-status defendant received lighter sanctions and was perceived as less responsible; but there was a corresponding "status liability" effect for the professionally related crimes, such that the high-status defendant received more severe sanctions and was perceived as more responsible. This pattern essentially held regardless of whether the crime itself was relatively major (rape) or minor (insurance fraud), and also whether the defendant had committed a criminal or a civil offense (Shaw & Skolnick, 1996). Defendants whose crimes are congruent with their occupations (e.g., a lawyer charged with embezzlement vs. auto theft) also receive a lower presumption of innocence (e.g., they are viewed as more likely to be guilty even prior to trial, are expected to have to offer more evidence to prove their innocence, etc.; Helgeson & Shaver, 1990).

The final possible moderator of the defendant status effect is whether the defendant shows remorse. In a pair of studies, Niedermeier, Horowitz, and Kerr (1999, Study 2; 2001, Study 2) found that an expression of remorse helped a low-status defendant (medical resident), but it hurt a high-status defendant (hospital medical director) charged with the same offense (administering unscreened blood during an emergency). The same pattern held for both individuals (Niedermeier et al., 1999, 2001) and deliberating mock jurors (Neidermeier et al., 1999).

The research on defendants' status suggests that religious defendants whose crimes were allegedly committed in the scope of their occupation—such as a nun embezzling from her church or a priest sexually abusing an altar boy—would be treated more harshly than similarly situated defendants who are charged with professionally unrelated offenses. That should be true whether the comparison group is comprised of religious figures committing the same offense in a professionally unrelated manner (e.g., a nun embezzling from the non–church-affiliated soup kitchen, or a priest sexually abusing a neighbor child), or laypersons committing the same offense (e.g., an embezzling accountant or a pedophile business owner). It might not be the case, however, if there is something special about clerical occupations, relating to assumptions people make about their character.

Defendants' Character

As discussed earlier, religion can be presented as positive (and sometimes negative) character evidence in an attempt to lessen punishment. Do jurors make religion-based inferences even when a defendant's religion is more in the background? To the extent that jurors hold positive stereotypes of clergy (or other religiously devout individuals) and view them to be of an upright moral character, they might be treated more leniently than similarly situated nonreligious defendants.

As with the variable of defendants' status, a number of specific variables fall under the rubric of "character," such as lifestyle, past behavior (criminal or noncriminal), honesty and related traits, moral values, and so on (Dane & Wrightsman, 1982; Lupfer & Gingrich, 1999; Park, 1998). Individuals of good character are seen as more deserving when good things happen to them than when they experience negative outcomes, whereas the reverse is true for individuals of bad character (Lupfer & Gingrich, 1999). This pattern is especially true when the outcome is under the individual's control (Lupfer & Gingrich, 1999). Legally, character evidence is permissible to substantiate some allegations (e.g., committing a particular crime in a certain trademark fashion) but not others (e.g., simply committing a particular kind of crime), and courts are freer to consider it in a trial's penalty phase than in the guilt or liability phase (Park, 1998). A few mock jury studies have examined these various manifestations of character, with the result that, in general, jurors are more likely to convict, and to recommend longer sentences for, defendants of low (versus high) moral character (Dane & Wrightsman, 1982).

Legal factfinders such as judges and juries might, of course, draw inferences about a defendant's character even in the absence of specific character evidence. Indeed, Feather and Atchison (1998) found that inferences about defendants' moral character mediated the effect of defendants' status on mock jurors' responsibility judgments. That is, relatively high-status defendants were seen as less responsible, and less deserving of punishment, to the extent that their status conferred higher moral character. These findings suggest that religious defendants would be treated more leniently than nonreligious defendants, insofar as factfinders make positive character judgments based on their religiosity.

Special Cases: Clergy Sexual Abuse, Religiously Motivated Terrorism, and Cults

Several of the cases with religious overtones have received a great deal of media and public attention. As in all of the cases from this category, the crime itself is nonreligious, but the defendants' religion is inextricably tied to their actions, perhaps more so than for the other exemplars. We therefore consider them separately.

There is a rapidly growing literature on the American Catholic Church sexual abuse scandal. It is not our purpose here to address the causes or consequences of such abuse; rather, we concentrate on that portion of the literature relevant to the legal disposition of cases.[23] Figures concerning how many cases exist are hard to come by. The most comprehensive study of the incidence of sexual abuse by priests concluded that 4392 priests were credibly accused of child sexual abuse between 1950 and 2002 (John Jay College of Criminal Justice, 2004). Through 2004, the number rises to an estimate in excess of 5000 priests, comprising approximately 4.75% of the priesthood (Frawley-O'Dea, 2007; Frawley-O'Dea & Goldner, 2007). Other studies place the figure as high as 6% (Plante, 2004a; van Wormer, 2008). These figures are likely to be low-end estimates, due to underreporting by both victims and church authorities (Frawley-O'Dea, 2007; Frawley-O'Dea & Goldner, 2007). Estimates of the number of victims are equally hard to make with precision, but reasonable estimates place the figure at 11,000–60,000, for the 1950–2004 time period (Frawley-O'Dea & Goldner, 2007; John Jay College of Criminal Justice, 2004).

The clergy abuse scandal has resulted in numerous lawsuits. The typical clergy sexual abuse lawsuit has multiple defendants, with the plaintiff suing the pastor who committed the abuse, the congregation that employed him, and the religious organization with which they were affiliated (Schiltz, 2003). As with the number of incidents, exact figures on the number of lawsuits are hard to come by, but the large settlements agreed to by several archdioceses give some idea of the scope of the litigation and provide evidence that the flood of litigation has not yet slowed down (Table 9.1). In the largest settlement to date, the Los Angeles archdiocese agreed in 2007 to pay $660 million to over 500 claimants ("L.A. archdiocese to settle suits," 2007; Dolbee, Sauer, & Krasnowski, 2007). Overall, the Catholic Church has paid more than $2 billion in compensation to American claimants for the abuse and subsequent cover-up by church authorities ("L.A. archdiocese to settle suits," 2007; van Wormer, 2008), and a number of dioceses have filed for bankruptcy protection. Several states have altered their statutes of limitations to allow additional prosecutions or compensation (Frawley-O'Dea, 2007; Plante, 2004a; Schiltz, 2003), and many priests have been found civilly or criminally liable at trial. Most penalties against the church itself (as opposed to individual priests) have been civil in nature, but in 2003, the archdiocese of Cincinnati was convicted of five misdemeanor counts of failure to report a felony (Frawley-O'Dea, 2007).

Table 9.1 Large Catholic Church Sexual Abuse Settlements

Amount (in $millions)	(Arch)Diocese	# of Victims	Year of Settlement
660	Los Angeles (CA)	508	2007
198	San Diego (CA)	14	2007
100	Orange County (CA)	87	2004
85	Boston (MA)	552	2003
84	Covington (KY)	361	2006
60	Los Angeles (CA)	45	2006
56	Oakland (CA)	56	2005
75	Portland (OR)	177	2007
48	Spokane (WA)	160	2007
35	Sacramento (CA)	33	2005
26	Louisville (KY)	243	2003

This table was adapted from material in Dolbee et al. (2007) and a number of online and print news sources.

Ultimately, there are likely to be hundreds and probably thousands of trials, and those trial outcomes will influence countless additional cases through their impact on settlement negotiations. How would priests fare as criminal or civil defendants, compared to other child sexual abuse defendants? Although the media abound with stories of individual trials featuring priest defendants, we are aware of no studies that have systematically compared trial outcomes for priests (or other clergy) versus lay defendants. The literature discussed earlier, on the role of defendants' status, occupation, and character, suggests competing hypotheses. On the one hand, clergy might benefit from jurors' assumptions about their good moral character; but on the other hand, the professional relatedness of such an allegation, in conjunction with the particular outrage jurors might experience at the alleged violation of the priest's pastoral duties, could lead to harsher treatment for priest defendants.

A second special case of religious defendants involves those accused of terrorism. Many recent defendants on trial for acts of terrorism were motivated by their religion. For instance, John Walker Lindh, who is sometimes known as the "American Taliban," was raised in America, but later traveled to the Middle East. He converted to Islam, went to a fundamentalist Islamic school, and voiced his support for jihad (i.e., holy war; "The case of the Taliban American," n.d.). Similarly, Zaccarias Moussaoui's strong religious beliefs led him to commit his crimes in support of the September 11th 2001 attacks (Dorf, 2005), and one of the "British shoebombers," Saajid Badat, once stated "I have a sincere desire to sell my soul to Allah in return for paradise." This desire led him to plan a terrorist attack, for which he pleaded guilty in 2005 (Raif & Dean, 2005). Or consider the case of Naveed Afzal Haq, who in 2006 shot one woman dead and wounded five people at the Jewish Federation of Greater Seattle. According to a witness, "He said 'I am a Muslim American, angry at Israel,' before opening fire on everyone."[24] Nor are such cases restricted to Islamist extremism. In 2005, Eric Rudolph was convicted of placing bombs at the Olympics and multiple abortion clinics ("Rudolph agrees to plea," 2005). Rudolph was a member of a fundamentalist church in Tennessee that opposed abortion ("Prosecutors allege link," 2005), and his crimes were directed at the federal government in retaliation for permitting abortions ("Eric Rudolph gets life," 2005).

For such defendants, their crimes' religious motivation would undoubtedly come up at trial and would most likely lead to harsher treatment than for comparable defendants whose crimes did not have a religious component. As with priests, however, we are aware of no research that has compared trials for religiously motivated versus non–religiously motivated terrorism (we are, of course, more familiar with the former, by virtue of the 9/11 attacks and similar events; but presumably the latter exists as well).

The last of the special cases involves religious cults, which are a recurrent concern for law enforcement. Cults such as the Unification Church ("Moonies"), Hare Krishnas, Mormon (Church of Latter Day Saints) fundamentalists, and Satanists have come under scrutiny for a wide variety of possible offenses, such as financial crimes, false imprisonment, child sexual abuse, and animal and even human sacrifice. The group labels themselves (e.g., "Moonies") trigger a set of negative perceptions, such that people make different attributions about the same behavior when it occurs in a cult than in a non-cult context (Pfeifer, 1992). For example, Pfeifer (1992) found that participants viewed a group's indoctrination process as more coercive, and more likely to involve brainwashing, when the group was characterized as Moonies than when it involved the Marines or a Catholic seminary—even though the group's behavior was exactly the same in all conditions. Not surprisingly, these differential perceptions influence how cult members are treated at trial. In a follow-up study, Pfeifer (1999) found that defendants who were associated with a satanic cult—whether their association was admitted or merely alleged—were seen as guiltier by mock jurors than defendants who had no cult involvement. This pattern held across two different types of crime (homicide and child sexual assault).

The study by Pfeifer (1999) is noteworthy because it experimentally compares treatment of defendants as a function of their religious affiliation. Without such systematic comparisons, it is difficult to know to what extent these "special cases" are really treated differently from similarly situated defendants, or if their cases are just more sensationalized. Pfeifer's results, in conjunction with those described previously, also suggest that a litigant's religion can have different effects depending on the type of litigation. It may be an advantage to belong to a marginal religion in pursuing a religious liberty claim—our first category of cases—but it appears to be a disadvantage in secular cases with religious overtones. The large, and growing, number of these "religious overtones" cases suggests that religion is finding its way into court in ever more guises. Religion is even increasingly an issue in child custody disputes, as in cases in which parents differ over their child's religious upbringing (Weiss, 2008). This raises the question: Are there any cases in which religion is *not* likely to come up? We turn now to such cases.

Litigants' Religion in Routine Secular Cases

The fourth, and final, category of cases in which litigants' religion can be an issue is routine secular cases. Social scientific research on the effect of litigants' characteristics in routine civil and criminal cases has explored the influence of a number of demographic and attitudinal variables (e.g., Greene & Bornstein, 2003; Vidmar & Hans, 2007), but it has generally ignored religion. Perhaps this is because, unlike other characteristics such as race, gender, and age, religion is generally not observable. Nonetheless, there are a number of ways that a litigant's religion could become known to, or inferred by, a jury. First, if clergypersons were involved in a trial, their occupation might be mentioned, or they might simply be known in the community. A good example of this is the trial of Victoria Osteen, co-pastor of Lakewood Church, an evangelical "megachurch" (with a television ministry, weekly attendance of approximately 40,000, and services held in a 16,000-seat basketball arena) in Houston.[25] A Continental Airlines flight attendant sued Osteen for an assault that allegedly occurred during a confrontation over a stain on her first-class seat. The plaintiff sought an apology and punitive damages equal to 10% of Osteen's net worth (which would have come to over $400,000). During voir dire, many of the venire-persons admitted knowing who Osteen was and even attending her church; so although her religious affiliation and occupation were irrelevant and might never have been mentioned at trial, jurors knew the information. In August 2008, the jury found in Osteen's favor.

Other highly publicized "preacher-defendant" cases include those of Anthony Hopkins (not the well-known actor by the same name), who, in 2008, was accused of killing his wife and storing her body in a freezer for nearly four years, as well as raping his daughter ("Preacher killed wife," 2008), and Edgar Ray Killen, a Ku Klux Klansman and Baptist preacher who, in 2005, was convicted of manslaughter in the 1964 deaths of three civil rights workers ("Former Klansman found guilty," 2005). The same sorts of issues arise in these cases as in those involving clergy charged with sexual abuse (see earlier discussion), namely, whether jurors would treat clerical defendants differently due to expectations related to their status, occupation, or presumed character.

One need not be a pastor for one's religion to be well-publicized. Consider, for instance, the recent raid in Texas on the compound of Warren Jeffs, leader of a fundamentalist Mormon sect. Authorities are investigating a number of charges against church members, most related to child neglect/abuse and child sexual assault.[26] In the trial of Dennis Rader, the serial killer who referred to himself as BTK ("bind, torture, and kill"), the fact that Rader was the president of his Lutheran church council was introduced into evidence ("Rader details how he killed," 2005). It is hard to imagine that in these cases, jurors would not be acquainted with the defendants' religious views.

The second way in which litigants' religion might become known to legal factfinders is if they display their religion in their appearance, especially their attire. Jurors could logically infer that a litigant wearing a yarmulke was Jewish, that one wearing a hijab or burkha was Muslim, that one with a long beard and turban was Sikh, that a woman with a sari and a bindi (the forehead decoration worn by many married Hindu women) was Hindu, or that one wearing a nun's habit was Catholic. Finally, they could make religious assumptions based on one's surname. Thus, they might assume that a litigant named Goldberg was Jewish, that one named al-Wahiri was Muslim, or that one named O'Donnell was Catholic. Surnames that suggest a particular ethnicity can activate ethnic stereotypes, leading jurors to make assumptions about a defendant's characteristics that color their decision making (Luscri & Mohr, 1998). Surname-based inferences are likely to be better than chance, but they are still prone to error and less reliable than inferences based on attire.

Of the four categories of cases, a litigant's religion is least likely to come up in these routine secular cases; but instances still occur in which it will become known to legal decision makers. When it does, the probable outcome is unclear. If the litigant is a clergyperson, then factfinders' expectations and assumptions regarding status and character might come into play, as with secular cases with religious overtones. If the litigant is a layperson, then religious stereotypes might influence factfinders' decisions. Ethnic and racial stereotypes have been found to influence mock juror decision making in run-of-the-mill cases (Bodenhausen & Lichtenstein, 1987; Luscri & Mohr, 1998), and it is reasonable to expect that religious stereotypes would operate in the same way.

Relationship Between Litigants' Religion and Jurors' Religion

The bulk of this chapter has considered litigants' religion in isolation; this isolation is useful for expository purposes, but it ignores the fact that the religion of various actors in the courtroom drama might interact. The defendant's religious identity would seem especially likely to interact with jurors' religious characteristics (see Chapters 3 and 4). Studies that have examined the matter indicate that such an interplay can and does occur, but with contradictory effects. Juror–litigant similarity can benefit defendants who share jurors' religion (i.e., a "leniency" effect), but it can also work to their detriment (i.e., a "black-sheep" effect).

There is a general tendency for jurors to treat litigants who resemble them in some respect (e.g., race, gender) more favorably (Greene & Bornstein, 2003). The standard explanation for this effect is that similarity breeds liking, which in turn breeds leniency (Greene & Bornstein, 2003; Kerr et al., 1995). Some evidence suggests that religion functions in this manner. For example, Kerr and colleagues (1995) found that both Jewish and Christian mock jurors were more lenient toward defendants who were members of their own religious group as compared to defendants of another religious group. Presumably, jurors see the defendant's choice of their own religious affiliation as a positive attribute.

There may be limitations to the leniency effect, however. Individuals can sometimes be *more* punitive toward ingroup members, especially when they violate group norms by engaging in especially egregious behavior. This phenomenon, called the *black-sheep* effect (Marques & Yzerbyt, 1988; Taylor & Hosch, 2004), hypothesizes that the misbehaving group member (the black sheep) reflects badly on the image of the entire group, thus leading ingroup members to judge him harshly in an attempt to distance themselves from him. In addition to making themselves feel better about their own group membership, the harsh treatment of deviant group members also sends a message to outsiders that the transgressor is not a typical member of the group (Kerr et al., 1995).

It follows from this interpretation that the black-sheep effect should be greatest when the case characteristics threaten the group's norms or members' group identification. Indeed, Begue (2001) found that highly religious Catholic participants were more punitive toward a woman who had had an abortion when she was Catholic than when her religious affiliation was not mentioned.[27] Johnson (1985; see Chapter 3) conducted a jury simulation study in which the defendant was charged with child abuse resulting in a skull fracture to his 2½-year-old son. The defendant's attorney either argued that because he was "a fine Christian man," he must be a good father, or made no mention of the defendant's religion. Mock jurors with a conservative Christian political orientation were more severe in their recommendation for punishment than other mock jurors, but only when the defendant used his religion as part of his defense. When the defendant did not make this claim, "Christian Rightists" did not differ from "non-Rightists." In other words, the Christian-right group tended to show a black-sheep effect toward a defendant accused of a heinous crime who went out of his way to claim he was just like them. Although juror–litigant religious similarity affected sentencing recommendations, it did not affect participants' verdicts.

Thus, although one might initially think that jurors would be more lenient toward members of their own religious group, the black-sheep effect suggests that it may not be that simple. The nature of the juror–litigant religion interaction is likely to depend on a number of factors, particularly type of case, strength of evidence, and whether the outcome is an individual or group decision. Kerr and colleagues (1995) propose that the black-sheep effect requires strong evidence against the defendant, as ingroup members should feel more threatened the more likely it is that the defendant actually committed the bad act. It follows, then, that the black-sheep effect should be more observable in jurors' sentencing recommendations—after the defendant's guilt has been established—than in their verdicts. The studies by Begue (2001) and Johnson (1985), which found a black-sheep effect in terms of punitiveness once the act itself was established, support this view.

The failure of some studies to obtain a black-sheep effect, especially in terms of verdict, could reflect case type effects. Some offenses would threaten a group's positive identification more than others (e.g., an illegal abortion for Catholics; child and sex crimes for virtually all religious groups). If this interpretation is true, then clergy accused of sex crimes would be treated especially harshly by members of their own denominations. For offenses that are less threatening to the group's values—such as simple assault, to use the Victoria Osteen example discussed earlier—one might expect, instead, a similarity-leniency effect.

Finally, Taylor and Hosch (2004) found no evidence of a black-sheep effect in their study of actual juries, and Miller and colleagues (2008) did not find a black-sheep effect in parole decisions, both of which contradict the findings from studies of individual (mock) jurors (e.g., Kerr et al., 1995, Study 2). As just noted, this could reflect the heterogeneous nature of their case sample, which included a variety of noncapital felonies; but it could also mean that the deliberation process itself or the type of decision (i.e., sentence vs. parole) attenuates the effect. Moreover, studies looking at multiple defendant characteristics have found a black-sheep effect for race but not for religion (see, e.g., Kerr et al., 1995, which found a leniency effect for religious similarity). Clearly, more research on the effects of juror–litigant religious similarity is necessary.

The Victim's Religion

It goes without saying that victims are a central feature of trials. In civil cases, victims take on the role of plaintiffs; in criminal cases, the victim is not officially a party to the case, but with the rare exception of victimless crimes, a victim is necessary for there to be a crime.[28] Moreover, victims usually attend trial and often testify. Thus, they share many characteristics of the litigants themselves, and it is reasonable to ask whether their religious characteristics would affect the trial's outcome.

Religion will likely play a role in cases in which the victim's religiosity is brought up at trial (Ariens, 1992). Although the identity of the victim is usually irrelevant from a legal standpoint, mock jurors tend to punish defendants more harshly when they cause harm to a victim who has positive traits or high moral character, compared to a victim who has less positive traits (Dane & Wrightsman, 1982; Greene & Bornstein, 2003; Jones & Aronson, 1973).

Thus, the identity of the victim, which possibly includes positively or negatively valenced religious traits, has the potential to affect jurors' decision making. This specific notion has not yet been scientifically tested; nevertheless, the religious beliefs of jurors are likely to be influential in such cases.

Except for hate crimes (discussed later), prosecutors generally cannot use a victim's religiosity to argue explicitly for more severe punishment, in the same way that they generally cannot use a defendant's religiosity (or lack thereof) to argue for more severe punishment (Ariens, 1992). For example, the South Carolina Supreme Court reversed a jury's death sentence in part because the prosecutor argued the defendant deserved the death penalty "because the victim was a religious man" (*Gathers v. State*, 1988, p. 144).[29] However, a victim's religion could exert a subtle influence even without explicit reference to it. For instance, in 2007, Mary Winkler was convicted of voluntary manslaughter for killing her husband, who was a popular minister in the Church of Christ in their Tennessee town (Rucker, 2007). It is possible that the victim's religiosity made the crime seem worse in the jurors' eyes. A victim's religiosity might also come up during victim impact statements, which can be introduced at sentencing to show how the crime has impacted the victim and his family. These are often statements that glorify the victim and could mention the victim's religious involvement (e.g., "Who will lead Bible study now? We will miss her beautiful voice in choir"). Thus, religion can enhance a victim's stature in the same way that, as described earlier, it can enhance a defendant's. Simply put, killing an individual with a presumably upright character, such as a pastor, may be seen as a more serious crime than killing someone with fewer socially desirable traits.

Just as with defendants, however, a victim's religiosity can have the opposite effect if jurors view the religion in question as a negative trait. In 2005, two teens named Paul Rotondi and Frank Scarpinito pleaded guilty to the second-degree assault of Daniel Romano, a member of the Church of Satan (Grinberg, 2005). The defendants allegedly yelled "Hey, Satan," to the victim before beating him with an ice scraper and a metal pipe. The teens could have received 15-year sentences for five counts of aggravated assault and use of a weapon. Instead, they received five years of probation and 150 hours of community service. Perhaps the relatively light sentence was due in part to the negative religious traits of the victim.

In cases in which a victim is targeted specifically because of his religion, the crime may qualify as a hate crime. For example, Jim Adkisson killed two people at a Unitarian church in Knoxville, Tennessee in 2008. He wrote a note indicating that his act was motivated by his disapproval of the church's liberal policies toward gays (Mansfield, 2008). Targeting the victims because of their religion would support a prosecutorial appeal for a stiffer penalty. This was precisely the prosecution's strategy in *People v. Lewis* (2006), in which the prosecution encouraged jurors to give the death sentence because the crime was against a church. Two defendants were convicted by jury of two counts of first-degree murder and of attempted murder of a third victim. Two gunmen, each carrying a shotgun, hooded and dressed in black, raided the Mount Olive Church of God in Christ in Los Angeles on July 21, 1989. While one assailant stood guard and shot at a bystander outside, the other one entered and shot three churchgoers, two of whom died. The prosecution argued:

> These criminals violated the one safe haven we have in this troubled world, the place where we go to enrich and glorify what is best in us, where we reaffirm our faith in all that is good and righteous, where we renew our souls and seek solace in the spiritual from a troubled world, a house of God. . . . Who would violate the sanctity of a house of God to commit the most heinous of crimes known to man? Only the most vile, soulless coward could commit crimes so foul and so evil. In these defendants, we have the very epitome of evil and cowardice. (*People v. Lewis*, 2006, p. 842, footnote 27)

The defendants argued at appeal that the prosecutor's religious references constituted prosecutorial misconduct (among other grounds for appeal), but the California Supreme Court affirmed their convictions.

As with litigants' religion, victims' religion cannot be treated completely in isolation, but could interact with the religion of other actors, especially jurors. For example, jurors with anti-Semitic sentiments would naturally have less sympathy for a Jewish victim, jurors with anti-Muslim prejudices would have less sympathy for a Muslim victim—especially if they were victimized precisely because of their religion—and so forth. These attitudes could then play out in differential conviction rates as a function of juror–victim similarity. Unfortunately, we know of no research that has addressed this issue specifically.

Conclusion

Catholic churches and priests as defendants in child sexual abuse litigation have garnered most of the attention lately, but religious figures and institutions can be participants in a variety of different kinds of cases. They can also play a number of different roles, including civil plaintiff, civil or criminal defendant, and victim. The effect of litigants' religion depends on which role they find themselves in, and even more so, on the kind of case.

The research suggests that, in free exercise litigation, claimants from marginal religions have an advantage, in that they are more likely to win their case than claimants from mainstream religions. The Free Exercise Clause also comes up in other kinds of cases, when defendants raise it as a defense against civil or criminal liability. The free exercise defense has had some, albeit mixed, success in civil cases, yet it rarely helps criminal defendants. Other religious defenses, such as using religion as a justification or excuse, likewise have, at best, only mixed success. In contrast, some research suggests that evidence of a religious conversion can mitigate punishment.

Other cases in which litigants' religion can be a factor are those we refer to as "routine secular" cases. Some of these cases have religious overtones (e.g., clergy accused of child sexual abuse), whereas others do not. Very little research addresses how defendants of different religious backgrounds are treated in such cases. What evidence does exist suggests that defendants from marginal religions (e.g., Muslim terrorists, cult members) are at a comparative disadvantage. Legal decision makers (i.e., judges and juries) are also likely to make assumptions about litigants' character based on their religious background and, in the case of clergy, their religious occupation. These assumptions, in turn, are likely to influence their decisions. Finally, there is some evidence of an interaction between litigants' and jurors' religion, but the precise nature of that interaction is unclear. What is abundantly clear, however, is that litigants' religion can influence trial outcomes in myriad ways.

10

Conclusion

Religion, including spirituality . . . , is a fascinating realm,
and that may be enough reason to study it. Of much greater
significance is the fact that religion is of the utmost importance
to people all over the earth.
  —Spilka et al., 2003, p. 1

Rather than simply reiterate, in digested form, the contents of the preceding chapters, in this concluding chapter we strive to do three things. First, we identify a number of key themes that run through the book and tie together some of the seemingly disparate topics. Second, we identify the most fruitful avenues for future research. And third, we revisit the question of "why religion at trial matters" in light of the empirical findings and address the issue from both descriptive and normative perspectives.

Key Themes

Choosing Perfection of the Life, or of the Work

The Yeats poem that opened Chapter 7 posed the dilemma religious attorneys may feel between choosing perfection of the life or of the work. Other chapters made it clear that this dilemma is not limited to attorneys and can affect other courtroom participants as well, such as jurors and judges. Religion is a salient factor in the majority of Americans' lives. It should come as no surprise, then, that those involved in the trial process not only have a hard time ignoring it, but often strive to incorporate it. Yet trials are often viewed, at least in an ideal sense, as a dispassionate process based on evidence and law. Hence, courtroom participants are faced with a conflict, a choice. In this section, we summarize the literature on how the various legal actors—attorneys, jurors, and judges—resolve this conflict.

The volume of material published under the aegis of the "Religious Lawyering Movement" attests to the significance of the issue in many attorneys' lives. As discussed in Chapter 7, many attorneys struggle to be both a devout religious observer and a successful and effective lawyer. The day-to-day practice of law affords little opportunity for spiritual growth, unless one makes a concerted effort in that direction (Allegretti, 1996, 1998b). Data are lacking on whether attorneys who subscribe to the tenets of the Religious Lawyering Movement are more successful in their careers or more satisfied in their lives, but the sheer number of books on the topic (see Chapter 7) suggests that a market exists for literature that can help lawyers to reconcile the demands of faith and career. The growing number of religious law schools and the infusion of religion into the law school curriculum are further evidence of the demand for integrating "perfection of the life" and "of the work" (Yeats, 1933/1962).

Unlike attorneys, jurors are only occasional (and maybe even one-time) participants in court; yet many of them likewise bring religion to their task. Jurors pray together, consult religious texts for guidance, quote scripture during deliberations, and consult religious authorities outside deliberations (see Chapter 5). They are especially likely to do so in difficult cases or those with potentially severe penalties, such as capital punishment. To be sure, not all jurors engage in these activities—which the courts may regard as juror misconduct—but they undoubtedly occur more often than the appellate record reflects. The appellate record contains only a small fraction of all cases, and it is necessarily slanted toward those in which the defendant was convicted, but the same religious texts and authorities could just as easily justify an acquittal (e.g., by emphasizing mercy or forgiveness). Thus, jurors' reliance on religion in making their decisions is likely more widespread than it might at first appear.

Judges, who make the same sorts of decisions as jurors (plus others, of course), report drawing on their religious values and beliefs as well (e.g., Gonzalez, 1996; Merz, 2004). Unlike juries, judges often explain their rationale in arriving at a particular decision, so that the factors they deem important can become part of the trial's official record. There are numerous examples of cases in which judges have explicitly relied on religious sources in giving a sentence (see Chapter 6). These religion-based sentences are controversial and have been grounds for appeal, but judges' freedom to quote scripture—in part because of their right to free speech—has generally been upheld (Wiehl, 2000). On the whole, there are fewer restrictions on judges' "bringing their religion to work" than there are for attorneys or jurors.

Judges Versus Jurors

As our discussion of this first theme suggests, the appellate courts have somewhat different views about what is acceptable behavior for judges and jurors. In general, a reliance on religion in decision making is considered more acceptable for judges than for jurors, although it is by no means excluded for the latter. Why the divergence? Judging is often portrayed as a dispassionate exercise based on facts and legal precedent; jurors, on the other hand, are regarded as less rational and more susceptible to extralegal influence (Greene & Bornstein, 2003; Vidmar & Hans, 2007). Thus, the courts might assume that judges could use their religious beliefs in an acceptable, nonprejudicial fashion, but that this would be beyond jurors' more limited capabilities. A direct comparison of how religion relates to decision making in the two groups can illuminate the issue.[1]

Studies of both judges and jurors show an association between religion and legal decisions. With respect to judges, Jewish judges tend to adopt relatively liberal positions, as do Catholic judges, albeit less consistently. Evangelical judges, on the other hand, make relatively conservative decisions. Mainline Protestants are harder to characterize as a group, perhaps reflecting the substantial diversity of denominations and beliefs in such a broad classification. This pattern characterizes both cases in which religion is explicitly at issue, as in religious freedom cases, and more mundane cases.

In the case of jurors, those from fundamentalist Protestant denominations, and who have fundamentalist beliefs, tend to be more punitive than other religious groups. In contrast, individuals who are high in evangelism (i.e., a proselytizing orientation) or devotionalism (i.e., personal religiosity or religious participation) tend to be less punitive. Although Judaism and Catholicism feature prominently in the judge studies, they have been less of a focus in the juror studies. Some studies that have addressed these religions have found that mock jurors tend to be more lenient toward defendants who share their religious heritage (e.g., Kerr et al., 1995), but other studies have found greater punitiveness toward same-religion defendants (i.e., a black-sheep effect; see Begue, 2001; Johnson, 1985). The exact contours of the juror–litigant religion interaction is likely to depend on a number of factors, such as case type and evidence strength (see Chapter 9).

Overall, the lack of comparability between studies of judge and juror decision making (e.g., different methods, different religions) makes it hard to draw conclusions about whether religion functions similarly in the two groups of decision makers. About the only conclusion we can reach with any confidence is that religious conservatives, such as evangelicals and fundamentalists—whether in the role of judge or juror—tend to be more punitive, especially in death penalty cases. Although other research may not have found additional similarities in terms of religion's influence on judges and jurors, it has also failed to find any discernible differences. This observation is consistent with research on judge–jury differences more generally, which has found that decision-making processes in the two groups are quite comparable (e.g., Bornstein, 2006; Robbennolt, 2005).

Using Religion to Tactical Advantage

We discussed several ways in which litigants attempt to use religion to their tactical advantage: by invoking the First Amendment's Free Exercise

Clause as a defense to civil or criminal liability, using religious beliefs to justify or excuse criminal conduct, or presenting evidence of a religious conversion to mitigate punishment. We do not mean to question the sincerity of these efforts—someone who claims to have killed at God's behest might really be suffering from hallucinations, and an avowed death-row conversion might be genuine. Nonetheless, we doubt that the individuals—unless they are severely mentally impaired—are oblivious to the instrumental value of these arguments. Thus, religion can be used—consciously or not—in a strategic manner. Even church–state separation claimants can avail themselves of this strategy. Anyone can challenge governmental actions on Establishment Clause grounds, and the research suggests that plaintiffs contemplating such a challenge would fare better if they designated a member of a marginal religion as the plaintiff of record (Ignagni, 1993).[2]

The question, of course, is: Does it work? As just noted, it can be effective in First Amendment litigation, where marginal religions fare better. There is not so clearly an advantage in other cases. Empirical data on the question are scant, but anecdotal evidence depicts a mixed picture. The Free Exercise Clause sometimes succeeds as a defense to civil liability (e.g., *Pleasant Glade Assembly of God v. Schubert,* 2008), but at other times it does not (e.g., the Westboro Baptist Church funeral picketing case; see Chapter 9), and it rarely, if ever, succeeds as a defense to criminal liability. Religion does not work as a justification (e.g., "committing this crime served the greater good of sparing the world God's wrath"), and it has had mixed success as an excuse in the context of an insanity defense. Religion not infrequently comes up in an attempt to mitigate punishment, but even here, a review of relevant cases fails to show a high success rate (Skaf, 2008), although some experimental evidence supports its effectiveness (Miller & Bornstein, 2006).

Attorneys have been known to use religion strategically as well, in making religious appeals at trial or in attempting to use religion as an aggravating factor in sentencing. As in the case of litigants' use of religion, there is little evidence for the effectiveness of these tactics. Biblical appeals (e.g., "an eye for an eye") are generally ineffective and may even backfire; they can also interfere with jurors' decision-making process (see Chapter 8). No research studies have addressed the effect of using defendants' religion in a negative light, but it does not matter much—defendants' religion can generally not be used to undermine their credibility or as an aggravating factor (Ariens, 1992; Ogletree, 1987). Thus, as often seems to be the case, attorneys might have certain intuitive beliefs about what is or is not likely to be effective, but those beliefs lack an empirical basis (cf. Fulero & Penrod, 1990).

Future Research Directions

It is a rare literature review that concludes "We now know the definitive answer to this question—the chapter is closed." The present work is no exception to this rule. Our review has identified a number of shortcomings in the extant literature. We hope that, if nothing else, our efforts will inspire future research on religion's role at trial. In this section, we identify what we believe are the most pressing research needs.

As mentioned in Chapter 4, studies of religious attitudes and characteristics use relatively few measures, different studies use different measures, and researchers have been unsystematic in their focus. This lack of focus might reflect the fact that research on religion and trial outcomes (and legal attitudes more generally) arises from so many different social scientific research traditions (e.g., sociology, political science, psychology), which tend to rely on different methodologies. Yet it creates a problem, in that "relatively crude conceptualizations of religious variables are frequently advanced and adopted by many social scientists, and this utilization of unrefined measures can prevent analysts from discerning important changes that may be taking place within and across different religious groups" (Smidt, 1989, p. 24). We are certainly not in a position to recommend the definitive measure(s) of religious beliefs that researchers should employ, but we do encourage future researchers to use more measures and to rely most heavily on those with known psychometric properties.

[handwritten margin note: problem]

Another complication is in terms of religious classification. Various researchers categorize religions differently. This is especially true for efforts to distinguish among Protestant denominations (e.g., evangelical vs. non-evangelical). Existing research is also somewhat piecemeal. For example, no comprehensive study asks participants from a large diversity of religions about their attitudes on legal matters such as punishment, rehabilitation, retribution, and the like. It is also important for research to draw from multiple geographical regions, as there can be differences in legal attitudes within a given religion across different parts of the United States (see Chapter 4).

As we described in the section on judges versus juries, researchers in different areas rely on different methodologies. To some extent, this reflects disciplinary biases: Most of the research on judges is done by political scientists, whereas most of the research on juries is done by psychologists. The differences are not trivial, and they make meaningful comparisons across topics difficult. For example, judge studies use archival analysis, whereas juror studies use surveys or experiments; judge studies use decisions as the outcome variable, whereas most juror studies use attitudes or beliefs; and the two clusters of studies break participants down into different religious categories. Some issues, such as attorneys' use of religion during voir dire and jurors' use of religion during deliberation, are almost entirely devoid of empirical data, forcing policy makers to rely on anecdotal evidence and intuition. That is obviously not a sound basis for formulating legal policy (Saks, 1989), but it is hard to blame the policy makers when the relevant data do not exist. It is incumbent on social scientists to provide empirical answers to the kinds of legal questions and assumptions raised throughout this volume.

Finally, our emphasis has been on religion's role in American courts. There are several reasons for this emphasis: nearly all of the literature on the topic comes from the United States; because of the high degree of religious diversity in the U.S. population and the doctrine of church–state separation, religious issues are probably more likely to arise in American courts than elsewhere; and, admittedly, we are simply unfamiliar with the legal systems of other countries. Nonetheless, religion is a politically salient factor in many parts of the world besides the United States (Bruce, 2003; Smidt, 1989). It is important to know whether religious differences in legal attitudes and decisions generalize across nations, or whether the relationships between religion and trial outcomes are somehow an outgrowth of the American legal system or American culture.

Based on this critique of existing research in the area, we make a number of specific recommendations for the most needed and promising research:

- *More measures of legally relevant religious attitudes, with the aim of developing standardized measures with known psychometric properties.* The area of religious attitudes, at least in the legal domain, includes few standard measures (see Chapter 4). Moreover, several studies have included these measures merely as add-ons while investigating other issues (e.g., personality or demographic variables). The field is wide open for researchers to develop reliable and valid measures of religious characteristics, such as those related to specific beliefs and devotionalism.
- *More diverse samples, with more reliable religious classifications.* For many studies, only major religious categories (e.g., Catholic, Jewish, Protestant) are included, which makes it impossible to know what is happening with other faiths (e.g., Islam, Buddhism, Hinduism) that are becoming increasingly prevalent in the U.S. population (Eck, 2001). It also obscures important differences across Protestant denominations. It is also difficult to make cross-study comparisons when one study includes a particular group, such as Mormons (Church of Latter Day Saints), among Protestant faiths, but another study does not. Even large-scale surveys suffer from this inconsistency in classification. We recommend that researchers adhere, insofar as possible, to the standard categories used by the General Social Survey or U.S. Census Bureau (see Chapter 3). Researchers interested in specific aspects of religious beliefs not captured by these measures, such as evangelicalism or fundamentalism, would naturally want to tailor the way in which they assess religious affiliation; but a greater reliance on standardized measures would at least provide a starting point and a more solid basis for comparison across studies.
- *More mixed methodologies.* For example, studies of judges should address attitudes as well as decisions, and vice versa for jury studies. A broad array of religions needs to be investigated for both samples. Much of this will not be easy. Judges' decisions are a matter of public record, whereas getting them to participate in experiments or surveys is harder to

accomplish. Information on judges' religious background is relatively easy to obtain, but it would be less so for jurors. Nonetheless, efforts in this direction could provide convergence within each sample (e.g., do differences in judges' religious attitudes and beliefs map onto religious differences in their decisions?), as well as address the important question of judge–jury differences. Any methodology for doing psycholegal research has its limitations and disadvantages (Bornstein, 1999, 2006; Bornstein & McCabe, 2005), so that using mixed methodologies can make researchers more confident in the inferences they draw.

- *More comparative analyses that seek both to replicate findings from American samples in other countries and to address questions that are only meaningful in a comparative context.* For example: Do attorneys in more secular countries than the United States, such as most of Europe, struggle to reconcile their work and their faith? Do judges and juries in more secular countries rely on religious texts or beliefs in making their decisions? Would Catholic priests charged with abuse be treated differently in countries with a larger (or smaller) Catholic population than the United States? Do litigants in other countries use religion as a defense in the same ways, or with the same frequency? Research on these and related questions would be interesting in its own right and would also help establish the generality of effects (or lack thereof) observed in the American legal context.

Why Religion Matters at Trial, Does It, and Should It?

As the epigraph that opens this chapter observes, religion is a prominent issue in the lives not only of the overwhelming majority of Americans but of people all over the world. Thus, religion matters at trial simply because it matters everywhere else. Beyond that, though, religion matters at trial because it raises a number of unique issues in the trial context. In this section, we reiterate some of those issues in arguing why social scientists and policy makers should worry about religion's role at trial.[3]

In this section, we also revisit the two critical questions, or approaches, regarding the topic of religion's role at trial: the descriptive question and the normative question. The descriptive approach is essentially a status report. It summarizes the available research and attempts to describe whether, the extent to which, and under what circumstances religion actually does relate to trial outcomes. The descriptive picture is often complicated—as it is in this case—by gaps in the literature, methodological shortcomings, and inconsistent findings, yet it is relatively straightforward and value-free. The normative approach, on the other hand, is very much concerned with values. The question of whether religion should factor into trial outcomes is independent of the question of whether it actually does, and it is harder to answer because it cannot be answered empirically. The norms reflect legal assumptions and policy considerations but not data. Throughout the book, we have emphasized the descriptive perspective, but we have touched on the normative perspective as well. In the following sections, we briefly summarize the two perspectives in light of the foregoing discussion.

Religion at Trial: Why Worry About It?

One answer to this question is: Why not? Religion matters virtually everywhere else, as evidenced by its importance in the lives and decision making of attorneys, jurors, and judges (reviewed earlier). Religion also serves as the foundation of most, if not all, legal systems (Berman, 2000; Hamburger, 1993; Marty, 2005; Segrest, 1994). Moreover, issues of church–state separation and religious liberty are cardinal issues in constitutional jurisprudence.

Another (and probably more legitimate) answer is that, as reviewed earlier, religion can and does influence trial outcomes in many ways. Although the number of trials has declined in recent years (Galanter, 2004; Ostrom et al., 2004), there are still hundreds of thousands of trials per year (Ostrom et al., 2004). Trials also have a profound impact on business and individual behavior, of both potential litigants (e.g., Crump, 1998; Galanter & Luban, 1993) and those already involved in litigation (Galanter, 1990; Gross & Syverud, 1996). Although we do not have good data on the frequency with which religious issues come up in various kinds of cases, our subjective impression is that the number of such cases is increasing. This seems to be especially true in cases in which religion is used as a defense, religious overtones are present, or religion comes up in routine secular cases. The apparently growing number of "religious overtones" cases (e.g., clergy sexual abuse, religiously motivated terrorism) suggests that religion is finding its way into court in ever more guises. At times, it seems as if there are very few cases in which religion is *not* likely to come up. Thus, there is much to be learned from a consideration of religion's role at trial and in legal practice more broadly.

The Descriptive Question: Does Religion Matter at Trial?

The short answer to this question is "Yes." The longer, and more precise, answer—as illustrated in the "Key Themes" section—is, "In some ways, in some cases, and to varying degrees." One of the more challenging, and more perplexing, aspects of doing research in psychology and law is the frequent lack of consistent findings, leading to generalizations that can be held with some degree of confidence, but with a need to explain exceptions and explore possible moderators. We have attempted to do this in our discussion of individual topics, reviewed in the "Key Themes" section, so we do not reiterate the major findings here. Rather, in the present section, we address the question of how large the effects concerning religion's role at trial are.

Before leaping to the conclusion that religion is very influential on jury decisions and is thus a good way to pick a jury or devise trial strategy, it is important to consider the magnitude of these effects. In general, individual differences such as attitudes and demographic characteristics are not strong predictors of juror verdicts (Greene & Bornstein, 2003; Vidmar & Hans, 2007). Several studies of the topic have found that demographic, personality, and attitude variables rarely explain more than approximately 15% of the variation in mock juror decisions (e.g., Applegate et al., 2000; Hans & Loftquist, 1994; Hastie, Penrod, & Pennington, 1983; Hepburn, 1980; Lieberman & Sales, 2006; Miller & Hayward, 2008; Mills & Bohannon, 1980; Moran & Comfort, 1986). Most of these studies have not included religion, although a few have (e.g., Miller & Hayward, 2008).

Nevertheless, one should not assume that religion does not have an impact on jury verdicts. Even if the effects of individual difference variables are small, they can still affect trials in significant ways, especially in close cases. Most cases that go to trial are reasonably close, because otherwise they would be settled or dismissed. And with so many trials, there are numerous cases in which religious factors will tip the scales in one direction or the other.

Moreover, as we argued in Chapter 1, there are reasons to expect religion to be associated more strongly with factfinders' decisions than other individual difference variables. The prominence of religion in the lives of many (indeed, most) Americans suggests that it is likely to be a more central element of many people's self-concept than other individual difference variables, such as age and socioeconomic status. It may even be as influential as race and gender, the two categories most relevant to people's self-identification. In addition, unlike most demographic variables, religious identification and beliefs color one's entire value system and worldview. Individuals do not generally think "because of my race/age/gender/socioeconomic status, how do I feel about this issue or make this decision," whereas individuals may be more likely to consult their religious teachings in developing their attitudes and making life decisions. Some of these beliefs are especially relevant to legal cases, such as beliefs about reproductive rights (e.g., abortion), parental autonomy, and the death penalty.

To be sure, religion matters less at trial, almost all the time, than the evidence. But in a large number of cases, religion *is* the evidence, or at least a major piece of it. This is true in religious liberties cases, as well as cases in which religion is used as a defense or that have religious overtones. And, in cases in which religion is not a primary issue, it is in the background, lurking in the minds of many attorneys, jurors, and judges. Thus, we can answer unequivocally that religion does matter at trial.

The Normative Question: What Role *Should* Religion Play at Trial?

Because the normative question is concerned with values and policy considerations, it is harder to answer than the descriptive question. Nonetheless, our immersion in the debates over religion's proper role at trial has led us to form some (at times tentative) opinions, which we share here. We organize this section around a number of "shoulds."

Should attorneys be able to use religion in voir dire? With few exceptions, attorneys may use jurors' religious affiliation or beliefs as a basis for excluding them during voir dire. Most jurisdictions that have considered the issue have not elevated religion to the status of race or gender, which are impermissible factors for peremptory challenges. We feel that this is a mistake, and that attorneys should not be allowed to strike prospective jurors on religious grounds. We say this with an awareness that such a policy would continue the slippery slope of further limiting attorneys' autonomy during the jury selection stage, and that it would be largely unenforceable.

The slippery slope argument goes roughly as follows: If race, gender, and now religion, why not age? Or political party? Or occupation? Or eye color? Ultimately, the slippery slope culminates in the abolition of peremptory challenges altogether. Indeed, several commentators have made just such a proposal (for review, see Ballesteros, 2002; Vidmar & Hans, 2007, pp. 100–102). Whether attorneys should be able to use peremptory challenges at all is a debate from which we respectfully abstain. Nonetheless, we favor sliding down the slope a little bit farther to encompass religion. The (un)enforceability argument maintains that laws against demographic-based (i.e., *Batson*-type) challenges are essentially useless because an attorney, if challenged, can always come up with an alternative reason for the challenge (e.g., "It's not that he's Muslim, Your Honor, but that he's a physician").

Despite the relative ease of circumventing a *Batson*-type challenge and the slippery slope problem, we favor adding religion to the list of off-limits categories because it sends an important message, just as with race and gender. The message is that democratic institutions, such as jury service, are open to all eligible citizens, regardless of their religion. As a nation founded, in part, on the principle of religious tolerance, this is an important theme for courts and legislators to reiterate when given the opportunity.[4] It is particularly apt in the early 21st century, when the United States is more religiously diverse than ever before (Eck, 2001). As a side benefit, barring religion-based challenges would likely encourage jury service among religious minorities. At a time when many courts struggle with maintaining an adequate jury pool in the face of budgetary constraints and low response rates (Diamond, 1993; Miller & Bornstein, 2004), that is no small benefit. The (un)enforceability argument also presumes that attorneys will invariably circumvent the law if they have reason to believe that jurors of a particular religious persuasion would be biased against their side of the case. To be sure, some will, but this presumption sells short the vast majority of attorneys who would respect and abide by the law, even if they could violate it, and benefit from the violation, without being caught.

Should judges be allowed to remove jurors based on their religion? Although we believe that lawyers should not be allowed to exclude prospective jurors based on their religion, that is not to say that religion should be a complete non-factor in voir dire. In certain circumstances, a judge may be warranted in removing a juror based on religious factors. Judges are allowed to exclude jurors for cause; that is, if there is a reason that a juror would be inherently and irremediably biased (see Chapter 2). Thus, a judge would be acting within his proper authority to remove a juror who attends the parish of a priest who is accused of sexual abuse, or a Jehovah's Witness who expresses that her religious beliefs are so strong that they would impair her ability to act as a juror.[5] Forcing jury duty upon members of religions that forbid it is not a good policy decision. In addition to possibly causing anxiety for the juror, there is the chance that justice will not be done because the juror would be unable to make a legally proper decision. It is also within the courts' authority to allow any juror to postpone jury duty if the trial is scheduled to overlap with religious holidays. Unless this causes a significant detriment to the court (e.g., by eliminating a large amount of the jury pool), such exemptions should be allowed, as they would likely affect only a small portion of individuals. Courts are generally in agreement with this position, which allows appropriate exceptions to the laws forbidding exclusion based on religion.

As discussed in Chapter 2, some states allow members of certain religions to opt out of jury duty.[6] We favor a case-by-case approach to judicial decisions about allowing jurors to opt out, rather than blanket legislative laws. Although it is true that some religions do not believe in judging, not all members may subscribe to that tenet equally. For instance, even though the Catholic church has officially stated its opposition to the death penalty, not all members (e.g., Supreme Court Justice Antonin Scalia) adhere to that doctrine. As the research in Chapter 3 illustrates, a huge variety in attitudes often exists even within a certain religious denomination, and Chapter 4 illustrates that religious beliefs are not always predictive of legal attitudes. Thus, even though one might belong to a group that does not believe in judging, one may still be willing and able to do so in some circumstances. Thus, the decision as to whether one should be excluded would best be made on a case-by-case basis.

Similarly, blanket rules excluding clergy are obsolete. It is not clear why a member of the clergy would be exempt simply because of his religious beliefs, but members of the clergy's congregation—who share those same beliefs—would not. It is also hard to imagine that the congregation would be unduly harmed by the clergy's short absence, as most trials are relatively short. Perhaps the congregation would be harmed by a long absence, as in the case of an extended trial (especially if the jury was sequestered), assuming no substitute clergy were available. As in the case of denominational opting out, such decisions are best made by judges on a case-by-case basis, rather than a "catch-all" exemption made by the legislature.

Should attorneys be allowed to make religious appeals during oral argument? Courts that forbid or restrict religious appeals generally voice one of two concerns: that the appeals violate defendants' constitutional rights, or that they are prejudicial (Miller & Bornstein, 2005).[7] The prejudice argument is essentially a descriptive, empirical question: Would religious appeals bias jurors' verdicts in one direction or another, or impair their ability to apply the law? Research on this question has found that although biblical appeals generally do not have their desired effect in terms of encouraging a particular verdict preference (and can even backfire), some evidence suggests that they do interfere with the process of jurors' decision making. From a policy perspective, it is obviously undesirable if a practice impairs jurors' ability to make legally proper decisions (e.g., to weigh aggravating and mitigating circumstances properly).

The constitutional concerns are partly empirical as well. For example, the argument that religious appeals violate the Eight Amendment prohibition of cruel and unusual punishment is predicated on the possibility that they would interfere with the jury's "channeled discretion." In other words, it would be cruel and unusual for the jury to make a punishment decision based on non–legally relevant factors. As noted earlier, this is an empirical question, and it is a concern for which some (although not a lot of) support exists. Other constitutional concerns, such as that religious appeals violate the Due Process Clause or defendants' right to a fair trial, are more normative. Yet, even though they cannot be readily addressed empirically, they are perfectly legitimate concerns (some would no doubt argue that they are the paramount concerns). Constitutional considerations are, naturally, a valid rationale for permitting or prohibiting some trial practice. In light of these concerns, as well as the potential for prejudice, and absent any evidence that religious appeals are in some way beneficial, we agree with those courts that restrict the use of religious appeals. We recognize that this is a limitation on the considerable freedom that attorneys otherwise enjoy in oral argument, but that freedom is not completely unfettered, and it is outweighed in this case by other considerations. It would help, furthermore, if jurisdictions were more consistent in their position regarding what is and is not allowed during oral arguments (Montz, 2001).

Should factfinders be allowed to rely on religious texts and beliefs in making their decisions? Another way of phrasing this question is whether it is desirable, or even reasonable, to expect legal actors to check their religious beliefs at the door. As we noted in Chapter 1, there is a subtle distinction between using religiously tinged morality to decide cases, which is generally permissible, and explicitly using religion to accomplish the same thing, which is generally not permissible. The courts have repeatedly acknowledged the impossibility of stripping legal factfinders of their values and experiences, which may have a religious component; moreover, these values and experiences have a legitimate role to play in helping them reach their decisions (e.g., *Young v. State*, 2000). In one sense, the distinction between implicit and explicit religious influence is a spurious one, as religion is influencing the factfinder's decision regardless. According to this view, it might therefore be better to acknowledge religion's role openly than to ignore it. The open use of religious values in legal decision making—especially by judges, who have more of an obligation than jurors to justify their decisions—can potentially improve the administration of justice by leading to richer decisions and greater accountability (e.g., Carter, 1989; Idleman, 1993). This argument of "if it's there anyway, we're better off getting it in the open where we can regulate it" has some persuasive intuitive logic in its favor.

Nonetheless, there is a sense in which the distinction between implicit and explicit religious influence is a meaningful one and worth maintaining. In a legal sense, the principle of church–state separation has generally been interpreted as barring the explicit use of religion in legal decision making. As Wiehl (2000) points out, this proscription is not difficult to circumvent, especially in the case of judicial decision making. Courts have upheld judges' right to rely on religious texts in sentencing, as long as they are not the sole basis for giving a particular sentence. Nonetheless, more widespread use of religious references in legal decision making would have serious constitutional implications. In addition, it would make it that much easier for legal decision makers to bring in other extraneous sources, such as nonreligious philosophical texts. Restricting the explicit use of religion keeps the emphasis on evidence and the law, where it belongs.

There is also another reason for preserving the distinction: Barring the explicit use of religion avoids the *appearance* of unfairness, even if no unfairness actually occurred (i.e., even if it could be considered "harmless error"). Appearances, no less in the courtroom than in other areas of life, are important. Americans have equal access to, and the right to equal treatment by, the courts regardless of their religious background. Imagine how a Hindu considering filing a lawsuit would feel about pursuing a claim if she knew the jury was going to look to the Judeo-Christian Bible for guidance; or how a Muslim defendant would feel after his sentence was justified by citing a religious text whose authority he did not recognize. Better still, imagine how an atheist would feel about a juror's receiving advice from her pastor on the disposition of her case, or how a Christian defendant would feel if a Muslim judge gave him a particular sentence because the Koran suggested it was the right one. On the one hand, one could argue that such perceptions and feelings on the part of litigants are not that important, as long as the outcome is legally defensible. Yet, on the other hand, a wealth of research on procedural justice shows that individuals' perceptions of how they were treated by a legal authority have profound implications for their willingness to obey the law, assist law enforcement (e.g., report crimes to the police), and accept adverse outcomes (see generally Lind & Tyler, 1988; Tyler, 2006). Thus, there is considerable value in keeping religious influences on legal decision making in the background.

Should there be a role for religion in legal education? Attorneys, like many other individuals, struggle with reconciling their career with their faith. Religious law schools are striving to aid them in this struggle, by incorporating religion and morality in law students' ethical training. Such training can provide new lawyers with an understanding of the rules of professional responsibility, an appreciation of the complex moral dilemmas that can occur in legal practice, and strategies for dealing with them when they do occur.

Despite these developments, we do not know the real extent to which the work–spirituality conflict is a source of dissatisfaction for lawyers, or whether graduates of religious law schools are better prepared than graduates of secular law schools to deal with the conflict. It is also unclear exactly how lawyers should bring religious values to bear on their work (Pearce & Uelmen, 2005–2006). Finally, although it is relatively easy for religious law schools to incorporate religious values in the curriculum, it is much more complicated for secular law schools, which would inevitably run afoul of the Establishment Clause if they attempted to do so. Our brief overview of religion in legal education (see Chapter 7) seems to suggest a movement toward two different types of law school curricula: one informed by religion (at religious law schools) and the other one not (at secular law schools). Only time, and systematic data collection, will tell whether one approach is more effective than the other.[8] Our qualified recommendation is that, in the marketplace of legal education, religious law schools are a legitimate alternative with the potential—as yet unproven—to make unique and valuable contributions to the legal profession.

Should litigants from different religious backgrounds be treated differently? At first blush, the answer to this question seems to be an obvious "of course not." Litigants' case disposition should depend on the evidence and the law, to neither of which religion is relevant in the vast majority of cases. One should not be judged more culpable or punished more severely for routine civil and criminal offenses simply by virtue of one's religious affiliation.

On further reflection, however, the answer to this question is not so obvious. A defendant who has had a born-again experience since committing a crime might seem less deserving of punishment than one who was not born-again, perhaps because the conversion makes any display of remorse seem more sincere. Or, a clergyman who committed child sexual abuse might seem more deserving of punishment than a stranger who committed the same crime, because of the greater violation of role expectations and greater breach of duty in the former instance. Free-exercise plaintiffs from marginal religions perhaps should be more likely to win than plaintiffs from mainstream religions, because the challenged restriction of religious expression really is more burdensome on them. Thus, legitimate legal reasons exist—in certain limited kinds of cases, and under specific circumstances—for taking litigants' religion into account. However, it is important to limit the role of litigants' religion to these special circumstances, so that it does not turn into blanket, unbridled religious prejudice.

The Final Word

All of these "shoulds" constitute our best assessment in light of the data available at the time. We reserve the right to modify our recommendations as additional data become available and the discourse on religion's role at trial increases. There seems to be little doubt that God is in the courtroom, and God is likely there to stay. We have argued that this is not necessarily a bad thing, but it is not necessarily a good thing either, and answering the question of whether God *should* be in the courtroom requires a nuanced exploration of a number of interrelated issues. This book is our attempt to add to that discussion.

We agree with the statement by Spilka and colleagues (2003), used as the epigraph to this chapter, that religion is "a fascinating realm." The enormous amount of discourse about religion, in both the academic literature and the popular media, suggests that we are not alone in our fascination. Yet, despite this fascination, empirical research on religion, especially in the legal domain, is rather scant. Our hope is that the present volume will inspire other social scientists to add to this fascinating and important topic.

Notes

Chapter 1

1. Chambers said that he filed the lawsuit to make a point about frivolous lawsuits (Bratton, 2007; "State Sen. Ernie Chambers sues God," 2007; Young, 2009). For more on the legislative career of this "irascible firebrand," who served for nearly four decades before being forced out by a newly passed term limits law, see Saulny (2008).

2. President Bush was not the first born-again Christian President (e.g., Jimmy Carter), and he might not even be the most religiously devout president, but he was probably more open than any other president about the role that religion played in his life and in his policy making.

3. Secularism, or not subscribing to any religion, does not necessarily imply atheism, which only a tiny percentage of U.S. adults (approximately 1%) use to describe themselves (Kosmin et al., 2001; Pew Forum on Religion and Public Life, 2008).

4. Despite the important differences between evangelicalism and fundamentalism, some researchers use the terms more or less interchangeably. In describing specific studies, we adhere to the terminology used by the researcher, but we otherwise strive to be as precise as possible in describing individuals' religious beliefs and affiliation.

5. We regret that a fuller comparative analysis is beyond our scope and expertise, as it offers the opportunity to address a number of interesting questions. For example, do religious differences in legal attitudes and decisions generalize across nations? Do attorneys in more secular countries than the United States, such as most of Europe, struggle to reconcile their work and their faith? Would Catholic priests charged with abuse be treated differently in more strongly Catholic nations, such as Ireland or Poland, than in the United States? Do litigants in other countries invoke religion as a defense or mitigating factor? We know of no research on these or related questions, which we hope future scholars will begin to address.

6. The remainder are not necessarily non-Christian, as many individuals describe themselves as religious but do not affiliate with any particular denomination.

7. Some commentators have made precisely this argument, as we describe in Chapter 6.

8. A number of legal journals pay particular attention to issues of church–state jurisprudence: *Rutgers Journal of Law and Religion, Journal of Law and Religion* (published by the Hamline University School of Law), *University of Maryland Law Journal of Race, Religion, Gender and Class,* and *Journal of Catholic Legal Studies* (formerly *Catholic Lawyer,* published by the St. John's Law School). The law reviews of the various religious law schools also publish frequent articles on these issues, especially the Catholic and evangelical law schools (for a list of law schools with a religious affiliation, see Chapter 7).

9. See, e.g., *International Journal for the Psychology of Religion, Journal for the Scientific Study of Religion, Journal of Psychology and Christianity, Journal of Psychology and Theology, Research in the Social Scientific Study of Religion,* and *Review of Religious Research.*

Chapter 2

1. Kissinger was the national security advisor to President Nixon and subsequently the Secretary of State.

2. It is difficult to know how effective scientific jury selection really is. It is impossible to try the case once using jury selection techniques and once without; thus, real-world tests of jury selection techniques are difficult to perform. Nonetheless, research can help determine whether jury selection based on specific techniques might be successful at helping a lawyer choose a favorable jury. For instance, Chapters 3 and 4 describe research about how religious affiliation and beliefs relate to legal attitudes and jury verdicts. Attorneys could use this research in selecting a jury. Chapter 10 discusses the magnitude of effects of these studies. As a whole, scientific jury selection appears to be somewhat beneficial (e.g., Posey & Wrightsman, 2005), although certainly other factors (e.g., the strength of the evidence) affect the trial more than the identity of the jurors.

3. Whether any empirical evidence supports this assumption is addressed in Chapter 3.

4. Many religions (especially Christianity) have a general prohibition against judging others—for example, "Judge not, that you be not judged" (Matthew 7:1), and "Let him who is without sin among you be the first to throw a stone" (John 8:7). These verses are generally interpreted not to proscribe any and all judging, merely unfair or improper judging; nor are they interpreted by mainstream religions as barring judging in the name of a recognized secular authority. However, some fundamentalist religions, such as the Amish, do interpret such scriptural passages as prohibiting judging for purposes of punishment on behalf of an authority other than God; it is for those religions that the exemption exists. We discuss these cases at greater length in the final section of this chapter.

5. Most statutes do not give reasons for excluding clergy. A clergy exemption may be based on community needs, such as concern that the congregation would be harmed if she was taken away from her occupational duties (similar to the reasons doctors are sometimes excluded because their patients need them). Perhaps some legislators also felt that a juror who was a member of the clergy would have undue influence on other jurors during deliberations because of her presumed moral authority.

Presumably, the reason for the exemption must be based on more than the clergy's beliefs about judging others. If that was the only basis, it is unclear why a clergy would be exempt, while her followers (who likely have similar beliefs) would not be exempt. In addition, a belief-based exemption would not necessarily exempt all clergy, as some laws do. Thus, the clergy exemptions are likely a result of the clergy's occupation, and not necessarily because of her religious beliefs.

6. This case was reviewed twice by the Minnesota Supreme Court and once by the U.S. Supreme Court. All decisions have the same name, and they all occurred in the same year. We refer to the initial Minnesota case as *In re Jenison I*, the subsequent U.S. Supreme Court case as *In re Jenison II*, and the ultimate disposition by the Minnesota Supreme Court as *In re Jenison III*.

7. See Chapter 4 for a more extensive discussion of how religious beliefs affect jurors' attitudes toward punishment and verdicts.

Chapter 3

1. The 3rd U.S. Circuit Court of Appeals will hear Prowel's appeal and decide whether the case will proceed to trial, but as of November 10, 2008, the court had not issued an opinion.

2. As discussed in Chapters 1 and 4, although "fundamentalist" and "evangelical" are often used interchangeably, they are not quite the same thing (Kellstedt, 1989).

3. For instance, Sandys and McGarrell used an Indiana sample, whereas the Grasmick studies used Oklahoma samples. Sandys and McGarrell contend that relationships among religious characteristics and legal attitudes may be stronger in places like Oklahoma, in part because of its location in the "Bible Belt."

4. Many other studies likely do not report null results if they do not find relationships among different religious groups.

5. Death-qualified participants would likely qualify to be jurors on a death penalty trial because their attitudes about the death penalty are not so strong that they would interfere with their duties as jurors.

6. We discuss this case, and others in which defendants have raised religion as part of an insanity defense, further in Chapter 9.

Chapter 4

1. Evangelism is often confused with evangelicalism, but the two are not the same. The former is simply a measure of whether one has proselytized, whereas the latter refers to a specific set of beliefs (Kellstedt, 1989). This includes believing in the importance of proselytizing, the divinity of Christ, Christ as the only way to attain eternal life/salvation, and an inerrant Bible. Many evangelicals report having had a "born-again" experience, but it is not an essential criterion (Kellstedt, 1989; Smidt, 1989). Further, evangelicalism subsumes a broad range of groups from across the political spectrum (i.e., liberal-conservative; see Kellstedt, 1989). All the studies reported here used the term "evangelism" to describe their measures, which investigate whether someone has personally proselytized others.

2. However, see Chapter 6 for a study about evangelicalism and judges, which uses membership in an evangelical church as a way to measure evangelicalism.

3. Death-qualified participants are those who would likely qualify as jurors in a death penalty trial.

4. In 2005, the U.S. Supreme Court found the juvenile death penalty to be unconstitutional (*Roper v. Simmons,* 2005); however, the penalty was allowed at the time these studies were conducted.

5. The scale was from 1 = "very religious" to 4 = "not religious at all."

6. Not surprisingly, believing in a punitive God is common among fundamentalist Protestants, who (as discussed in Chapter 3) are also more supportive of corporal punishment and spanking.

7. This is an interesting finding, considering that one might expect that the results would depend on participants' affiliation. For instance, a Catholic who based her death penalty attitudes on her religious beliefs would likely be opposed to the death penalty, whereas a Southern Baptist who based her death penalty attitudes on her religious beliefs would likely be supportive of the death penalty. The results of this measure (as with many of the measures) may be dependent on the sample and particular question wording. Even so, it is interesting that the overall effect indicates that those who say they base their attitudes toward the death penalty on their religious beliefs—regardless of what their beliefs are—are less punitive.

8. However, it is important to note that, in general, fundamentalism is related to increased punitiveness, whereas evangelism is related to decreased punitiveness.

9. See Chapter 10 for a more in-depth discussion of effect sizes associated with these studies.

Chapter 5

1. In Chapter 8, we consider attorneys' reliance on these same scriptural guidelines in making oral arguments.

2. In determining whether contact with an outside source is more than just harmless error, these cases fail to distinguish between an individual juror and collective jurors. It would seem to be a less serious error if an individual juror gets outside information, which he does not share and which might influence his judgment alone, than if he also shares that information with the rest of the jury—thereby influencing others' judgments as well.

3. Additionally problematic is the fact that the juror admittedly relied on the defense attorney's conduct in reaching a verdict. Even if the attorney's conduct did bear a relationship to the defendant's guilt—which it almost certainly did not—it was not evidence and should therefore not influence the verdict.

4. A similar argument has been made against attorneys quoting scripture in arguing for the death penalty; see Chapter 8.

5. In some countries (e.g., Canada), much stricter rules are in place about whom a juror may consult outside of the trial. In some countries, jurors cannot discuss the trial with anyone—including family, media, or pastors—even after the trial has concluded. Thus, the issue of religious consultation outside the jury room is less of a concern in such countries.

6. Actual jurors receive similar instructions.

7. Note, however, that another study in this same book indicated that mock juror participants who read an appeal given by a prosecuting attorney did not rely more on personal religious beliefs or biblical authority.

Chapter 6

1. Nearly all of these couples obtain a state-sanctioned divorce as well.
2. This is obviously less true for appellate judges, who decide cases as a group. Although judicial conferences might resemble jury deliberations in some respects, individual judges are nonetheless considerably more autonomous than individual jurors (e.g., each judge can write his own opinion).
3. See, e.g., recent interviews of Scalia (http://www.cbsnews.com/stories/2008/04/24/ 60minutes/main4040290_page4.shtml; retrieved 10/24/08), and Thomas (http://www. cbsnews.com/stories/2007/09/27/60minutes/main3305443.shtml).
4. A wealth of biographical information is available on Supreme Court justices, much of which covers their religion, especially when it is relevant to their selection, as in the case of Catholic and Jewish justices. We rely primarily on works that have focused specifically on justices' religion; for more general biographical sources, see Abraham (1992); Stephenson (1994).
5. These data are taken from "Religious affiliation of the U.S. Supreme Court," http:// www.adherents.com/adh_sc.html, which lists the religion of the first 108 Supreme Court justices. We have added Chief Justice Roberts and Associate Justice Alito to the tally. Some justices changed their affiliation or had more than one affiliation; they are listed according to their primary affiliation. Figures do not equal 100% due to rounding. See also Abraham (1992, p. 64); Hitchcock (2004, Vol. 2, Ch. 4).
6. President Ford did consider nominating a Mormon—Dallin Oaks, president of Brigham Young University—to replace William O. Douglas in 1975, but chose not to, fearing a confirmation battle on the grounds of Oaks' religion. Ford ultimately nominated John Paul Stevens instead (Hitchcock, 2004, Vol. 2; Yalof, 1999).
7. The nominees answered that their religious beliefs would play no role in their judging (Levinson, 2006).
8. Brandeis was offered the presidency of the World Zionist Organization in 1920, but he refused to resign from the Supreme Court to assume that position (Auerbach, 1990).
9. For comparison purposes, consider that losing Democratic Presidential candidate Al Smith garnered 72% of the Jewish vote in the 1928 election (Perry, 1991).
10. McReynolds is doubtless not the only religious bigot to have served on the Court. For example, Hugo Black had pronounced anti-Catholic sentiments and ties to the Ku Klux Klan, but there is no evidence that it adversely affected his interactions with his Catholic colleagues (Hitchcock, 2004, Vol. 2).
11. The main factor was his admission of past marijuana use, although presidential mismanagement—in the wake of the failed Robert Bork nomination immediately prior— may also have contributed to Ginsburg's unsuccessful nomination (Massaro, 1990).
12. Robertson declined to identify the justices by name, but two of the three were evidently Justices Stevens and Ginsburg, both of whom are still on the Court as of this writing.
13. A revised version of Segal and Spaeth's statement of the attitudinal model was published in 2002 as *The Supreme Court and the Attitudinal Model Revisited*.
14. Recent Catholic nominees for federal judgeships, including Supreme Court nominees, have been questioned about their position on issues on which the Catholic Church has taken an unequivocal position, such as abortion and capital punishment (Dlouhy, 2003; Levinson, 1990, 2006; Myers, 1991). As a rule, they have been evasive and/or relied on legal precedent in responding, refusing to allow their personal beliefs to become part of the process.

15. They also examined a number of other social background, environmental, community, and school district variables that are not relevant to the present discussion.

16. This is the same reasoning that some lawyers used in determining that Jews would be sympathetic to plaintiffs (see Chapters 2 and 3).

17. Although this result supports the social background model, it should be noted that the sample was relatively small (14 justices), and only three of the justices were non-Protestant. Two were Catholic (Murphy and Brennan), and one was Jewish (Frankfurter). In their analysis of Supreme Court voting behavior in civil rights and economics cases over a longer time period (1916–1988), Tate and Handberg (1991) found no difference between Protestant and non-Protestant justices.

18. The terminology in these cases can be confusing. Those who favor accommodations in free exercise cases generally vote in favor of claimants arguing that their religious liberty has been infringed upon; however, "accommodationists" in establishment cases generally vote to allow government support of religion, in opposition to claimants arguing for separation.

19. We consider the role of litigants' religion in Chapter 9.

20. These figures are averages. Exact figures vary depending on the particular survey. The American Religious Identification Survey found that 24.5% of American adults were Catholic and 16.3% were Baptist (Kosmin et al., 2001). More recently, the U.S. Religious Landscape Survey, released in February 2008 by the Pew Forum on Religion and Public Life, found that 23.9% of American adults were Catholic and 12.7% were Baptist (the latter figure combines Evangelical and Mainline Baptists, who were classified separately; results are available at http://religions.pewforum.org).

21. Although they are accommodationist on the matter of the Establishment clause, Scalia and Thomas have come into conflict with the Catholic Church on other issues, most notably in their support for the constitutionality of capital punishment (Berg & Ross, 1998; Hitchcock, 2004, Vol. 2; Lithwick, 2002). For a discussion of the relationship between Catholicism and judges' role in capital sentencing, see Garvey and Coney (1998), and Merz (2004).

22. The Model Code, which was originally promulgated in 1990 and amended most recently in 2004, is available at http://www.abanet.org/cpr/mcjc/home.html.

23. Note that much of the difficulty in this debate lies in the determination of what, exactly, is better, more just, or more humane.

24. This figure comes from a 1996 article in which Judge Quirk was interviewed, so the current number is probably much higher. According to the Lake Charles City Court website, Judge Quirk is still on the bench and presumably still allowing defendants to choose church over other penalties (http://www.lccitycourt.org/Pages/Quirk.htm, last modified 4/14/08, retrieved 11/14/08).

25. See "A brief guide to Alcoholics Anonymous," available at http://www.aa.org/en_pdfs/p-42_abriefguidetoaa.pdf.

26. Note that this is the same judge who, as described at the beginning of this chapter, was subsequently removed from office for actions involving his religious beliefs—primarily installation of a monument to the Ten Commandments in the rotunda of the Alabama State Judicial Building (Idleman, 2005).

27. Leviticus 20:13 states: "If a man lies with a male as one lies with a woman, the two of them have done an abhorrent thing." Elsewhere in the opinion, Moore cited Genesis and St. Thomas Aquinas's *Summa Theologica*.

Chapter 7

1. Baker and Floyd (1998) use this poem to introduce their book *Can a Good Christian Be a Good Lawyer?* As it nicely captures the challenges faced by many religious attorneys, we have borrowed it here.

2. By way of analogy, Levinson (1993/2003) gives the wonderful example of Sandy Koufax, who refused to pitch the opening game of the 1965 World Series for the Los Angeles Dodgers because it fell on Yom Kippur, but who could not be said to have "pitched like a Jew."

3. For example, Chapter 3 describes the case of a lesbian pastor who was tried by the Methodist church for violating the church's policy on gay pastors.

4. Droel (1989) observes that as a rabbi, Jesus was also part of this "Jewish lawyer" tradition.

5. This is not to argue that the "justice imperative" is a peculiarly Jewish invention. Similar statutes existed in Mesopotamia as far back as 2400 B.C.E., in the Code of Hammurabi seven centuries later, and in pre-Israelite Canaanite literature (Auerbach, 1990).

6. The first Jewish ABA president was Bernard G. Segal (1969–1970); recent Jewish presidents include Roberta C. Ramo (1995–1996; also the first woman to hold the office) and Jerome Shestack (1997–1998).

7. They split Protestants into two groups: those "of higher socioeconomic status, from older immigrant stock" (e.g., Presbyterians, Episcopalians, and Congregationalists), and those of lower socioeconomic status (e.g., Lutherans, Methodists, and Baptists; Heinz & Laumann, 1982, p. 15). The size of the two groups was roughly equal (13.0% in Group 1 and 12.2% in Group 2).

8. It is important to note that the data from Heinz and colleagues' follow-up study, although published in 2005, were collected in 1995. We were unable to find more recent data, and it is entirely possible that the picture has changed in the last 10–15 years. It is also possible that the Chicago bar is not representative of the population of American lawyers. Given how little the picture changed between their two studies, conducted 20 years apart, and in light of comparable findings from other locales (e.g., Dinovitzer, 2006; Lena, Roach, & Warkov, 1993; Smigel, 1964), we doubt that the situation is much different now, in Chicago or elsewhere; but we wholeheartedly support additional research on the topic.

9. From the Association's website, http://www.intjewishlawyers.org/html/about.asp. The Association has an American affiliate, the American Association of Jewish Lawyers and Jurists, organized in 1983 (http://www.jewishlawyers.org/).

10. From the Guild's Welcome page, http://www.clgc.org/ (retrieved 6/19/08).

11. http://www.clsnet.org/clsPages/vision08.php (retrieved 6/19/08).

12. The sizeable number of Catholic divorce lawyers (26%) might seem surprising, in light of the Catholic Church's prohibition of divorce; or it might not, considering the relatively high degree of acceptance of the practice among American Catholics.

13. According to van Hoy (1997, pp. 27–28), franchise law firms "can be best understood as part of a process [of] 'McDonaldization.' McDonaldization combines the principles of franchises, bureaucracies, scientific management and assembly lines to achieve a maximum level of rationalization in the creation and delivery of products and services. Within the context of law this means organizing the law firm and legal work to minimize the efforts of lawyers as experts and put more responsibility into the hands of

support staff." Franchise firms offer a limited menu of standardized, prepackaged services.

14. By referring to this as a "perception," we do not mean to imply that it is necessarily inaccurate, but merely that we cannot vouch for its accuracy because of the absence of objective data on the question.

15. The ethnic community in this study had linguistic and geographical, as well as religious components, as the study participants were mostly English-speaking Quebecois who had relocated from Montreal to Toronto.

16. On the issue of stratification in the legal profession, see also Auerbach (1976).

17. The RALS conference traditionally alternates between Catholic and Protestant institutions; see http://law.baylor.edu/rals/index.htm (retrieved 6/23/08).

18. Regent was founded by Pat Robertson, who is himself a Yale Law School graduate, and Liberty was founded by Jerry Falwell. Liberty is so new that its ABA accreditation is still provisional (as of June 24, 2008).

19. This dichotomy is, of course, a simplification and obscures a more finely graduated continuum.

20. The author of this particular article, Rex Lee, was founding dean of the Brigham Young University Law School and later served as the university's president.

21. From the Ave Maria Mission Statement, available at http://www.avemarialaw.edu/index.cfm?event=about.mission (retrieved 6/2/08).

22. From the Baylor Law School Mission Statement, available at http://law.baylor.edu/MissionStatement.htm (retrieved 6/2/08).

23. From the Regent Law School Dean's Message, available at http://www.regent.edu/acad/schlaw/dean/home.cfm (retrieved 6/18/08). For specific examples of how Regent accomplishes this goal, see Scarlato and Kohm (1998–1999).

24. From "Law at BYU," available at http://www.law2.byu.edu/admissions/law_at_byu.php (retrieved 6/18/08).

25. Most states have adopted some variation of either the ABA Model Code of Professional Responsibility (adopted 1981) or the ABA Model Rules of Professional Conduct (adopted 1983).

26. For example, Fordham's Institute on Religion, Law & Lawyer's Work; Pepperdine's Institute for Law, Religion and Ethics; and Regent's Institute for Christian Legal Studies.

27. For example, these same eight law schools appear in the top 30 spots on www.lawsch001100.com, which bills its rankings as "based on qualitative, rather than quantitative, criteria" (retrieved 6/24/08). They are in more or less the same order, with the main exception that Georgetown is the highest ranked religious law school, at #7.

28. At http://www.ilrg.com/rankings/law (retrieved 6/24/08).

29. It is important to compare a school's rate to the state average because, as the table shows, state passage rates vary considerably (from 92% in Oklahoma to 62% in Wyoming).

30. According to the school's website, http://www.faulkner.edu/admissions/jonesLaw.asp (retrieved 6/24/08).

31. The Justice Department's report on the hiring scandal, "An investigation of allegations of politicized hiring by Monica Goodling and other staff in the office of the Attorney General," is available at http://www.usdoj.gov/oig/special/s0807/final.pdf. In the related firing scandal, Attorney General Michael Mukasey appointed a special prosecutor in September 2008 to lead an investigation (Palazzolo, 2008).

32. The most recent ABA Young Lawyers Division Career Satisfaction Survey, released in 2000, is available at http://www.abanet.org/yld/satisfaction_800.doc. The Division

has also written a guide for dealing with young lawyers' dissatisfaction, "Life in the balance: Achieving equilibrium in professional and personal life" (available at http://www.abanet.org/yld/about/writtenguide.html).

33. These tensions and dilemmas naturally hold true for nonreligious attorneys as well (Lesnick, 2003), but religious attorneys, to the extent that they reflect more on such issues, might feel them more keenly.

34. The article by Rice (1999) consists of advice to aspiring Catholic lawyers, but one could easily imagine similar advice being given to (and by) devout attorneys of other faiths.

35. The term "spirituality," so central to this issue, is one of those words that everyone uses and understands but is hard to define. A working definition is that it "refers to all of the ways in which we seek and respond to God's presence. Spirituality is the style, the awareness with which we orient ourselves to God" (Droel, 1989, p. 12).

36. It is worth noting that forming a stronger attachment to clients carries risks as well. If lawyers get too attached to their clients, they may suffer *vicarious trauma*. Vicarious trauma is a form of secondary traumatic stress that can happen when someone becomes too attached to another person and takes on a caretaker role (Saakvitne, Tennen, & Affleck, 1998). This could occur, for example, with a lawyer who is working on behalf of an injured client. The lawyer might identify with the client's suffering and take on the role of caretaker, thinking he will be able to "provide" for the client; if the client loses the case, then the lawyer could suffer too.

37. Needless to say, one does not have to be personally religious to engage in this kind of work, but in the words of many of the practitioners themselves, it helps (e.g., Ball, 1998).

38. As Moore (2007) describes, there is no requirement that religiously minded legal advocacy groups be Christian, but the vast majority of them are; specifically, nearly all of them are staffed by evangelical Protestants.

39. In one of the more widely publicized nonreligious efforts, the Rutherford Institute represented Paula Jones in her sexual harassment suit against President Bill Clinton, because it provided "a great opportunity for Christians to say, 'We really do care about sexual harassment in the workplace'" (Whitehead, 1999, p. 4; see also Moore, 2007).

40. Shaffer (1998, p. 202) observes that "[w]e lawyers know who the oppressed are, if only because we know whom we oppress."

Chapter 8

1. This verse is very similar to Matthew 18:6, which judges have used in sentencing (see Chapter 6).

2. The prosecutor stated that the only murders that are acceptable to God are murders in self-defense, as in the case of David slaying Goliath. Because the defendant's murder was not self-defense, he deserved to be punished.

3. The prosecutor compared the crimes of the defendant with the deeds of Peter, who denied Christ three times; this was meant as an indication of the defendant's undesirable character, which presumably indicated that he deserved to be punished.

4. In addition to showing a lot of hubris on the part of the attorney, this sort of argument places a great deal of pressure on jurors, as it implies that they are responsible for the defendant's eternal soul.

5. For more on the effects of a defendant's religious conversion and religious behavior in court, see Chapter 9.

6. The defense attorney in *State v. Patterson* (1996) wanted to tell this story, but the judge would not allow it.

7. And, of course, lawyers who use biblical appeals hope that the appeals will affect jurors' decisions.

Chapter 9

1. Sorauf (1976) also examined the relationship between case outcomes and the religion of judges and attorneys; we describe these findings in Chapters 6 and 7, respectively.

2. Most of the reports were of appellate court decisions, but the sample did include some federal district (trial) court cases.

3. The reference group for their statistical analyses was "general Christians," a category that consisted of numerous non-Baptist Protestant denominations. This study also addressed the role of judges' religion; see Chapter 6.

4. Data on the question are not completely unanimous. Brent (1999) analyzed free exercise cases decided in U.S. Courts of Appeals from 1987–1996 and found that claimants from what he termed "mainstream" Christian faiths (Catholics, Presbyterians, Baptists, Lutherans, Episcopalians, etc.) actually won their cases *more* often (38.9%) than nonmainstream claimants (24.5%). Because the various studies examined different time periods and courts and categorized religions somewhat differently, it is hard to explain the discrepancy in findings; but it might reflect the fact that Brent's study concentrated on cases decided immediately before and after two controversial milestones in free exercise jurisprudence: the U.S. Supreme Court's decision in *Employment Division v. Smith* (1990) and passage of the Religious Freedom Restoration Act (RFRA; 1993). The RFRA effectively overturned *Smith*, which was viewed as overly restrictive of free exercise claims (Brent, 1999); the RFRA was itself declared unconstitutional only a few years later, in *City of Boerne v. Flores* (1997).

5. "Religious shunning is a practice in which religious adherents break off contact with a member or former member of their religious body to some degree at the order of their church" (Merkin, 2001, p. 372).

6. The Texas Supreme Court held that the First Amendment would not protect the church from liability for a plaintiff's physical injuries. Although the plaintiff in *Pleasant Glade* did allege some minor physical injuries (e.g., scrapes and bruises), the trial dealt solely with her emotional injuries (*Pleasant Glade v. Schubert*, 2008).

7. As with any high-profile news story, the Snyder trial and general activities of the Westboro Baptist Church have been covered extensively. The primary sources we relied on were news articles by Castaneda (2007), Hotakainen (2007), and MSNBC ("Funeral war pickets lose verdict," 2008), as well as information on the Anti-Defamation League website ("Fred Phelps and the Westboro Baptist Church," available at http://www.adl. org/special_reports/wbc.default.asp, retrieved 8/22/08).

8. In addition to Jehovah's Witnesses and Christian Scientists, members of the Church of God and Pentecostal Free Will Baptist Church also refuse certain kinds of medical treatment. According to the U.S. Census Bureau, these groups together constitute 4.5% of the U.S. population (Parobek, 2006–2007). These cases can raise other constitutional issues in addition to religious freedom, such as the right to privacy.

9. *Employment Division v. Smith* (1990) was not specifically about peyote. The plaintiffs were fired because they used peyote; they then applied for unemployment benefits and were denied. They sued because they felt that the denial of benefits was because of their religion. The Supreme Court held that the state could deny unemployment benefits to a person fired for violating a state prohibition on the use of peyote, even though the use of the drug was part of a religious ritual. The Court reasoned that although states have the *power* to accommodate otherwise illegal acts done in pursuit of one's religious beliefs, they are not *required* to do so. Thus, the case was seen as a failure to protect the right to use peyote for religious purposes.

10. Lest one think that exorcisms are exceedingly rare, and failed exorcisms even rarer, a Google search for the phrase "exorcism trial" (on August 29, 2008) yielded approximately 549,000 hits. These trials, in which a person has allegedly been injured, and in some cases killed, during an exorcism, occur all over the world. Even more frightening, evidence suggests that interest in the practice is growing (see, e.g., "Australia Catholic Church," 2008). The entertainment industry has taken notice. The book and film "The Exorcist" (original film released in 1973, with multiple sequels) were hugely popular; more recently, the Hollywood film "The Exorcism of Emily Rose" (2005) depicted a case—loosely based on actual incidents in Germany—in which a girl died from starvation after repeated exorcism sessions, and the priest who performed the exorcism was subsequently tried for negligent homicide.

11. Because polygamists, especially those from fundamentalist religious sects, rarely formally marry more than one spouse, they are usually prosecuted for other crimes, such as statutory rape, sexual assault, or child abuse.

12. Consider, for example, Ray Hemphill's sentence of only 2½ years for causing the death of his exorcism victim, or the relatively light sentences handed down in polygamy cases, especially when the judge or jurors are also polygamists (http://www.cnn.com/2006/LAW/08/03/polygamist.sentenced/index.html).

13. Hill became the first person to be executed for anti-abortion violence in 2003 ("Abortion doctor's murderer dies," 2003).

14. In cases like Yates,' part of the reason an excuse defense such as insanity seems more compelling than a justification defense is the assumption that in reality, her children would not actually go to hell if she failed to kill them. We are entirely comfortable with this assumption, but we also note that religious texts contain numerous examples of the dire consequences—just as hard to prove—that will befall adherents who fail to follow certain religious precepts.

15. An incompetency judgment does not mean that a defendant is set free. In most cases, such as Mitchell's, the person is confined to a mental health treatment center. If a future court determines that his mental health has improved enough to stand trial, Mitchell will face charges of kidnapping, sexual assault, and burglary. Likewise, defendants who successfully plead not guilty by reason of insanity are not necessarily liberated and on average are confined for periods as long as, if not longer than, defendants found guilty of comparable crimes (Greene et al., 2007). A federal judge ordered a new competency evaluation for Mitchell in November, 2008 (Dobner, 2008), but the evaluation had not been completed by the time this book went to press.

16. This is the case for capital sentencing, the arena in which religious conversions have received the most attention; the role of aggravators and mitigators in non-capital cases is somewhat more complicated.

17. Although defendants sometimes convert to religions other than Christianity, the clear majority of cases involve a Christian conversion.

18. As is typically the case, the conversion was described more as a "born-again" experience than as a conversion from one religious denomination to another. We cover other aspects of this study in Chapter 8.
19. We discuss the relationship between juror and litigant religion later in this chapter.
20. The situation might be different if the cult actively engaged in or endorsed violent acts, which it did not in *Flanagan*.
21. See "Omaha nun sentenced to prison" (2008), and "Nun asks to take back guilty plea" (2008).
22. Only in the rarefied world of medicine could dermatology be considered a low-status occupation. This example is proof that every profession has its own internal hierarchy.
23. Many excellent sources exist that cover the topic from multiple perspectives. See, e.g., Frawley-O'Dea (2007); Frawley-O'Dea and Goldner (2007); Plante (2004b).
24. Available at http://www.komonews.com/news/archive/4192846.html (retrieved 10/4/08).
25. See the church's website, www.lakewood.cc, and "Victoria Osteen trial" (2008). We also discuss this case in Chapter 2.
26. We distinguish these "routine secular" charges from polygamy (discussed earlier), which is also a prominent issue in these cases, because defendants are likely to make a free exercise defense to any polygamy charges. In July, 2008, a Texas grand jury indicted Jeffs and four of his followers on charges of sexual assault of a child ("Sect leader Jeffs indicted," 2008). One of the followers was also charged with bigamy, and a fifth follower was indicted for failure to report child abuse.
27. In Begue's (2001) study, the black-sheep effect occurred only in some situations (i.e., when the abortion produced negative consequences and when she had been under social pressure to have the abortion).
28. It is debatable whether any crime is truly victimless. When people refer to victimless crimes, they usually mean such offenses as violations of sexual prohibitions (e.g., sodomy, prostitution, public nudity), health protections (e.g., seat belt and helmet laws), etc. For a more comprehensive list, see http://www.ldp.org.au/federal/policies/victimlessCrimes.html (retrieved 9/24/08).
29. The U.S. Supreme Court affirmed the reversal on other grounds (*South Carolina v. Gathers*, 1989; see Ariens, 1992).

Chapter 10

1. Studies of the two populations tend to use different research methodologies. The judge studies are exclusively archival analyses of actual judicial decisions, whereas the jury studies tend to be surveys of people from different religious backgrounds (who could become jurors, but who are not jurors at the time of the study) or experimental studies of mock jurors. We return to this and related methodological issues in the Future Research Directions section, later.
2. As discussed in Chapter 9, free exercise claimants from marginal religions are also likely to be more successful than claimants from mainstream religions; but because free exercise claims tend to be more idiosyncratic (e.g., a prohibition against wearing a head covering would affect members of some religions but not others), less opportunity exists for potential plaintiffs to use religion in a strategic fashion than in establishment claims.

3. We do not use the term "worry" here in the sense that people should fret about it (although in some respects, maybe they should); rather, we use it in the sense of "consider" or "attend to."

4. As discussed in Chapter 2, many states have adopted specific legislative acts forbidding individuals from being excluded based on their religion.

5. Religious beliefs in such cases would operate in much the same way as death penalty attitudes in capital cases, which can be used to exclude prospective jurors if they would prevent them from applying the law (see Chapter 2).

6. It is interesting that some laws forbid excluding jurors based on religion, whereas other laws allow members of religious groups to opt out. Although these are seemingly opposite messages, they quite likely can live comfortably in tandem if one views the former law as a protection against discrimination and the latter as an accommodation for those who have very strong religious reasons not to perform jury duty.

7. This is a broad-brush distinction; in actuality, there are subtypes within each category (see Chapter 8).

8. Among other things, any researchers who investigate this question will have to answer "effective in what way?" There are numerous possible criteria, such as job satisfaction, job stability, earnings, and the like, and many of the criteria are hard to operationalize.

References

ABA Young Lawyers Division. (2000). Career satisfaction survey. *American Bar Association.* Retrieved May 9, 2008, from http://www.abanet.org/yld/satisfaction_800.doc.

Abortion doctor's murderer dies by lethal injection (2003, September 3). *FoxNews.com.* Retrieved November 17, 2008, from http://www.foxnews.com/story/0,2933,96286,00.html.

Abraham, H. J. (1992). *Justices and presidents: A political history of appointments to the Supreme Court* (3rd ed.). New York: Oxford University Press.

A.C.L.U. sues judge for church sentence (1994, November 24). New York Times. Retrieved February 17, 2008, from http://query.nytimes.com/gst/fullpage.html?res=9507EEDF1730F937A15752C1A962958260.

al-Hibri, A. (1996). On being a Muslim corporate lawyer. *Texas Tech Law Review, 27,* 947–961.

Allegretti, J. G. (1996). *The lawyer's calling: Christian faith and legal practice.* New York: Paulist Press.

Allegretti, J. G. (1998a). Lawyers, clients, and covenant: A religious perspective on legal practice and ethics. *Fordham Law Review, 66,* 1101–1129.

Allegretti, J. G. (1998b). Neither curse nor idol: Towards a spirituality of work for lawyers. In T. E. Baker & T. W. Floyd (Eds.), *Can a good Christian be a good lawyer? Homilies, witnesses, and reflections* (pp. 147–158). Notre Dame, IN: University of Notre Dame Press.

Allegretti, J. G. (2001a). A Christian perspective on alternative dispute resolution. *Fordham Urban Law Journal, 28,* 997–1006.

Allegretti, J. G. (2001b). The lawyer's calling revisited: Second look or second thoughts? *St. John's Law Review, 75,* 267–272.

Allegretti, J. G. (2002). The role of a lawyer's morals and religion when counseling clients in bioethics. *Fordham Urban Law Journal, 30,* 9–34.

Alley, R. S. (1988). *The Supreme Court on church and state.* Oxford: Oxford University Press.

American Law Institute. (2000). *A concise restatement of torts.* St. Paul, MN: American Law Institute Publishers.

Applegate, B. K., Cullen, F. T., Fisher, B. S., & Vander Ven, T. (2000). Forgiveness and fundamentalism: Reconsidering the relationship between correctional attitudes and religion. *Criminology, 38,* 719–753.

Appleman, J. A. (1952). *Successful jury trials: A symposium.* Indianapolis: Bobbs-Merrill.

Ariens, M. (1992). Evidence of religion and the religion of evidence. *Buffalo Law Review, 40,* 65–111.

Ashenfelter, O., Eisenberg, T., & Schwab, S. J. (1995). Politics and the judiciary: The influence of judicial background on case outcomes. *Journal of Legal Studies, 24,* 257–281.

Ashley, G. M. (2002). Theology in the jury room: Religious discussion as "extraneous material" in the course of capital punishment deliberations. *Vanderbilt Law Review, 55,* 127–163.

Auerbach, J. S. (1976). *Unequal justice: Lawyers and social change in modern America.* New York: Oxford University Press.

Auerbach, J. S. (1990). *Rabbis and lawyers: The journey from Torah to Constitution.* Bloomington, IN: Indiana University Press.

Australia Catholic Church trains more exorcists due to growing demand. *FoxNews.com.* Retrieved August 29, 2008, from http://www.foxnews.com/story/0,2933,330955,00.html.

Baker, T. E., & Floyd, T. W. (1998). *Can a good Christian be a good lawyer? Homilies, witnesses, and reflections.* Notre Dame, IN: University of Notre Dame Press.

Ball, W. B. (1998). On hoping to be, being, and having been. In T. E. Baker & T. W. Floyd (Eds.), *Can a good Christian be a good lawyer? Homilies, witnesses, and reflections* (pp. 42–46). Notre Dame, IN: University of Notre Dame Press.

Ballesteros, S. G. (2002). Don't mess with Texas voir dire. *Houston Law Review, 39,* 201–241.

Banerjee, N. (2007, September 22). Episcopal Church remains divided on gay issues. *New York Times.* Retrieved October 28, 2008, from http://www.nytimes.com/2007/09/22/us/22episcopal.html?fta=y.

Barkan, S. E., & Cohn, S. F. (1994). Racial prejudice and support for the death penalty by whites. *Journal of Research in Crime and Delinquency, 31,* 202–209.

Barkan, S. M. (1995). The first conference of religiously affiliated law schools: An overview. *Marquette Law Review, 78,* 247–254.

Barringer, D. (1996, December). Higher authorities: Religious faith ordinarily is a personal matter. *ABA Journal, 82,* 68.

Bartkowski, J. P, & Wilcox, W. B. (2000). Conservative Protestant child discipline: The case of parental yelling. *Social Forces, 79,* 265–290.

Bartol, C. R., & Bartol, A. M. (2004). *Psychology and law: Theory, research, and application* (3rd ed.). Belmont, CA: Wadsworth Publishing.

Barton, B. (1995). Religion-based peremptory challenges after *Batson v.* Kentucky *and* J.E.B. v. Alabama. *Michigan Law Review, 94,* 191–216.

Batson, C. D., & Ventis, W. L. (1982). *The religious experience: A social-psychological perspective.* New York: Oxford University Press.

Baumer, E. P., Messner, S. F., & Rosenfeld, R. (2003). Explaining spatial variation in support for capital punishment: A multilevel analysis. *American Journal of Sociology, 108,* 844–875.

Baylor Institute for Studies of Religion. (2006). *American piety in the 21st century: New insights to the depth and complexity of religion in the U.S.* Waco, TX: Baylor Institute for Studies of Religion.

Begue, L. (2001). Social judgment of abortion: A black-sheep effect in a Catholic sheepfold. *Journal of Social Psychology, 141,* 640–649.

Bell, C. W. (2000, June 17). Some juicy ironies at Fla. Baptist meet. *NYDailyNews.com.* Retrieved October 16, 2008, from http://www.nydailynews.com/archives/news/2000/06/17/2000–06–17_some_juicy_ironies_at_fla__b.html.

Belli, M. (1963). *Modern trials* (Abridged Ed.). Indianapolis: Bobbs-Merrill.

Berg, T. C., & Ross, W. G. (1998). Some religiously devout justices: Historical notes and comments. *Marquette Law Review, 81,* 383–409.

Berman, H. J. (2000). *Faith and order: The reconciliation of law and religion.* Grand Rapids, MI: William B. Eerdmans Publishing Co. (Original work published 1993).

Biber, E. (2004). The price of admission: Causes, effects and patterns of conditions imposed on states entering the Union. *American Journal of Legal History, 46,* 119–219.

Bjarnason, T., & Welch, M. R. (2004). Father knows best: Parishes, priests, and American Catholic parishioners' attitudes toward capital punishment. *Journal for the Scientific Study of Religion, 43,* 103–119.

Blum, V. (2005, July 8). Putting Islam on the stand. *Law.com.* Retrieved June 27, 2008, from http://www.law.com/jsp/article.jsp?id=1120727114514.

Blume, J. H., & Johnson, S. L. (2000). Don't take his eye, don't take his tooth, and don't cast the first stone: Limiting religious arguments in capital cases. *William and Mary Bill of Rights Journal, 9,* 61–104.

Blumstein, A., & Cohen, J. (1980). Sentencing of convicted offenders: An analysis of the public's views. *Law and Society Review, 14,* 223–261.

Bodenhausen, G., & Lichtenstein, M. (1987). Social stereotypes and information-processing strategies: The impact of task complexity. *Journal of Personality and Social Psychology, 48,* 267–282.

Borg, M. J. (1997). The southern subculture of punitiveness? Regional variation in support for capital punishment. *Journal of Research in Crime and Delinquency, 34,* 24–45.

Borg, M. J. (1998). Vicarious homicide victimization and support for capital punishment. *Criminology, 36,* 537–568.

Bornstein, B. H. (1999). The ecological validity of jury simulations: Is the jury still out? *Law and Human Behavior, 23,* 75–91.

Bornstein, B. H. (2006). Judges vs. juries. *Court Review, 43,* 56–58.

Bornstein, B. H., & McCabe, S. G. (2005). Jurors of the absurd? The role of consequentiality in jury simulation research. *Florida State University Law Review, 32,* 443–467.

Bornstein, B. H., & Miller, M. K. (2005). Does religion predict juror decisions? Implications for peremptory challenges. *APA Monitor, 36,* 92.

Bornstein, B. H., Miller, M. K., Nemeth, R. J., Page, G. L., & Musil, S. M. (2005). Juror reactions to jury duty: Perceptions of the system and potential stressors. *Behavioral Sciences and the Law, 23*, 321–346.

Bost, T. G., & Perrin, L. T. (2005). Practicing law as a Christian: Restoration movement perspectives. *Pepperdine Law Review, 32*, 419–437.

Bratton, A. J. (2007, September 21). "God" gets an attorney in lawsuit. *Associated Press*. Retrieved July 24, 2008, from http://abcnews.go.com/print?id=3637469.

Breen, J. M. (2006). The Catholic lawyer: "Faith" in three parts. *Notre Dame Journal of Law, Ethics & Public Policy, 20*, 431–441.

Brent, J. C. (1999). An agent and two principals: U.S. Court of Appeals responses to *Employment Division, Department of Human Resources v. Smith* and the Religious Freedom Restoration Act. *American Politics Quarterly, 27*, 236–266.

Britt, C. L. (1998). Race, religion and support for the death penalty: A research note. *Justice Quarterly, 15*, 175–191.

Brooks, E. A. (1999). Thou shalt not quote the Bible: Determining the propriety of attorney use of religious philosophy and themes in oral arguments. *Georgia Law Review, 33*, 1113–1180.

Bruce, S. (2003). *Politics and religion*. Cambridge, U.K.: Polity Press.

Bullis, R. K. (1991). The spiritual healing "defense" in criminal prosecutions for crimes against children. *Child Welfare, 70*, 541–555.

Burt, C. (2006, May 25). Cold Bay 'heaven' for three children. *Oakland Tribune*. Retrieved May 21, 2007, from http://findarticles.com/p/articles/mi_qn4176/is_20060525/ai_n16439032.

Burt, R. A. (1988). *Two Jewish justices: Outcasts in the promised land*. Berkeley, CA: University of California Press.

Burtchaell, J. T. (1998). *The dying of the light: The disengagement of colleges and universities from their Christian churches*. Grand Rapids, MI: William B. Eerdmans.

Butler, B. (2007). The role of death qualification in capital trials involving juvenile defendants. *Journal of Applied Social Psychology, 37*, 549–560.

Buzzard, L. R. (1995). A Christian law school: Images and vision. *Marquette Law Review, 78*, 267–282.

Capehart, J. (2007). Michael Vick's self-defeat. Retrieved November 22, 2008 from http://www.washingtonpost.com/wp-dyn/content/article/2007/08/28/AR2007082801447.html.

Carter, S. L. (1989). The religiously devout judge. *Notre Dame Law Review, 64*, 932–943.

Carter, S. L. (1998). All that we do. . . . In T. E. Baker & T. W. Floyd (Eds.), *Can a good Christian be a good lawyer? Homilies, witnesses, and reflections* (pp. 3–10). Notre Dame, IN: University of Notre Dame Press.

Cartwright, R. E. (1977). Jury selection. *Trial, 13*, 29–31.

Cascarelli, J. C. (2000). The Catholic's role in the legal profession in republican government. *Catholic Lawyer, 39*, 291–316.

The case of the Taliban American (n.d.). *CNN.com*. Retrieved November 29, 2005, from http://www.cnn.com/CNN/Programs/people/shows/walker/profile.html.

Casson, A. K., & Curran, R. F. (1984). Secular orthodoxy and sacred freedoms: Accreditation of church-related law schools. *Journal of College and University Law, 11*, 293–322.

Castaneda, R. (2007, November 1). $11 million awarded in funeral protest suit. *Washington Post.* Retrieved August 22, 2008, from http://www.washingtonpost.com.

Chamberlain, J., Miller, M. K., & Jehle, A. (2006). Celebrities in the courtroom: Legal responses, psychological theory and empirical research. *Vanderbilt Journal of Entertainment and Technology Law, 8,* 551–572.

Champagne, A., & Nagel, S. S. (1982). The psychology of judging. In N. L. Kerr & R. M Bray (Eds.), *The psychology of the courtroom* (pp. 257–283). New York: Academic Press.

Chase, H. W., Green, M. J., & Mollan, R. (1960, September 26). Catholics on the Court. *New Republic,* pp. 13–15.

Chavez, H. L., & Miller, M. K. (in press). Religious references in death sentence phases of trials: Two psychological theories that suggest judicial rulings and assumptions may affect jurors. *Lewis & Clark Law Review.*

Chermak, S., & Chapman, N. M. (2007). Predicting crime story salience: A replication. *Journal of Criminal Justice, 35,* 351–363.

Chopko, M. E. (1998). Public lives and private virtue. In T. E. Baker & T. W. Floyd (Eds.), *Can a good Christian be a good lawyer? Homilies, witnesses, and reflections* (pp. 11–16). Notre Dame, IN: University of Notre Dame Press.

Church trial acquits gay pastor: Methodist clergy vote to keep lesbian minister (2004, March 21). *CBSnews.com.* Retrieved October 16, 2008, from http://www.cbsnews.com/stories/2004/03/22/national/main607701.shtml.

Cohen, A. B., Malka, A., Rozin, P., & Cherfas, L. (2006). Religion and unforgivable offenses. *Journal of Personality, 74,* 85–117.

Collett, T. S. (2000). The king's servant, but God's first. *South Texas Law Review, 41,* 1277–1297.

Conkle, D. O. (1998a). Professing professionals: Christian pilots on the river of law. *Catholic Lawyer, 38,* 151–183.

Conkle, D. O. (1998b). Religiously devout judges: Issues of personal integrity and public benefit. *Marquette Law Review, 81,* 523–531.

Cook, K. J., & Powell, C. (2003). Christianity and punitive mentalities: A qualitative study. *Crime, Law & Social Change, 39,* 69–89.

Corbett, M., & Corbett, J. M. (1999). *Politics and religion in the United States.* New York: Garland.

Court: Bible in jury room was wrong, death sentence stands (2008, August 20). *USAtoday.com.* Retrieved October 27, 2008, from http://www.usatoday.com/news/religion/2008–08–20-bible-jury_N.htm.

Court: Exorcism is protected by law (2008, June 28). *MSNBC.com.* Retrieved July 24, 2008, from http://www.msnbc.com/id/25423465/.

Coyle, M. (2006, September 8). Judicial surveys vex the bench. *National Law Journal.* Retrieved September 8, 2006, from http://www.law.com/jsp/law/LawArticleFriendly.jsp?id=1157629870187.

Crocker, C. B., & Kovera, M. B. (in press). In R. L. Wiener and B. H. Bornstein (Eds.), *Trial consulting: A psychological handbook.* New York: Springer.

Cromartie, J. L. (1998). Reflections on vocation, calling, spirituality and justice. In T. E. Baker & T. W. Floyd (Eds.), *Can a good Christian be a good lawyer? Homilies, witnesses, and reflections* (pp. 139–146). Notre Dame, IN: University of Notre Dame Press.

Crump, D. (1998). Evidence, economics, and ethics: What information should jurors be given to determine the amount of a punitive-damage award? *Maryland Law Review, 57,* 174–235.

Daicoff, S. S. (2004). *Lawyer, know thyself: A psychological analysis of personality strengths and weaknesses.* Washington, DC: American Psychological Association.

Dane, F. C., & Wrightsman, L. S. (1982). Effects of defendants' and victims' characteristics on jurors' verdicts. In N. L. Kerr & R. M. Bray (Eds.), *The psychology of the courtroom* (pp. 83–115). New York: Academic Press.

Darrow, C. (1936, May). Attorney for the defense. *Esquire, 5,* 36.

Davis, R. (2005). *Electing justice: Fixing the Supreme Court nomination process.* Oxford: Oxford University Press.

Dawkins, R. (2006). *The God delusion.* London: Bantam Press.

Dembo, M. H., & McAuliffe, T. J. (1987). Effects of perceived ability and grade status on social interaction and influence in cooperative groups. *Journal of Educational Psychology, 79,* 415–423.

Dennett, D. C. (2006). *Breaking the spell: Religion as a natural phenomenon.* New York: Viking.

Descant, E. (2006, December 9). Defense calls for mistrial after Bible left in jury room. *Dispatch Starkville Bureau.* Retrieved May 18, 2007, from http://www. cdispatch.com/articles/2006/12/09/local_news/loca102.txt.

Deutsch, L. (2004, November 2). Questionnaires used to reduce jury pool in Robert Blake case. *North County Times.* Retrieved August 5, 2008, from http:// www.nctimes.com/articles/2004/11/03/news/state/20_18_3211_2_04.txt.

Diamond, S. S. (1993). What jurors think: Expectations and reactions of citizens who serve as jurors. In R.E. Litan (Ed.), *Verdict: Assessing the civil jury system* (pp. 282–305). Washington, DC: Brookings Institution.

Dinovitzer, R. (2006). Social capital and constraints on legal careers. *Law & Society Review, 40,* 445–479.

DiSalvo, C. R., & Droel, W. L. (1998). Reflections on the contents of the lawyer's work: Three models of spirituality—and our struggle with them. In T. E. Baker & T. W. Floyd (Eds.), *Can a good Christian be a good lawyer? Homilies, witnesses, and reflections* (pp. 127–138). Notre Dame, IN: University of Notre Dame Press.

Dlouhy, J. A. (2003, August 2). Religion takes center stage in fight over judicial nominees. *CQ Weekly, 61,* 1964–1965.

Dobner, J. (2008, November 12). Judge OKs new mental test in Elizabeth Smart case. *USA Today.* Retrieved November 17, 2008, from http://www.usatoday. com/news/nation/2008–11–12–3938074532_x.htm?loc=interstitialskip.

Dobranski, B. (2002). New lawyers for a new century—legal excellence and moral clarity: The founding of Ave Maria School of Law. *University of Toledo Law Review, 34,* 55–64.

Dolbee, S., Sauer, M., & Krasnowski, M. (2007, July 15). Los Angeles archdiocese will settle abuse suits. *San Diego Union-Tribune.* Retrieved September 19, 2008, from http://www.signonsandiego.com/news/state/20070715–9999– 1n15settle.html.

Dorf, M. C. (2005, April 27). Why Al Qaeda conspirator Zacarias Moussaoui's guilty plea probably won't save his life. *FindLaw.com.* Retrieved August 5, 2008, from http://writ.news.findlaw.com/dorf/20050427.html.

Dressler, J. (2007). *Cases and materials on criminal law* (4th ed.). St. Paul, MN: West.

Drinan, R. F. (2000). Religious organizations and the death penalty. *William and Mary Bill of Rights Journal, 9*, 171–177.

Droel, W. L. (1989). *The spirituality of work: Lawyers.* Chicago: ACTA Publications.

Duffy, B. C. (1997). Prosecutors' use of religious arguments in the sentencing phase of capital cases. *Vanderbilt Law Review, 50*, 1335–1385.

Duin, J. (2008, October 26). Episcopal Church losing members. *The Washington Times.* Retrieved October 28, 2008, from http://www.washingtontimes.com/ news/2008/oct/26/episcopal-church-losing-members/.

Ebrahim, M. (2006, May/June). The Bible bench. *Mother Jones, 31(3)*, 54–57, 81–83.

Echols, M. (2005). Is the courtroom the right place for religion? Difficulties in restricting religious arguments during the sentencing phase of Pennsylvania death penalty cases: *Commonwealth v. Spotz. University of West Los Angeles Law Review, 36*, 254–269.

Eck, D. L. (2001). *A new religious America: How a "Christian country" has now become the world's most religiously diverse nation.* San Francisco: HarperCollins.

Edwards, D. (1998). Reflections on three stories: "Practicing" law and Christianity at the same time. In T. E. Baker & T. W. Floyd (Eds.), *Can a good Christian be a good lawyer? Homilies, witnesses, and reflections* (pp. 17–27). Notre Dame, IN: University of Notre Dame Press.

Egland, T. T. (2004). Prejudiced by the presence of God: Keeping religious material out of death penalty deliberations. *Capital Defense Journal, 16*, 337–366.

Eisenberg, D., Thomas, C. B., Calabresi, M., Novak, V., Steptoe, S., Padgett, T., & Tortora, A. (2005, May 23). The posse in the pulpit. *Time, 165(21)*, 32–33.

Eisenberg, H. B. (1998–1999). Mission, marketing, and academic freedom in today's religiously affiliated law schools: An essay. *Regent University Law Review, 11*, 1–16.

Eisenberg, T., Garvey, S. P., & Wells, M. T. (2001). Forecasting life and death: Juror race, religion, and attitude toward the death penalty. *Journal of Legal Studies, 30*, 277–311.

Elkins, J. R. (1987). Reflections on the religion called legal education. *Journal of Legal Education, 37*, 522–528.

Ellison, C. G. (1991). An eye for an eye? A note on the southern subculture of violence thesis. *Social Forces, 69*, 1223–1241.

Ellison, C. G., & Sherkat, D. E. (1993). Conservative Protestantism and support for corporal punishment. *American Sociological Review, 58*, 131–144.

Epstein, S. (1990). Cognitive-experiential self-theory. In L. Pervin (Ed.), *Handbook of personality: Theory and research* (pp. 165–192). New York: Guilford.

Epstein, S. (1994). Integration of the cognitive and the psychodynamic unconscious. *American Psychologist, 49*, 709–724.

Eric Rudolph gets life without parole (2005, July 18). *Fox News.* Retrieved November 29, 2005, from http://www.foxnews.com/story/0,2933,162790,00. html.

Evans, T. D., & Adams, M. (2003). Salvation or damnation?: Religion and correctional ideology. *American Journal of Criminal Justice, 28*, 15–36.

Everson, G. (1919). The human element in justice. *Journal of the American Institute of Criminal Law and Criminology, 10,* 90–94.

Failinger, M., Allegretti, J., Emmerich, C., Kaliff, M., Quraishi, A., Reber, R., & Schorr, N. H. (1999). Panel discussion: Models of successful "religion and lawyering" programs. *Fordham Urban Law Journal, 26,* 917–960.

Falbo, T., New, B. L., & Gaines, M. (1987). Perceptions of authority and power strategies used by clergymen. *Journal for the Scientific Study of Religion, 26,* 499–507.

Feather, N. T., & Atchison, L. (1998). Reactions to an offence in relation to the status and perceived moral character of the offender. *Australian Journal of Psychology, 50,* 119–127.

Feldman, S. M. (2006). Empiricism, religion, and judicial decision-making. *William & Mary Bill of Rights Journal, 15,* 43–57.

Finamore, F., & Carlson, J. M. (1987). Religiosity, belief in a just world, and crime control attitudes. *Psychological Reports, 61,* 135–138.

Finkel, N. J. (1995). *Commonsense justice.* Cambridge, MA: Harvard University Press.

Finkel, N. J. (2001). When principles collide in hard cases: A commonsense moral analysis. *Psychology, Public Policy, and Law, 7,* 515–560.

Fischer, H. (2008, August 1). Ruling: No religious right to marijuana. *AZstarnet. com.* Retrieved October 16, 2008, from http://www.azstarnet.com/ metro/250846.

Fitzgerald, J. J. (2001). Today's Catholic law schools in theory and practice: Are we preserving our identity? *Notre Dame Journal of Law, Ethics & Public Policy, 15,* 245–306.

Fitzgerald, R., & Ellsworth, P. C. (1984). Due process v. crime control: Death qualification and jury attitudes. *Law and Human Behavior, 8,* 31–51.

Flanagan, T. J., & Jamieson, K. M. (1988). *Sourcebook of criminal justice statistics—1987.* U.S. Department of Justice. Washington D.C.: Bureau of Justice Statistics.

Flowers, R. B. (1993). Government accommodation of religious-based conscientious objection. *Seton Hall Law Review, 24,* 695–736.

Flowers, R. B. (2007). *That Godless court? Supreme Court decisions on church–state relationships* (2nd ed.). Louisville, KY: Westminster John Knox Press.

Foley, L. A., & Pigott, M. A. (1997). The influence of forepersons and nonforepersons on mock jury decisions. *American Journal of Forensic Psychology, 15,* 15–17.

Former klansman found guilty of manslaughter: Conviction coincides with 41st Anniversary of civil rights killings (2005, June 22). *CNN.com.* Retrieved November 29, 2005, from http://www.cnn.com/2005/LAW/06/21/mississippi. killings/index.html.

Frawley-O'Dea, M. G. (2007). *Perversion of power: Sexual abuse in the Catholic Church.* Nashville, TN: Vanderbilt University Press.

Frawley-O'Dea, M. G., & Goldner, V. (2007). Abusive priests: Who they were and were not. In M. G. Frawley-O'Dea & V. Goldner (Eds.), *Predatory priests, silenced victims: The sexual abuse crisis and the Catholic Church* (pp. 21–34). Mahwah, NJ: The Analytic Press.

Fred, M. A. (1998). Yerwal religion. *Journal of Legal Education, 48,* 140–144.

Fukuno, M., & Ohbuchi, K. (1998). How effective are different accounts of harm-doing in softening victim's reactions? A scenario investigation of the effects of severity, relationship, and culture. *Asian Journal of Social Psychology*, *1*, 167–178.

Fulero, S. M., & Penrod, S. D. (1990). Attorney jury selection folklore: What do they think and how can psychologists help? *Forensic Reports, 9*, 233–259.

Funeral war pickets lose verdict (2007, October 31). *MSNBC.com.* Retrieved August 22, 2008, from http://www.msnbc.msn.com/id/21566280/.

Gaffney, E. M. (1986). Biblical law and the first year curriculum of American legal education. *Journal of Law and Religion, 4*, 63–95.

Galanter, M. (1990). The civil jury as regulator of the litigation process. *University of Chicago Legal Forum, 1990*, 201–271.

Galanter, M. (1999). A vocation for law? American Jewish lawyers and their antecedents. *Fordham Urban Law Journal, 26*, 1125–1147.

Galanter, M. (2004). The vanishing trial: An examination of trials and related matters in federal and state courts. *Journal of Empirical Legal Studies, 1*, 459–570.

Galanter, M., & Luban, D. (1993). Poetic justice: Punitive damages and legal pluralism. *American University Law Review, 42*, 1393–1463.

Galanter, M., & Palay, T. (1991). *Tournament of lawyers: The transformation of the big law firm.* Chicago: University of Chicago Press.

Garvey, J. H., & Coney, A. B. (1998). Catholic judges in capital cases. *Marquette Law Review, 81*, 303–341.

Gaudet, F. J. (1938/1964). Individual differences in the sentencing tendencies of judges. In G. Schubert (Ed.), *Judicial behavior: A reader in theory and research* (pp. 352–367). Chicago: Rand McNally & Co.

George, T. E. (2001). Court fixing. *Arizona Law Review, 43*, 9–62.

George, T. E., & Epstein, L. (1992). On the nature of Supreme Court decision making. *American Political Science Review, 86*, 323–337.

Gerdy, K. B. (2006). "The irresistible force meets the immovable object": When antidiscrimination standards and religious belief collide in ABA-accredited law schools. *Oregon Law Review, 85*, 943–991.

Giles, M., & Walker, T. (1975). Judicial policy-making and southern school segregation. *Journal of Politics, 37*, 917–936.

Ginsburg, R. B. (1994). Introduction. In J. M. Lowe (Ed.), *The Jewish justices of the Supreme Court revisited: Brandeis to Fortas* (pp. 3–4). Washington, DC: The Supreme Court Historical Society.

Glickstein, H. A. (1995). A Jewish-sponsored law school: Its purposes and challenges. *Marquette Law Review, 78*, 481–486.

"God" responds to legislator's lawsuit (2007, November 28). *CNN.com.* Retrieved July 24, 2008, from http://www.cnn.com/2007/US/law/09/20/swing.god.ap/index.html.

Goldman, S. (1966). Voting behavior on the United States Courts of Appeals, 1961–1964. *American Political Science Review, 60*, 374–383.

Goldman, S. (1975). Voting behavior on the United States Courts of Appeals revisited. *American Political Science Review, 69*, 491–506.

Goldman, S. (1997). *Picking federal judges: Lower court selection from Roosevelt through Reagan.* New Haven, CT: Yale University Press.

Goldstein, I. (1935). *Trial technique.* Chicago: Callaghan.

Gonzales, M. H., Haugen, J. A., & Manning, D. J. (1994). Victims as "narrative critics": Factors influencing rejoinders and evaluative responses to offenders' accounts. *Personality and Social Psychology Bulletin, 20*, 691–704.

Gonzalez, R. A. (1996). Climbing the ladder of success: My spiritual journal. *Texas Tech Law Review, 27*, 1139–1157.

Gonzalez-Perez, M. (2001). A model of decisionmaking in capital juries. *International Social Science Review, 76*, 79–91.

Goode, B. P. (2003–2004). Religion, politics, race and ethnicity: The range and limits of voir dire. *Kentucky Law Journal, 92*, 601–712.

Grasmick, H. G., Bursik, R. J., & Blackwell, B. S. (1993). Religious beliefs and public support for the death penalty for juveniles and adults. *Journal of Crime and Justice, 16*, 59–86.

Grasmick, H. G., Bursik, R. J., & Kimpel, M. (1991). Protestant fundamentalism and attitudes toward corporal punishment of children. *Violence and Victims, 6*, 283–298.

Grasmick, H. G., Cochran, J. K., Bursik, R. J., & Kimpel, M. L. (1993). Religion, punitive justice and support for the death penalty. *Justice Quarterly, 10*, 289–314.

Grasmick, H. G., Davenport, E., Chamlin, M. G., & Bursik, R. J. (1992). Protestant fundamentalism and the retributive doctrine of punishment. *Criminology, 30*, 21–45.

Grasmick, H. G., & McGill, A. L. (1994). Religion attribution style, and punitiveness towards juvenile offenders. *Criminology, 32*, 23–46.

Grasmick, H. G., Morgan, C. S., & Kennedy, M. B. (1992). Support for corporal punishment in the schools: Comparison of the effects of S.E.S. and religion. *Social Science Quarterly, 73*, 177–187.

Green, E. (1964). Judicial attitudes in sentencing. In G. Schubert (Ed.), *Judicial behavior: A reader in theory and research* (pp. 368–388). Chicago: Rand McNally & Co.

Greenawalt, K. (1995). *Private consciences and public reasons.* New York: Oxford.

Greenawalt, K. (1998). Judicial resolution of issues about religion conviction. *Marquette Law Review, 81*, 461–472.

Greene, E., & Bornstein, B. H. (2003). *Determining damages: The psychology of jury awards.* Washington, D.C.: American Psychological Association.

Greene, E., & Dodge, M. (1995). The influence of prior record evidence on juror decision-making. *Law and Human Behavior, 19*, 67–78.

Greene, E., Heilbrun, K., Fortune, W. H., & Nietzel, M. T. (2007). *Wrightsman's psychology and the legal system* (6th ed.). Belmont, CA: Thomson/Wadsworth.

Greene, E., & Wrightsman, L. (2003). Decision making by juries and judges: International perspectives. In D. Carson & R. Bull (Eds.), *Handbook of psychology in legal contexts* (2nd ed., pp. 401–422). Chichester, England: Wiley.

Greer, T., Berman, M., Varan, V., Bobrycki, L., & Watson, S. (2005). We are a religious people; We are a vengeful people. *Journal for the Scientific Study of Religion, 44*, 45–57.

Griffen, W. L. (1998). The case for religious values in judicial decision-making. *Marquette Law Review, 81*, 513–519.

Grinberg, E. (2005, July 15). Teens in satanist case enter plea. *CNN.com*. Retrieved November 29, 2005, from http://www.cnn.com/2005/LAW/07/15/ctv.satanist. case/index.html.

Gross, S. R., & Syverud, K. D. (1996). Don't try: Civil jury verdicts in a system geared to settlement. *UCLA Law Review, 44*, 1–64.

Hadfield, G. K. (2004). Where have all the trials gone? Settlements, nontrial adjudications, and statistical artifacts in the changing disposition of federal civil cases. *Journal of Empirical Legal Studies, 1*, 705–734.

Hagan, J., Huxter, M., & Parker, P. (1988). Class structure and legal practice: Inequality and mobility among Toronto lawyers. *Law & Society Review, 22*, 9–55.

Hall, D. (2005). *The spiritual revitalization of the legal profession: A search for sacred rivers*. Lewiston, NY: Edwin Mellen Press.

Hall, M. G., & Brace, P. (1992). Toward an integrated model of judicial voting behavior. *American Politics Quarterly, 20*, 147–168.

Hamburger, P. A. (1993). Natural rights, natural law, and American constitutions. *Yale Law Journal, 102*, 907–960.

Hamilton, M. (2004, July 29). The marriage debate and polygamy: Several Utah cases challenge whether anti-polygamy laws are constitutional. *FindLaw. com*. Retrieved September 19, 2008, from http://writ.news.findlaw.com/ hamilton/20040729.html.

Hans, V. P., & Lofquist, W. S. (1992). Jurors' judgments of business liability in tort cases: Implications for the litigation explosion debate. *Law and Society Review, 26*, 85–115.

Hans, V. P., & Lofquist, W. S. (1994). Perceptions of civil justice: The litigation crisis attitudes of civil jurors. *Behavioral Sciences and the Law, 12*, 181–196.

Hans, V. P., & Vidmar, N. (1986). *Judging the jury*. New York: Plenum Press.

Harrington, D. C., & Dempsey, J. (1969). Psychological factors in jury selection. *Tennessee Law Review, 37*, 173–178.

Harris, P. W. (1986). Over-simplification and error in public opinion surveys on capital punishment. *Justice Quarterly, 3*, 429–455.

Hastie, R., Penrod, S., & Pennington, N. (1983). *Inside the jury*. Cambridge, MA: Harvard University Press.

Heinz, J. P., & Laumann, E. O. (1982). *Chicago lawyers: The social structure of the bar*. New York: Russell Sage Foundation & Chicago: American Bar Foundation.

Heinz, J. P., Nelson, R. L., Sandefur, R. L., & Laumann, E. O. (2005). *Urban lawyers: The new social structure of the bar*. Chicago: University of Chicago Press.

Heinz, J. P., Paik, A., & Southworth, A. (2003). Lawyers for conservative causes: Clients, ideology, and social distance. *Law & Society Review, 37*, 5–50.

Heinz, J. P., Schnorr, P. S., Laumann, E. O., & Nelson, R. L. (2001). Lawyers' roles in voluntary associations: Declining social capital? *Law & Social Inquiry, 26*, 597–629.

Helgeson, V. C., & Shaver, K. G. (1990). Presumption of innocence: Congruence bias induced and overcome. *Journal of Applied Social Psychology, 20*, 276–302.

Heller, R. (2008). Passage of Prop. 8 reveals rift between denominations. *The Jewish Journal*. Retrieved November 17, 2008, from http://www.jewishjournal. com/elections/article/passage_of_prop_8_reveals_rift_between_ denominations_20081112/.

Henson, M. (2001). Carruthers v. State: Thou shalt not make direct religious references in closing arguments. *Mercer Law Review, 52,* 731–744.

Hepburn, J. R. (1980). The objective reality of evidence and the utility of systematic verdicts. *Law and Human Behavior, 4,* 89–102.

Hindelang, M. J. (1974). Public opinion regarding crime, criminal justice, and related topics. *Journal of Research in Crime and Delinquency, 21,* 101–116.

Hitchcock, J. (2004). *The Supreme Court and religion in American life* (Vols. 1 & 2). Princeton, NJ: Princeton University Press.

Honeymar, M. G. (1997). Alcoholics Anonymous as a condition of drunk driving probation: When does it amount to establishment of religion? *Columbia Law Review, 97,* 437–472.

Horowitz, I. A., Kerr, N. L., & Niedermeier, K. E. (2002). The law's quest for impartiality: Juror nullification. *Brooklyn Law Review, 66,* 1207–1256.

Horowitz, I. A., Kerr, N. L., Park, E. S., & Gockel, C. (2006). Chaos in the courtroom reconsidered: Emotional bias and juror nullification. *Law and Human Behavior, 30,* 163–181.

Horrigan, D. (2002, August 19). Answering to a higher calling: A religious practice. *National Law Journal, 24(48),* p. C4.

Hotakainen, R. (2007, October 30). Antigay church revels in trial publicity. *Lincoln Journal Star,* p. 8A.

Howard, W. G., & Redfering, D. (1983). The dynamics of jury decision-making: A case study. *Social Behavior and Personality, 11,* 83–89.

Huff, T. P. (1986). A heresy in the ordinary religion: Jurisprudence in the first year curriculum. *Journal of Legal Education, 36,* 108–116.

Idleman, S. C. (1993). The role of religious values in judicial decisionmaking. *Indiana Law Journal, 68,* 433–487.

Idleman, S. C. (1998). The limits of religious values in judicial decisionmaking. *Marquette Law Review, 81,* 537–565.

Idleman, S. C. (2005). The concealment of religious values in judicial decisionmaking. *Virginia Law Review, 91,* 515–534.

Ignagni, J. A. (1993). U.S. Supreme Court decision-making and the Free Exercise Clause. *Review of Politics, 55,* 511–529.

Jaasma, K. (1995). The religious freedom restoration act: Responding to *Smith;* reconsidering *Reynolds. Whittier Law Review, 16,* 211–300.

James, W. (1902). *The varieties of religious experience.* Cambridge, MA: Harvard University Press (republished 1985).

Jenkins, M., Moore, B., Lambert, E., & Clarke, A. (2005). DUI treatment programs and religious freedom: Does Cutter v. Wilkinson change the analysis? *University of Maryland Law Journal of Race, Religion, Gender and Class, 5,* 351–385.

John Jay College of Criminal Justice. (2004). The nature and scope of the problem of sexual abuse of minors by Catholic priests and deacons in the United States. *United States Conference of Catholic Bishops.* Retrieved October 28, 2008, from http://www.usccb.org/nrb/johnjaystudy/.

John the Evangelist? The church-state divide. (2005, August 27). *The Economist, 376(8441),* 25–26.

Johnson, S. D. (1985). Religion as a defense in a mock-jury trial. *Journal of Social Psychology, 125,* 213–220.

Jones, C., & Aronson, E. (1973). Attribution of fault to a rape victim as a function of respectability of the victim. *Journal of Personality and Social Psychology, 26,* 415–419.

Judge gives offenders option of church (2005, May 31). *Boston Globe.* Retrieved November 29, 2005, from http://www.boston.com/news/nation/articles/2005/05/31/judge_gives_offenders_option_of_church/?rss_id=Boston.com±/±News.

Juror: Sympathy spared Nichols (2004, June 15). *CNN.com.* Retrieved April 23, 2005, from http://www.cnn.com/2004/LAW/06/12/nichols.react/index.html.

Jury finds Yates not guilty by reason of insanity (2006, July 27). *USA Today.* Retrieved November 17, 2008, from http://www.usatoday.com/news/nation/2006–07–26-yates-trial_x.htm.

Jury prayer didn't violate killer's rights: Judge rules rapist-murderer isn't entitled to resentencing (2004, March 30). *Toledo Blade.* Retrieved April 4, 2004, from http://www.toledoblade.com.

Kahneman, D., Slovic, P., & Tversky, A. (1982). *Judgment under uncertainty: Heuristics and biases.* Cambridge: Cambridge University Press.

Karfunkel, T., & Ryley, T. W. (1978). The Jewish seat: Anti-Semitism and the appointment of Jews to the Supreme Court. Hicksville, NY: Exposition Press.

Kaufman, A. L. (1994). Benjamin N. Cardozo, Sephardic Jew. In J. M. Lowe (Ed.), *The Jewish justices of the Supreme Court revisited: Brandeis to Fortas* (pp. 35–59). Washington, DC: The Supreme Court Historical Society.

Kellstedt, L. A. (1989). The meaning and measurement of evangelicalism: Problems and prospects. In T. G. Jelen (Ed.), *Religion and political behavior in the United States* (pp. 3–21). Westport, CT: Praeger.

Kelly, M. J. (2007). *Lives of lawyers revisited: Transformation and resilience in the organizations of practice.* Ann Arbor, MI: University of Michigan Press.

Kerr, N. L., Hymes, R. W., Anderson, A. B., & Weathers, J. E. (1995). Defendant–juror similarity and mock juror judgments. *Law and Human Behavior, 19,* 545–567.

Klein, A. L. (1976). Changes in leadership appraisal as a function of the stress of a simulated panic situation. *Journal of Personality & Social Psychology, 34,* 1143–1154.

Knee, J. A. (1993, August 16). Ginsburg's ascent heralds death of the "Jewish seat." *New Jersey Law Journal, 134*(16), p. 17.

Kosmin, B. A., Mayer, E., & Keysar, A. (2001). American religious identification survey, 2001. Retrieved March 26, 2008, from City University of New York, The Graduate Center Web site: http://www.gc.cuny.edu/faculty/research_briefs/aris/key_findings.htm.

Krakauer, J. (2003). *Under the banner of heaven: A story of violent faith.* New York: Doubleday.

Kramer, G. P., Kerr, N. L., & Carroll, J. S. (1990). Pretrial publicity, judicial remedies, and jury bias. *Law and Human Behavior, 14,* 409–438.

Kravets, D. (2006, May 18). U.S. judge did not call for Jews to be kept off death penalty jury, justices say. *Findlaw.com.* Retrieved June 12, 2006, from http://public.findlaw.com/pnews/news/ap/o/51/05–18–2006/59ce000793fcfacd.html.

Kraybill, D. B., Nolt, S. M., & Weaver-Zercher, D. L. (2007). *Amish grace: How forgiveness transcended tragedy.* San Francisco, CA: Jossey-Bass.

236 References

Kressel, J. J., & Kressel, D. F. (2002). *Stack and sway: The new science of jury consulting.* Cambridge, MA: Westview Press.

Kuljol, K. L. (2002). Where did Florida go wrong? Why religion-based peremptory challenges withstand constitutional scrutiny. *Stetson Law Review, 32,* 171–203.

L.A. Archdiocese to settle suits for $660 million (2007, July 14). *MSNBC.com.* Retrieved September 19, 2008, from http://www.msnbc.com/id/19762878/.

Lambert, W. W., Triandis, L. M., & Wolf, M. (1959). Some correlates of beliefs in the malevolence and benevolence of super natural being: A cross cultural study. *Journal of Abnormal and Social Psychology, 48,* 162–169.

Larson, E. J. (1997). *Summer for the Gods: The Scopes trial and America's continuing debate over science and religion.* Cambridge, MA: Harvard University Press.

Lee, R. E. (1995). Today's religious law school: Challenges and opportunities. *Marquette Law Review, 78,* 255–265.

Lee, R. (1998–1999). Faith through lawyering: Finding and doing what is mine to do. *Regent University Law Review, 11,* 71–135.

Leiber, M. J., & Woodrick, A. C. (1997). Religious beliefs, attributional styles, and adherence to correctional orientation. *Criminal Justice and Behavior, 24,* 495–511.

Leiber, M. J., Woodrick, A. C., & Rhoudebush, E. M. (1995). Religion, discriminatory attitudes and the orientations of juvenile justice personnel: A research note. *Criminology, 33,* 431–449.

Lena, H. F., Roach, S. L., & Warkov, S. (1993). Professional status at midcareer: The influence of social and academic origins on lawyers' achievement. *Sociological Forum, 8,* 365–382.

Lesnick, H. (2003). No other Gods: Answering the call of faith in the practice of law. *Journal of Law and Religion, 18,* 459–485.

Levine, S. J. (1996). The broad life of the Jewish lawyer: Integrating spirituality, scholarship and profession. *Texas Tech Law Review, 27,* 1199–1210.

Levine, S. J. (2006). A look at American legal practice through a perspective of Jewish law, ethics, and tradition: A conceptual overview. *Notre Dame Journal of Law, Ethics & Public Policy, 20,* 11–26.

Levinson, S. (1990). *The confrontation of religious faith and civil religion: Catholics becoming justices. DePaul Law Review,* 39, 1047–1081. Reprinted in S. Levinson (2003). *Wrestling with diversity* (pp. 192–232). Durham, NC: Duke University Press.

Levinson, S. (1993). *Identifying the Jewish lawyer: Reflections of the construction of professional identity. Cardozo Law Review,* 14, 1577–1612. Reprinted in S. Levinson (2003). *Wrestling with diversity* (pp. 124–162). Durham, NC: Duke University Press.

Levinson, S. (2006). Is it possible to have a serious discussion about religious commitment and judicial responsibilities? *University of St. Thomas Law Journal, 4,* 280–295.

Lewis, N. A. (2007, June 14). Justice Dept. reshapes its civil rights mission. *New York Times.* Retrieved May 9, 2008, from http://www.nytimes.com/2007/06/14/washington/14discrim.html.

Lichtblau, E. (2008, July 29). Report faults aides in hiring at Justice Department. *New York Times.* Retrieved October 10, 2008, from http://www.nytimes.com/2008/07/29/washington/29justice.html.

Lieberman, J., & Sales, B. (2006). *Scientific jury selection*. Washington, DC: American Psychological Association.

Lin, A. (2005). Can the "Jewish law firm" success story be duplicated? *New York Law Journal*. Retrieved on May 17, 2006, from http://www.law.com.

Lind, E. A., & Tyler, T. R. (1988). *The social psychology of procedural justice*. New York: Plenum.

Lindsay, S. (2003, May 24). Harlan's sentence tossed: Killer's death penalty thrown out because jurors used Bible. *Rocky Mountain News*, p. 4A.

Lindsey, S. C., Miller, M. K., Hayward, R. D., Jehle, A., Singer, J. A., & Summers, A. (2008). How attorneys can use religion to be more effective at trial. *The Jury Expert, 20(2)*, 33–50.

Linowitz, S. M., & Mayer, M. (1994). *The betrayed profession: Lawyering at the end of the twentieth century*. New York: Charles Scribner's Sons.

Liptak, A. (2004, November 22). Giving the law a religious perspective. *New York Times*. Retrieved April 30, 2008, from http://www.nytimes.com/2004/11/22/national/22law.html.

Lithwick, D. (2002). Justice Salia vs. the Pope: Should every Catholic judge in America quit? *Slate*. Retrieved January 22, 2008 from http://www.slate.com.

Litowitz, D. (2006). *The destruction of young lawyers: Beyond One L*. Akron, OH: University of Akron Press.

Loeffler, R. L., & Lawson, T. J. (2002). Age and occupational status of defendant in relation to mock juror sentencing recommendations. *Current Psychology: Developmental, Learning, Personality, Social, 21*, 289–292.

Loewy, A. H. (2000). Religious neutrality and the death penalty. *William and Mary Bill of Rights Journal, 9*, 191–200.

Lubet, S. (2004). *Modern trial advocacy: Analysis and practice* (3rd ed.). USA: National Institute for Trial Advocacy.

Lupfer, M. B., & Gingrich, B. E. (1999). When bad (good) things happen to good (bad) people: The impact of character appraisal and perceived controllability on judgments of deservingness. *Social Justice Research, 12*, 165–188.

Luscri, G., & Mohr, P. B. (1998). Surname effects in judgments of mock jurors. *Psychological Reports, 82*, 1023–1026.

Lutherans to allow pastors in gay relationships (2007, August 11). *Reuters*. Retrieved October 16, 2008, from http://www.reuters.com/article/domesticNews/idUSN1131383720070811

MacLean, P. A. (2005, May 2). Judge's religious ties issue in fight over paper: As trio vies for paper, a judge's involvement with Mormon church raised. *National Law Journal, 27(34)*, p. 6, col. 1.

Mansfield, D. (2008, July 28). Police: Man shot churchgoers over liberal views. *Associated Press*. Retrieved August 5, 2008, from http://ap.google.com/article/ALeqM5jOAQKzY-aOBqDspFkEAV_Z065vZAD9275DI80.

Mansfield, J. H. (2004). Peremptory challenges to jurors based upon or affecting religion. *Seaton Hall Law Review, 34*, 435–473.

Margolick, D. (1994, February 4). At the bar; more than a century after its founding, a new honorific at the A.B.A.: Madam President. *New York Times*. Retrieved June 4, 2008, from http://query.nytimes.com/gst/fullpage.html?res=9C06E6DC1139F937A35751C0A962958260&sec=&spon=&pagewanted=all.

Markon, J. (2005, November 29). Moussaoui's prosecutors draft slew of questions for jury pool. *Washingtonpost.com*. Retrieved May 31, 2007, from http://www. washingtonpost.com/wpdyn/content/article/2005/11/28/AR2005112801591. html.

Marques, J., & Yzerbyt, V. (1988). The black sheep effect: Judgmental extremity towards ingroup members in inter- and intragroup situations. *European Journal of Social Psychology, 18,* 287–292.

Marty, M. E. (2005). The religious foundations of law. *Emory Law Journal, 54,* 291–323.

Marty, M. E. (2007). Foreword. In R.J. Moore, *Suing for America's soul: John Whitehead, the Rutherford Institute, and conservative Christians in the courts*. Grand Rapids, MI: William B. Eerdmans Publishing Co.

Massaro, J. (1990). *Supremely political: The role of ideology and presidential management in unsuccessful Supreme Court nominations*. Albany, NY: SUNY Press.

Matheny, T. H. (1998). My faith and my law. In T. E. Baker & T. W. Floyd, *Can a good Christian be a good lawyer? Homilies, witnesses, and reflections* (pp. 66–73). Notre Dame, IN: University of Notre Dame Press.

Mathis, A. B. (2004). Judges, thou shall not use thine own religion in thy opinions. *Mississippi College Law Review, 23,* 131–155.

Mauet, T. A. (2002). *Trial techniques* (6th ed.). USA: Aspen Publishing.

Mazzella, R., & Feingold, A. (1994). The effects of physical attractiveness, race, socioeconomic status, and gender of defendants and victims on judgments of mock jurors: A meta-analysis. *Journal of Applied Social Psychology, 24,* 1315–1344.

McConnell, M. W. (2000). The problem of singling out religion. *DePaul Law Review, 50,* 1–28.

McDonough, M. (2006). No more excuses. Indiana among several states to cut jury duty exemptions. *ABA Journal E-Report, 5,* 3–4.

McFarland, S. (1989). Religious orientation and the targets of discrimination. *Journal for the Scientific Study of Religion, 28,* 324–336.

McGraw, S. L., & Foley, L. A. (2000). Perceptions of insanity based on occupation of defendant and seriousness of crime. *Psychological Reports, 86,* 163–174.

McMurry, K. (1998). Balancing scales: Small firms seek diversity. *Trial, 34,* 12–16.

McNeil, H. L. (1996). Problems identified: The bar surveys. In J. R. Simmons (Ed.), *Life, law and the pursuit of balance: A lawyer's guide to quality of life* (pp. 9–15). Phoenix, AZ: Maricopa County Bar Association.

McNulty, P. J., Spencer, R. A., Novak, D. J., & Raskin, D. (2005, November 28). Government's proposed jury questionnaire: *U.S. v. Zacarias Moussaoui*. Retrieved May 31, 2007, from http://news.lp.findlaw.com/hdocs/docs/ moussaoui/usmouss112805juryq.pdf.

Mega-preacher's wife sued over loss of faith (2008, August 7). *CNN.com*. Retrieved August 7, 2008, from http://www.cnn.com/2008/US/08/07/osteen.wife.trial. ap/index.html.

Merkin, N. (2001). Getting rid of sinners may be expensive: A suggested approach to torts related to religious shunning under the Free Exercise Clause. *Columbia Journal of Law and Social Problems, 34,* 369–403.

Merrick, J. C. (1994). Christian Science healing of minor children: Spiritual exemption statutes, First Amendment rights, and fair notice. *Issues in Law & Medicine, 10*, 321–342.

Merz, M. R. (2004). Conscience of a Catholic judge. *University of Dayton Law Review, 29*, 305–318.

Michaelson, J. (2006, November 3). Two lawyers, three opinions: On the Jewishness of law, and vice versa. *The Jewish Daily Forward.* Retrieved May 9, 2008, from http://www.forward.com/articles/two-lawyers-three-opinions/.

Miller, J. T. (1999). Free exercise v. legal ethics: Can a religious lawyer discriminate in choosing clients? *Georgetown Journal of Legal Ethics, 13*, 161–182.

Miller, M. K. (2006). *Religion in criminal justice.* New York: LFB Publishing.

Miller, M. K., & Bornstein, B. H. (2004). Juror stress: Causes and interventions. *Thurgood Marshall Law Review, 30*, 237–269.

Miller, M. K., & Bornstein, B. H. (2005). Religious appeals in closing arguments: Impermissible input or benign banter? *Law and Psychology Review, 29*, 29–61.

Miller, M. K., & Bornstein, B. H. (2006). The use of religion in death penalty sentencing trials. *Law and Human Behavior, 30*, 675–684.

Miller, M. K., & Dolson, S. (in press). Two studies test the effects of religious hallucinations on perceptions of insanity. In F. Columbus (Ed.), *Religion and psychology.* Hauppauge, NY: Nova.

Miller, M. K., Greene, E., Dietrich, H., Chamberlain, J. C., & Singer, J. A. (2008). How emotion affects the trial process. *Judicature, 92*, 56–64.

Miller, M. K., & Hayward, R. D. (2008). Religious characteristics and the death penalty. *Law and Human Behavior, 32*, 113–123.

Miller, M. K., Jehle, A., & Summers, A. (2007). From Kobe Bryant to Saddam Hussein: A descriptive examination and psychological analysis of how religion likely affected twenty-five recent high-profile trials. *Florida Coastal Law Review, 9*, 1–33.

Miller, M. K., Lindsey, S. C., & Shamblin, S. (2008). *How a prisoner's religious conversion affects release decisions of actual and mock parole board members.* Unpublished manuscript.

Miller, M. K., Singer, J., & Jehle, A. (2008). Identification of circumstances under which religion affects each stage of the trial process. *Applied Psychology in Criminal Justice, 4*, 135–171.

Mills, C., & Bohannan, W. (1980). Juror characteristics: To what extent are they related to jury verdicts? *Judicature, 64*, 23–31.

Modak-Truran, M. C. (2004). Reenchanting the law: The religious dimension of judicial decision making. *Catholic University Law Review, 53*, 709–800.

Montz, C. L. (2001). Why lawyers continue to cross the line in closing arguments: Examination of federal and state cases. *Ohio Northern University Law Review, 28*, 67–131.

Moore, R. J. (2007). *Suing for America's soul: John Whitehead, the Rutherford Institute, and conservative Christians in the courts.* Grand Rapids, MI: William B. Eerdmans Publishing Co.

Moran, G., & Comfort, J. (1986). Neither "tentative" nor "fragmentary": Verdict preference of impaneled felony jurors as a function of attitude toward capital punishment. *Journal of Applied Psychology, 71*, 146–155.

Murphy, D. E. (2005, March 16). Case stirs fight on Jews, juries, and execution. *The New York Times*, p. A1.

Murphy, W. F., Pritchett, C. H., Epstein, L., & Knight, J. (2006). *Courts, judges, and politics: An introduction to the judicial process* (6th ed.). Boston: McGraw Hill.

Murphy-Cowan, T., & Stringer, M. (2001). Religious affiliation and attitudes toward the use of corporal punishment in Northern Ireland. *Irish Journal of Psychology, 22,* 55–62.

Mushlin, M. B. (2007). Bound and gagged: The peculiar predicament of professional jurors. *Yale Law and Policy Review, 25,* 239–288.

Myers, R. S. (1991). The Supreme Court and the privatization of religion. *Catholic University Law Review, 41,* 19–80.

Nagel, S. S. (1964). The relationship between the political and ethnic affiliation of judges, and their decision-making. In G. Schubert (Ed.), *Judicial behavior: A reader in theory and research* (pp. 234–264). Chicago: Rand McNally & Co.

Nagel, S. S. (1969). *The legal process from a behavioral perspective.* Homewood, IL: Dorsey.

Nanda, V. P. (1996). Hinduism and my legal career. *Texas Tech Law Review, 27,* 1229–1235.

Nelson, J. F. (1996). The spiritual dimension of justice. *Texas Tech Law Review, 27,* 1237–1249.

Nelson, R. L. (1988). *Partners with power: The social transformation of the large law firm.* Berkeley, CA: University of California Press.

Niedermeier, K. E., Horowitz, I. A., & Kerr, N. L. (1999). Informing jurors of their nullification power: A route to a just verdict or judicial chaos? *Law and Human Behavior, 23,* 331–351.

Niedermeier, K. E., Horowitz, I. A., & Kerr, N. L. (2001). Exceptions to the rule: The effects of remorse, status, and gender on decision making. *Journal of Applied Social Psychology, 31,* 604–623.

Nisbett, R. E., & Wilson, T. D. (1977). Telling more than we can know: Verbal reports on mental processes. *Psychological Review, 84,* 231–259.

Nolt, S. M. (2007, October 2). *Why the Amish forgave a killer.* Retrieved October 16, 2008, from Goshen College Web site: http://www.goshen.edu/news/pressarchive/10–02–07-nolt-convo/speech.html.

North, G., & DeMar, G. (1991). *Christian reconstruction: What it is. What it isn't.* Tyler, TX: Institute for Christian Economics.

Nun asks to take back guilty plea (2008, July 23). *KETV.com.* Retrieved July 24, 2008, from http://www.ketv.com/news/16968550/detail.html.

Oakland mother convicted of second-degree murder (2007, January 17). *Oakland Tribune.* Retrieved May 20, 2007, from http://findarticles.com/p/articles/mi_qn4176/is_20070117/ai_n17132133.

Ogletree, C. J. (1987). Reverend Moon and the Black Hebrews: Constitutional protection of a defendant's religion in criminal cases. *Harvard Civil Rights-Civil Liberties Law Review, 22,* 191–229.

Omaha nun sentenced to prison for theft (2008, July 11). *KETV.com.* Retrieved July 24, 2008, from http://www.ketv.com/news/16858170/detail.html.

O'Neil, K. M., Patry, M. W., & Penrod, S. D. (2004). Exploring the effects of attitudes toward the death penalty on capital sentencing verdicts. *Psychology, Public Policy, and Law, 10,* 443–470.

Osborn, R. L. (2006). Beliefs on the bench: Recusal for religious reasons and the model code of judicial conduct. *Georgetown Journal of Legal Ethics, 19,* 895–905.

Osler, M. (2005). The lawyer's humble walk. *Pepperdine Law Review, 32,* 483–496.

Osler, M. (2007). Christ, Christian and capital punishment. *Baylor Law Review, 59,* 1–40.

Ostrom, B. J., Strickland, S. M., & Hannaford-Agor, P. L. (2004). Examining trial trends in state courts: 1976–2002. *Journal of Empirical Legal Studies, 1,* 755–782.

Palazzolo, J. (2008, September 30). Mukasey appoints special prosecutor to investigate U.S. attorney firings. *Law.com.* Retrieved October 1, 2008, from http://www.law.com/jsp/law/LawArticleFriendly.jsp?id=1202424889914.

Park, R. C. (1998). Character at the crossroads. *Hastings Law Journal, 49,* 717–779.

Parobek, J. (2006–2007). God v. the mitigation of damages doctrine: Why religion should be considered a pre-existing condition. *Journal of Law and Health, 20,* 107–138.

Parrish, M. E. (1994). Justice Frankfurter and the Supreme Court. In J. M. Lowe (Ed.), *The Jewish justices of the Supreme Court revisited: Brandeis to Fortas* (pp. 61–80). Washington, DC: The Supreme Court Historical Society.

Paxton, M. (2004). Gone fishin': A framing analysis of the fight over a small town's city seal. *Journal of Media and Religion, 3,* 43–55.

Pearce, R. G. (1996). The Jewish lawyer's question. *Texas Tech Law Review, 27,* 1259–1270.

Pearce, R. G. (1998). The religious lawyering movement: An emerging force in legal ethics and professionalism. *Fordham Law Review, 66,* 1075–1082.

Pearce, R. G. (2001). Faith and the lawyer's practice. *St. John's Law Review, 75,* 277–281.

Pearce, R. G., & Uelmen, A.J. (2004). Religious lawyering in a liberal democracy: A challenge and an invitation. *Case Western Reserve Law Review, 55,* 127–161.

Pearce, R. G., & Uelmen, A. J. (2005–2006). Religious lawyering's second wave. *Journal of Law and Religion, 21,* 269–281.

Perry, B. A. (1991). *A "representative" Supreme Court? The impact of race, religion, and gender on appointments.* New York: Greenwood Press.

Pew Forum on Religion and Public Life. (2008). *U.S. Religious landscape survey.* Retrieved October 21, 2008, from http://religions.pewforum.org/reports.

Pfeifer, J. E. (1992). The psychological framing of cults: Schematic representations and cult evaluations. *Journal of Applied Social Psychology, 22,* 531–544.

Pfeifer, J. E. (1999). Perceptual biases and mock juror decision making: Minority religions in court. *Social Justice Research, 12,* 409–419.

Pinello, D. R. (2003). *Gay rights and American law.* Cambridge, UK: Cambridge University Press.

Plante, T. G. (2004a). Introduction. In T. G. Plante (Ed.), Sin against the innocents: Sexual abuse by priests and the role of the Catholic Church (pp. xvii–xxvii). Westport, CT: Praeger.

Plante, T. G. (2004b). *Sin against the innocents: Sexual abuse by priests and the role of the Catholic Church.* Westport, CT: Praeger.

Police: Teacher attacked over witch claim (2008, October 8). *WDIV Detroit.* Retrieved October 9, 2008, from http://www.clickondetroit.com/news/17655770/detail.html?taf±det.

Posey, A. J., & Wrightsman, L. S. (2005). *Trial consulting*. Oxford: Oxford Press.

Power, S. (2009). The enforcer: A Christian lawyer's global crusade. *The New Yorker*. Retrieved February 25, 2009 from http://www.newyorker.com/reporting/2009/01/19/090119fa_fact_power.

Preacher killed wife, stuffed body in freezer, police say (2008, July 31). *CNN.com*. Retrieved August 5, 2008, from http://www.cnn.com/2008/CRIME/07/31/preacher.freezer/index.html.

Pritchett, C. H. (1964). Division of opinion among Supreme Court justices. In G. Schubert (Ed.), *Judicial behavior: A reader in theory and research* (pp. 319–324). Chicago: Rand McNally & Co.

Prosecutors allege link between bomb defendant Rudolph and anti-abortion figure (2005, March 29). *USA Today*. Retrieved August 5, 2008, from http://www.usatoday.com/news/nation/2005-03-29-rudolph_x.htm.

Putney, S., & Middleton, R. (1961). Dimensions and correlates of religious ideologies. *Social Forces, 39*, 285–290.

Rader details how he killed 10 people: Killer had "sexual fantasies" while picking victims (2005, June 28). *CNN.com*. Retrieved November 29, 2005, from http://www.cnn.com/2005/LAW/06/27/btk/index.html.

Raif, S. & Dean, N. (2005). Repentant shoebomber jailed for 13 years. *The Press Association Limited*. Retrieved from Lexis Nexis, July 17, 2005.

Ramsay, M. (2007). The religious beliefs of tort victims: Religious thin skulls or failures of mitigation? *Canadian Journal of Law and Jurisprudence, 20*, 399–427.

Reed, J. P. (1965). Jury deliberation, voting, and verdict trends. *Southwest Social Science Quarterly, 45*, 361–370.

Reynolds, D. (2004, August 20). Hemphill sentenced over boy's "exorcism" death. *Inclusion Daily Express*. Retrieved August 29, 2008, from http://www.mnddc.org/news/inclusion-daily/2004/08/082004wiabusecottrell.htm.

Rhode, D. L. (2000). *In the interests of justice: Reforming the legal profession*. Oxford: Oxford University Press.

Rice, C. E. (1999, May/June). Being a Catholic lawyer today. *Catholic Dossier*. Retrieved September 19, 2006, from http://www.catholic.net/RCC/Periodicals/Dossier/MAYJUN99/lawyer.html/.

Richardson, J. T., & DeWitt, J. (1992). Christian Science spiritual healing, the law, and public opinions. *Journal of Church and State, 34*, 549–561.

Richey, W. (2008, October 7). Supreme Court lets stand death sentence after Bible reading. *The Christian Science Monitor*. Retrieved October 27, 2008, from http://www.csmonitor.com/2008/1007/p25s17-usju.html.

Riley, N. S. (2005). *God on the quad: How religious colleges and the missionary generation are changing America*. New York: St. Martin's Press.

Ringenberg, W. C. (2006). *The Christian college: A history of Protestant higher education in America* (2nd ed.). Grand Rapids, MI: Baker Academic.

Robbennolt, J. K. (2005). Evaluating juries by comparison to judges: A benchmark for judging? *Florida State University Law Review, 32*, 469–509.

Roberts, S. V. (1987, October 31). Ginsburg choice renews tension between factions in White House. *New York Times*. Retrieved February 28, 2008, from http://query.nytimes.com/gst/fullpage.html?res=9B0DE0DB103DF932A0575 3C1A961948260.

Robertson asks God to oust liberal justices. (2003, August 9). *Christian Century, 120*(16), p. 13.

Roche, T. (2002, March 18). Andrea Yates: More to the story. *Time.* Retrieved October 1, 2008, from http://www.time.com/time/nation/ article/0,8599,218445,00.html.

Rogers, B., & Lezon, D. (2008, August 15). Megachurch pastor's wife wins case. *Houston Chronicle.* Retrieved August 25, 2008, from http://www.mysanantonio. com/news/local_news/megachurch_pastors_wife_acquitted100.html.

Romero, S. (2005). Scrushy: Finding religion or saving self? Retrieved November 22, 2008, from http://www.iht.com/articles/2005/02/17/business/scrushy.php.

Rosoff, S. M. (1989). Physicians as criminal defendants: Specialty, sanctions, and status liability. *Law and Human Behavior, 13*, 231–236.

Rucker, B. (2007, April 10). Winkler jury selection focuses on abuse issues. Associated Press. Retrieved May 25, 2007, from http://www.tennessean.com/ apps/pbcs.dll/article?AID=/20070410/NEWS03/704100347.

Rudolph agrees to plea agreement: Deal would allow accused bomber to avoid death penalty (2005, April 8). *CNN.com.* Retrieved November 29, 2005, from http://www.cnn.com/2005/LAW/04/08/rudolph.plea/index.html.

Russell, J. J. (2004, April 4). Mental illness, bad religion a deadly mix for young mothers. *San Antonio Express,* p. 1H.

Russo, C. J., & Thro, W. E. (2007). The constitutional rights of politically incorrect groups: *Christian Legal Society v. Walker* as an illustration. *Journal of College & University Law, 33*, 361–386.

Ryan, H. (2004). Williams will not testify. Attorneys for ex-NBA star rest case. *CNN.com.* Retrieved July 18, 2005, from cnn.com/2004/law/04/01/jayson. williams/index.html.

Saakvitne, K. W., Tennen, H., & Affleck, G. (1998). Exploring thriving in the context of clinical trauma theory: Constructivist self-development theory. *Journal of Social Issues,* 279–299.

Saks, M. J. (1989). Legal policy analysis and evaluation. *American Psychologist, 44,* 1110–1117.

Sandys, M., & McGarrell, E. F. (1997). Beyond the Bible belt: The influence (or lack thereof) of religion on attitudes toward the death penalty. *Journal of Crime and Justice, 20,* 179–190.

Saulny, S. (2008, April 29). An irascible firebrand, quieted by term limits. *New York Times.* Retrieved July 24, 2008, from http://www.nytimes. com/2008/04/29/us/29nebraska.html?emc=rss&partner=rssnyt.

Savage, C. (2007, April 8). Scandal puts spotlight on Christian law school. *Boston Globe.* Retrieved April 30, 2008, from http://www.boston.com/news/education/ higher/articles/2007/04/08/scandal_puts_spotlight_on_christian_law_school/.

Scalia escalates attacks on church–state separation at New York conference (2005). *Church & State, 58(1),* 16–17.

Scalia sticks to his guns, says Catholic judges opposed to death penalty should resign (2002, February 5). *CBSnews.com.* Retrieved October 16, 2008, from http://www.cbsnews.com/stories/2002/02/05/deathpenalty/main328253.shtml

Scarlato, M. C., & Kohm, L. M. (1998–1999). Integrating religion, faith, and morality in traditional law school courses. *Regent University Law Review, 11*, 49–69.

Scheiber, N. (2005, October 17). Merit scholars. *New Republic, 233(16),* 6.

Schiltz, P. J. (1998). Legal ethics in decline: The elite law firm, the elite law school, and the moral formation of the novice attorney. *Minnesota Law Review 82,* 705–792.

Schiltz, P. J. (1999). On being a happy, healthy, and ethical member of an unhappy, unhealthy, and unethical profession. *Vanderbilt Law Review, 52*, 871–951.

Schiltz, P. J. (2003). The impact of clergy sexual misconduct litigation on religious liberty. *Boston College Law Review, 44*, 949–975.

Schiltz, P. J. (2004). Making ethical lawyers. *South Texas Law Review, 45*, 875–889.

Schopp, R. F. (1993). Justification defenses and just convictions. *Pacific Law Journal, 24*, 1233–1321.

Schubert, G. (1964). *Judicial behavior: A reader in theory and research.* Chicago: Rand McNally & Co.

Schubert, G. (1974). *The judicial mind revisited: Psychometric analysis of Supreme Court ideology.* New York: Oxford University Press.

Schulman, J., Shaver, P., Colman, R., Emrich, B., & Christie, R. (1987). Recipe for a jury. In L. S. Wrightsman, S. M. Kassin, & C.E. Willis (Eds.), *In the jury box: Controversies in the courtroom* (pp. 13–47). Newbury Park, CA: Sage.

Schutt, M. P. (2007). *Redeeming law: Christian calling and the legal profession.* Downers Grove, IL: IVP Academic.

Sect leader Jeffs indicted in child sex case (2008, July 23). *CNN.com.* Retrieved Oct. 2, 2008, from http://www.cnn.com/2008/CRIME/07/22/jeffs.indictment/index.html.

Segal, J. A., & Spaeth, H. J. (1993). *The Supreme Court and the attitudinal model.* Cambridge: Cambridge University Press.

Segrest, D. (1994). *Conscience and command: A motive theory of law.* Atlanta, GA: Scholars Press.

Severed-arm baby mom said incompetent (2005, February 15). *Fox News.* Retrieved November 29, 2005, from http://www.foxnews.com/story0,2933,147633,00.html.

Shaffer, T. L. (1981). *On being a Christian and a lawyer: Law for the innocent.* Provo, UT: Brigham Young University Press.

Shaffer, T. L. (1987). *Faith and the professions.* Provo, UT: Brigham Young University Press.

Shaffer, T. L. (1989). Should a Christian lawyer serve the guilty? *Georgia Law Review, 23*, 1021–1034.

Shaffer, T. L. (1993). Erastian and sectarian arguments in religiously affiliated American law schools. *Stanford Law Review, 45*, 1859–1879.

Shaffer, T. L. (1995). Why does the church have law schools? *Marquette Law Review, 78*, 401–411.

Shaffer, T. L. (1998). Maybe a lawyer can be a servant; if not. . . . In T. E. Baker & T. W. Floyd, *Can a good Christian be a good lawyer? Homilies, witnesses, and reflections* (pp. 193–206). Notre Dame, IN: University of Notre Dame Press.

Shaw, J. I., & Skolnick, P. (1996). When is defendant status a shield or a liability? Clarification and extension. *Law and Human Behavior, 20*, 431–442.

Sherbine, E. L. (2006). Does *Cutter v. Wilkinson* change the analysis of mandated DUI treatment programs? A critical response. *University of Maryland Law Journal of Race, Religion, Gender & Class, 6*, 223–249.

Shively, N. G. (2008). Divine intervention? The threat of religious discussion in the context of capital sentencing deliberations: *Fields v. Brown*, 503 F.3d 755 (9th Cir. 2007). *University of Cincinnati Law Review, 76*, 1401–1430.

Shuman, D. W., & Champagne, A. (1997). Removing the people from the legal process: The rhetoric and research on judicial selection and juries. *Psychology, Public Policy, and Law, 3*, 242–258.

Silverstein, M. (1994). *Judicious choices: The new politics of Supreme Court confirmations.* New York: WW Norton & Co.

Simmonds, A. R. (2004). Measure for measure: Two misunderstood principles of damages, Exodus 21:22–25, "Life for life, eye for eye," and Matthew 5:38–39, "Turn the other cheek." *St. Thomas Law Review, 17,* 123–171.

Simon, R. J. (1967). *The jury and the defense of insanity.* Boston: Little, Brown.

Simons, M. A. (2004). Born again on death row: Retribution, remorse and religion. *Catholic Lawyer, 43,* 311–337.

Simson, G. J., & Garvey, S. P. (2001). Knockin' on heaven's door: Rethinking the role of religion in death penalty cases. *Cornell Law Review, 86,* 1090–1130.

Singer, J., & Miller, M. K. (2008, April). *Effects of religion on jurors' decisions.* Presented at the Western Social Science Association conference, Denver, CO.

Singer, N. (2008, June 5). Judge declares mistrial in Haq case: Jewish Federation jury couldn't agree. *Seattle Times.* Retrieved September 5, 2008, from http://seattletimes.nwsource.com/html/localnews/2004458503_haq05m.html.

Sisk, G. C., Heise, M., & Morriss, A. P. (2004). Searching for the soul of judicial decisionmaking: An empirical study of religious freedom decisions. *Ohio State Law Journal, 65,* 491–594.

Skaf, L. (2008). Is religion an effective mitigating factor in capital cases? Near miss Christian factors and disregarded Muslim ones. *Rutgers Journal of Law & Religion, 9,* 13–29.

Skeem, J. L., & Golding, S. L. (2001). Describing jurors' personal conceptions of insanity and their relationship to case judgments. *Psychology, Public Policy, and Law, 7,* 561–621.

Skolnick, P., & Shaw, J. I. (1994). Is defendant status a liability or a shield? Crime severity and professional relatedness. *Journal of Applied Social Psychology, 24,* 1827–1836.

Skolnick, P., & Shaw, J. I. (1997). The O.J. Simpson criminal trial verdict? Racism or status shield? *Journal of Social Issues, 53,* 503–516.

Skovron, S. E., Scott, J., & Cullen, F. T. (1989). The death penalty for juveniles: An assessment of public support. *Crime and Delinquency, 35,* 546–561.

Smart's accused kidnapper ruled incompetent: Judge orders man confined for mental treatment (2005, July 26). *CNN.com.* Retrieved November 29, 2005, from http://edition.cnn.com/2005/LAW/07/26/smart.suspect.

Smidt, C. (1989). Identifying evangelical respondents: An analysis of "born-again" and Bible questions used across different surveys. In T. G. Jelen (Ed.), *Religion and political behavior in the United States* (pp. 23–43). Westport, CT: Praeger.

Smigel, E. O. (1964). *The Wall Street lawyer: Professional organization man?* New York: Free Press.

Smith, T. W. (1990). Classifying Protestant denominations. *Review of Religious Research, 31,* 225–245.

Songer, D. R., & Tabrizi, S. J. (1999). The religious right in court: The decision making of Christian evangelicals in State Supreme Courts. *Journal of Politics, 61,* 507–526.

Sorauf, F. J. (1976). *The wall of separation: The constitutional politics of church and state.* Princeton, NJ: Princeton University Press.

Soss, J., Langbein, L., & Metelko, A. R. (2003). Why do white Americans support the death penalty? *Journal of Politics, 65,* 397–421.

Spaeth, J. M. (2008). The impact of religion on verdicts. *Arizona Jury Research*. Retrieved August 5, 2008, from www.azjuryresearch.com/pdf_docs/pubs_rsrch_dem_factors/TheImpactofReligion.doc.

Spilka, B., Hood, R.W., Hunsberger, B., & Gorsuch, R. (2003). *The psychology of religion* (3rd ed.). New York: Guilford Press.

Spiller, C. (2005). *People v. Harlan:* The Colorado Supreme Court takes a step toward eliminating religious influence on juries. *Denver University Law Review, 83,* 613–638.

Springer, J. (2004, April 5). Jury accepts insanity defense for mother who stoned sons. *Court TV*. Retrieved November 29, 2005, from http://www.courttv.com/trials/laney/040304_verdict_ctv.html.

Stack, S. (2003). Authoritarianism and support for the death penalty: A multivariate analysis. *Sociological Focus, 36,* 333–352.

State Sen. Ernie Chambers sues God (2007, September 17). *KETV.com*. Retrieved July 24, 2008, from http://www.ketv.com/news/14133442/detail.html.

Steblay, N., Hosch, H.M., Culhane, S.E., & McWethy, A. (2006). The impact on juror verdicts of judicial instruction to disregard inadmissible evidence: A meta-analysis. *Law and Human Behavior, 30,* 469–492.

Steinhaus, R. (2004, March 8). Martha Stewart faces prison, uncertain future. Retrieved October 16, 2008, from http://www.courttv.com/trials/stewart/verdict_ctv.html.

Stephenson, D. G. (1994). Five Jewish justices: A bibliographical essay. In J. M. Lowe (Ed.), *The Jewish justices of the Supreme Court revisited: Brandeis to Fortas* (pp. 127–140). Washington, DC: The Supreme Court Historical Society.

Stewart, M. N., & Tolley, H. D. (2004). Investigating possible bias: The American legal academy's view of religiously affiliated law schools. *Journal of Legal Education, 54,* 136–155.

Stipanovich, T. J. (2004). ADR and the "vanishing trial": The growth and impact of "alternative dispute resolution." *Journal of Empirical Legal Studies, 1,* 843–912.

Summers, A., Hayward, R. D., & Miller, M. K. (in press). How death qualification systematically excludes jurors based on religious characteristics, justice philosophy, cognitive processing, and demographics. *Journal of Applied Social Psychology*.

Sundby, S. E. (2005). A life and death decision: Jury weighs the death penalty. New York: Palgrave Macmillan.

Tate, C. N. (1981). Personal attribute models of the voting behavior of United States Supreme Court justices: Liberalism in civil liberty and economic decisions, 1946–1978. *American Political Science Review, 75,* 355–367.

Tate, C. N., & Sittiwong, P. (1989). Decision making in the Canadian Supreme Court: Extending the personal attributes model across nations. *Journal of Politics, 51,* 900–916.

Taylor, T. S., & Hosch, H. M. (2004). An examination of jury verdicts for evidence of a similarity-leniency effect, an out-group punitiveness effect or a black sheep effect. *Law and Human Behavior, 28,* 587–598.

Texas evangelist cleared of assault (2008, August 15). *USA Today*, p. 3A, col. 1.

Tyler, T. R. (2006). *Why people obey the law*. Princeton, NJ: Princeton University Press (Reissue; originally published 1990).

Tyler, T. R., & Weber, R. (1982). Support for the death penalty: Instrumental response to crime or symbolic attitude? *Law and Society Review, 17,* 21–44.

Uelmen, A. J. (2004). An explicit connection between faith and justice in Catholic legal education: Why rock the boat? *University of Detroit Mercy Law Review, 81*, 921–938.

Uelmen, G. F. (2005). Catholic jurors and the death penalty. *Journal of Catholic Legal Studies, 44*, 355–378.

Ulmer, S. S. (1970). Dissent behavior and the social background of Supreme Court justices. *Journal of Politics, 32*, 580–598.

Ulmer, S. S. (1973). Social background as an indicator to the votes of Supreme Court justices in criminal cases: 1947–1956 terms. *American Journal of Political Science, 17*, 622–630.

Ulmer, S. S. (1986). Are social background models time-bound? *American Political Science Review, 80*, 957–967.

United States District Court for the District of Colorado (1997, September 30). *U.S. v. Nichols*, 96-CR-68, Reporter's Transcript. *CNN.com.* Retrieved on August 5, 2008, from http://www.cnn.com/US/9703/okc.trial/transcripts/september/093097.pm.html.

Unnever, J. D., & Cullen, F. T. (2006). Christian fundamentalism and support for capital punishment. *Journal of Research in Crime and Delinquency, 43*, 169–197.

Urofsky, M. I. (1994). Justice Louis Brandeis. In J. M. Lowe (Ed.), *The Jewish justices of the Supreme Court revisited: Brandeis to Fortas* (pp. 9–34). Washington, DC: The Supreme Court Historical Society.

Van Hoy, J. (1997). *Franchise law firms and the transformation of personal legal services.* Westport, CT: Quorum Books.

Van Voorhis, P., Braswell, M., & Lester, D. (2007). *Correctional counseling & rehabilitation.* Cincinnati, OH: Anderson Publishing.

Van Wormer, K. (2008). Family safety—how social workers help: About priest/clergy sexual abuse—trauma and healing. *National Association of Social Workers.* Retrieved September 16, 2008, from http://www.helpstartshere.org/Default.aspx?PageID=1216.

Victoria Osteen trial (2008, August 6). *Chicago Tribune.* Retrieved August 20, 2008, from www.chicagotribune.com/news/nationalworld/chi-joel-victoria/osteen-wife-080806-ht,0,5371781.story.

Vidmar, N. (1974). Retributive and utilitarian motives and other correlates of Canadian attitudes toward the death penalty. *The Canadian Psychologist, 15*, 337–356.

Vidmar, N., & Hans, V. P. (2007). *American juries.* Amherst, NY: Prometheus Books.

Vines, K. (1964). Federal district judges and race relations cases in the South. *Journal of Politics, 26*, 337–357.

Visser, R. C. (2007). Collision course?: Christian Legal Society v. Kane could create a split over the right of religious student groups to associate in the face of law school antidiscrimination policies. *Hamline Law Review, 30*, 449–487.

Vogel, B. (2003). Support for life in prison without the possibility of parole among death penalty proponents. *American Journal of Criminal Justice, 27*, 263–275.

Waggoner, C. A. (2004). Peremptory challenges and religion: The unanswered prayer for a Supreme Court opinion. *Loyola University of Chicago Law Journal, 36*, 285–328.

Walker, A. D. (2003). "The murderer shall surely be put to death:" The impropriety of Biblical arguments in the penalty phase of capital cases. *Washburn Law Journal, 43*, 197–225.

Ward, P. R. (2008, September 28). Gay man takes bias claim to appeals court. *Pittsburgh Post-Gazette*. Retrieved October 16, 2008, from http://www. post-gazette.com/pg/08272/915738–54.stm.

Ward, S. F. (2008). Faith's rewards: Some lawyers find religion a righteous marketing tool. *ABA Journal, 94*(8), 34.

Way, F., & Burt, B. J. (1983). Religious marginality and the Free Exercise Clause. *American Political Science Review, 77*, 652–665.

Weiss, D. C. (2008, Feb. 13). Judges increasingly asked to weigh religion in custody battles. *ABA Journal*. Retrieved May 9, 2008, from http://www.abajournal. com/news/judges_increasingly_asked_to_weigh_religion_in_custody_battles/.

White, J. P. (1995). Religiously affiliated law schools: Their role in American legal education. *Marquette Law Review, 78*, 371–375.

Whitehead, J. W. (1999). *Slaying dragons: The truth behind the man who defended Paula Jones*. Nashville, TN: Nelson.

Wiehl, L. (2000). Judges and lawyers are not singing from the same hymnal when it comes to allowing the bible in the courtroom. *American Journal of Trial Advocacy, 24*, 273–296.

Wilkey, M. R. (1973). Judicial background and decision-making. In G. R. Winters (Ed.), *Selected readings: Judicial selection and tenure* (Rev. ed., pp. 171–181). Chicago: American Judicature Society.

Wiltshire, A. T. (1998). Religion and lifework in the law. In T. E. Baker & T. W. Floyd, *Can a good Christian be a good lawyer? Homilies, witnesses, and reflections* (pp. 74–82). Notre Dame, IN: University of Notre Dame Press.

Witte, J. (2005). *Religion and the American constitutional experiment* (2nd ed.). Boulder, CO: Westview Press.

Wolfe, C. (1995). The ideal of a (Catholic) law school. *Marquette Law Review, 78*, 487–505.

Wrightsman, L. S. (2006). *The psychology of the Supreme Court*. Oxford: Oxford University Press.

Yalof, D. A. (1999). *Pursuit of justices: Presidential politics and the selection of Supreme Court nominees*. Chicago: University of Chicago Press.

Yarnold, B. M. (2000). Did circuit courts of appeals judges overcome their own religions in cases involving religious liberties? 1970–1990. *Review of Religious Research, 42*, 79–86.

Yates found guilty of murdering her children (2002, March 13). *CNN.com*. Retrieved March 13, 2002, from http://www.cnn.com/2002/law/03/13/yates. trial/index.html.

Yeats, W. B. (1933/1962). *Selected poems and two plays* (ed. by M.L. Rosenthal). New York: Macmillan [originally published in The winding stair and other poems, 1933].

Young, J. (2009, February 28).Chambers hits end of line with God lawsuit. *Lincoln Journal Star*, p. 1B.

Young, R. L. (1992). Religious orientation, race and support for the death penalty. *Journal for the Scientific Study of Religion, 31*, 76–88.

Young, R. L. (2000). Symposium: Religion's role in the administration of the death penalty: Punishment at all costs: On religion, convicting the innocent, and supporting the death penalty. *William & Mary Bill of Rights Journal, 9*, 237–245.

Cases Cited

Adams v. Texas, 448 U.S. 38 (1980).
Arizona v. Hardesty, 2008 Ariz. App. LEXIS 121 (2008).
Batson v. Kentucky, 476 U.S. 79 (1986).
Bennett v. Angelone, 92 F.3d 1336 (Va. 1996).
Bieghler v. State, 690 N.E. 2d 188 (Ind. 1997).
Boyd v. French, 147 F.3d 319 (4th Cir. 1998).
Boyd v. State, 2003 WL 22757932 (NC 2003).
Bradley v. State, 79 So. 651 (Fla. 1920).
Branch v. State, 882 So.2d 36 (Miss. 2004).
Brown v. Board of Education, 347 U.S. 483 (1954).
Brown v. Payton, 544 U.S. 133 (2005).
Bussard v. Lockhart, 32 F.3d 322 (8th Cir. 1994).
Buttrum v. Black, 721 F.Supp. 1268 (Ga. 1989).
Caldwell v. Mississippi, 472 U.S. 320 (1985).
Call v. Polk, 454 F.Supp. 2d 475 (N.C. 2006).
Camp v. United States, 413 F.2d 419 (5th Cir. 1969).
Carruthers v. State, 528 S.E.2d 217 (Ga. 2000).
Casarez v. State, 913 S.W.2d 468 (Tex. 1995).
Chambers v. State, 724 S.W.2d 440 (Tex. 1987).
City of Boerne v. Flores, 521 U.S. 507 (1997).
Coe v. Bell, 161 F.3d 320 (6th Cir. 1998).
Colorado v. Harlan, 546 U.S. 928 (2005).
Commonwealth v. Brown, 711 A.2d 444 (Pa. 1998).
Commonwealth v. Chambers, 599 A.2d 630 (Pa. 1991).
Commonwealth v. Cook, 676 A.2d 639 (Pa. 1996).
Commonwealth v. Cooper, 941 A.2d 655 (Pa. 2007).

Joseph v. State, 636 So.2d 777 (Fla. 1994).
Juarez v. State, 277 S.W. 1091 (Tex. 1925).
Lockett v. Ohio, 438 U.S. 586 (1978).
Lucero v. Texas, 129 S.Ct. 80 (2008).
Lynch v. Donnelly, 465 U.S. 668 (1984).
Manning v. State, 929 So.2d 885 (Miss. 2006).
McNair v. State, 653 So.2d 320 (Ala. 1997).
Melson v. State, 775 So.2d 857 (Ala. 1999).
Miles v. United States, 103 U.S. 304 (1880).
Miller v. State, 583 F.2d 701 (N.C. 1978).
Minnesota v. Davis, 504 N.W.2d 767 (Minn. 1993).
Miniel v. Cockrell, 339 F.3d 331 (Tex. 2003).
Minor v. State, 914 So.2d 372 (Ala. 2004).
O'Connor v. California, 855 F.Supp. 303 (C.D. Cal. 1994).
Oliver v. Quarterman, 541 F.3d 329 (Tex. 2008).
People v. Bradford, 929 P.2d 544 (Cal. 1997).
People v. Clark, 857 P.2d 1099 (Cal. 1993).
People v. Danks, 82 P.3d 1249 (Cal. 2004).
People v. Eckles, 404 N.E.2d 358 (Ill. App. Ct. 1980).
People v. Freeman, 882 P.2d 249 (Cal. 1994).
People v. Gajadhar, 880 N.E.2d 863 (N.Y. 2007).
People v. Hale, 173 Misc.2d 140 (N.Y. 1997).
People v. Harlan, 109 P.3d 616 (Colo. 2005).
People v. Hill, 839 P.2d 984 (Cal. 1992).
People v. Hughes, 39 P.3d 432 (Cal. 2002).
People v. Jackson, 920 P. 2d 1254 (1996).
People v. Lewis, 28 P.3d 34 (Cal. 2001).
People v. Lewis, 140 P.3d 775 (Cal. 2006).
People v. Mahaffey, 651 N.E.2d 1055 (Ill. 1995).
People v. Martin, 64 Cal. App. 4th 378 (1998).
People v. Malone, 570 N.E.2d 584 (Ill. 1991).
People v. Payton, 839 P.2d 1035 (Cal. 1992).
People v. Rohn, 296 N.W.2d 315 (Mich. Ct. App. 1980).
People v. Roldan, 110 P.3d 289 (Cal. 2005).
People v. Samuels, 113 P.3d 1125 (Cal. 2005).
People v. Sandoval, 841 P.2d 862 (Cal. 1992).
People v. Serravo, 823 P.2d 128 (Colo. 1992).
People v. Slaughter, 47 P.3d 262 (Cal. 2002).
People v. Viera, 106 P.3d 990 (Cal. 2005).
People v. Wash, 861 P.2d 1107 (Wash. 1993).
People v. Wheeler, 583 P.2d 748 (Cal. 1978).
People v. Williams, 148 P.3d 47 (Cal. 2006).
People v. Wrest, 839 P.2d 1020 (Cal. 1992).
People v. Zambrano, 163 P. 3d 4 (Cal. 2007).
Pleasant Glade Assembly of God v. Schubert, 2008 Tex. LEXIS 620 (2008).
Remmer v. United States, 347 U.S. 227 (1954).
Republican Party of Minnesota v. White, 536 U.S. 762 (2002).
Robinson v. State, 900 P.2d 389 (Okla. Crim. App. 1995).
Roper v. Simmons, 543 U.S. 551 (2005).

Sandoval v. Calderon, 241 F.3d 765 (9th Cir. 2000).
Scott v. Dugger, 891 F.2d 800 (11th Cir. 1989).
Shell v. State, 554 So.2d 887 (Miss. 1989).
Smith v. Phillips, 455 U.S. 209 (1982).
South Carolina v. Gathers, 490 U.S. 805 (1989).
State v. Arnett, 724 N.E.2d 793 (Ohio 2000).
State v. Artis, 384 S.E.2d 470 (N.C. 1989).
State v. Barden, 572 S.E.2d 108 (N.C. 2002).
State v. Berry, 141 S.W.3d 549 (Tenn. 2004).
State v. Cauthern, 1996 WL 937660 (Tenn. Crim. App. 1996).
State v. Cribbs, 967 S.W. 2d 773 (Tenn. 1998).
State v. Daniels, 446 S.E.2d 298 (N.C. 1994).
State v. Debler, 856 S.W.2d 641 (Mo. 1993).
State v. DeMille, 756 P.2d 81 (Utah 1988).
State v. Fuller, 862 A.2d 1130 (N.J. 2004).
State v. Gell, 524 S.E.2d 332 (N.C. 2000).
State v. Gentry, 888 P.2d. 1105 (Wash. 1995).
State v. Graham, 422 So.2d 123 (La. 1982).
State v. Haselden, 577 S.E.2d 594 (N.C. 2003).
State v. Hodge, 726 A.2d 531 (Conn. 1999).
State v. Holden, 488 S.E.2d 514 (N.C. 1997).
State v. Lafferty, 20 P.3d 342 (Utah 2001).
State v. Lockhart, 664 P.2d 1059 (Okla. 1983).
State v. Lundgren, 653 N.E.2d 304 (Ohio, 1995).
State v. Middlebrooks, 995 S.W.2d 550 (Tenn. 1999).
State v. Messiah, 538 So.2d 175 (La. 1988).
State v. Moose, 313 S.E.2d 507 (N.C. 1984).
State v. Norman, 808 P.2d 1159 (Wash. 1991).
State v. Patterson, 482 S.E.2d 760 (S.C. 1996).
State v. Phillips, 940 S.W.2d 512 (1997).
State v. Purcell, 18 P.3d 113 (Ariz. 2001).
State v. Ramsey, 311 S.C. 555 (S.C. 1993).
State v. Roache, 595 S.E.2d 381 (N.C. 2004).
State v. Shafer, 531 S.E.2d 524 (S.C. 2000).
State v. Sidden, 491 S.E.2d 225 (N.C. 1997).
State v. Walters, 588 S.E.2d 344 (N.C. 2003).
State v. Wangberg, 136 N.W.2d 853 (Minn. 1965).
State v. Williams, 510 S.E.2d 626 (N.C. 1999).
State v. Williams, 832 N.E.2d 783 (Ohio 2005).
State v. Worthy, 532 So.2d 541 (La. 1988).
Taylor v. Louisiana, 419 U.S. 522 (1975).
Thompson v. State, 581 So.2d 1216 (Ala. 1991).
Thorson v. State, 721 So. 2d 590 (Miss. 1998).
Todd v. State, 410 S.E.2d 725 (Ga. 1991).
United States v. Bakker, 925 F.2d 728 (4th Cir. 1991).
United States v. Bauer, 84 F.3d 1549 (9th Cir.1996).
United States v. DeJesus, 347 F.3d 500 (3rd Cir. 2003).
United States v. Giry, 818 F.2d 120 (1st Cir. 1987).
United States v. Gooch, slip op. 2006 WL 3780781 (D.D.C. 2006).

United States v. Hasting, 461 U.S. 499 (1983).
United States v. Hillyard, 52 F.Supp. 612 (E.D. Wash. 1943).
United States v. Kirk, 41 M.J. 529 (C.G.C.M.F. 1994).
United States v. Lemon, 723 F.2d 922 (D.C. Cir. 1983).
United States v. Mitchell, 502 F.3d 931 (Cal. 2007).
United States v. Myrick, 1998 U.S. Dist. LEXIS 18861 (N.D. Ill. 1998).
United States v. Stafford, 136 F.3d 1109 (7th Cir.1998).
United States v. Webster, 162 F.3d 308 (5th Cir. 1998).
Wainwright v. Witt, 469 U.S. 412 (1985).
Ward v. Dretke, 420 F.3d 479 (Tex. 2005).
Warner v. Orange County Department of Probation, 115 F.3d 1068 (2d Cir. 1996).
West Virginia v. Everly, 146 S.E.2d 705 (W. Va. 1966).
Wilcher v. State, 863 So.2d 776 (Miss. 2003).
Witherspoon v. Illinois, 391 U.S. 510 (1968).
Young v. State, 12 P.3d 20 (Okla. 2000).

Index

Page numbers followed by *t* indicate a table; by an *n* a note.

Jewish seat. *See* Jewish Supreme Court justices
Judaism/Jews, 3–4, 97, 106, 131, 187–88
    Anti-Semitism, 93–94, 185, 191
    As jurors, 20, 23–26, 32, 35, 37, 40–41,
        43–45, 48–49, 51–52
    As religious liberties claimants, 166
    Jewish judges' decision making, 100,
        102–5, 195
    Jewish Supreme Court justices, 92–95
Judges' decision making, 85–111
    Attitudinal model, 96–97
    Compared to jurors, 194–95, 198–99
    Extralegal model, 97
    Legal model, 96–97
    Religious differences in, 86–87,
        96–105, 195
    Social background variables, 96–97
    Religious freedom cases, 102
    Use of religion in, 105–110, 194, 204–5
Judicial selection, 85, 87–96
Juror-litigant similarity, 187–89, 195
Jury composition, 15–34
Jury deliberations. *See* Deliberation, jury
Jury decision making
    Consultation with religious figures,
        69, 75–76, 79, 205
    Reliance on religious beliefs, 15–18,
        21–24, 26, 30–32, 43–51, 55–59,
        61, 63, 67–69, 79, 160, 194, 204–5
Jury duty, religious exemptions from,
    16, 28–33, 203
Jury nullification. *See* Nullification, jury
Jury selection/voir dire, 16–27, 35,
    43–44, 65, 67
    Folklore, 15, 20–21
    Peremptory challenges, 15, 16,
        18–20, 22, 24–27, 202
    Challenges for cause, 18–19
    Permissibility of religious challenges,
        24–27, 202–3
    Pretrial questionnaires, 17–18
Justification defense, 173–74, 196

KARAMAH: Muslim Women Lawyers for
    Human Rights, 118

Latter-Day Saints. *See* Mormons
Legal education, 120–30, 205–6
    Catholic law schools, 122, 123–24*t*, 125–26
    Evangelical law schools, 122, 123–24*t*,
        126–27, 129
    Jewish law schools, 123–24*t*, 126–27
    Measures of success, 128–30
    Religious law schools, listed by
        denomination, 123–24*t*

Legal ethics
    In practice, 127, 130–38, 206
    Teaching, 127–28, 205–6
Literal interpretism, 3, 22, 33,
    55, 57, 58–60, 64–65
Lutherans, 4, 15, 20–21, 36, 39*t*, 43,
    101–3, 187

Mainline Protestants, 4, 41, 102–4, 195, 206
    As religious liberties claimants,
        166–67, 218*n*.4
Marginal religions, 166–67, 196
Methodists, 21, 28, 36, 39*t*, 43–44,
    101–2, 215*n*.3
Miers, Harriet, 90, 96
Mitigation, 72, 76, 196, 175–76.
    See also Death penalty
Moore, Roy, 85, 89, 109–110
Mormons, 4, 27, 39*t*, 51, 106–7, 174, 186–87

National Association of Muslim Lawyers, 118
Native American religions, 171–72, 178–79
Nazarenes, 102
Non-U.S. countries, 4, 86, 101, 120, 171,
    198–99, 209*n*.5, 212–13*n*.5
Normative perspective. *See* Descriptive vs.
    normative perspective
Nullification, jury, 5

Obscenity, 101

Parachurch organizations, 139–40
Parole decisions, 176–77, 189
Pentecostals, 22, 24, 166
Poland Act, 27
Polygamy, 16, 27, 172, 220*n*.26
Presbyterians, 4, 20–21, 39*t*, 43, 44, 101–2
Protestants. *See* Mainline Protestants;
    see also entries for specific denominations
Punitiveness, 37–38, 40, 43–44, 47,
    50, 52, 57–64, 159, 195

Rabbinical court, 86, 115
Race relations, 98
Race, relationship with religion, 46
Rastafarians, 172
Recusal
    Attorneys, 132
    Judges, 103, 106
Religions' positions on social issues, 39*t*.
    See also Catholicism/Catholics
Religious classification, problems of,
    40–41, 64, 197
Religious diversity in the legal
    profession, 114–20